PRACTICING ORGANIZATION DEVELOPMENT

A Guide for Consultants

PRACTICING ORGANIZATION DEVELOPMENT

A Guide for Consultants

Edited by

William J. Rothwell
Roland Sullivan
Gary N. McLean

With a Foreword by

Kathleen D. Dannemiller and Robert W. Jacobs

Johannesburg • London
San Diego • Sydney • Toronto

Published by Pfeiffer & Company
8517 Production Avenue
San Diego, California 92121
United States of America

Editorial Offices
(619) 578-5900, FAX (619) 578-2042

Orders
U.S.A. (606) 647-3030
FAX (606) 647-3034

This book is printed on acid-free, recycled stock that meets
or exceeds the minimum GPO and EPA specifications for
recycled paper.

"The linking of key competencies to stages of change is a major contribution to current practitioners and to the development of the next generation of change agents."
> —*Charles and Edie Seashore,*
> Partners,
> Seashore Consultants

"This is one of the most exciting OD books that has been developed. We need a definitive statement about the relevant OD skills needed in this field, and this book does it eloquently. I fully expect that it will become a classic."
> —*Dr. Joanne C. Preston,*
> Director of MSOD Program for
> the School of Business and Management,
> Pepperdine University

"This book is a real service to the OD profession. It strengthens the foundation of OD by telling us what this mysterious profession is and is not."
> —*Geoff Bellman,*
> Principal,
> GMB Associates, LTD.

"Readers will find in these pages a variety of approaches to organizational change, and will thrive on the diversity of viewpoints. Clearly stated objectives guide the consultant through carefully researched and well-written chapters."
> —*Timothy J. Costello,*
> Consultant,
> IDS Financial Services, Inc.

"Long overdue. A clear and instructive accounting of all basic elements in OD. Provides a terrific classification of competencies and an invaluable list of references."
> —*René F. Pino,*
> Co-Administrator,
> National OD Network

"This is an extremely valuable and practical resource for those of us internal consultants who have been learning OD on our own and in workshops. It provides the best overall change-management framework that I have come across."
>—*Paul Pelkola,*
>OD Facilitator,
>Minnesota Mining and Manufacturing

"Rothwell, McLean, and Sullivan have done a masterful job of cataloging and describing the essential skills that OD practitioners must have in order to effectively transform cultures."
>—*Dan Stone,*
>Chief of OD,
>US Department of Agriculture

"Change management is one of the 'hot' careers of the future. This book is a valuable addition to the OD profession. It is essential reading for persons interested in or practicing in our field."
>—*Dr. Peter Sorensen,*
>Director of Management and Organizational Behavior,
>Illinois Benedictine College

"With rapid change impacting business today, we need operations professionals to be even more familiar with organization development. This book is a terrific and comprehensive overview of key OD concepts beneficial for both OD practitioners and line managers."
>—*James O'Hern,*
>Director of Training and Organization Development,
>Marriott International Lodging

"This book is a comprehensive and valuable guide to concepts, skills, and strategies used by OD practitioners. It is a welcome edition to the OD library."
>—*Linda Thorne,*
>OD Consultant

DEDICATION

This book is dedicated to Robert Tannenbaum for:

- Facilitating the first team-building session in 1952 and publishing about team building in 1954;
- Being involved in the first university program to train OD practitioners;
- Continuing to place value on the individual;
- Helping consultants to be self-aware and to see themselves as intervention instruments; and
- Being one of the most loved, respected, and "spirited" mentors of OD practitioners.

This book is also dedicated to Richard Beckhard for:

- Facilitating one of the first large-scale interactive change conferences at the 1950 White House conference for youths and children;
- Bringing leadership training to Europe in 1954;
- Coining the phrase organization development in 1958;
- Developing one of the first nondegree training programs in OD at NTL in 1958;

- Creating with Edgar Schein the still popular Addison-Wesley Series on Organization Development; and

- Leading the effort of bringing OD to top management through his teaching at MIT and elsewhere.

FOREWORD

The field of organization development (OD) has developed over the last thirty years and it is now firmly established as a field of study. As a new generation of OD consultants enters the field, we believe that it is time to review what we have learned and to determine what we need to learn. Ronald Lippitt, a significant mentor and a founding father of OD, believed deeply in promoting collaborative learning among OD consultants. To that end, he developed a process he called *sharing the practices* which is a means of passing on experience and wisdom. His influence is still felt, and this book is, in part, a tribute to the value of it.

In this book, an eclectic group of experienced OD consultants demonstrates the value of sharing the practices by offering its insights on steps in the OD intervention process. The book will benefit those new to the field as well as those who have been practicing OD for years. Moreover, *Practicing OD: A Guide for Consultants* takes a hands-on approach to the issues and challenges confronting OD consultants. Although real learning in OD occurs on the front lines—contracting with clients, planning interventions, and working through the difficult issues inherent in any change effort—proper preparation is the key to success.

This book provides a solid, practical preparation for facilitating a change process and supporting those who make change happen. Given the increasing rate and scope of change unfolding in the world, opportunities exist for OD consultants to play significant roles in creating the futures of corporations, governments, communities, and nonprofit organizations. This book adds value by documenting what has been learned in the OD field and by exploring the competencies required by present and future change agents. We recommend it to you and believe it will make a welcome contribution to your library.

Kathleen D. Dannemiller   Robert W. Jacobs
Ann Arbor, MI   Ann Arbor, MI
November, 1994   November, 1994

CONTENTS

C H A P T E R 9

Person-Focused Interventions   **265**

Udai Pareek

C H A P T E R 10

Evaluation   **311**

Gary N. McLean, Roland Sullivan, and William J. Rothwell

C H A P T E R 11

Adoption   **369**

W. James Smith and Jack A. Tesmer

CHAPTER 12

Separation   395

Ann Van Eron and W. Warner Burke

PART III
CHAPTER 13

International OD   421

David C. Wigglesworth

PREFACE

The paradox of our times is that change has become the only constant. Changes occur in organizations every day. Organizations are started, some evolve, and some dissolve. Some undergo mergers, takeovers, or buyouts; some go bankrupt. Changes in corporate ownership may result in corporate rightsizing, downsizing, early retirement offers, or various other staffing alterations. To cope with the fierce competition organizations face, senior managers are taking innovative steps by introducing total quality management (TQM), self-directed work teams, skill-based pay, and business process reengineering.

Practicing OD: A Guide for Consultants is about facilitating these and other organizational changes. But this book is not about just any type of organizational change; rather, it focuses on planned, systematic, and educationally oriented change that is carried out for organizational improvement. The book is about organization development (OD). *Organization development* is defined as "a series of planned processes by which human resources are identified, utilized, and developed in ways that strengthen organizational effectiveness by increasing problem-solving capabilities and planning" (*Organization Development,* 1991, p. 4). Although the book addresses organizational change, many principles described in it also apply to change efforts with individuals, with teams, or across organizations.

The Audience for the Book

This book has three intended audiences: OD consultants, human resource development practitioners, and managers and executives.

The primary audience is OD consultants. There are two levels of OD consultants: practitioners and master practitioners. This book is geared to the *practitioner*, someone who is already carrying out the role of change agent but needs more formal grounding in organization development theory and practice. This includes students enrolled in courses on OD, organizational behavior, or organizational change. A master practitioner may also find this book useful as a guide to OD literature and as a tool to help him or her orient, train, and mentor other OD consultants.

Our second audience is human resource development (HRD) practitioners. Some HRD practitioners specifically train employees. They devote their attention largely to increasing employees' job knowledge and to improving individual performance in organizational settings. But some HRD practitioners go beyond training to ensure that identified training needs take organizational and work-group cultures into account. In addition, results-oriented HRD practitioners are aware that individual performance improvement can only occur when the surrounding work environment supports it. The theory and practice of changing organizational and work-group cultures are OD topics. To do their jobs and achieve results, HRD practitioners sometimes need to apply competencies associated with OD (London, 1988).

Our third audience consists of managers and executives. In today's dynamic business environment, they must know how to introduce and consolidate change successfully if they are to realize their visions for organizational improvement.

When executives or managers lack competence in change theory, they will never see their visions realized.

The Purpose and Objectives of the Book

The purpose of *Practicing OD: A Guide for Consultants* is to build the readers' competencies in diagnosing the need for—and facilitating implementation of—change in organizational settings. When readers finish this book, they should be able to do the following:

1. Define OD;
2. Define action research, its eight steps, and explain how it is related to OD;
3. Describe the competencies necessary to conduct each step in the action research model;
4. Apply, at a minimum level, the competencies necessary to conduct each step in the action research model; and
5. Define intervention as it is used in the OD field and describe typical OD interventions.

Theoretical Foundation of the Book

This book is based on research about the activities of internal and external consultants functioning as change agents. The research results are described in a report entitled "The Essential Competencies of Internal and External Organization Development Consultants" ("The Essential Competencies") that is issued by the Organization Development Institute's (ODI) committee to define OD knowledge and skills. An early draft of this report was prepared by Roland Sullivan and Erin Threlkeld and was subsequently revised by Gary N. McLean and Roland Sullivan. A later draft was published in the *OD Practitioner* (McLean & Sullivan, 1990).

"The Essential Competencies" developed from an attempt to combine previous efforts to describe what change agents do as they diagnose the need for change and participate in planned-change efforts. The study began in the late 1970s with a review of OD literature and has been updated annually, based on continuing literature reviews. It has been repeatedly scrutinized in feedback sessions held at Pepperdine University, Malibu, California; the southern Minnesota Chapter and Region 6 Conference of the American Society for Training and Development (ASTD); the Minnesota OD Network; the OD Interorganization Group Worldwide in Austria; and annual ODI conferences. In 1988 the study was examined by a committee of twenty top OD consultants under the auspices of ODI.

Practicing OD: A Guide for Consultants takes up where "The Essential Competencies" and McLean and Sullivan (1990) leave off. Practice is emphasized in the book and that word is imbued with multiple meanings. As Kinnunen (1992) points out, to practice can mean any or all of the following:

- To do frequently or by force of habit;
- To use knowledge and skill in a profession or occupation;
- To adhere to a set of beliefs or ideals;
- To do repeatedly to become proficient; and
- To drill in order to give proficiency (p. 6).

This book explains the competencies described, in abbreviated form, in "The Essential Competencies" as they have been most recently updated. But the other meanings of practice listed above can also apply to the editors' intentions in assembling this book.

The Structure of the Book

What are the competencies of an effective OD consultant? That is the central question addressed by this book. This book is structured in four parts:

Part I, The Introduction, provides essential background information about OD and planned change.

Part II, Steps in OD, focuses on the OD intervention process as described by Burke (1982). Chapters in Part II address entry, start-up, assessment and feedback, action planning, intervention, evaluation, adoption, and separation.

Part III, International Competencies and Ethics in OD, describes unique competencies needed by internal and external OD consultants in a global marketplace and the ethical issues that confront OD consultants.

Part IV, OD and the Future, addresses the competencies that may be required of OD consultants in the future.

In Chapter 1, contributing editors William J. Rothwell, Roland Sullivan, and Gary N. McLean introduce the book. The chapter defines OD, provides an overview of key terms, summarizes the history of OD, places OD in the context of other human resource fields, and clarifies when OD should be used. Chapter 2, which is also written by the contributing editors, describes three models for organizational change and summarizes the steps in most OD interventions.

In Chapter 3, author Richard Alan Engdahl focuses on the first step in any OD intervention: entry. He covers such essential issues in consulting as writing a mission statement, developing a marketing strategy, acting on the marketing strategy, "selling" during an initial contact, and the contracting process.

In Chapter 4, David Jamieson reviews the start-up step of most OD interventions. He identifies the following nine key outcomes to be achieved by OD consultants:

- Identifying client(s) and sponsor(s);
- Getting oriented to the client's world;
- Establishing consultant competence and credibility;
- Developing open and trusting relationships;
- Assessing alignment of values;
- Connecting with the organization's political system;
- Completing a preliminary diagnostic scan;
- Contracting for:

    A. The work to be done;
    B. The psychosocial relationships with those people the consultant will be working with directly and those who are critical stakeholders;
    C. The consultant's support needs; and
    D. The financial or other exchange that is expected.

- Introducing the intervention and consultant(s).

In Chapter 5, Jerry Franklin describes the OD consultant's competencies in the assessment and feedback step of OD interventions. He also covers some information-gathering methods that are appropriate for assessment and feedback, and he summarizes key advantages and disadvantages of using each method.

In Chapter 6, Don Warrick directs attention to developing an action plan. He identifies the following key issues in developing an action plan:

- Involving strategic people in the planning process;
- Evaluating relevant data;
- Agreeing on what is to be changed or improved;
- Developing a change strategy;
- Developing a system for monitoring and managing the change process, and
- Clarifying change roles.

Chapters 7, 8, and 9 address the intervention step. In Chapter 7, Tom Cummings and Ann E. Feyerherm examine interventions in large systems. The authors define what is meant by large-system interventions, summarize their characteristics, and cite examples of selected interventions of this kind. Roland Loup provides information about large-scale interventions in Appendix IV.

In Chapter 8, W. Brendan Reddy turns to interventions in small systems and addresses such questions as:

- What is a small group?
- What developmental model describes the competencies needed by OD consultants in working with small groups?
- What is a small-group intervention?

He then identifies seven lessons he has learned to ensure successful small-group interventions:

- Clarify the client;
- Clarify the contract;
- Assess the group;
- Focus on joint problem solving;
- Focus on modest goals;
- Model appropriate behavior; and
- Provide follow-up.

Chapter 9 focuses on person-focused interventions. In this last of three chapters on intervention, Udai Pareek offers a typology of person-focused interventions. He distinguishes between participant-active interventions and consultant-active interventions. Participant-active interventions literally require the participants in a change effort to take an active role, and consultant-active interventions require consultants to take an active role. Pareek briefly reviews each intervention.

In Chapter 10, the contributing editors define evaluation, cite its advantages, review factors discouraging its use, define levels of evaluation, identify key evaluation competencies, and describe the key steps in developing appropriate evaluation instruments.

In Chapter 11, W. James Smith and Jack Tesmer turn to the next step in most OD interventions: adoption. They cite five issues to be considered to ensure that change is adopted by an organization. These issues are as follows:

- Change should be based on business strategy and business needs;
- Change must balance planning with flexibility;
- Change should not rely exclusively on outside expertise;

- Change should be the center of attention; and

- Change must become strategy driven rather than project driven.

Chapter 12 is about separation, the final step in most OD interventions. Chapter authors Ann Van Eron and W. Warner Burke define the term separation, identify competencies associated with it, clarify the competencies that OD consultants need to conduct separation successfully, and review the separation process.

Chapters 13 and 14 focus on international OD competencies and the ethics of OD consultants. In Chapter 13, author David Wigglesworth describes international OD competencies. He identifies fifteen requisite skills for successful international OD work, key factors affecting OD practice, and cultural determinants of OD success. In Chapter 14, Susan H. DeVogel and the contributing editors define professional ethics in OD, summarize practical ethical issues and dilemmas in OD, offer decision-making methods, and list essential ethical competencies for OD consultants.

In Chapter 15, the final chapter, authors Saul Eisen, Hoy Steele, and Jeanne Cherbeneau examine what competencies they believe OD consultants will need for the future. They summarize the key themes from their research, which they believe will necessitate new OD competencies in the future:

- Broadened frameworks in a global environment;
- Clients and client systems;
- Cultural and demographic diversity and change;
- Values and ethics; and
- Trends within the OD field.

The chapter includes a series of self-assessment and planning instruments for OD consultants to use in preparing for future challenges.

References

Burke, W. (1982). *Organization development: Principles and practices.* Boston, MA: Little, Brown & Co.

Kinnunen, G. (1992, November). The practice of practice. *NSPI Insight,* p. 6.

London, M. (1988). *Change agents: New roles and innovation strategies for human resource professionals.* San Francisco, CA: Jossey-Bass.

McLean, G., & Sullivan, R. (1989). *Essential competencies of internal and external OD consultants.* Unpublished manuscript.

McLean, G., & Sullivan, R. (1990). OD skills: An ongoing competency list. *OD Practitioner, 22*(2), 11-12.

Organization development: A straightforward reference guide for executives seeking to improve their organizations. (1991). Chesterland, OH: The Organization Development Institute.

Acknowledgments

No book is the product of its author(s) or editor(s) alone. This book is no different. Accordingly, we would especially like to thank Dr. Don Cole, president of the Organization Development Institute, for his support of this project. Although he did not see the many drafts of this work, he was supportive of it. It was his original idea to define the knowledge and skill necessary for competence in OD.

We would also like to thank the participating authors for their willingness to write their chapters and respond to our repeated demands for revisions. However, we must accept ultimate responsibility for any mistakes or misstatements made in this volume because we read all the chapters and revised them so as to maintain consistent writing styles.

Finally, we would like to thank our wives and children for their patience over the four years in which this volume was in the making. Without their emotional support and encouragement, the volume would never have been published.

William J. Rothwell
University Park, Pennsylvania

Roland Sullivan
Deephaven, Minnesota

Gary N. McLean
St. Paul, Minnesota

Contributors

W. Warner Burke, Ph.D., is president of W. Warner Burke Associates, Inc., a consulting firm based in Pelham, New York. He is also a professor of psychology and education and coordinator for the graduate program in organizational psychology at Teachers College, Columbia University.

Jeanne Cherbeneau is president and principal consultant of Cherbeneau and Associates, a consulting firm based in Berkeley, California, that specializes in management, human resources, and organization development. She specializes in strategic planning, planning and managing complex organizational change, valuing workforce diversity, and management coaching and team building.

Donald W. Cole, Ph.D., is president of the Organization Development Institute and a management/clinical psychologist. He has been practicing OD as both an internal and external consultant since 1965. In 1988, he was given the Outstanding OD Consultant of the Year award for his leadership in building OD into a profession.

Thomas G. Cummings, Ph.D., is a professor of management and organization in the School of Business Administration, University of Southern California. His consulting and research interests are designing complex organizations and systems approaches to management.

Kathleen D. Dannemiller is a partner in Dannemiller Tyson Associates, Inc., where she has been a consultant to business, industry, and community organizations since 1968. She is a professional member of the National Training Laboratory and a member of the Michigan OD Network, National OD Network, and World Future Society.

Susan Harrington DeVogel, Ph.D., is president of the Ivy Consulting Group, Inc., in Minneapolis, Minnesota. She has worked with organizations of all sizes in the private and public sectors. Her consulting practice includes general OD services and quality transformations using Deming's philosophy and methods.

Saul Eisen, Ph.D., is a professor of management and coordinator of the Organization Development Master's Degree Program at Sonoma State University. An international consultant to organizations in various industries, he has published and presented widely. The focus of his consulting includes the integration of strategic planning and OD and sociotechnical work redesign.

Richard Alan Engdahl, Ph.D., is an associate professor of management at the Cameron School of Business Administration, University of North Carolina at Wilmington, and a consultant with Organization Imagineering in Wilmington, North Carolina. He is a registered organization development consultant (RODC).

Ann E. Feyerherm, Ph.D., is a faculty member in the MSOD program for the School of Business and Management at Pepperdine University. She worked for Procter and Gamble for eleven years as a manufacturing manager and OD manager. Her current research interests are leadership in changing systems and environmental management.

Jerry Franklin, Ph.D., has worked with major organizations in the United States, Canada, and South America. Much of his professional activity has involved the development of diagnostic and feedback procedures as the basis for large-scale OD projects. In 1983, he formed Jerry Franklin & Associates, which is based in San Diego, California. He has published numerous books and articles about organizational behavior and OD.

Robert W. Jacobs is a partner in Dannemiller Tyson Associates, Inc., where he has been a consultant since 1985. Before 1985 he was an employee-involvement consulting specialist in the electrical and electronics division at Ford Motor Company.

David W. Jamieson is president of the Jamieson Consulting Group, based in Los Angeles. His interests include facilitating change, organizational culture, managing for quality and service, and facilitating executive development. His most recent book is *Managing Workforce 2000: Gaining the Diversity Advantage* (Jossey-Bass, 1991).

Roland Loup, Ph.D., is a consultant and a trainer. He has been a partner in Dannemiller Tyson Associates, Inc. since 1987. His practice is focused on large-scale systems change and training related to large-scale interventions. He has consulted with service and manufacturing, health care, universities, government and public utilities.

Gary N. McLean, Ed.D., a contributing editor to this book, is a professor and head of business and marketing education and coordinator of training and development at the University of Minnesota, St. Paul. He has been an independent consultant, primarily in training and organization development, for over twenty years and is a registered organization development consultant (RODC). A frequent speaker and the author of over a hundred articles and eighteen books, he is the editor of the *Human Resource Development Quarterly*.

Udai Pareek, Ph.D., is currently the president of the National HRD Network (India) and has been president of the Indian Society of Applied Behavioral Science. He has been a Fellow of NTL Institute for Applied Behavioral Science and he is on the editorial boards of several international professional journals. He consults with organizations in the areas of training and organization development.

W. Brendan Reddy, Ph.D., is a professor of psychology and director of the Institute for Consultation and Training at the University of Cincinnati and a senior consultant in Reddy & Phillips, an international consultation and training company. He is a Fellow of the American Psychological Association and a professional member of the NTL Institute. Author of numerous articles and book chapters, he co-edited *Training Theory and Practice* and *Team Building: Blueprints for Productivity and Satisfaction* (NTL Institute and University Associates, 1987 and 1988).

William J. Rothwell, Ph.D., senior contributing editor of this book, is an associate professor of human resource development in the College of Education at The Pennsylvania State University in University Park. He is an active consultant in OD, management development, and employee training. He has achieved life designation as a senior professional in human resources (SPHR) and is a registered organization development consultant (RODC). He has authored, co-authored, or edited numerous articles, books, and training packages.

W. James Smith, founder of his own consulting business, is the former corporate manager of organizational development for 3M Company, where he worked for almost a decade in HRD and corporate quality and manufacturing services. He was also senior consultant for Bell Northern Research in Ottawa, Canada, and has consulted extensively with organizations in many industries.

Hoy Steele, Ph.D., is a senior partner with The Results Group. He specializes in OD, mediation, and training in management and conflict-resolution skills. He also serves as adjunct faculty and member of the Visiting Committee for the Master's degree program in OD at Sonoma State University and as adjunct faculty in OD at Greenwich University.

Kristine Sullivan, is co-president of OD Corp. She received her degree in MSOD from Pepperdine University and she teaches OD at the University of St. Thomas in Minneapolis. She specializes in building teams and organizations and is currently working on revising the OD competencies list for the OD Practitioner.

Roland Sullivan, a contributing editor of this book, is co-president of OD Corp. A widely-known OD consultant, he has also participated in extensive and intensive learning at the NTL Institute and has worked with over 400 organizations, ranging from multinational Fortune 500 corporations to small and midsize organizations. Currently he chairs the Organization Development Institute's Committee to define the essential competencies for the OD profession and is a registered organization development consultant (RODC). In addition, he leads an effort with twelve professional, OD-related associations to define the OD profession's change-management competencies.

Jack A. Tesmer began his own consulting firm in 1972. He has directed the corporate OD function in a Fortune 100 company and has served several clients from the Fortune 100 as well as diverse organizations in such industries as healthcare, manufacturing, insurance, and finance. Jack is also a founding partner of the Center for the Advancement of Professional Associations (CAPA) and a principal with the Brussels-based AEON GROUP.

Ann M. Van Eron, Ph.D., is principal of Potentials, an OD and management consulting firm she founded in 1984. Her research and practice focus on leadership, managing change, workforce diversity, and OD.

D.D. (Don) Warrick, Ph.D., is a professor of management and organization change at the University of Colorado at Colorado Springs and is president of the Warrick Agency Training and Development Company. He has received such national awards as Outstanding OD Practitioner of the Year and Outstanding Human Resources Professional of the Year, has been named the Outstanding Teacher in the College of Business at his university eight times, and was awarded the lifetime title of President's Teaching Scholar by the University of Colorado. He is the author of four books and numerous articles.

David C. Wigglesworth, Ph.D., is an external consultant and president of D.C.W. Research Associates International in Foster City, California. He is also affiliated with the Prosper Consortium in the U.K. He has taught at universities in Latin America, Southeast Asia, sub-Saharan Africa, and North Africa. His writings appear frequently in professional journals around the world.

P A R T   I

INTRODUCTION

Part I consists of Chapters 1 and 2. It sets the stage for the book by doing the following:

- Defining organization development (OD);
- Defining such important terms as *change, change agent, client, culture, intervention,* and *system;*
- Summarizing the history of OD;
- Distinguishing differences between OD and other human-resource fields;
- Describing when OD should and should not be used; and
- Summarizing key steps in an OD intervention.

INTRODUCTION

*William J. Rothwell, Roland Sullivan, and
Gary N. McLean*

Organization development (OD) is one approach to change, but it is not the only approach. To begin appreciating how OD differs from other approaches to change, read the following case study.

A Case Study

The top managers of a bank in the rural midwestern U.S. were feeling pressure to cut operating expenses and boost income. The bank's board of directors believed that coping with these pressures was essential if the bank was to survive the conditions that have rocked the foundations of many financial institutions in recent years.

One board member advised the bank president to call in a consulting firm that specializes in performing efficiency studies in white-collar settings. The bank president agreed. She met with representatives of the consulting firm to request help.

Soon afterward the president called a meeting of the bank's management employees. She opened the meeting with a few brief remarks about the competitive pressures under which the bank and the banking industry had been operating, emphasizing the need to cut costs and improve operating efficiency. Then she introduced the consultants and concluded by voicing her support for them. Their efforts, she explained, would eventually strengthen the bank, making it more competitive and better able to survive difficult economic conditions.

The chief consultant followed the bank president to the podium and explained that her staff members would review banking operations by observing employees as they carried out their daily work. She listed by name the bank departments that would first undergo operational reviews and explained that the reviews would begin immediately after the meeting.

Within an hour of the meeting's adjournment, the consultants were peering over the shoulders of bank employees as they worked. Bank officers had no chance to explain to their employees what was going to happen during the reviews, so the effect on employee morale was devastating. Rumors were rampant. On the same day two key officers announced their long-pending retirements, fueling employees' grim speculations about the future.

The president was soon inundated with complaints about the way in which the consultants entered work areas without warning; spied on employees, disrupting operations and unsettling employees and customers alike; and then announced their recommendations without first discussing those recommendations with bank personnel who could predict the consequences.

Listening quietly to these complaints, the president never defended what the consultants did. Nor did she demand compliance from her officers. However, she did allow the consultants to continue with their work. Eventually, many came to believe that she was just paying lip service to the consultants' recommendations so that she could mollify the board of directors.

The consultants worked in the bank for a year. Nearly two hundred of the bank's eight hundred employees were laid off during that time. When the consultants were ready to leave, they pointed with pride to numerous changes they had introduced and recommendations they had made to increase efficient operations. However, they did not mention that few of their recommendations were successfully implemented.

Within one week of the consultants' departure, the changes they had introduced were unceremoniously discarded. The consultants left triumphant and enriched, having received a sizable bonus for the two hundred employees who had been laid off. However, employee overtime expenses had increased dramatically and so had employee absenteeism and turnover. Exit interviews conducted with employees who resigned consistently revealed a pattern of morale problems from every department.

Conclusions About the Case Study

How different would the case study have been if the consultants had used a more participative approach? They could have applied the theory and techniques of OD, and that approach would have facilitated efforts within the bank to identify and solve problems. In the process, the consultants would have modeled another way to handle problem solving, created recognition of a need for change, and built ownership in the change effort. In all likelihood, an OD approach would have created the impetus for progress while institutionalizing changes already made.

Definitions of OD

Organization development has been defined by just about every author who has written about it. Here are a few definitions:

> Organization Development is an effort (1) planned, (2) organization-wide, and (3) managed from the top, to (4) increase organization effectiveness and health through (5) planned interventions in the organization's "processes," using behavioral-science knowledge. (Beckhard, 1969, p. 9)

> Organization Development is a response to change, a complex educational strategy intended to change the beliefs, attitudes, values, and structure of organizations so that they can better adapt to new technologies, markets, and challenges, and the dizzying rate of change itself. (Bennis, 1969, p. 2)

> Most people in the field agree that OD involves consultants who try to help clients improve their organizations by applying knowledge from the behavioral sciences—psychology, sociology, cultural anthropology, and certain related disciplines. Most would also agree that OD implies change and, if we accept that improvement in organizational functioning means that change has occurred, then, broadly defined, OD means organizational change. (Burke, 1982, p. 3)

> Organization Development focuses on assuring healthy inter- and intra-unit relationships and helping groups initiate and manage

change. Organization Development's primary emphasis is on relationships and processes between and among individuals and groups. Its primary intervention is influence on the relationship of individuals and groups to effect an impact on the organization as a system. (McLagan, 1989, p. 7)

Organization Development is a top-management-supported, long-range effort to improve an organization's problem-solving and renewal processes, particularly through a more effective and collaborative diagnosis and management of organization culture—with special emphasis on formal work team, temporary team, and intergroup culture—with the assistance of a consultant-facilitator and the use of the theory and technology of applied behavioral science, including Action Research. (French & Bell, 1990, p. 17)

Organization Development has been defined as a series of planned processes by which human resources are identified, utilized, and developed in ways that strengthen organizational effectiveness by increasing problem solving capabilities and planning. (*Organization Development: A Straightforward Reference Guide for Executives Seeking to Improve Their Organizations*, 1991, p. 4)

These definitions imply several key points deserving elaboration. First, OD is long-range in perspective. It is not a "quick-fix" strategy for solving short-term performance problems, as employee training is often inappropriately perceived to be. Many U.S. managers are becoming acutely aware of the need to move beyond quick and unworkable solutions to complex organizational problems (Kilmann, 1984; Naisbitt, 1982). Organization development is a means to bring about complex change. In many organizations OD is coupled with strategic business planning, a natural fit because both are long-range in scope.

Second, OD should be supported by top managers. They are usually the chief power brokers and change agents in any organization; top managers control an organization's resources and reward systems. Although OD efforts can be undertaken at any organizational level without direct top-management participation (Beer, 1980), OD is less likely to succeed if it does not have at least tacit approval from top management.

Third, OD effects change chiefly, though not exclusively, through education. Organization development expands people's ideas, beliefs, and behaviors so that they can apply new approaches to old problems. Even more importantly, OD change efforts go beyond employee-training interventions and concentrate on the work group or organization in which new ideas, beliefs, or behaviors are to be applied.

Fourth, OD emphasizes employee participation in diagnosing problems, considering solutions, selecting a solution, identifying change objectives, implementing planned change, and evaluating results. In this sense OD differs from other methods that hold managers or consultants responsible for the success or failure of a change effort.

In OD, everyone in an organization who is affected by change should have an opportunity to contribute to—and accept responsibility for—the continuous-improvement process. Indeed, the results of one study revealed that most OD consultants believe in "empowering employees" by giving them a say, if not the chief say, in decision making, "creating open communication," "facilitating the ownership of [change] processes and outcomes," "promoting a culture of collaboration," and "promoting inquiry and continuous learning" (Van Eynde, Church, Hurley, & Burke, 1992, p. 44). Organizational effectiveness and humanistic values meet as employee ownership increases in change processes and outcomes.

Key Terms in OD

Organization development consultants use special terms as shorthand. Although these terms can create barriers to understanding and may be potential sources of suspicion for those not versed in them, they are useful when consultants are communicating with one another rather than with clients.

Change

Change is a departure from the status quo. It implies movement toward a goal, an idealized state, or a vision of what should be and movement away from present conditions, beliefs, or attitudes.

Different degrees of change exist (Golembiewski, 1990). *Alpha change* implies constant progress, a shift from a pre-change state to a post-change state in which variables and measurement remain constant. It is sometimes associated with incremental change.

Beta change implies variable progress, a shift from a pre-change state to a post-change state in which variables and measurement methods themselves change. For example, as members of an organization participate in a change effort, they become aware of emerging issues that were unknown to them at the outset. The members change their vision of what should be and thereby alter the course of the change effort itself.

Gamma change implies, in addition to beta change, a radical shift from what was originally defined as a pre-change state and a post-change state. It is sometimes called transformational change, a radical alteration from the status quo, a quantum leap, or paradigm shift. It involves a complete revolution in "how we do things" or "what results we strive to achieve."

Change Agent

A change agent is a person or team responsible for beginning and maintaining a change effort. Change agents may come from inside an organization, in which case they are called *internal consultants,* or they may come from outside an organization, in which case they are called *external consultants.*

Warren Bennis (1969) notes that "change agents are for the most part, but not exclusively, external to the client system" (p. 12). The reason is that "external consultants can manage to affect...the power structure in a way that most internal change agents cannot" (p. 12). Although external consultants may be less familiar with an organization's power networks, key decision makers, and culture than internal consultants, external consultants are less subject to implicit and explicit rewards or punishments.

Client

The client is the organization, group, or individuals whose interests the change agent primarily serves. The client authorizes an OD change effort and supports it as it is carried out. The consultant, either internal or external, is accountable to the client.

Although consultants often think of the client as the one who authorized the change effort and pays their bills, they are not always certain whose purposes are to be served. For this reason, a key question for any OD consultant to consider is

"Who is the client?" (Varney, 1977). On occasion, the "client" may not be the one who originally sponsored or participated in the change effort.

Culture

The focus of most OD change efforts is on changes in an organization's culture. Prior to the early 1980s, the issue of culture was restricted to anthropology and OD circles, but *culture* became a popular buzzword after the publication of *Corporate Cultures: The Rites and Rituals of Corporate Life* (1982) by Deal and Kennedy and *In Search of Excellence: Lessons from America's Best-Run Companies* (1982) by Peters and Waterman. Peters and Waterman provided numerous examples demonstrating the importance of culture in many of the best-known and best-run companies in the United States at that time. Generally, culture means the following:

> ...*basic assumptions* and *beliefs* that are shared by members of an organization, that operate unconsciously, and that define in a basic "taken-for-granted" fashion an organization's view of itself and its environment. These assumptions and beliefs are *learned* responses to a group's problems. They come to be taken for granted because they solve those problems repeatedly and reliably. (Schein, 1985, pp. 6-7)

Intervention

In the nomenclature of OD, an intervention is a change effort or a change process. It implies an intentional entry into an ongoing system for the purpose of initiating or introducing change.

Organizational Development

Not to be confused with OD—as it often is—organizational development refers to any effort to improve an organization. Unlike OD, it does not imply assumptions about people, organizations, or the change process.

Sponsor

One who underwrites, legitimizes, and champions a change effort or OD intervention.

Stakeholder

One who has an interest in an OD intervention. Stakeholders may include customers, suppliers, distributors, employees, and government regulators.

Subsystem

A subsystem is a part of a system. In one sense, subsystems of an organization (a system) may include work units, departments, or divisions. In another sense, subsystems may cut across an organization and encompass activities, processes, or structures. It is thus possible to focus on an organization's maintenance, adaptive, or managerial subsystems (Katz & Kahn, 1978), among others.

System

In the simplest sense, a system is a series of interdependent components (Burke, 1980). For example, organizations may be viewed as social systems because they depend on interactions among people (Katz & Kahn, 1978). In addition, any organization that receives information from the environment is an open system. Organizations take in inputs (raw materials, capital, information, or people), act on them through a transformation process (production or service-delivery methods), and release them into the environment as outputs (finished goods, services, information, or people). (See Exhibit 1-1.) This transformation cycle must continue if an organization is to survive.

Exhibit 1-1: A Model of a System

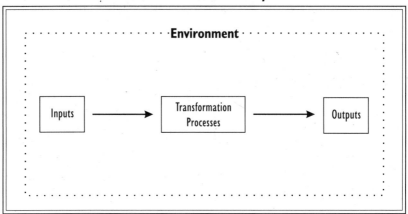

The History of OD

The history of OD is one of gradual evolution. It can be viewed from two separate but related perspectives.

The first perspective is philosophical: The basic assumptions of OD were influenced largely by a philosophy about people, work, organizations, and change that swept through many disciplines during the late 1950s and the 1960s. This philosophy is called the Human Resources School of Management Thought (Rothwell & Sredl, 1992; Wren, 1979). Its influence remains important and widespread.

The second perspective is methodological: The basic techniques of OD stemmed from experiments conducted by applied social scientists in the early Twentieth Century. Many OD techniques were introduced during this period.

The following section briefly reviews both perspectives. Primary emphasis is placed on the evolution of management thought since the beginning of the Twentieth Century, although this emphasis is not meant to imply that the evolution of management thought did not begin until that time (George, 1968). Understanding OD's history makes it easier to understand its present state and likely future.

Philosophical Influences

Management thinking in the United States has undergone three major stages of evolution (Miles, 1975). Each stage presented a different view of people, work, organizations, and change. Some understanding of all three stages or "schools of thought" is important as background for a deeper understanding of OD.

The Classical School of Thought

The first stage was the Classical School of Thought. This school of thought dominated management thinking from the late Nineteenth Century until the early 1930s, and many of its precepts still strongly affect management practice. This philosophy developed from two sources: Social Darwinism and populist interpretations of work by Frederick Taylor, Frank and Lillian Gilbreth, and Henry L. Gantt. The Social Darwinists,whose views were most clearly set forth by the philosopher Herbert Spencer, provided a key assumption on which the Classical School of Thought was based.

> [They] argued strongly that with man [sic], as with other species, not only do the fittest survive but that they should survive, as they can and do contribute disproportionately to their numbers. Conversely, efforts made to preserve and improve the lot of the inept are not only expensive but are potentially damaging to the natural evolutionary progress of mankind. (Miles, 1975, p. 36)

Populists, interpreting the work of practical theorists, added to this pessimistic view of human nature. For instance, Frederick Taylor's work "propagated a view of efficiency which, until recently, was markedly successful—so long as 'success' was measured in terms of unit costs and output" (*Work in America: Report of a Special Task Force to the Secretary of Health, Education, and Welfare,* 1973, p. 17).

Taylor's ideas were translated into management practices in such a way that they yielded "simplified tasks for those who are not simple-minded, close supervision by those whose legitimacy rests only on a hierarchical structure, and jobs that have nothing but money to offer" (p. 18). As Rue and Byars (1989) note, "Taylor and scientific management were (and still are) attacked as being inhumane and interested only in increased output" (p. 38). Although the views of Taylor and his followers were not as pessimistic about human nature as they have been interpreted to be (Wren, 1979), populists did lead U.S. managers to believe that employees find work generally distasteful, that they value monetary rewards more than other rewards, and that few of them are really suited for creative tasks (Miles, 1975).

Human Relations School of Thought

The second stage was the Human Relations School of Thought. It was a partial rejection of the Classical School of Thought, though it retained many of the Classical School's key assumptions. The Human Relations School emerged from a series of experiments at a Western Electric plant in Hawthorne, Illinois. These experiments began in 1924 and were designed to study how employee productivity would be affected when working conditions were altered. At first the researchers lowered the lighting and expected productivity to decrease, but instead productivity increased. Researchers repeated the experiments for many months, only to find that productivity consistently increased.

In 1927 a new team of researchers entered the Hawthorne plant. For five years the researchers conducted hundreds of experiments and altered many aspects of the working conditions, such as the length of the work day, the wages paid, and the length of rest periods. Productivity continued to increase. However, the increases did not seem to be directly tied to the changes made to the working conditions. After much consideration, the researchers concluded that employees respond more to the way they are treated than they do to environmental conditions. Indeed, the researchers thought "that employees in a congenial work group, interacting and involved with supportive supervisors, either increased their output or maintained it at high levels" (Miles, 1975, p. 40).

From this finding, which critics later found to be flawed, the Hawthorne researchers concluded that workers want socially sensitive supervision and a feeling of camaraderie in the workplace. Unfortunately, "this school (which has many adherents in personnel offices today) ignores the technological and production factors involved in a business. This approach concentrates on the enterprise as a social system—the workers are to be treated better, but their jobs remain the same" (*Work in America,* 1973, p. 18).

Human Resources School of Thought

The third stage was the Human Resources School of Thought. It emerged as a direct response to an economic recession that began in 1957 and to evidence that the Human Relations School had not generated effective workplace applications (Wren, 1979).

The intellectual precursors of the Human Resources School can be traced to numerous sources well before the 1950s. One source is humanism, the key values of which include a firm belief in human rationality, human perfectibility through learning, and the importance of self-awareness.

Another source is applied social science, which began making its first empirical investigations of human behavior in industry early in the Twentieth Century. Through these investigations, social scientists gradually recognized that "each individual, highly variable and complex due to a unique genetic composition and family, social, and work experiences, becomes even more variable and complex when placed in interaction with other unique individuals" (Wren, 1979, p. 348).

During the 1950s and later, the advocates of the Human Resources School of Thought articulated their beliefs in many disciplines. In economics, Eli Ginzberg (1958) stressed the importance of human effort and creativity in the production process. He added a new dimension to the debate about the values of land, labor, and capital. In the process he laid the groundwork for a Human Capital Theory of Economics, which examines human contributions to productivity improvement.

In psychology, Carl Rogers (1942) and Abraham Maslow (1943, 1954) championed a new view of people and change. Rogers' central assumption was that people have a lasting desire to improve themselves and satisfy their needs. Building on the earlier work of Henry Murray (1938), Maslow also contributed new ideas about human motivation that suggested an evolutionary pursuit of needs fulfillment. According to Maslow, people are motivated to meet their needs, which are arranged in a hierarchy. (See Exhibit 1-2.)

Maslow's ideas about motivation are positive, much like those that characterize the later work of Frederick Herzberg, Bernard Mausner, Barbara Snyderman, and Douglas McGregor. (See Exhibit 1-3 for a summary of Herzberg's theory; see Exhibit 1-4 for a summary of McGregor's theory.) These positive ideas about motivation challenged the more negative and generally pessimistic assumptions made by Freud and by the behavioralist, B.F. Skinner. According to Freudians, people are enslaved to their pasts and must be reconciled to them in order to be freed from the burdens created by them; according to behavioralists, people are captives of their environments and must adapt to them to survive and prosper.

In education, Cyril Houle (1961) and Malcolm Knowles (1972) focused new attention on assumptions about the learning process and the learners themselves. Houle researched why people learn. He discovered three primary reasons and categorized learners by their chief orientation to the learning experience. The three primary reasons are as follows:

1. The love of learning itself,
2. The desire for social relationships, and
3. The desire for practical information to use in solving immediate problems.

Exhibit 1-2: Maslow's Need Hierarchy

In Maslow's need hierarchy, as each lower-level need is satisfied, a higher-order need arises to motivate individuals:

Self-Actualization Needs (Highest Order)
1. Achieving one's potential
2. Sense of accomplishment
3. Satisfaction of curiosity
4. Realization of creativity

Esteem Needs
1. Recognition
2. Prestige
3. Confidence stemming from leadership

Social Needs
1. Acceptance
2. Feelings of belonging
3. Love/affection

Safety Needs
1. Security
2. Physical comfort
3. Economic well-being

Physiological Needs (Lowest-Order)
1. Food
2. Water
3. Air
4. Rest
5. Bodily requirements and sex

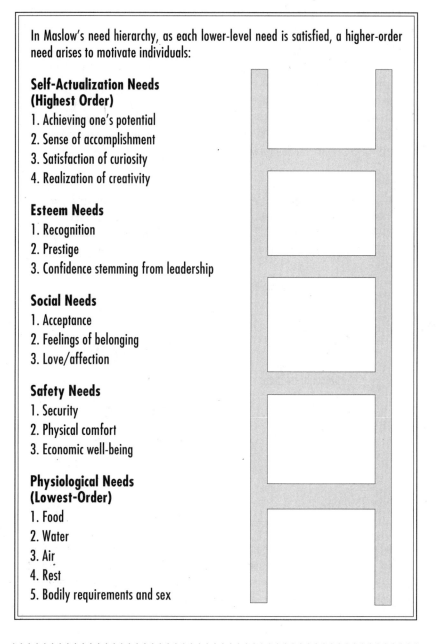

Exhibit 1-3: Herzberg's Two-Factor Theory of Motivation

Herzberg's theory—called by various names, such as dual-factor theory, motivation-hygiene theory, and motivation-maintenance theory—was initially based on interviews with engineers and accountants. Through analysis of interview results, the researchers found that some factors were viewed positively while others were viewed negatively. Interestingly, those factors viewed positively were often associated with the work itself; those viewed negatively were often associated with the work environment. The following is an example:

Factors Associated with the Work Environment (Hygiene Factors)	Factors Associated with the Work Itself (Motivation Factors)
• Policies and administration	• Achievement
• Supervision	• Recognition
• Working conditions	• Challenging work
• Interpersonal relations	• Increased responsibility
• Personal life	• Advancement
• Money	• Personal growth
• Status	
• Security	

Motivation stems from individual actions, not management actions. When hygiene factors are satisfied, individuals are not satisfied; rather, they experience no dissatisfaction. Individuals are motivated to act by motivation factors, assuming that hygiene factors are not giving rise to dissatisfaction.

Exhibit 1-4: McGregor's Theories X and Y

One of the best-known and classic expressions of management theory was the result of Douglas McGregor's work. He developed two descriptions of management philosophy that he claimed many leaders ascribe to, whether or not they articulate what they believe. These he called Theory X and Theory Y, and they were fully described in *The Human Side of Enterprise* (McGregor, 1960).

Theory X leaders assume that people

- Have a genuine distaste for work
- Must be prodded, coerced, or threatened into work because it is so unpleasant
- Prefer to be closely supervised
- Avoid as much responsibility as they can
- Have little ambition
- Value security above all else

In contrast, Theory Y leaders assume that people

- Want to work because working is natural
- Will exercise self-control if they are committed to the results to be achieved by their efforts
- Will be motivated to achieve goals if they value those goals
- Share imagination and creativity, traits that are not limited solely to management
- Are "boxed in" by bureaucratic job descriptions and are capable of realizing more potential than they are typically given a chance to realize

Knowles suggested that adults learn in ways significantly different from those used by children. Successful adult learning experiences must take into account adult learners' experiences and values.

In management, new ideas about work, workers, and organizations were espoused by Chris Argyris (1962, 1964), among others. Argyris believed that bureaucratic organizations foster individual dependence and passivity. People in them tend to be locked into distinct roles and subjected to an authority structure that makes action and creativity difficult to exercise. The chief assumptions and implications of the three schools of management thought are summarized in Exhibit 1-5.

Methodological Influences

Another common way to view the history of OD stresses its emergence from three separate but related behavioral-science applications:[1] (1) laboratory training, (2) survey research and feedback, and (3) Tavistock Sociotechnical Systems. Newer applications that warrant inclusion are total quality management and business process reengineering.

Laboratory Training

An early precursor of OD, laboratory training is associated with unstructured, small-group sessions in which participants

---

[1] This part of the chapter is based on lengthier descriptions of OD's history appearing in Burke (1987), French (1972), French and Bell (1984), and Patten (1990).

Exhibit 1-5: A Summary of the Chief Assumptions of Three Schools of Management Thought

The Classical School	The Human Relations School	The Human Resources School
Assumptions		
1. Work is inherently distasteful to most people.	1. People want to feel useful and important.	1. Work is not inherently distasteful. People want to contribute to meaningful goals which they have helped establish.
2. What workers do is less important than what they earn for doing it.	2. People desire to belong and to be recognized as individuals.	2. Most people can exercise far more creative, responsible self-direction and self-control than their present jobs demand.
Policies		
1. The manager's basic task is to supervise and closely control subordinates.	1. The manager's basic task is to make each worker feel useful and important.	1. The manager's basic task is to coach and to make use of "untapped" human resources.
2. The manager must break down tasks into simple, repetitive, easily-learned operations.	2. The manager should keep subordinates informed and listen to their objections to the manager's plans.	2. The manager must create an environment in which all members may contribute to the limits of their abilities.
3. The manager must establish detailed work routines and procedures and enforce these firmly and fairly.	3. The manager should allow subordinates to exercise some self-direction and self-control on routine matters.	3. The manager must encourage full participation on important matters, continually broadening subordinate self-direction and control.

Exhibit 1-5: A Summary of the Chief Assumptions of Three Schools of Management Thought (continued)

The Classical School	The Human Relations School	The Human Resources School
Expectations		
1. People can tolerate work if the pay is decent and the boss is fair.	1. Sharing information with subordinates and involving them in routine decisions will satisfy their basic needs to belong and feel important.	1. Expanding subordinate influence, self-direction, and self-control will lead to direct improvements in operating efficiency.
2. If tasks are simple enough and people are closely controlled, they will produce up to standard.	2. Satisfying these needs will improve morale and reduce resistance to formal authority; subordinates will " willingly cooperate."	2. Work satisfaction may improve as a "by-product" of subordinates' making full use of their resources.

From Miles, R. E. (1975). *Theories of Management: Implications for Organizational Behavior and Development.* New York: McGraw-Hill, p. 35. Reproduced with permission of McGraw-Hill, Inc.

share their experiences and learn from their interactions. Bradford, Gibb, and Benn (1964) explain this application in the following way:

> The term "laboratory" was not idly chosen. A training laboratory is a community dedicated to the stimulation and support of experimental learning and change. New patterns of behavior are invented and tested in a climate supporting change and protected for the time from the full practical consequences of innovative action in ongoing associations. (p. 3)

Unlike employee-training sessions, which focus on increasing individual knowledge or skill in conformance with the participant's job requirements, laboratory-training sessions focus on group processes and group dynamics. The first laboratory-training sessions were carried out in the 1940s. In particular, the work of the New Britain Workshop in 1946, under the direction of such major social scientists as Kurt Lewin, Kenneth Benne, Leland Bradford, and Ronald Lippitt stimulated much interest in laboratory training. The leaders and members of the workshop accidentally discovered that providing feedback to groups and to individuals at the *end of each day* produced more real learning about group dynamics than did lectures. The groundbreaking work of the New Britain Workshop led to the founding of the National Training Laboratories (NTL Institute for Applied Behavioral Science).

Early laboratory-training sessions were usually composed of participants from different organizations, a fact that led such groups to be called Stranger T-groups. (The term "T-group" is an abbreviation of "training group.") Bradford, Gibb, and Benn (1964) define such a group in the following manner:

> A T-Group is a relatively unstructured group in which individuals participate as learners. The data for learning are not outside these individuals or removed from their immediate experience within the T-Group. The data are transactions among members, their own behavior in the group, as they struggle to create a productive and viable organization, a miniature society; and as they work to stimulate and support one another's learning within that society. (p. 1)

Behavioral scientists later discovered that the participants had difficulty transferring insights and behavioral changes to their work lives. This transfer-of-learning problem increased interest in conducting such sessions in a single organization, a technique that has evolved into what is now called *team building*.

Laboratory training was an important forerunner of OD because it focused attention on the dynamics of group or team interaction. In addition, it provided a basis for team building, which is still an important OD intervention.

Survey Research and Feedback

Survey research and feedback also made an important contribution to the evolution of OD. This approach to change was developed and refined by the Survey Research Center at the University of Michigan under the direction of Rensis Likert. Likert, who directed the Survey Research Center from 1950 to 1970, became widely recognized for his innovative use of written survey questionnaires to collect information about an organization and its problems, provide feedback to survey respondents, and stimulate joint planning for improvement. This technique is called survey research and feedback or survey-guided development.

Likert's method began evolving when he observed that many organizations seldom used the results from attitude surveys to guide their change efforts. Managers authorized the surveys but did not always act on the results. This "ask-but-don't-act" approach produced greater frustration among employees than not asking for their opinions in the first place.

The centerpiece of Likert's approach was a technique called the *interlocking conference*. Survey results were given to top managers during the first conference, and then other conferences were held to inform the organization's successively lower levels. In each conference, group members worked together to establish an action plan to address problems or weaknesses revealed by the survey. This top-down strategy of feedback and performance planning ensured that the action plan devised by each group was tied to those at higher levels.

A philosophy about organizational systems governed much of Likert's work. He believed that any system—that is, an organization or a component part of an organization—can be categorized into one of four types based on eight key characteristics. The four organizational types (Exhibit 1-6) are as follows:

- System 1: Exploitive-Authoritarian;
- System 2: Benevolent-Authoritative;
- System 3: Consultative; and
- System 4: Participative.

The eight characteristics are as follows:

- Leadership
- Motivation
- Communication
- Interaction
- Decision making
- Goal setting
- Control
- Performance

Likert developed a fifty-one-item questionnaire to measure these characteristics.

Likert believed that System 4 was the "ideal" organization. In Likert's System 4 organization, leadership is based on influence, not authority or power. Employees are motivated through the intrinsic rewards stemming from the work itself. Communication is balanced, with a great deal of two-way interaction between managers and employees. Likert (1961) justified System 4 as a norm or ideal because he found that "supervisors with the best records of performance focus their primary attention on the human aspects of their subordinates' problems and on endeavoring to build effective work groups with high performance goals" (p. 7).

Exhibit 1-6: Characteristics of Likert's Four Types of Organizations

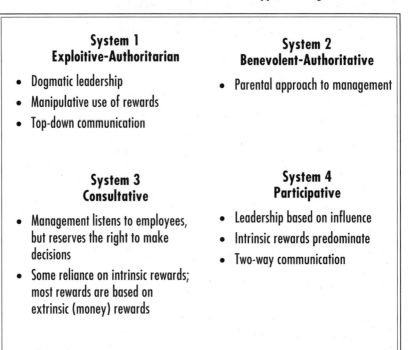

Likert's views, described in his two major books, *New Patterns of Management* (1961) and *The Human Organization* (1967), have had a profound influence on OD. He demonstrated how information can be collected from members of an organization and used as the basis for participative problem solving and action planning. In addition, he advocated pursuit of a norm for organizational functioning (System 4) that has since prompted others to pursue similar norms for organizations. In some respects, Likert's views about the System 4 organization are important precursors to modern-day interest in self-directed work teams and high-performance work environments.

Tavistock Sociotechnical Systems

Another major contributor to the evolution of OD is Tavistock Sociotechnical Systems. Tavistock, founded in 1920, is a clinic in England. Its earliest work was devoted to family therapy in which both child and parents received simultaneous treatment.

An important experiment in work redesign was conducted for coal miners by a team of Tavistock researchers at about the same time that laboratory training was introduced in the United States. Before the experiment, coal miners worked closely in teams of six. They maintained control over who was placed on a team and were rewarded for team, not individual, production. New technology was introduced to the mine, changing work methods from a team to an individual orientation. The result was a decrease in productivity and an increase in absenteeism. The Tavistock researchers recommended that the new technology could be used by miners grouped into teams. The researchers' advice, when implemented, improved productivity and restored absenteeism rates to historic levels in the organization.

Tavistock Sociotechnical Systems' key contribution to OD was an emphasis on social subsystems. The Tavistock researchers believed that organizations are composed of key subsystems. One such subsystem is the people in an organization. Their needs must be taken into account if a change is to be successful. Consequently, to effect change successfully, OD should focus on how a proposed change might impact work methods.

Quality Management and Business Process Reengineering

Newer contributions to the evolution of OD are total quality management (TQM) and business process reengineering. Total quality management has benefitted from the philosophical contributions of W. Edwards Deming and the technical contributions of Philip Crosby and Joseph M. Juran. Total quality management has focused attention on the creative potential of human beings and their ability to improve the work that they do.

However, business process reengineering has created new interest in radical organizational change and restructuring. Reengineering has encouraged managers and employees to rethink what they do and how they do it as a means to achieve an advantage in a fiercely competitive, global marketplace.

OD and Other Human Resource Fields

Organization development is part of a larger human resource (HR) field that is unified in its focus on people—primarily people in organizational settings. However, OD's central focus differs from that of other HR fields. It is worth considering the relationship between OD and these other fields because OD activities are affected by—and, in turn, affect—other HR activities.

Leonard Nadler (1980, 1989) is one prominent authority who has attempted to explain these relationships. He distinguishes between human resource development (HRD), human resource management (HRM), and human resource environment (HRE) activities. Taken together, they encompass all HR fields.

Human Resource Development

Human resource development, according to Nadler (1989), consists of training, education, and development. It is defined as "organized learning experiences provided by employers within a specified period of time to bring about the possibility of performance improvement and/or personal growth" (p. 6). Training is a short-term change effort intended to equip individuals with the knowledge, skills, and attitudes they need to perform their jobs better. Education is an intermediate-term change effort intended to prepare individuals for promotions (vertical career progression) or for enhanced technical abilities in their current jobs (horizontal career progression). Development is a long-term change effort intended to broaden individuals through experience and to give them new insights about themselves and their organizations. All HRD efforts share a common goal of bringing about "the possibility of performance improvement and/or personal growth" (p. 6).

Human Resource Management

Nadler believes that HRM includes all activities traditionally linked with the personnel function except training. Human resource management is thus associated with recruitment, selection, placement, compensation, benefits, appraisal, and HR information systems. According to Nadler, all HRM efforts share one common goal: to increase organizational productivity by using the talents of its current employees.

Human Resource Environment

Human resource environment includes OD and job- or work-redesign efforts. According to Nadler, HRE activities focus on changing working conditions and interpersonal relationships when they interfere with performance or impede employee creativity. Unlike other HR fields, HRE activities share one goal: to improve the work environment through planned, long-term, and group-oriented change in organizational structures or interpersonal relations.

Human Resource Wheel

Leonard Nadler has not been alone in describing relationships among HR fields. A study of HRD competencies, entitled *Models for HRD Practice* (McLagan, 1989), provides another way to conceptualize the relationships. The study provides a "Human Resource Wheel" to identify major HR fields and show their relative emphases. (See Exhibit 1-7.)

As the Human Resource Wheel indicates, training and development (T & D), organization development, and career development (CD) are related fields. Each is a key component of HRD according to McLagan (1989), who defines HRD as "the integrated use of training and development, Organization Development, and career development to improve individual, group, and organizational effectiveness. Those three areas use development as their primary process" (p. 6).

Training and Development. Training and development focuses on "identifying, assuring, and—through planned learning—helping develop the key competencies that enable individuals to perform current or future jobs" (p. 6). The key words in this definition are "learning" and "individuals." The field of T & D is directed toward individuals, and learning is its key method of inducing change.

Organization Development. Organization development is intended to "assure healthy inter- and intra-unit relationships and help groups initiate and manage change." Groups is the key word in this definition. Organization development is thus geared to initiating and managing change within and between groups of people. In this respect it differs from training, which focuses primarily on individuals.

Career Development. Career development is a third component of HRD.

> [It] focuses on assuring an alignment of individual career planning and organizational career management processes to achieve an optimal match of individual and organizational needs. Career development's primary emphasis is on the person as an individual who performs and shapes his or her various work roles (McLagan, 1989, p. 6).

Career development is not directed toward individuals and their jobs, like T & D, or toward individuals/groups and inter- and intra-unit relationships, like OD. Instead, CD is intended to ensure a match between individual and organizational needs.

Each HR area on the Human Resource Wheel is related to others. However, according to the model T & D, OD, and

Exhibit 1-7: The Human Resource Wheel

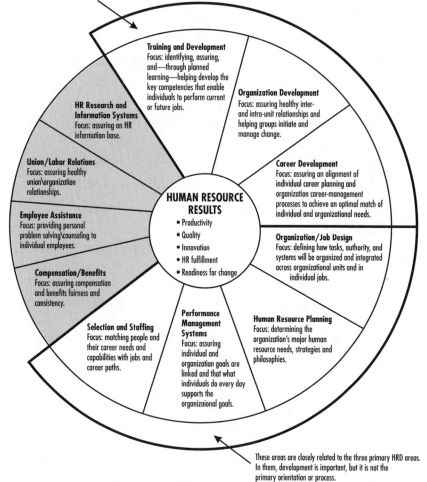

HRD

HRD is the integrated use of training and development, organization development, and career development to improve individual, group, and organizational effectiveness. Those three areas use development as their primary process, and are the focal point of this study.

Training and Development
Focus: identifying, assuring, and—through planned learning—helping develop the key competencies that enable individuals to perform current or future jobs.

HR Research and Information Systems
Focus: assuring an HR information base.

Organization Development
Focus: assuring healthy inter- and intra-unit relationships and helping groups initiate and manage change.

Union/Labor Relations
Focus: assuring healthy union\organization relationships.

Career Development
Focus: assuring an alignment of individual career planning and organization career-management processes to achieve an optimal match of individual and organizational needs.

Employee Assistance
Focus: providing personal problem solving\counseling to individual employees.

HUMAN RESOURCE RESULTS
• Productivity
• Quality
• Innovation
• HR fulfillment
• Readiness for change

Organization/Job Design
Focus: defining how tasks, authority, and systems will be organized and integrated across organizational units and in individual jobs.

Compensation/Benefits
Focus: assuring compensation and benefits fairness and consistency.

Selection and Staffing
Focus: matching people and their career needs and capabilities with jobs and career paths.

Performance Management Systems
Focus: assuring individual and organization goals are linked and that what individuals do every day supports the organizaional goals.

Human Resource Planning
Focus: determining the organization's major human resource needs, strategies and philosophies.

These areas are closely related to the three primary HRD areas. In them, development is important, but it is not the primary orientation or process.

McLagan, P. (1989). *The models.* A volume in *Models for HRD practice.* Alexandria, VA: American Society for Training and Development, p. 6. Used by permission of the American Society for Training and Development.

CD are closely aligned to such other areas as organization/job design, human resource planning, performance-management systems, and selection and staffing. Training and development, organization development, and career development are less closely aligned to compensation/benefits, employee assistance, union/labor relations, and HR research and information systems.

Knowledge Requirements of HR Practitioners

A large-scale research project was undertaken by the Personnel Accreditation Institute (since renamed the Human Resource Certification Institute) and affiliated organizationally with the Society for Human Resource Management (SHRM) to identify the "body-of-knowledge" requirements of HR practitioners (Tornow, 1988). Basing results on six thousand questionnaires returned by SHRM members in early 1988, the researcher concluded that of all HR practitioners, OD specialists require the most general knowledge.

More surprisingly, in light of the conclusions in *Models for HRD Practice,* the researcher concluded that "OD and HR Planning have similar Body-of-Knowledge profiles." Comparing factor scores from the questionnaires, Tornow ranked the areas of HR practice that OD consultants indicated were most important to successful OD practice. They were, in order of importance, as follows:

1. OD,
2. Human resource planning,
3. T & D,
4. Employment and personnel practices,
5. Compensation and benefits,

6. Personnel research,
7. Collective bargaining,
8. Human resource information systems, and
9. Health and safety.

When Will OD Be Successful?

Sometimes, novices interested in OD mistakenly assume that any problem lends itself to a solution through an OD intervention. When OD is applied to the wrong situations or is an instrument for manipulation, it can fail as dramatically as other methods intended to initiate or manage change (Mirvis & Berg, 1977). It is worth considering when OD will be successful—and when it will not be successful—in change efforts.

When OD Will Be Successful

Generally speaking, OD may be used effectively when the following conditions exist:

- At least one key decision maker in the organization perceives a need for change, and top managers do not actively oppose change.
- The perceived need or problem is caused, in whole or in part, by conditions in the work environment, such as relations between or among individuals or intact work groups.
- Managers in the organization are willing to commit to long-term improvement.
- Managers and employees are willing to listen with open minds to the key assumptions of OD as articulated by

an internal consultant, an external consultant, or a team of internal and external consultants.

- Some trust and cooperation exist in the organization.

- Top management is willing to provide the resources necessary to support expertise either inside or outside the organization.

When OD Will Not Be Successful

OD may not be an appropriate solution for introducing change when the conditions previously listed are not met or when the change agent behaves unethically or manipulatively. Consider options to OD interventions when the following conditions exist:

- Nobody, apart from a consultant, feels a need for change. The decision makers have closed minds, rejecting the notion that change is appropriate. They prefer the way things are.

- Managers in the organization prefer appearances to reality. They seek "quick fixes" designed to give the illusion that management supports change.

- Managers or employees are unwilling to listen to key assumptions and values of OD, preferring coercion or persuasion.

- Distrust is so prevalent among decision makers that they are unwilling to speak to one another to begin resolving conflicts. In these cases, organizational members would rather leave the setting than resolve their problems. Alienation of affection, comparable to what is experienced in cases of irreconcilable differences in divorce proceedings, is apparent.

- The organization's culture is so strong that managers are reluctant to call in expertise from outside the organization when qualified talent is not available inside.

In these cases, someone must lay the groundwork for change or an OD effort. This task, which often falls to personnel or HRD staff members (London, 1988), may be accomplished by demonstrating a need for change, focusing attention on reality rather than on appearances, explaining OD methods, building trust, or making the case for using external consultants when necessary.

Alternatives to OD

When the goal is planning and implementing change, there are alternatives to OD. Although these alternatives are not the chief focus of this book, they are worth mentioning so that OD consultants will be familiar with other possibilities.

The Legalistic Approach

The legalistic approach to change is based on a comparison between existing laws and organizational practices. When differences are noted, management changes organizational practices to bring them into compliance with applicable legal standards. For example, concerned citizens, consumers, special-interest groups, or disgruntled employees can file lawsuits against private, public, or not-for-profit organizations if the organizational practices in question are illegal. Government agencies can perform investigations, and courts may eventually compel organizational changes to be made. Another example of this approach to change is that managers can authorize their own internal or external performance audits to ensure that their organizations are complying with laws and good management practices (Herbert, 1979; Rothwell, 1981).

The Dialectic Approach

Change can also be brought about by a dialectic approach (Mason & Mitroff, 1981). For instance, management may authorize two employees or management groups to examine different sides of an issue and debate them in an open forum. A fundamental assumption of this approach is that superior ideas emerge through conflict between two or more contrasting opinions. Indeed, conflict is prized because it subjects issues to uncensored consideration from all angles.

The Leadership Change Approach

Another way to initiate and implement change is to appoint a new leader (Gilmore, 1988). Each person brings to a leadership role his or her own attitudes, values, and beliefs that underlie subsequent actions. If an organization selects a leader whose beliefs are in line with its intended direction for change, the organization's strategic direction may be changed (Dlugos & Weiermair, 1981; Glueck & Jauch, 1984). When an organization needs to make a radical change, it should appoint a leader who has no stake in preserving the organization's existing conditions. That often means appointing someone from outside the organization (Gerstein & Reisman, 1983). Later, once a change has been made, the leader may have to be replaced by someone who can consolidate the gains that have been made in the organization (Schein, 1978).

The Persuasive Approach

People will change when they are convinced that change is in their best interests (Chin & Benne, 1969). Advocates of persuasion as a change strategy advise managers to examine who will be affected by proposed changes and then to make a concerted effort to explain how those affected will benefit. Unfortunately, persuasion will probably not work well as a change strategy when people do not know what goals are being sought, do not believe they can attain rewards if they do achieve goals that are clearly spelled out, or do not value the rewards they think they will receive (Vroom, 1964).

The Coercive Approach

People will also change if they are threatened with punishment, such as discipline or dismissal. This technique is called a coercive approach to change (Chin & Benne, 1969). Coercion is usually a counterproductive change strategy because it creates anxiety, fear, and stress and it may provoke sabotage. In addition, turnover and absenteeism tend to increase. However, there may be occasions in which coercive change is the only approach that will work. It is usually considered a change strategy of last resort.

References

Argyris, C. (1962). *Interpersonal competence and organizational effectiveness.* Belmont, CA: Dorsey Press.

Argyris, C. (1964). *Integrating the individual and the organization.* New York: John Wiley & Sons.

Beckhard, R. (1969). *Organization development: Strategies and models*. Reading, MA: Addison-Wesley.

Beer, M. (1980). *Organization change and development: A systems view*. Santa Monica, CA: Goodyear.

Bennis, W. (1969). *Organization development: Its nature, origin and prospects*. Reading, MA: Addison-Wesley.

Bradford, L., Gibb, J., & Benne, K. (1964). *T-group theory and laboratory method: Innovation in re-education*. New York: John Wiley & Sons.

Bradford, L., Gibb, J., & Benne, K. (1964). Two educational innovations. In L. Bradford, J. Gibb, & K. Benne, *T-group theory and laboratory method: Innovation in re-education* (pp. 1-14). New York: John Wiley & Sons.

Burke, W. (1980). Systems theory, gestalt therapy, and organization development. In T. Cummings (Ed.), *Systems theory for organization development* (pp. 209-222). Chichester, UK: John Wiley & Sons.

Burke, W. (1982). *Organization development: Principles and practices*. New York: Little, Brown & Co.

Burke, W. (1987). *Organization development: A normative view*. Reading, MA: Addison-Wesley.

Chin, R., & Benne, K. (1969). General strategies for effecting changes in human systems. In W. Bennis, K. Benne, & R. Chin (Eds.), *The planning of change* (2nd ed.) (pp. 32- 59). New York: Holt, Rinehart & Winston.

Deal, T., & Kennedy, A. (1982). *Corporate cultures: The rites and rituals of corporate life*. Reading, MA: Addison-Wesley.

Dlugos, G., & Weiermair, K. (Eds.). (1981). *Management under differing value systems: Political, social and economical perspectives in a changing world*. New York: Walter de Gruyter.

French, W. (1972). The emergence and early history of organizational development: With reference to influences on and interaction among key actors. *Group and Organizational Studies, 7*(3), 261-277.

French, W., & Bell, C., Jr. (1984). *Organization development: Behavioral science interventions for organization improvement* (3rd. ed.). Englewood Cliffs, NJ: Prentice-Hall.

French, W., & Bell, C., Jr. (1990). *Organization development: Behavioral science interventions for organization improvement* (4th. ed.). Englewood Cliffs, NJ: Prentice-Hall.

George, C., Jr. (1968). *The history of management thought.* Englewood Cliffs, NJ: Prentice-Hall.

Gerstein, M., & Reisman, H. (1983). Strategic selection: Matching executives to business conditions. *Sloan Management Review, 24*(2), 33-49.

Gilmore, T. (1988). *Making a leadership change: How organizations and leaders can handle leadership transitions successfully.* San Francisco, CA: Jossey-Bass.

Ginzberg, E. (1958). *Human resources: The wealth of a nation.* New York: Simon & Schuster.

Glueck, W., & Jauch, L. (1984). *Business policy and strategic management* (4th ed.). New York: McGraw-Hill.

Golembiewski, R. (1990). *Ironies in organizational development.* New Brunswick, NJ: Transaction Publishers.

Herbert, L. (1979). *Auditing the performance of management.* Belmont, CA: Lifetime Learning Publications.

Herzberg, F., Mausner, B., & Snyderman, B. (1959). *The motivation to work.* New York: John Wiley & Sons.

Houle, C. (1961). *The inquiring mind.* Madison, WI: University of Wisconsin Press.

Katz, D., & Kahn, R. (1978). *The social psychology of organizations* (2nd ed.). New York: John Wiley & Sons.

Kilmann, R. (1984). *Beyond the quick fix: Managing five tracks to organizational success.* San Francisco, CA: Jossey-Bass.

Knowles, M. (1972). *The modern practice of adult education: Andragogy versus pedagogy.* New York: Association Press.

Likert, R. (1961). *New patterns of management.* New York: McGraw-Hill.

Likert, R. (1967). *The human organization: Its management and value.* New York: McGraw-Hill.

London, M. (1988). *Change agents: New roles and innovation strategies for human resource professionals.* San Francisco, CA: Jossey-Bass.

Maslow, A. (1943). *A theory of human motivation. Psychological Review, 50,* 370-396.

Maslow, A. (1954). *Motivation and personality.* New York: Harper & Row.

Mason, R., & Mitroff, I. (1981). *Challenging strategic planning assumptions: Theory, cases and techniques.* New York: John Wiley & Sons.

McGregor, D. (1960). *The human side of enterprise.* New York: McGraw-Hill.

McLagan, P. (1989). *Models for HRD practice.* Alexandria, VA: American Society for Training and Development.

Miles, R.E. (1975). *Theories of management: Implications for organizational behavior and development.* New York: McGraw-Hill.

Mirvis, P., & Berg, D. (1977). *Failures in organization development and change.* New York: John Wiley & Sons.

Murray, H. (1938). *Explorations in personality.* New York: Oxford University Press.

Nadler, L. (1980). *Corporate human resources development.* New York: Van Nostrand Reinhold.

Nadler, L. (1989). *Developing human resources* (3rd ed.). New York: Van Nostrand Reinhold.

Naisbitt, J. (1982). *Megatrends: Ten new directions transforming our lives*. New York: Warner Books.

Organization development: A straightforward reference guide for executives seeking to improve their organizations. (1991). Chesterland, OH: The Organization Development Institute.

Patten, T., Jr. (1990). Historical perspectives on organization development. In W. Sikes, A. Drexler, & J. Gant (Eds.), *The emerging practice of organization development* (pp. 3-14). Alexandria, VA: NTL Institute for Applied Behavioral Science/San Diego, CA: Pfeiffer & Company.

Peters, T., & Waterman, R. (1982). *In search of excellence: Lessons from America's best-run companies*. New York: Harper & Row.

Rogers, C. (1942). *Counseling and psychotherapy*. Boston, MA: Houghton-Mifflin.

Rothwell, W. (1981). Alternatives to organization development. *Training and Development Journal, 35*(12), 119-124.

Rothwell, W., & Sredl, H. (1992). *The ASTD reference guide to professional HRD roles and competencies*. (2nd ed.). 2 vols. Amherst, MA: Human Resource Development Press.

Rue, L., & Byars, L. (1989). *Management: Theory and application* (5th ed.). Homewood, IL: Irwin.

Schein, E. (1978). *Career dynamics: Matching individual and organizational needs*. Reading, MA: Addison-Wesley.

Schein, E. (1985). *Organizational culture and leadership*. San Francisco, CA: Jossey-Bass.

Van Eynde, D., Church, A., Hurley, R., & Burke, W. (1992). What OD practitioners believe. *Training and Development, 46*(4), 41, 44-46.

Varney, G. (1977). *Organization development for managers*. Reading, MA: Addison-Wesley.

Vroom, V. (1964). *Work and motivation*. New York: John Wiley & Sons.

Work in America: Report of a special task force to the secretary of health, education, and welfare. (1973). Cambridge, MA: MIT Press.

Wren, D. (1979). *The evolution of management thought* (2nd ed.). New York: John Wiley & Sons.

CHAPTER 2

MODELS FOR CHANGE AND STEPS IN ACTION RESEARCH

William J. Rothwell, Roland Sullivan, and
Gary N. McLean

A model for change is a simplified representation of the general steps in initiating and carrying out a change process. This chapter reviews three models for change, placing special emphasis on the steps in action research, the change model on which most of the remaining chapters are based.

Models for Change

Three change models, relying primarily on a normative, reeducative approach in which behavioral change results from learning, have been mentioned in OD literature: critical research,

Shewhart's (1924) Plan, Do, Check, and Act cycle, and action research. However, most OD consultants rely on action research as the change model underpinning their efforts.

Critical Research

Critical research (CR) stems from Marxist practices. The key idea underlying CR is similar to a dialectic approach to change. Critical research assumes that every organization or group has an ideology, a more or less consistent rationale about how decisions should be made, how resources should be used, how people should be managed, and how the organization should respond to the environment in which it functions. Katz and Kahn (1978) describe ideology as "generated to provide justification for the organization's existence and functions" (p. 101). In one sense, an ideology is a step above culture, and "culture is the manifestation of ideology, giving 'life' to ideology" (Lang, 1992, p. 191).

A natural tension develops between what people believe should be happening and what they believe is actually happening. The basic thrust of CR is to identify this discrepancy. Because individual perceptions differ within groups, CR builds an impetus for change by dramatizing differences between the organization's ideology about what should be and actual situations contradicting its ideology—thereby underscoring the need for change. Critical research heightens the tension by pointing out inconsistency.

Although critical research has not been widely used in OD (Rothwell, 1981), OD interventions such as confrontational meetings lend themselves to it. (A confrontation meeting brings together two conflicting groups to discuss their differences and to arrive at ways of working together more effectively.)

Critical research views conflict between ideology and actual practices as constructive, leading to self-examination and to change. The steps in applying CR to a change effort are listed in Exhibit 2-1.

Exhibit 2-1: Steps in Applying Critical Research to OD

1. Describe the Ideology.
   (How do people believe the organization or group should be functioning?)

2. Identify Situations, Events, or Conditions That Conflict with the Ideology.
   (What is actually happening?)

3. Identify Individuals or Groups Desiring Progressive Change.
   (Who wants to challenge the ideology and/or actual situations to create an impetus for progressive change?)

4. Confront Proponents of the Ideology with Conflicting Situations, Events, or Conditions.

5. Devise a New Ideology or Action Steps to Correct Inconsistency.

6. Help the Client Establish a Timetable for Change.

7. Implement the Change.

8. Ask the Client to Monitor the Change, Identifying Opportunities for Continuous Improvement as Necessary.

Shewhart's PDCA Cycle

Recent interest in total quality management (TQM) has drawn attention to a change model that was developed in 1924. This model, Shewhart's PDCA Cycle, takes its name from its inventor, Thomas Shewhart, and from the steps in the change cycle itself: Plan, Do, Check, and Act. Shewart's PDCA Cycle is associated widely with W. Edwards Deming's ideas about continuous improvement.

Review the PDCA model shown in Exhibit 2-2. The model can be applied to an OD intervention or to phases within an intervention.

Exhibit 2-2: Shewhart's PDCA Cycle

Cycles of Transformation Efforts

Though no hard and fast rules exist, there seems to be adequate testimony and experience to roughly describe the first "cycles of transformation" for a typical organization. We have chosen "cycles of transformation" as the descriptive phrase because transformation is an iterative process and the Shewhart cycle is an elegant model. Each iteration of the cycle includes:

ACT: Does the data confirm the "plan"? Are other "causes" operating? Are the "risks" of proceeding to further change necessary and worthwhile?

PLAN: What could be? What changes are needed? What obstacles need to be overcome? What are the most important results needed? etc. Are data available? What new information is needed?

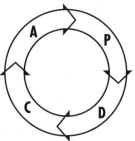

CHECK: Measure and observe "effects" of change or test.

DO: Small scale implementation of change or test to provide data for answers.

From Schultz, L., & Parker, B. (1988). Visioning the Future. In G. McLean & S. DeVogel (Eds.), *The Role of Organization Development in Quality Management and Productivity Improvement: Theory-to-Practice Monograph* (pp. 47-67). Alexandria, VA: American Society for Training and Development, p. 53. Used by permission of the American Society for Training and Development.

Action Research

Action research is the foundation for most OD interventions. It is both a model and a process. As a model, action research can be seen as a simplified representation of the complex activities that occur in a change effort. The model serves as a road map to consultants facilitating change. It helps the consultants track where they are and where they are going. Exhibit 2-3 illustrates a model of action research.

Exhibit 2-3: A Model of Action Research

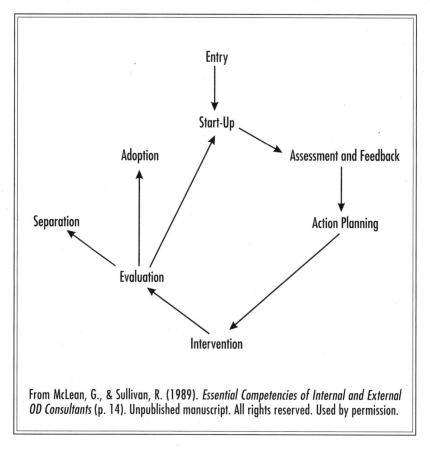

Action research may also be understood as a process, a continuing series of events and actions. French and Bell (1990) define this interpretation of action research in the following manner:

> [It is] the process of systematically collecting research data about an ongoing system relative to some objective, goal, or need of that system; feeding these data back into the system; taking actions by altering selected variables within the system based both on the data and on hypotheses; and evaluating the results of actions by collecting more data. (p. 99)

As a process, action research is thus a cycle in which research is followed by change activities, the results of which are fed into further research.

Steps in OD Interventions

The eight steps in any OD intervention are based on those in action research and are listed in Burke (1982) and *Essential Competencies of Internal and External OD Consultants* (McLean & Sullivan, 1989). The steps in are as follows:

Step	Brief Description
1. Entry	The need for change in an organization becomes apparent. A problem is discovered. Someone or a group of people in the organization look for a person who is capable of examining the problem or facilitating change.
2. Start-Up	The change agent enters the picture, working to clarify issues surrounding the problem and to gain commitment to a change effort.

Step	Brief Description
3. Assessment and Feedback	The change agent gathers information about the problem and gives decision makers and those having a stake in the change process feedback about the information.
4. Action Planning	The change agent works with decision makers and stakeholders to develop a corrective-action plan.
5. Intervention	The action plan is implemented. The change process is carried out.
6. Evaluation	The change agent helps decision makers and stakeholders assess the change effort's progress.
7. Adoption	Members of the organization accept ownership for the change, and the change is implemented throughout the organization.
8. Separation	The change agent prepares to leave the change effort. As part of the process, the change agent works to disengage while ensuring that improvement will continue after his or her departure. This step is possible because the knowledge and skills of the change agent have been transferred to the organization.

Although the length and depth of each step may vary across interventions, the steps are usually present in one form or another.

The steps in an OD intervention and the essential competencies for carrying them out are discussed further in subsequent chapters. However, a brief overview of both follows. For more information about the steps in OD interventions and competencies of OD consultants, core OD literature should be consulted (Varney, 1990).

Entry

During this first step, a consultant identifies an organization or parts of an organization that needs help and desires change. Entry can be viewed appropriately as a searching and marketing stage. An internal consultant may be approached for help by an operating manager with specific problems, and perhaps even specific solutions. An internal consultant may also suggest OD interventions when conditions warrant them.

On the other hand, an external consultant may be so successful with one or more past clients that he or she is referred to other organizations that need help in a change effort. An external consultant may also scan the business environment to identify organizations presently undergoing crisis or about to undergo crisis.

Crisis is often the single best indicator of readiness for change (Beer, 1980). Examples of such crises include dramatic and widespread industry deregulation, the introduction of new competitors in an otherwise stable industry, the introduction of new technology in work methods, the appointment of a new CEO, a mismatch between corporate strategy and results, downsizing, a merger, an acquisition, and a takeover. An external consultant may directly approach a firm undergoing such a change to describe the help that he or she can offer.

Once the organization or organizational component is identified, the consultant should first investigate its background. Following are some typical questions to consider:

- What is the organization's size?
- What is the organization's general reputation in the industry?
- What is the organization's business?

- What are its product lines?

- Who are the key decision makers? What biographical information about them is available? What are their values? visions for the organization? shared beliefs?

- What is reported in industry publications about the organization's history? missions and goals? strategies in the marketplace or industry? structure ?

- How well has the organization been doing? Is it financially sound?

Other questions may be developed from numerous published guides available on diagnosing organizations (Levinson, 1972; Manzini, 1988; Weisbord, 1978).

Once background research has been completed, the consultant contacts the key decision makers to explain the services that he or she can perform. (Alternatively, the client may contact the consultant.) In this process the consultant may have to summarize what OD is, why it is a change strategy worth considering, and what results have been achieved by OD in similar organizations. The consultant should also state his or her qualifications, particularly stressing any track record of achievement in working with similar firms or addressing similar problems.

Start-Up

In the second step of an OD intervention, the consultant enters the organization and lays the groundwork for the change effort by determining, in broad terms, what change is desired, when it is desired, who desires it, who opposes it, what reasons account for the desired change, and what reasons exist for opposing the change. The consultant should form a psychological contract with the client during this step, forging cooperation and collaboration.

During start-up, the consultant becomes familiar with the organization's culture through discussions with key decision makers and others in the organization. The consultant steeps himself or herself in the organization by observing rituals; listening to stories about the problem, the organization, the change effort, key people, key issues confronting the industry or the organization; and observing how people in the organization interact. The consultant needs to remain as objective as possible during this process, much like an anthropologist entering a foreign culture (Geertz, 1973), collecting information but taking care to verify through other sources any major issues or problems that are identified in the process.

Of course, the consultant also exerts some influence on the organization, a process called *personalization* (Wanous, 1980). By serving as a leader and a catalyst favoring change, the consultant has the opportunity to influence the organizational culture through his or her own values, beliefs, and attitudes. The consultant should be straightforward about his or her personal motivations, expectations, capabilities, and limitations so that these are not mistaken as a reflection of viewpoints advocated by top managers or others in the organization. The consultant's real aim is to encourage those in the client organization to reflect on their own motivations. The client's desire for change, wrought through a careful consideration of the reasons for it, is critical to a change effort.

In the second step, the consultant also works with the client to prepare a tentative, flexible, written plan for guiding the change effort. The plan specifies the purpose for the change, the objectives to be achieved in the change effort, and the measures for determining movement toward desired goals. It also includes identifiable steps and/or activities in the change effort, times for implementing change, desired results, and resources needed for implementing the change effort (including a detailed budget when necessary). The plan is prepared with the direct participation of all affected people and groups so that they share ownership in it. The process of developing the plan can be a first key step in creating an impetus for the change and support in making it. This process makes the vision of "what should be" tangible, realistic, clear, and achievable.

Assessment and Feedback

The third step in an OD intervention is assessment and feedback, perhaps best understood as a process of collecting information about an existing or pending problem and helping members of the client organization identify its cause(s). If any step in an OD intervention is crucial, it is this one: If the assessment is handled improperly, if it is not performed, or if feedback is inadequate, then the resulting change effort will be a waste of time and organizational resources.

During assessment, the consultant determines what domains of the organization are to be examined, uses appropriate processes to collect data about the problem, observes and documents current conditions, analyzes and interprets data about the problem, gives the client feedback about the data, and begins to select an intervention strategy appropriate for dealing with root causes and not just symptoms.

Feedback is crucial at this point. Feedback is simply information about problems or actions—responses to questions such as "What is the problem?" (Bell & Zemke, 1992). The consultant must give feedback that is pertinent, appropriate, energetic, impactful, clear, understandable, valid, specific, descriptive, and owned by the client (Nadler, 1977). However it is offered, feedback should include participation from those involved in the change effort, should reflect sensitivity and compassion, and should facilitate problem-solving rather than manipulating behavior. Indeed, feedback that is given appropriately encourages healthy preparation for change and involves those who provided input. Feedback serves two key purposes: It validates the accuracy of assessment and it builds ownership in the data that have come from employees.

Action Planning

The fourth step of an OD intervention is action planning. This is the process of finalizing the corrective-action plan. During this step the consultant works with the client to brainstorm options. Action planning should be highly participative; it often requires interaction with people at many different organizational levels.

To carry out this step successfully, the consultant should do the following:

- Guide participants' thoughts away from the pain and problems associated with the change effort and guide their thoughts toward comfort and possible solutions.
- Help participants brainstorm activities that will generate the greatest amount of desirable change.
- Help participants judge possible solutions critically, thinking beyond short-term solutions to long-term consequences.
- Help participants rehearse the change effort in advance in order to foresee possible problems that may arise and

ways to sidestep them or deal with them before they derail the change effort.

The consultant should also work with the client to finalize the plan for change that was tentatively established in the third step. In this process he or she ensures that the plan is concrete, cost effective, measurable, simple, and sequenced in logical order.

Intervention

The fifth step of an OD change effort is intervention. Intervention involves the implementation of the action plan and is the step in which the desired change is effected. Organization development interventions may vary by what problems are to be solved, who or what is to be changed, and how the change is carried out.

Special terminology is used when referring to such issues: Problems to be solved are called *diagnostic problems,* the individual or groups to be changed are called the *focus of attention,* and the way the OD intervention is carried out is called the *mode of intervention.* Twenty years ago an influential model was devised to help OD consultants conceptualize these issues and classify OD interventions. That model is called the OD Cube (Schmuck & Miles, 1971), and it is still widely used. (See Exhibit 2-4.)

As the cube illustrates, OD interventions may address diagnostic problems having to do with goals and plans, communication, culture or climate, leadership and authority, problem solving, decision making, conflict or cooperation, role definition, or other matters. The focus of attention may be an individual, a role, a pair or a trio, a team or a group, an intergroup situation, or the entire organization. Modes of intervention include training or education, process consultation or coaching, confrontation, data feedback, problem solving, plan making, establishing an OD task force, or technostructural activity. There are thus many kinds of interventions, each suited for dealing with a specific problem. A partial list of interventions appears in Exhibit 2-5. At present, the most common OD intervention is group development (Fagenson & Burke, 1990).

During the intervention step, the consultant sets out to make sure that there are a few early, highly visible successes in the intervention to increase support for the change effort. Quick and highly visible successes will also help win over skeptics and build infectious enthusiasm among supporters.

Timing is particularly crucial in any intervention. The consultant should carefully examine work cycles in advance, planning an intervention to begin at a time when the work cycle is not at a peak. A peak work cycle will draw attention away from the change effort, thereby reducing the initial momentum and leading to possible failure (Mirvis & Berg, 1977).

Evaluation

The sixth step in an OD intervention is evaluation. Two evaluation methods are needed: one to assess the progress of the intervention as it occurs (formative) and another to assess the overall results of the intervention (summative).

Frequently, evaluation is minimized in OD interventions. One reason for this is because OD consultants fear that enthusiastic reports heralding success will only build unrealistic expectations for future interventions and, thus, potentially

Exhibit 2-4: The OD Cube: A Scheme for Classifying OD Interventions

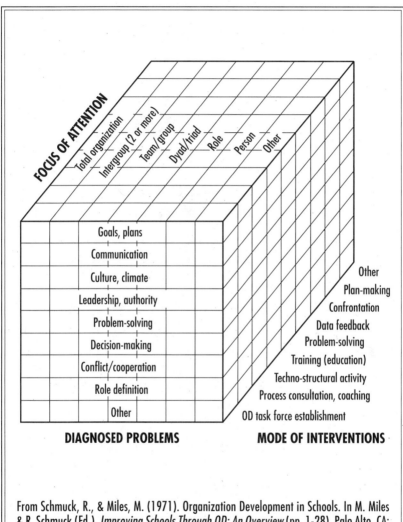

FOCUS OF ATTENTION

Total organization
Intergroup (2 or more)
Team/group
Dyad/triad
Role
Person
Other

Diagnosed Problems:
- Goals, plans
- Communication
- Culture, climate
- Leadership, authority
- Problem-solving
- Decision-making
- Conflict/cooperation
- Role definition
- Other

Mode of Interventions:
- Other
- Plan-making
- Confrontation
- Data feedback
- Problem-solving
- Training (education)
- Techno-structural activity
- Process consultation, coaching
- OD task force establishment

DIAGNOSED PROBLEMS   **MODE OF INTERVENTIONS**

From Schmuck, R., & Miles, M. (1971). Organization Development in Schools. In M. Miles & R. Schmuck (Ed.), *Improving Schools Through OD: An Overview* (pp. 1-28). Palo Alto, CA: National Press Books. Used by permission of the publisher. The OD Cube was originally published in *Organization Development in Schools,* p. 8, (1971). San Diego, CA: Pfeiffer & Company. For subsequent development of the OD Cube, see Schmuck, R., & Runkel, P. (1985). *The handbook of organization development in schools* (3rd ed.). Prospect Heights, IL: Waveland Press.

Exhibit 2-5: A List of OD Interventions

Type	Brief Description
	Individual
Counseling/Coaching	An intervention designed to formalize/ increase helping relationships in which individuals may relate their problems to sympathetic listeners or be advised how to deal with work or interpersonal problems.
Training	An intervention designed to provide individuals with knowledge, skills, or attitudes that may be applied immediately on the job.
Individual Goal Setting	An intervention intended to increase planning for performance improvement between employees and their immediate supervisors.
Performance-Appraisal Systems	An intervention intended to change or improve methods for measuring employee performance and providing feedback to employees about their performance.
Statistical Process Control (SPC)	A technique used to track production/performance and its variations.
Job Descriptions	An intervention intended to analyze duties performed by job incumbents and to describe what results they are to achieve. Changes in job descriptions may affect individual behaviors and accomplishments.
Values Clarification	An intervention designed to help assess or determine individual or group values.

From McLean, G., & Sullivan, R. (1989). *Essential Competencies of Internal and External OD Consultants*, p.8. Unpublished manuscript.

Exhibit 2-5: A List of OD Interventions (continued)

Type	Brief Description
Life and Career Planning	An intervention designed to help individuals plan for their lives or careers.
People-Policy Development	An intervention designed to establish broad guidelines for action to be followed by employees when they encounter common problems in the course of their work.
Procedures Manuals	An intervention designed to establish or formalize methods of handling common problems encountered by people in an organization. The procedures stem from the organization's policies.
Process Improvement	An intervention designed to change the way in which processes are performed to make them more effective or efficient.
Team or Unit	
Team Building	An intervention designed to increase cohesiveness / cooperation of people who work together.
Job Enrichment	An intervention designed to change job duties and expected results, providing job incumbents with greater responsibilities.
Quality of Work Life	An intervention designed to improve working conditions and to increase employee participation in decisions that affect them and theirorganizations.
Quality Circles	An intervention designed to use small groups, often work groups, to identify methods of improving production or to solve work problems.

Exhibit 2-5: A List of OD Interventions (continued)

Type	Brief Description
Unit Goal Setting	An intervention designed to help members of a work group to establish goals (often involving production output) for their work group.
Conflict Management	An intervention designed to reduce destructive conflict between members of a work unit.
Open-System Mapping	An intervention designed to identify relevant inputs, outputs, and transformation processes of an organization.
Process Consultation	An intervention designed to focus attention on how individuals or groups interact.
Intergroup	
Work-Flow Planning	An intervention designed to plan the flow of work between two or more components of an organization.
Scheduling Review	An intervention designed to assess how work is scheduled.
Interorganizational Development	An intervention in which two groups or organizations work together to establish and/or maintain more effective relationships.
Intergroup-Conflict Management	An intervention designed to deal with destructive conflict between two or more work units.
Third-Party Intervention	An intervention designed to improve relationships that have been marred by previous conflict.

Exhibit 2-5: A List of OD Interventions (continued)

Type	Brief Description
Cross-Functional Training	An intervention designed to provide individuals or groups with the knowledge they need to function with another unit or organization.

Total Organization

Type	Brief Description
Strategic Planning	An intervention designed to improve establishment of long-term organizational goals, objectives, and direction.
Confrontation Meetings	An intervention designed to bring together two or more groups to resolve destructive conflict.
Culture Transformation	An intervention designed to change assumptions about the "right" and "wrong" ways of doing things.
Reengineering	An intervention also known as process innovation and core process redesign—a radical redesign of business process to achieve breakthrough results.
Work Redesign	An intervention in which the work itself is changed.
Quality and Productivity Systems	An intervention designed to improve quality and productivity continually across an organization.
Survey Feedback	An intervention designed to collect information from members of an organization, report the results, and use the results as the starting point for action planning for improvement.
Structural Change	An intervention designed to alter reporting relationships and the purposes/objectives of componentparts of an organization.

Exhibit 2-5: A List of OD Interventions (continued)

Type	Brief Description
Structural Change	An intervention designed to alter reporting relationships and the purposes/objectives of component parts of an organization.
Customer-Service Development	An intervention designed to increase the sensitivity of employees to the importance of efficient, courteous customer service and to give employees the means by which to carry out effective customer service.
Sociotechnical Systems	An intervention designed to improve the link between employees and the work technology used in the organization.
Large-Scale Technology/ Future Search Conferences	An intervention designed to bring together three hundred to twenty-three hundred employees from all levels of an organization to create an ideal future for the organization.
Societal/Planetary	
Transcultural Planning Processes	An intervention designed to improve planning across national or cultural groups.
Transnational Community Building and Problem Solving	An intervention designed to improve trust and collaboration across national or cultural groups.

jeopardize the success of those interventions. Yet, ironically, evidence suggests that success rates for OD interventions exceed 50 percent (Golembiewski, 1990). Formative evaluation keeps the intervention on track by allowing for continual improvement and feedback during the change effort.

Summative evaluation occurs near the point at which the consultant is preparing to disengage from involvement and allow the change to continue through the support of appointed members in the client organization. In summative evaluation the consultant can ask specific questions such as the following:

- What changes occurred?
- To what extent was the action plan implemented successfully?
- What dollars were saved or earned as a result of the change effort?
- Was there a match between estimated and actual consulting time and expense?
- How much has pain been reduced?

Adoption

Adoption is the seventh step of an OD intervention and it is defined as the process of stabilizing change. During adoption, the OD consultant works to establish a continual-improvement effort within an organization, secures commitment from top managers and others to continue the change effort, and gives special attention to areas in which slippage is likely to occur. (Slippage refers to change reversals, movements back to pre-change states.) This step is the true test of any change effort because change must be transplanted and institutionalized into the organization's culture, traditions, and rites if the change effort is to endure.

The organization development consultant uses several strategies to increase the likelihood of success in this step:

- One strategy is centered in the people of the organization: The consultant secures pledges from top managers and other stakeholders to continue the change effort after the consultant leaves.

- A second strategy is centered in the structure of the organization: Top managers charge specific people with an explicit mandate to ensure continuation of the change effort. Some people are delegated responsibilities associated with maintaining the effort and they are thereafter held accountable for its success.

- A third strategy is to redesign methods of measuring results and allocating rewards. Those who achieve results consistent with the direction of the change effort are rewarded.

- A fourth and final strategy is to reexamine the organization for slippage and take appropriate action to rectify the situation. Slippage is common and should be watched for carefully, both during and after the change effort.

Of course, all four strategies may be used together.

Separation

The eighth and final step of an OD intervention, separation, is associated with the departure of the consultant from the setting. Just prior to this step, the consultant recognizes that separation is desirable. After all, there is a point at which continued assistance in facilitating change can actually be counterproductive because it leads to client dependence.

During separation, the consultant provides feedback to the client on the change process by summarizing progress to date. Responsibility for continuing progress is transferred to the client, often most effectively through a "going-away ritual" such as a meeting or luncheon. Finally, the consultant clarifies both appropriate and inappropriate conditions under which he or she may be called back by the client for additional support.

General Competencies

Essential Competencies of Internal and External OD Consultants, like several other studies, describes what a consultant should know or do to conduct each step of an OD intervention successfully. Much has also been written about the competencies necessary for successful performance as an OD consultant (for example, Carey & Varney, 1983; Egan, 1985, 1988a, 1988b; Eubanks, Marshall, & O'Driscoll, 1990; Hamilton, 1988; Hitt & Mathis, 1983; McDermott, 1984; Neilsen, 1984; *Organization Development Practitioner,* 1983; Shepard & Raia, 1981; Varney, 1980; Warrick & Donovan, 1979; White & Wooten, 1986). The competencies are also summarized in Appendix I.

During each step in an OD intervention, a consultant makes use of general competencies. More specifically, the consultant acts ethically (White & Wooten, 1986), uses computers to support his or her activities, employs statistical analysis for problem solving, and interprets cross-cultural influences among organizations, work units, and individuals. To demonstrate each general competency successfully, an OD consultant may find that he or she requires specialized education and training.

References

Beer, M. (1980). *Organization change and development: A systems view.* Santa Monica, CA: Goodyear.

Bell, C., & Zemke, R. (1992). On-target feedback. *Training, 29*(6), 36-38, 44.

Burke, W. (1982). *Organization development: Principles and practices.* Boston: Little, Brown & Co.

Carey, A., & Varney, G. (1983). Which skills spell success in OD? *Training and Development Journal, 37*(4), 38-40.

Egan, G. (1985). *Change agent skills in helping and human service settings.* Pacific Grove, CA: Brooks/Cole.

Egan, G. (1988a). *Change agent skills A: Assessing and designing excellence.* San Diego, CA: Pfeiffer & Company.

Egan, G. (1988b). *Change agent skills B: Managing innovation and change.* San Diego, CA: Pfeiffer & Company.

Eubanks, J., Marshall, J., & O'Driscoll, M. (1990). A competency model for OD practitioners. *Training and Development Journal, 44*(11), 85-90.

Fagenson, E., & Burke, W. (1990). The activities of organization development practitioners at the turn of the decade of the 1990s. *Group and Organization Studies, 15*(4), 366-380.

French, W., & Bell, C., Jr. (1990). *Organization development: Behavioral science interventions for organization improvement* (4th ed.). Englewood Cliffs, NJ: Prentice-Hall.

Geertz, C. (1973). *The interpretation of cultures.* New York: Basic Books.

Golembiewski, R. (1990). *Ironies in organizational development.* New Brunswick, NJ: Transaction Publishers.

Hamilton, E. (1988). The facilitation of organizational change: An empirical study of factors predicting change agents' effectiveness. *Journal of Applied Behavioral Science, 24*(1), 37-59.

Hitt, M., & Mathis, R. (1983). Survey results shed light upon important developmental tools. *Personnel Administrator, 28*(2), 87-88, 90, 92, 97.

Katz, D., & Kahn, R. (1978). *The social psychology of organizations* (2nd ed.). New York: John Wiley & Sons.

Lang, D. (1992). Organizational culture and commitment. *Human Resource Development Quarterly, 3*(2), 191-196.

Levinson, H. (1972). *Organizational diagnosis.* Cambridge, MA: Harvard University Press.

McDermott, L. (1984). The many faces of the OD professional. *Training and Development Journal, 38*(2), 14-19.

McLean, G., & Sullivan, R. (1989). *Essential competencies of internal and external OD consultants.* Unpublished manuscript.

Manzini, A. (1988). *Organizational diagnosis: A practical approach to company problem solving and growth.* New York: AMACOM.

Mirvis, P., & Berg, D. (1977). *Failures in organization development and change.* New York: John Wiley & Sons.

Nadler, D. (1977). *Feedback and organization development: Using data-based methods.* Reading, MA: Addison-Wesley.

Neilsen, E. (1984). *Becoming an OD practitioner.* Englewood Cliffs, NJ: Prentice-Hall.

Organization development practitioner: Self development guide. (1983). Alexandria, VA: American Society for Training and Development.

Rothwell, W. (1981). Alternatives to organization development. *Training and Development Journal, 35*(12), 119-124.

Shepard, K., & Raia, A. (1981). The OD training challenge. *Training and Development Journal, 35*(4), 90-96.

Varney, G. (1990). A study of the core literature in organization development. *Organization Development Journal, 8*(3), 59-66.

Varney, G. (1980). Developing OD competencies. *Training and Development Journal, 34*(4), 30-35.

Wanous, J. (1980). *Organizational entry: Recruitment, selection and socialization of newcomers.* Reading, MA: Addison-Wesley.

Warrick, D., & Donovan, T. (1979). Surveying OD skills. *Training and Development Journal, 33*(9), 22-25.

Weisbord, M. (1978). *Organizational diagnosis: A workbook of theory and practice.* Reading, MA: Addison-Wesley.

White, L., & Wooten, K. (1986). *Professional ethics and practice in organization development: A systematic analysis of issues, alternatives, and approaches.* New York: Praeger.

PART II

STEPS IN OD INTERVENTIONS

Part II covers key steps in OD interventions and the competencies that OD consultants need to carry out those steps. It includes chapters on entry, start-up, assessment and feedback, action planning, interventions in large systems and small systems, person-focused interventions, evaluation, adoption, and separation.

CHAPTER 3

ENTRY

Richard Alan Engdahl

E ntry is the process of locating an organization or part of an organization that desires change and needs assistance with it (Jackson, 1987). Marketing is the process of attracting, maintaining, and enhancing client relationships (Engdahl, Howe, & Cole, 1991). Marketing includes executing a formal or informal agreement between an external or an internal consultant and his or her client. After the consultant and the client reach agreement, the external consultant must be concerned with legal matters linked to contracting services; these legal matters rarely are a consideration for an internal consultant.

Entry and marketing issues continue throughout organization development (OD) interventions as consultants develop psychological contracts with their clients, continue to educate members of client organizations about OD, and cultivate trust in their skills. If successful, entry and marketing lead not only to effective interventions but also to further business with clients or to new consulting engagements through referrals from clients.

Marketing Concepts and Relationships

Organization development consultants seldom are hired solely on the strength of their advertising campaigns. Consultants are in the business of marketing their services to people who are the "experts" about their organizations. A consultant must work collaboratively with his or her client, demonstrating specialized expertise about OD intervention concepts and using expert interpersonal skills. Thus, OD consultants essentially market an assurance that they know how to work with clients and organizations to bring about change and to achieve participatively determined outcomes from change efforts.

The Importance of Self-Knowledge

Consultants will find building trust about what they can do and how they can do it to be difficult if they do not understand their own values and beliefs. Organization development consultants also must know what they believe about OD and have a sense of how well they can make use of OD intervention techniques before they begin to offer advice to clients. They will need to be clear about what they believe about OD because marketing OD services consists largely of educating prospective clients about the services that the OD consultants are selling.

Developing a Personal Definition of OD

To communicate effectively with prospective clients, OD consultants must know which OD concepts and skills are essential. They also must be clear about which options are available to them in particular situations. What consultants do is more important than what they say: Role modeling is the most powerful means of educating people, and everything OD consultants do should model what clients are asked to accept. For this reason OD consultants must ask themselves this important question: "How well do I understand and demonstrate through my behavior the concepts and skills I am trying to market?"

As OD consultants attempt to market their services, they face a major problem: lack of widespread agreement among managers about what OD is. As consultants develop understanding of their own "brands" of OD, they also must understand their clients' perspectives. Notwithstanding the classic definitions of OD presented in Chapter 1, consultants must be prepared to adapt their terminology to client environments and to explain what they do to those who may be unfamiliar with OD.

When OD consulting developed in the 1950s and 1960s, consultants offered a more distinct package of services than they do today. Consultants worked largely with the social side of organizations to overcome the ill effects of rigid bureaucracies as manifested in poor communication, wrongheaded decision making, and ineffective team work (Glassman & Cummings, 1991).

Over the years, however, OD's horizons have expanded beyond Lewin's "action research," primarily on the social side of organizations, to encompass "concepts and techniques from strategic management, human resources management, corporate culture, and organization theory.... OD values of humanism and organization effectiveness [have] expanded to include concern for environmental relations and external stakeholders, such as customers, competitors, owners, and government regulators" (Glassman & Cummings, 1991, p. 2). Organization development continues to expand its horizons as the global interdependence of organizations becomes a factor in organizational evolution.

Understanding that OD may be unfamiliar to some managers and that misconceptions about it may exist among those who think they are familiar with it, OD consultants should ask themselves the following questions:

- What do I do as an OD consultant?
- What is my unique brand of OD?

Unfortunately, there are some OD consultants who have a limited repertoire of OD concepts and skills. Such consultants concentrate on a piece of the OD field, applying one intervention tool to every situation. For example, they may frame every organizational problem in terms of scores on a specific standardized test or in terms of team-building. These consultants can damage the OD profession by touting one intervention as synonymous with OD itself and as a panacea for all ills.

Because some prospective clients may have limited perceptions about OD, consultants may have to introduce clients to alternative, and perhaps more appropriate, OD techniques. As Metzger (1989) points out, "Given the new sophistication of clients, the unfortunate experience of some at the hands of charlatans and 'pop management' hucksters, and the enormous increase in the number of consultants, it is no wonder that marketing consulting services has become a very challenging task" (p. 61).

Reaching a Personal Understanding

Organization development consultants must reach a personal understanding about themselves and how their behaviors are observed by others.

As with most people in the "helping professions," OD consultants may regularly need to seek the support of therapists or support groups in order to maintain healthy and accurate views of themselves so that individual issues do not hinder their ability to provide objective and clear professional help to client organizations. By learning more about themselves through therapy or support groups, OD consultants become better equipped to help others.

Reviewing Personal Knowledge

Consultants should periodically review classic works of OD, such as those listed in the Chapter 1 references. Taken together, those works represent the collective wisdom of the OD field. One way consultants can review the different definitions of OD that have evolved is to study them and then write their own definitions of OD. They can then review what they know and what they can do against the backdrop of well-known classics in OD. Among other questions consultants may consider are the following:

- How well can I use the action research model or another model to guide change?
- How well can I explain my change model to a client?
- Do I approach clients with a predetermined intervention in mind or do I approach all situations with an open mind?

- Do I conduct background research on a prospective client organization or part of an organization before making initial contact or reaching agreement about next steps?

Contrary to what sometimes is said about OD's pure focus on process and interpersonal relationships, most clients also expect OD consultants to be familiar with the nature of their businesses. How else could consultants be expected to understand client problems?

Reviewing Personal Skills

Organization development consultants must be able to build client trust. Clients learn to trust or distrust consultants based on their general experiences with consultants and their particular experiences with individual consultants. By communicating inappropriate or insufficient information, consultants can fail to inspire trust in themselves or their services.

Being able to model trust is a key competency of OD consultants. According to Jack Gibb (1991), trust is the most significant factor in human and organizational relationships. When trust is high consultants can transcend apparent limits and discover new and unimagined abilities. The formation of trust releases energy, excitement, and brings about higher performance.

To build trust and to demonstrate what it means, consultants should review their experiences so they are familiar with what they can do and how they can relate their abilities to the apparent needs of prospective clients. One way to review their abilities is to compare what they know and what they can do to the list of competencies in Appendix I.

Merely identifying skills is not enough. Consultants should also be able to communicate what they can do to meet their clients' expectations and needs, and what results they can help to achieve. Writing these descriptions is helpful because they become clear to the consultants and then can be communicated clearly to prospective clients. This step is essential in developing an effective marketing strategy.

Exhibit 3-1 provides references to self-evaluation tools that consultants can use to explore their management styles, psychological types, OD process awareness, intervention knowledge, and problem-solving capabilities. These instruments are not foolproof, but they can evoke insights about self. (Additionally, OD consultants should be aware of these instruments because they can be especially valuable in evoking clients' insights during OD interventions.)

Writing a Mission Statement

Once OD consultants know who they are and what they are capable of doing, they may find it useful to write mission statements for themselves and their consulting business. This step is advisable for several reasons.

1. Mission statements provide anchors in times of doubt and amid conflicting priorities.
2. They serve as rallying points that create enthusiasm.
3. They are anchor points for addressing ethical questions.
4. They help consultants—as they help organizations—to define their markets, their services, quality standards appropriate for their services, and the values added by those services.

Exhibit 3-1: An Overview of Self-Assessment Instruments[1]

Survey of Behavioral Characteristics

The survey's purpose is to help an individual consider his or her behavioral characteristics and the influence they might have on the individual and on his or her interactions with others. Behavioral characteristics also are likely to influence learning and productivity.

Survey of Managerial Style

The survey's purpose is to measure aspects of an individual's managerial style in comparison with others' managerial styles so that patterns of behavior can be understood in likely interactions.

Myers-Briggs Type Indicator

This instrument is based on the personality topographics of Carl Jung. It produces sixteen personality "types" or temperaments based on combinations of the following "Type Dimensions":

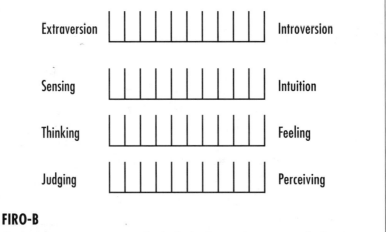

Extraversion		Introversion
Sensing		Intuition
Thinking		Feeling
Judging		Perceiving

FIRO-B

This instrument examines an individual's fundamental interpersonal-relations orientation in terms of behavior by measuring self-perceptions of how an individual

---

[1] The following instruments are found in *Self-Assessment and Career Development* by J. Clawson, J. Kotter, V. Faux, & C. McArthur, 1992, Englewood Cliffs, NJ: Prentice-Hall.

Exhibit 3-1: An Overview of Self-Assessment Instruments (continued)

relates to other people. It yields information about how the respondent sees himself or herself behaving in interpersonal relationships and it can be used to facilitate effectiveness in those relationships. It examines three dimensions of human relations: inclusion, control, and openness. The instrument is widely used in a variety of settings and is useful in understanding an individual's entry into and developing relationships within a group.

Interpersonal-Style Inventory

This instrument helps an individual learn more about his or her interpersonal style by utilizing a self-report and then comparing it with perceptions collected from five other people.

The Predisposition Test

This test explores psychological predispositions felt to be important because psychological tendencies shape behavior, especially in work settings.

The 24-Hour Diary

This exercise produces information on what an individual actually does on a daily basis. This activity enables the individual to recognize habits and patterns of behavior from which it is possible to draw inferences that can be used to learn to interact more effectively with others.

The Strong Interest Inventory

This instrument is one of the most widely used vocational-interest instruments. It reveals similarities between an individual's interests and those of people who are successful in a variety of careers. This is useful for consultants in developing awareness of those types of clients with whom they are more likely to perform content-expert roles rather than process-expert roles.

Dyad Exercise

This exercise is an exchange of data between two partners, followed by thorough analysis and feedback designed to give each partner greater skill in inductively analyzing complex data and to obtain his or her partner's perspective. Another instrument available for this purpose is "Dyadic Encounter: A Program for Developing Relationships" (Pfeiffer & Jones, 1974).

The purpose of the mission statement is "to set the organizational context within which strategic decisions will be made—in other words, to give the organization strategic focus and direction.... All strategic decisions flow from the mission statement" (Hill & Jones, 1989, p. 30).

A mission should consist of the following three parts:

1. A definition of the OD consulting business (or for internal consultants, the services they offered);
2. A statement of goals; and
3. A statement of philosophy.

Abell (1980) suggests that a consultant's business or role can be defined by answering three simple questions:

- Who is to be satisfied? (client groups)
- What is to be satisfied? (client needs)
- How are clients to be satisfied? (technologies)

This approach is very client oriented. But consultants should be careful to consider all stakeholders whose interests might be affected by their consulting activities.

The mission statement should also clarify the consultants' ethical standards and underlying values. Various professional associations in the OD field have published codes of ethics. (Several of them are reproduced in Appendix III.) These codes can help consultants as they articulate their own personal ethics and values.

There is no "right" OD mission statement. Each is tailored to the needs, desires, beliefs, knowledge, skills, and experiences of the consultant involved. The process of developing the mission statement is probably more valuable than the statement itself.

Considerations in Developing a Marketing Strategy

Consultants should consider the ways in which OD practices and skills fit into their missions, value systems, and capabilities. They also should be aware of current issues in the OD field and should think about them carefully.

Tailored Versus Universal Approaches

Organization development interventions evolve; there is no "right way" to start out. This fact can be maddening to some managers who seek quick fixes or who possess preconceived notions about interventions that they believe are appropriate to rectify perceived problems. Under such circumstances consultants may be tempted to sell the requested interventions to their clients quickly and easily. However, this approach is similar to patients asking their doctors for prescription drugs to cure problems that the doctors have not diagnosed. In such situations, the consultants' mission statements and ethics can serve as anchors. Ethical OD consultants talk with their clients about how the clients perceive that problems exist, what various causes could be contributing to the problems, what types of problems the requested intervention might solve, and what other intervention options might be appropriate.

If a consultant perceives a problem to be different from that identified by his or her client or pinpoints a solution different from that requested by the client, the consultant must decide how much to attempt to relabel the requested intervention so that it meets the client's preconceived ideas. The consultant must judge how much to attempt to influence the client to accept the consultant's perceptions and whether it is possible to develop a mutually agreeable solution. Such decisions require a thorough knowledge of OD and of one's own capabilities and values.

Organization Development and Power

Organization development involves acquiring and exercising power because power must be exerted to influence people in the change process. Consultants need to understand the types of and sources of power. They need to know how those sources can be utilized to facilitate positive change and to empower others to create change. They also need to know their own sources of power.

Effective OD consultants, like effective managers, draw power from two primary sources: expertise and charisma (French & Raven, 1989). Line managers obtain their power from content expertise (knowledge of the work), and OD consultants draw their power from process expertise (knowledge of OD). Charisma grows out of admirable personal characteristics and reputation. It fosters close, trusting relationships and collaboration. Charisma also fosters credibility, which is, in turn, paramount to building trust. The ability of consultants to bring their process expertise to bear on problems depends, to a considerable extent, on the interpersonal relationships they establish with their clients.

Who Is the Client?

Organization development consultants are responsible for facilitating processes that will enable effective changes to occur in the ways in which client organizations accomplish their missions. Consultants are change agents but they are not the changers. Only managers in client organizations possess the necessary authority and power to create and support change. Therefore, OD consultants should be able to identify and work with people in positions of power. Often those with whom consultants have initial contact during marketing and contracting activities are not those who have the power to effect change. Ultimately, in a philosophical sense, the organization itself or a part of it is the client. But consultants work with people. Organization development consultants must be able to identify who has power and who is the client. To do that they must answer the following two key questions:

- Who are the leaders?
- Who are the beneficiaries?

They also must be able to establish and maintain collaborative relationships with sponsors of change who occupy key roles.

Consultants As Role Models

Consultants must model the behaviors they prescribe for others if they are to be effective at entry and are to prosper in their marketing. They must recognize their individual needs and subordinate them to the accomplishment of their purposes. Organization development consultants need a high tolerance for uncertainty. They must be capable of dealing with others who have poor interpersonal skills, while making use of proper feedback techniques and participative-management techniques. If organization development consultants are to remain physically and mentally healthy, they also must develop and model effective ways to manage their workloads and cope with stress.

Organization development consultants must ask themselves whether they have the skills, awareness, and stress tolerance to play multiple roles—from process facilitator, to nondirective counselor, to content expert on specific knowledge about process, to analyst of organizational functions, to formal trainer, to on-the-spot conflict resolver.

The act of entering organizations with the intention of helping is intrusive. Furthermore, ethical dilemmas are common in OD. Conflicting perspectives, values, and desires for particular outcomes can create these dilemmas, making it difficult for consultants to know what is "right" for clients, employees, communities, and themselves. In particular, access to highly privileged, highly confidential information may create moral dilemmas for consultants about justice, fairness, and social responsibility.

To succeed, OD consultants must be clear about their roles, needs, and desires. That can be difficult, especially when management becomes overly dependent or abdicates responsibility. Personal mission statements can be helpful guides for consultants when they are doubtful about their involvement in certain situations. These issues underscore the need for consultants to anchor their values solidly in self-awareness and in agreements made mutually with clients.

Approaches to Marketing OD Services

The marketing of OD really occurs at two levels, usually simultaneously. The first level is institutional marketing in which consultants develop marketplace awareness of their names, expertise, and the OD field itself. The second level is client-specific marketing, in which consultants approach individual clients to sell services.

Institutional Marketing

For the individual consultant—whether working internally or externally—institutional marketing centers around educating prospective clients about himself or herself and about OD processes, purposes, and values. Of critical importance is finding a means to link education about OD and its benefits with awareness of the consultant and his or her expertise.

Public speaking and seminars are perhaps the most effective means to create market awareness about the OD field and the consultants' capabilities. The results of one survey of 280 professional internal and external OD consultants revealed that 89 percent of them rated public speaking and seminars as their most important contacts with potential clients (Engdahl et al., 1991). As Sheehan and O'Toole (1985) point out, "Eighty percent of the people in America who make over $50,000 are those who are good on their feet, who can speak in front of others" (p. 5).

Consultants should take full advantage of public-speaking engagements and seminars by doing the following:

- Developing speeches focused on current issues of interest to organizations in their market areas;

- Adding personal experiences and descriptions of personal expertise so the consultants sell themselves through their presentations;

- Approaching local organizations, identified through newspapers and trade journals, to volunteer for speaking engagements. (Chambers of commerce and convention bureaus are useful sources of information about conferences and trade shows where consultants might be able to speak.);

- Approaching professional societies, such as the American Society for Training and Development, the National Society for Performance and Instruction, the Organization Development Network, the Organization Development Institute (ODI), the American Management Association, and other important groups, regarding possible speaking engagements;

- Surveying organizations in their market areas about needed training or other OD interventions and how much financial support organizations might be able to provide for such efforts. The results can then be used to develop a seminar or workshop to meet perceived marketplace needs. (To be ethical, such surveys should note the purposes for which the results will be used.); and

- Contacting news media to request public-service coverage that promotes not only the consultants' services or seminars but also the OD field.

Organization development consultants may also take other actions to market their services. They can, for example, invest in professional business cards, service brochures, printed letterhead and envelopes, and printed invoices. In the 1991 survey conducted by Engdahl et al., approximately 66 percent of the respondents indicated that they make use of business cards, service brochures, printed letterhead, and printed invoices. Although they are not necessarily marketing tools, they do make a positive first impression with prospective clients.

Another way consultants can market themselves is to demonstrate their competence through registration. For centuries people have been establishing organizations and procedures to legitimize their professions and ensure competence so that others can rely on them. Registration provides consultants with a marketing edge because it demonstrates some measure of competence.

The ODI has developed credentialing procedures (with the help of W. Warner Burke) that are validated by a committee of one hundred top OD consultants. To qualify as a registered organization development professional (RODP), an OD consultant needs to agree to abide by the ODI's Code of Ethics (see Chapter 16). To qualify as a registered organization development consultant (RODC), an OD consultant must meet the following experience requirements: [2]

- A Doctoral degree in psychology or an allied field and the equivalent of two years of full-time experience in OD, or

- A Master's degree in psychology, business administration, or an allied field and the equivalent of four years of full-time experience in OD, or

- A Bachelor's degree and the equivalent of six years of full-time experience in OD. Two of these six years must have been spent working closely with a person who has met the previously listed requirements or who has completed a training program in OD recognized by ODI.

---

[2] These requirements are listed with permission of the ODI and are found in the *International Registry of Organization Development Professionals* and *Organization Development Handbook*, 1992-1993.

- In addition to the previously listed requirements, a professional consultant must have demonstrated competence in OD as evidenced by letters from two qualified OD consultants stating that they are familiar with the consultant's work and that they consider the consultant to be fully competent in OD. (Applicants who are not graduates of an organizational-behavior [OB] or OD program approved by the ODI will be expected to pass a written test[3] on their knowledge and understanding of OD.)

Yet another way for OD consultants to market themselves is to write articles for newspapers or trade journals, prepare monographs to be made available at trade conferences or business meetings, conduct and publish research on OD practices, or publish books. When writing, the consultants' objectives should be to be quoted in other media, thereby giving them additional credibility and obtaining publicity for their efforts.

Consultants also should invest time in networking through trade groups, professional associations, and computer bulletin boards. Indeed, networking with anyone in a position to promote their professional images and unique "brands" of OD is advisable. (Of course, word-of-mouth recommendations from previous clients are most effective.)

Client-Specific Marketing

Gaining entry into a specific organization is a goal-directed activity. Consultants may gain access as a result of network

---

[3] The published version of the written test, which is under revision as this book goes to press, appeared in the *Organization Development Journal* (Burke, 1984).

referrals or contacts they initiate. However access is gained, preentry research on prospective clients should include the following items about the organizations:

- History;
- Current market position;
- Stage of organization/product/service life cycle; and
- Leaders.

For help in understanding how to conduct preentry research, consultants are advised to refer to Porter's *Competitive Strategy* (1985), Hofer's "Towards a Contingency Theory of Business Strategy" (1975), and Andreason's *Cheap but Good Marketing Research* (1988). In addition, consultants will find it valuable to ask their prospective clients questions about their organizations' previous experiences with other OD and management consultants. For instance, consultants may need to know who the consultants were, what they did, and what the results of their efforts were.

Other valuable sources of information can be obtained about prospective clients and their industries by doing the following:

- Visiting public and university libraries;
- Reading prospective clients' annual reports;
- Phoning personnel or human resources departments for information about organizations;
- Obtaining copies of organizational charts to see the organizations' formal structures and published reporting relationships;
- Scanning recent newspapers and trade publications for any mention of prospective clients' organizations;

- Investigating organizations' products or services, particularly how they compare to the products or services of their competitors, how their products or services are delivered to their customers, and customer perceptions of quality or satisfaction;

- Identifying organizations' suppliers, wholesalers, and retailers, if appropriate; and

- Determining the ownership of organizations (for example, public or private, profit or not-for-profit, part of a larger organization or independent).

The important point is that the more consultants know about an organization and its problems, the more likely they will be able to identify and work with the "true client" and the leaders to effect change. Knowledge of an organization makes consultants appear more credible to prospective clients as well.

One apparent trend in recent years is that the growing complexity of the world has led to leaner, flatter organizational structures and a greater focus on "general managers and administrators as the key agents of change...[and] business-related concerns as the primary change targets" (Glassman & Cummings, 1991, p. 4). Organization development consultants must therefore learn to associate themselves with bottom-line results, as defined in business terms, and not with flashy or vaguely defined fads. In preparing for initial contacts, organization development consultants should frame potential outcomes in language and measures that are meaningful to specific client organizations.

In most organizations in the United States, managers have grown accustomed to tailoring solutions to fit problems. Managers expect the same from OD consultants. For this reason, it is imperative that the OD process be tailor-made to fit each client organization. Above all, consultants should view each intervention as unique to one organizational culture.

One way to do that is to ask prospective clients some questions about what has worked in the past. By hearing stories about past successes, organization development consultants can identify key elements in the organizational cultures that can lead to successful interventions, such as the inclusion of the "right" people or use of the "right" approaches. An especially effective technique is asking the clients why they think particular ventures succeeded.

A Two-Stage Selling Process

Marketing OD services to prospective clients can be viewed as a two-stage selling process. The first stage is initial contact; the second stage is the contracting process.

During initial contact, the consultant faces the challenge of gaining access to someone in the organization or a part of the organization who has sufficient authority to reach an agreement with the consultant about services. During contracting, the consultant's challenge is to negotiate a formal (written) or informal (unwritten) agreement with the client that specifies details of an OD intervention and covers the issues surrounding start-up (discussed in Chapter 4). At this point, the consultant needs to establish ground rules with the client that define the consulting relationship.

The Initial Contact

Initial contact occurs in two phases—notwithstanding calling an unfamiliar potential client, which is the least effective form of initial contact, according to Engdahl et al. (1991). The first phase of initial contact is a nonplanned contact between consultant and client. This often happens when a member of the prospective client organization attends a seminar hosted by the consultant, reads a thought-provoking quotation from the consultant, or hears about the consultant by word-of-mouth from a mutual acquaintance. The second phase of initial contact occurs when the consultant and prospective client meet to develop a contract for an OD intervention.

Many institutional marketing activities result in nonplanned contacts that bring together consultants and prospective clients. In particular, training seminars offer consultants ample opportunities to showcase their talents and build their self-confidence. For many managers, seeing is believing. For this reason, successful OD consultants literally practice what they preach—that is, they model the principles, values, and skills they brings to the marketplace—and they do so in a manner that exhibits confidence in their abilities. Once the opportunity is lost to make a good first impression, it cannot be recovered. Consultants can enhance their abilities to capitalize on nonplanned contacts by developing their networking skills, listening skills, memory techniques, and note-taking techniques.

Making successful targeted contacts is a planned process. Research conducted by Engdahl et al. (1991) indicates that the most successful initial contacts are those made by the consultant based on a suggestion by a colleague after that colleague has made the prospective client aware of the consultant and what the consultant does. Networking is the process in which a consultant creates awareness of himself or herself and his or her unique "brand" of OD and explicitly makes himself or herself available for such referrals. A major goal of networking is to become the recipient of "matchmaking" by fellow net-workers.

Before meeting with a prospective client, a consultant must consider where, when, and how long to meet. During the first face-to-face meeting, the consultant faces four essential tasks:

1. Conveying information about what the consultant does and how it compares with traditional OD consulting efforts;

2. Establishing client confidence and trust in the consultant;

3. Learning enough about the client's organization—or how to obtain that information—to be able to make a credible proposal; and

4. Obtaining commitment to a follow-up meeting to make the proposal or continue the discussion.

The fourth task is the most important. Without it, an agreement can never be reached and a "sale" can never be closed.

Because OD consulting is a service commodity, success-ful marketing most often occurs at the client's convenience—usually in the client's office. Although this is not a neutral area, it does allow a consultant the opportunity to practice observa-tional skills and to gather initial data. Obviously, the longer the visit, the greater the opportunity for the consultant to gather information about the client and the problem(s) facing the client. A good rule for consultants to remember is to ask prospective clients to block out at least one hour of uninter-rupted time for the meetings. Indeed, more than 80 percent of initial, successful contacts last for that length of time (Eng-dahl et al., 1991). The consultant should remember that he or she is involved in a mutual assessment of a potential relationship. This assessment involves judging interpersonal qualities that can be difficult to quantify; only by extended exposure can the consultant begin to "feel" how compatible he or she can be with representatives of a prospective client organization.

How initial contact time is spent also is important. Time should be spent talking about the client's organization and needs rather than the consultant's capabilities. In initial contact situations the client is likely to be one manager, and it is the consultant's responsibility to develop trust so that both parties can broaden their perspectives and see the organization as the client. Therefore, the consultant can best display his or her capabilities by reflecting on the client's situation and reframing it in terms of options with specific consequences. The idea is to convey the OD consultant's role as one of facilitator-educator rather than advice giver.

Planning the initial contact meeting is essential. Armed with data from initial research efforts on the client, a consultant should plan to use the following strategy in his or her presentations.

1. The first step is to get the client's attention. A good way to accomplish this is to demonstrate that research has been conducted and that the consultant is at least familiar with the organization.

2. The second step is to establish the client's need for OD.

3. The third step is to set up the consultant's role as solution facilitator.

4. The fourth step is action, a commitment to next steps, and a follow-up meeting.

In most cases the prospective client will find it difficult to refuse an additional meeting to review and discuss the consultant's written proposal. After all, the prospective client is usually highly motivated to discuss problems or issues confronting it or the organization—particularly with a third-party consultant from outside the department, division, or organization. So the client has a stake in talking to someone—so long as the client feels that he or she will not be charged exorbitant fees solely for that privilege. Successful initial contacts also result from the consultant's use of effective interpersonal skills, such as active listening and questioning.

Contracting

Once a consultant has received a referral, he or she needs to work on developing and closing a sale. Success depends on the consultant's ability to make a favorable first impression while helping the client to focus on specific needs.

During the initial contact, the consultant's focus should be on client needs. During subsequent meetings, the consultant's focus should gradually shift to setting a mutual agenda. As French and Bell point out in *Organization Development* (1978, p. 200), issues for a mutual agenda relate to the following questions:

- Who is the client?
- How much trust exists in the organization about the change effort?
- What is the nature of the consultant's expertise?
- What will the contract be and how will the contact be established?

- How can the problem be diagnosed and an appropriate intervention be selected?
- What should the depth of the intervention be?
- How can the consultant avoid being absorbed by the culture?
- How can the consultant serve as a role model during the intervention?
- What are the steps of action research and the OD process?
- How should client dependence be handled and how should the relationship be terminated?
- What are the implications of OD for the client?

The key ingredient to successful negotiation and contracting during the entry stage is discussion of client-consultant relations. During such discussions the consultant should focus on reaching agreement with the client. When that cannot be reached easily, the consultant should think back to the point where they were last in agreement to see what issues led them astray. Common reasons for not reaching contractual agreement include the following:

- Client resistance to interventions proposed by the consultant;
- Lack of understanding by the client of the OD process;
- Lack of commitment by the client to going beyond the assessment phase of the OD process;
- Lack of agreement on a time commitment; and
- Lack of acceptance of financial arrangements.

The OD consultant faces a major challenge to educate the client in those areas in which the client has strong preconceived notions or hidden agendas. Educating a client is a metamarketing strategy. Creating awareness and understanding of the OD process is further complicated by the consultant's need to gain the support of the necessary level of management to focus on the organization or a major subelement of it as the client.

Reaching agreement on the details of the consulting relationship is part of forging the psychological contract between client and consultant that is so important to subsequent success in the OD intervention. Once that psychological contract has been established, the consultant should provide the details of the arrangement in a written proposal (see Appendix II), contract, or letter of agreement. Such an agreement should clarify issues associated with the following:

- Consulting fees;
- Billing times;
- Expense reimbursements;
- Responsibilities for materials and logistical support;
- Approximate time frames of the OD intervention;
- Provisions for renegotiating the contract due to a changing situation; and
- Methods of negotiating areas of concern stemming from discoveries made during the OD process.

External consultants may prefer binding legal agreements. These agreements are best drafted and reviewed by attorneys, based on information provided by the parties in interest, although it is advisable to develop a standard form to meet the needs of individual organization development consultants. Internal consultants may prefer less formal agreements, although they will still need to clarify who is paying for what and how each party to the agreement is responsible for successful results.

References

Abell, D. (1980). *Defining the business: The starting point of strategic planning.* Englewood Cliffs, NJ: Prentice-Hall.

Andreason, A. (1988). *Cheap but good marketing research.* Homewood, IL: Business One Irwin

Burke, W. (1984). Assessment questionnaire for knowledge and understanding of organization development. *Organization Development Journal, 2*(4), 37-42.

Engdahl, R., Howe, V., & Cole, D. (1991). Marketing OD: What now works and what does not. *Organization Development Journal, 9*(2), 32-40.

French, W., & Bell, C. (1978). *Organization development* (2nd ed.). Englewood Cliffs, NJ: Prentice-Hall.

French, J., & Raven, B. (1989). The bases of social power. In J. Ott (Ed.), *Classic readings in organizational behavior* (pp. 440-453). Pacific Grove, CA: Brooks/Cole Publishing.

Gibb, J. (1991). *Trust: A new vision of human relationships for business, education, family and personal living.* North Hollywood, CA: Newcastle Publishing.

Glassman, A., & Cummings, T. (Eds.). (1991). *Cases in organization development.* Homewood, IL: Irwin.

Hill, C., & Jones, G. (1989). *Strategic management theory.* Boston, MA: Houghton-Mifflin.

Hofer, C. (1975). Towards a contingency theory of business strategy. *Academy of Management Journal, 18,* 784-810.

International registry of organization development professionals and organization development handbook. (Annual). Chesterland, OH: The Organization Development Institute.

Jackson, C. (Ed.). (1987). *Entry: Beginning the OD consultation process.* Alexandria, VA: American Society for Training and Development.

Metzger, R. (1989). *Profitable consulting.* Reading, MA: Addison-Wesley.

Pfeiffer, J., & Jones, J. (1974). Dyadic encounter: A program for developing relationships. In *A handbook of structured experiences for human relations training.* (Vol. I, pp. 90-100). San Diego, CA: Pfeiffer & Company.

Porter, M. (1985). *Competitive strategy: Techniques for analyzing industries and competitors.* New York: The Free Press.

Sheehan, D., & O'Toole, J. (1985). *Becoming a superstar seller.* New York: AMACOM.

CHAPTER 4

Start-Up

David W. Jamieson

When organization development (OD) consultants initially engage with clients to facilitate change efforts, the consultants need to ensure that many activities go right because much can go wrong. It is most important that the clients and the consultants clarify their expectations about what will happen. Clarifying expectations will facilitate subsequent steps of OD interventions.

The following situations are common at the outset of most change efforts:

- Visible support may be minimal in an organization;

- Managers and employees may feel vulnerable;

- There can be differing—and often biased—perspectives about what is working well and what is not working well; and

- There are usually more "unknowns" than "knowns."

In typical situations, both internal and external OD consultants find that they are not sure what they should do, with whom they should work, how they should conduct OD interventions, how fast interventions should be carried out, or what the results should look like. However, within this context, consultants must work with their clients to establish rapport quickly, gain credibility, validate key issues, and diagnose needs.

All OD consultants must contract for the work to be done, build or clarify their relationships with clients, and be sure they understand the client organizations, the organizations' industries, and their informal systems and power networks. Although internal consultants may need to do less in some of these respects, they should not make assumptions about the perspectives of their clients. External consultants generally have to do more about becoming familiar with client organizations and contracting about financial arrangements.

The Start-Up Step

The start-up step rarely falls neatly, distinctly, and sequentially between the entry and assessment and feedback steps. In fact, the start-up step overlaps and bridges those steps in most OD interventions (see Exhibit 4-1.) Generally, OD consultants are developing some credibility while they are marketing themselves and learning about client organizations, even when making initial contacts. Likewise, preliminary diagnostic scanning is necessary during start-up to validate organizational issues and develop change plans.

For purposes of this chapter, the start-up step will be regarded as the beginning of an OD intervention—when an OD consultant clearly has a client, a desire to do work, and

Exhibit 4-1: The Relationships Among the Entry, Start-Up, and Assessment and Feedback Steps of OD Work

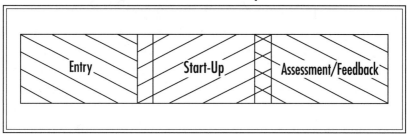

activities associated with marketing, selling, and closing have been completed. The start-up step concludes when an OD consultant and a client have clarified the nature of the change effort, their working relationship, and their plan for conducting an extensive assessment of the organization. Some elements of start-up may never conclude and may require continuing discussion and negotiation. Examples include changing work scopes, handling new issues that come up during interventions, changing players, or changing expectations in the consulting relationship. It is also common for the start-up step to repeat or recycle as an OD intervention moves to new parts of the organization or as new people are included.

One slogan is popular among OD consultants: "You are the instrument" (Jamieson, 1991). That slogan is significant, serving to emphasize that OD consultants are change agents who have to rely on their thoughts, feelings, strengths, and weaknesses throughout OD interventions. In the start-up step, the "instrument" is evident and critical. What consultants say and do affects their credibility, provides the basis for building relationships, generates support, or initiates resistance.

The work consultants do is affected by how quick they are to judge, criticize, or conclude. Communicating, listening, and probing effectively will increase their understanding and ease client fears. Confronting others appropriately and giving timely and effective feedback will increase their clients' clarity about issues and their authenticity in approaching problems and solutions. How well consultants adapt to their clients' cultures may determine the success of their interventions. Moreover, OD consultants' front-end work—that is, reaching agreement for successful OD interventions—will be greatly improved by their ability to elicit hope, facilitate discussions, work collaboratively, empathize, and assert their points of view.

The Importance of the Start-Up Step

During start-up, a consultant must clarify his or her expectations and make agreements concerning the work to be done and the client-consultant working relationship. Reaching agreement with the client on these issues is critical to the success of the change effort. To reach successful outcomes and use resources effectively—both the consultant's and the client's—the consultant will need to ensure that he or she is working on the "right" issues, problems, or needs and is working within the appropriate boundaries, using the correct methods, working within the specified time, and eliciting the proper support. The consultant and the client will become frustrated if the consultant devotes his or her efforts only to part of a problem or only to symptoms of the problem or if the consultant understands only the causes of the problem. Resources such as time and money are valuable, and it is the responsibility of the consultant and the client to avoid misusing them.

For example, an owner of a successful, growing service organization contracted with a consultant to look at her company's future prospects, facilitate strategic planning, and develop senior management. After the consultant had collected data, designed a process that worked well in terms of planning and team building, and conducted the intervention, the participants, including the owner, expressed satisfaction with present conditions and commitment to future improvements. A few months later, the owner sold the company to a competitor. Both the consultant and members of the client organization felt great frustration.

Developing Working Relationships

Developing an effective working relationship is essential for a consultant to gain client trust, build support from power brokers, and ensure appropriate consultant influence.

Most organizations are generally quick to reject outsiders, especially consultants. If clients find it difficult to work with consultants or to understand them, that creates an additional barrier. Clients often experience mixed feelings (including desire, fear, and risk) about a change effort, and consultants can either be helpful in dealing with these feelings or aggravate them. Feelings of satisfaction and comfort during OD interventions are affected by how clients want to be included and informed, how they want to receive inputs from consultants, and what consultants want from their clients. Many of the feelings experienced by clients and consultants are associated with their availability to one another, their priorities, and their levels of commitment to the change effort.

For example, in one situation a client was expecting a written report from the consultant. The consultant, however, had prepared an oral presentation, complete with overhead transparencies and a handout. Shortly thereafter the client began to quarrel with the consultant over billed time because the client did not believe that the consultant was using his time appropriately. There was obviously lack of clarity and agreement about how the report should be presented and how time was being used.

Elements of the Start-Up Step

When the entry step is complete, the consultant should establish a working relationship and a work plan with his or her client. During this process, the consultant should focus on the following nine key outcomes:

1. Identifying the client and the sponsor(s);
2. Becoming oriented to the client's world;
3. Establishing the consultant's competence and credibility;
4. Developing open and trusting relationships;
5. Assessing alignment of values;
6. Understanding the organization's political system;
7. Completing a preliminary diagnostic scan;
8. Contracting for the following items:
   a. The work to be done (what, how, who, when, and where) and the critical success factors for measuring results. Contracting for work to be done often needs to be handled in two stages. The first stage consists of contracting for the content and the process of diagnosis and assessment. The second stage focuses on the design and intervention work, and possibly the evaluation phase.
   b. The psychosocial relationships with those people with whom the consultant will be working directly and those who are critical stakeholders but are not

directly involved in the work, such as sponsors, key political players, or people who may become more important or more involved as the work progresses;

c. The consultant's resource and support needs; and

d. The financial arrangements. Most OD consultants bill the client for their services, but it is possible to barter or to receive a mixture of money, learning, or use of developed materials. Several mutually beneficial arrangements are possible.

9. Introducing the intervention and the consultant to the appropriate members of the organization (the client and others who will be affected).

Outcome 1: Identifying the Client and the Sponsor(s)

The consultant should clarify—as early as possible—who the client will be. It is not always possible to know all the key players in the client organization immediately, but those who are known and those who are possible key players should be the focus of the consultant's attention. Of course, the consultant may find that there is an individual client, a group of clients, or even multiple clients. He or she may find that the client at the outset of the OD intervention will be replaced by subsequent clients as the intervention progresses. The consultant may even find a primary client who is directly involved in the work and secondary clients who are influenced by results of the work.

Although no two interventions start or progress in the same way, the first step is usually a meeting with one person from the organization. The second step is a meeting with a small group of key sponsors, a management team, or an employee committee. These group members may or may not continue as clients, but they will most assuredly remain as intervention sponsors. Depending on how the intervention is designed, a new group may become the client (for example, a design team). The consultant may also be asked to work jointly, as a co-consultant, with others from inside or outside the organization or department.

These co-relationships can become problematic. Those who work with the consultant can range from clerical support, to a colleague, to the "real" client. The consultant will need to clarify roles and relationships if he or she is placed in such a situation.

For example, some OD consultants contracted with the president and his senior staff of a company that was one of three owned by a parent company. The consultants believed that their clients were the president and the senior staff. Not long after the intervention began, the president of the parent company began to make late-night telephone calls to the consultants for information about the client organization and to ask how well the president and senior staff members were working with the consultants. It was no longer clear to the consultants who the client was, so they called a meeting with the two presidents. The consultants were able to clarify in the meeting that the primary client was the company in which direct intervention was occurring, but that the parent company was, indeed, a secondary client. An arrangement was made for the consultants to meet monthly with both presidents in order to update them on the intervention.

Clients and sponsors can have different perspectives, work styles, and levels of influence. The consultant may need to work with people who cannot make necessary intervention-related decisions. The consultant may sometimes listen too much to one group and not enough to other groups. The consultant's direct clients may not be in agreement with a key sponsor. If all the players are known, then all viewpoints need to be included; if the consultant is unknowingly not in contact with all of the key players, he or she may embark on inappropriate courses of action or be derailed by powerful groups or persons who were excluded. Thus, one important goal during start-up is to create alignment in the contracting among all the clients and sponsors.

Outcome 2: Becoming Oriented to the Client's World

People in an organization operate from their perceptions, which, in turn, are influenced by their own experiences and their organization's history and culture. People's perceptions are influenced by many things: their organization's work technology and processes; beliefs and realities about their own world, the industry, and the organization's competitors; and beliefs about how they should perform their work. The consultant must understand and appreciate the client's world and how the client perceives his or her world.

Becoming oriented to the client's world involves asking questions about it, observing it, and reading about it. Some key questions that the consultant should consider are as follows:

- What is happening in the client's environment (for example, issues involving regulation, competition, increased or decreased customer demand, changing customer profiles, and the economy)?

- What pronouncements are made in the client organization's annual report, state-of-the-organization messages, or recent studies?

- Who are the competitors and the heroines of the client's organization and the client's industry?

- What crises and/or achievements has the client experienced?

- What was the client's previous experience with other consultants and planned-change efforts?

In addition to the client's external context and history, the consultant should also familiarize himself or herself with the client organization's work, structure, technology, culture, and people. Because organizations are systems, their parts are interconnected. A change has to be viewed in its larger context:

- What other departments, functions, or people will the change influence?

- What potentially limits the change?

- What leverage points affect the change?

- What alignments are needed to make change work?

The consultant should find out the following about the client organization:

- What does the organization produce or do?

- How does the organization make its product or provide its service?

- How is the organization structured?

- What problems/issues does the organization typically have to deal with?

- What does the organization do especially well?

The consultant needs to learn about the role of technology in the organization's work, the values and behavioral norms that operate in the workplace, and the key players in the formal or informal social network.

In finding out about the client's world, the consultant needs to know what else the organization is doing, working at, or changing. The change effort needs to be integrated and coordinated with the efforts of different divisions or departments. It must be positioned and linked to what is already occurring.

Becoming oriented to the client's world provides the consultant with a foundation, a way of understanding the client's language, fears, desires, and frustrations. The foundation gives the consultant a basis for introducing alternative thinking, different frameworks, and new ideas. It demonstrates that the consultant cares and it helps him or her to connect with people through their reality. The foundation also helps the consultant to talk about change or desired future states because it is grounded in the organization's reality, and the consultant is not having to be corrected so often that the he or she loses credibility.

For example, while working with a utility company, an OD consultant found it helpful to have someone explain the current drive to develop alternative energy sources and the trend toward deregulation. She was able to use this information to introduce change by explaining how relevant the trends were to the organization and that the organization needed to be more innovative, take more risks, and be more entrepreneurial to seize opportunities presented by the trends.

In another situation, the OD consultant discovered that a previous consultant was perceived by organizational members to have violated confidentiality, so the consultant was careful to give that issue greater attention and visibility during the change effort.

In the start-up step, the consultant will not have detailed information about the client organization. The assessment phase is, of course, designed to fill in the information gaps that are apparent during start-up.

Outcome 3: Establishing the Consultant's Competence and Credibility

The consultant's knowledge, skills, experience, and work style must fit the OD intervention and the client's requirements. It is an ineffective and unethical use of resources for a consultant to work on an OD intervention for which he or she lacks necessary competence. An OD intervention that is outside or beyond a consultant's competence can best be handled under the guidance of someone more experienced or in a team arrangement. In this way, the requisite skills are available to the client, and the consultant can learn and develop greater competence.

The client is also vulnerable during a change effort and is rightfully concerned about receiving the appropriate help for what it needs. The client's anxiety is increased when the consultant's credibility is questionable—either in performing the necessary work or in working effectively with the client. In the same way that it is important for the consultant to know the client's world, the client will find it important to learn about the consultant's education, experience, and personal values. The client should also know how the consultant acquired his or her expertise, what he or she has done that is related to the change effort, what he or she knows that is relevant to the intervention, and how he or she feels about the possibilities for success.

Authenticity, honesty, and confidence contribute to the consultant's credibility. The consultant may not have worked with many clients before, but he or she may have compelling ideas about how to approach the OD intervention. He or she even may have conducted a similar intervention before that did not work well, but from which the consultant learned valuable lessons that could affect the success of the current change effort. The consultant's credibility also can be enhanced when he or she describes his or her strengths and limitations with the client, voices his or her concerns, and expresses confidence or enthusiasm about the assignment.

The consultant's competence may come from various areas. It may result from his or her expertise in a particular content area needed for the intervention, such as total quality management or work-process redesign. Competence also may result from the consultant's expertise in process design and facilitation, such as ability to involve people or generate new ideas. It also may be based on the outcomes of the consultant's previous interventions, his or her understanding of the client's situation, or his or her writings or teachings.

Credibility is associated with more than just having the right knowledge and skills. It also stems from the consultant's ability to relate to the client and complete activities leading to a successful change effort. Credibility grows from the consultant's ability to organize action, such as what steps to take and how to sequence them. It reflects the client's assessment of the potential for success, incorporating the ability to work well with the consultant. Ultimately, the success of an OD intervention will depend both on what is done and on the effectiveness of the client-consultant relationship.

For example, in one client situation, a consultant found it necessary to assume a leadership role in the first meeting. She pulled out a piece of paper and drew a simple model so she could discuss with her clients the relationship among the problems that the client organization was experiencing. These clients were confused and needed to feel they were receiving expert help, and the consultant was able to provide this by guiding the clients through their problem.

Competence and credibility easily can be underplayed or overplayed. If the consultant devotes too much time displaying his or her credentials, talking about past successes, or naming bigger clients, some clients may become intimidated. On the other hand, the consultant's competence and credibility need to be conveyed, and he or she should describe his or her strengths or experiences in order to build client confidence and comfort.

Outcome 4: Developing Open and Trusting Relationships

The client-consultant relationship must be built on a foundation of openness and trust. Openness is important to the relationship because the client and the consultant need to share all information affecting the change effort. That includes important information about the organization and the personal concerns, fears, and opinions of key clients, sponsors, and the consultant.

Trust is also essential. The consultant must feel that his or her skills are being properly used; the client must feel that its proprietary or confidential data will be properly handled. The client must also believe that the consultant is really working in its best interests. A foundation of openness and trust is important because, over the course of the OD intervention, the consultant and the client must rely on each other and work to achieve an unimpeded flow of information so they can make informed decisions.

Two major barriers to openness and trust stem from a client's negative past experiences with other consultants or other people and from the client's vulnerability during the OD intervention. Both barriers can impede the client's ability to enter an OD intervention in an open, trusting way. For this reason, the consultant will need to take initiative in showing support, sharing realistic concerns, expressing reservations or optimism, modeling openness and authenticity, talking honestly about what has worked and what has not, and discussing their working relationship. The consultant is always a role model, and he or she must model the behaviors he or she wants to find in the relationship.

In creating openness and trust, the consultant will find it helpful to discuss the following with the client:

- Expected time lines;
- Real barriers or challenges;
- Personal hopes;
- Possible problems;
- Possible risks in the change effort; and
- Personal commitments and values as they relate to the change effort.

Openness and trust emanate from a foundation of alignment (seeing things the same way) and honesty (saying what is real). In order to establish such a foundation, the client and the consultant have to maintain a continuing dialogue about what is meaningful, significant, compelling, or scary. Openness and trust grow from sharing experiences. The client and the consultant should talk about specific issues, not unreachable goals. They must also talk about what forces support the success of the OD intervention, what forces resist the intervention, what motivations underlie the change effort, and what they find exciting about the desired future.

The client and consultant do not have to agree on every-thing at the outset of the change effort, but they do need to confront their differences, discuss their implications, clarify viewpoints, and show respect for each other's viewpoints.

For example, in one situation the consultant found it useful to alert a top manager about issues that could be surfaced about her role and the consultant's role in the prob-lems that had been identified. This lead-in enabled the leader to share her concerns about her contribution to the problems and to express a willingness to change.

In another situation, the consultant was honest about not having performed a particular type of work before. The con-sultant shared the approach she planned to use and asked for the client's approval and commitment to the change effort. The consultant's honesty engendered client trust and permit-ted important collaboration between them.

Outcomes 5 and 6: Assessing Alignment of Values and Understanding the Organization's Political System

Values in an organization are created and maintained through the power system. The power system comprises people who command leverage, influence, and authority over key systems and processes, rewards and incentives, and people. The con-sultant needs to know the client's values that are relevant to a change effort, such as the client's values about people, work, success, diversity, and so on,and how compatible those values are with the consultant's.

Those entering a planned change effort rarely do so from a value-free perspective; rather, everyone operates with de-sired results in mind. The OD consultant often brings to a change effort his or her own perspective, which is loaded with such value-based principles as a high regard for employee involvement, employee empowerment, and respect for human dignity. Although the consultant's values should not singularly drive the OD intervention, the client and consultant may not work together effectively if their values are incompatible. Without some alignment, conflict is likely to result over the intervention's goals and means, and that conflict will influence decisions about the OD intervention.

The consultant must understand the organization's power system and its politics (Greiner & Schein, 1988). He or she must find out who has significant influence, what decision-making policies are used in the organization, and who has expertise pertinent to the change effort. The consultant must also learn about the motives, perspectives, and values of those in power so he or she understands the political dynamics inherent in the organization's culture (for example, dependencies, tradeoffs, deals, and incentives).

Powerful people attain their status through formal or informal means. The consultant needs to learn about the power/political dimensions of the organization and gain access to key people in appropriate ways during the start-up step. Greiner and Metzger (1983) refer to this aspect of start-up as "meeting the power structure."

For example, in one consulting situation an OD intervention was terminated when a pending invoice was rejected because a new chief financial officer (CFO) had not been involved in the early stages of the intervention. The client and the consultant had proceeded without paying attention to a key change in the power system and, in this case, the emergence of a new perspective on the value of the work being performed.

In another intervention, the human-resource client got into trouble with the head of data processing by launching an

OD intervention on people issues in implementing technological change without first obtaining the support and approval of the high-powered head of data processing. Even the organization's president, who initially supported the OD intervention, overlooked the importance of involving this power player. The head of data processing discredited early work on the intervention and convinced the president to withdraw support. The intervention was terminated after the initial phase. In this case, the consultant needed to test the political system rather than rely on the client's belief that everyone necessary supported the OD intervention.

Outcome 7: Completing a Preliminary Diagnostic Scan

In a preliminary diagnostic scan, the consultant's interest should be threefold:

1. Understanding and validating issues and needs;
2. Identifying resistance and support; and
3. Clarifying competence and commitment.

In the start-up step, the consultant attempts to learn enough about the client and its problem to contract effectively for the work. The consultant should seek information from more than his or her initial contact. He or she may find it helpful to hear from—or about—people who may be causing, affected by, or have a stake in the issues.

The consultant should, for instance, seek information to answer such questions as the following:

- What is the problem?
- What is the apparent cause of the problem?
- Why is the present state as it is?

- How do people feel about it?

Whenever possible, the consultant should obtain this information directly from those closest to the problem, event, situation, or cause. At minimum, the consultant should be able to question credible sources for their perceptions about how the people involved in the issues would answer the questions previously listed.

In a preliminary scan, the consultant should not strive to obtain great detail about the problem; rather, he or she should seek to understand the issues generally and reach conclusions about relationships among them. In part, the consultant is trying to achieve clarity and elevate his or her confidence about what to work on while also sharpening the client's understanding. The consultant is also trying to establish the validity of presenting problems and determine the commonality of perceptions and distinctions among different viewpoints. Greiner and Metzger (1983) label this approach as "probing the problem."

Initially, the consultant is trying to simplify the problem in order to design an approach to diagnosis. In this process he or she should talk to a few key people or meet with key stakeholder groups. The consultant may have to facilitate discussions so as to surface real issues and challenge beliefs. The consultant may also review studies, memos, or other documents that relate to the issues, needs, and viewpoints. The consultant may find it helpful to observe some regular meetings or to tour work areas to see the operations, interactions, and culture at work. Investing a little energy in the preliminary scan will help the consultant place the OD intervention on the right path.

When performing the diagnostic scan, the consultant should also note who appears to support or resist the change effort and why they feel the way they do. Identifying supporters and resisters helps to crystallize motives and personal agendas. Supporters and resisters may also dramatize the real hurdles to be encountered or identify key considerations in designing the content and process of the change effort.

When performing the preliminary scan, the consultant should assess the organization's commitment and capability for change. He or she should try to gauge the organization's level of commitment (attitude and energy toward change) and the capability of its members (their knowledge and skills contributing to the change effort). Knowing the commitment of key stakeholders is important because it helps the consultant determine whether the organization is ready for change or if other steps will be needed to create an impetus for it. Commitment can be viewed as levels of energy applied toward or against change. People can be against the change direction, somewhat neutral about letting it happen, passively for it, or wanting to make it happen (Beckhard & Harris, 1987).

Assessing the commitment to change by those involved in the issues—even as "best guess" perceptions—helps the consultant ascertain how much readiness building is needed and how strong the champions of change are. The capability of organizational members is measured by their knowledge or experience with planned change and change processes and their level of needed skills, such as their ability to participate, work productively in groups, function in an open way, think creatively, and demonstrate flexibility.

Change could be utterly new to some organizations, participation could be countercultural, and the people may be highly rigid. However, other organizations may be accustomed to change, their members may have undergone extensive training in interpersonal communication and small-group management, and these organizations may have employees who seek variety and experimentation.

When a consultant is familiar with an organization's change competence, he or she can more easily determine how much education should be included in the intervention strategy, how to use the organization's human resources to help other parts of the organization change, and how to provide needed skills.

For example, a preliminary diagnostic scan will often move the client from wanting a simple training solution to wanting a more complex reexamination of the organization's work structure or culture. Alternatively, the problems presented by the client may be full of attributions and can be seen more accurately only by surfacing the real causes of why a system is not working, why products are of poor quality, or why services are fraught with delays. The consultant also may find that some form of education or readiness-building is essential prior to launching an in-depth diagnosis because of the real potential for sabotage or invalid data to affect a change effort.

The results of skipping or shorting the preliminary diagnostic scan can be disastrous. If a consultant hurries to begin the intervention, resistance may be elevated and the wrong problems may be addressed. The consultant must therefore help the client identify real issues and attitudes. Only then is it possible to contract appropriately and design the intervention strategy effectively.

Outcome 8: Contracting

The next important element of start-up is contracting. The information that has been learned so far provides a foundation for the contracting process and data for the content of the work and psychological contracts (Boss, 1985).

The process of contracting needs to be a primary focus in the start-up step. But contracting can be ongoing in some respects and reopened as conditions change. Contracting means establishing and clarifying expectations about the change effort, the working relationship(s), consultant support needs, and financial or other arrangements.

Block (1981) refers to contracting as an explicit agreement about what the consultant and the client should expect and how they should work together. That agreement results from discussions in which the wants, offers, and concerns of the client and the consultant are clarified. Differences are negotiated, and agreement is reached.

Contracting is of utmost importance in organization development work (Weisbord, 1973). It sets the tone for the entire OD intervention (Block, 1981). The parties with whom the consultant should contract will depend on who is identified as the client(s), sponsor(s), and key player(s) in the power system. A consultant may sometimes need to perform primary contracting for all aspects of a change effort and relationship, and auxiliary contracting for parts of the change effort or limited relationship needs.

The consultant should start the OD intervention by agreeing with the client about desired goals or outcomes, the nature of the change effort and the methods to be used. As part of these discussions, the consultant and the client should establish critical success factors (what will it take to be successful?) which can later be used in the evaluation step. Critical success factors can include objective, measurable outcomes such as reduced turnover, higher margins, or quality improvements, and more subjective attitude or behavior outcomes such as more participation among a group's members, improved morale, or shared perceptions of what is valued and rewarded. Caution may be needed, however; there is no guarantee of improvement. The consultant should keep in mind the mutual nature of the contracting process. No matter how well the consultant does, there can be no change or improvement without the full support of the client organization. Both Boss (1985) and Schein (1988) have stressed the importance of emphasizing the joint responsibility of clients and consultants during contracting.

Developing consensus on the nature of the change effort and methods will produce more detailed information on whom to work with, whom to include, where the OD work will take place, when the work should be performed, in what sequence OD intervention activities should happen, and approximately how long the change effort will take. The consultant should be sure that flexibility is incorporated in the contractual language.

In contracting for the OD work, the client and the consultant should agree on the overall strategy for approaching the intervention. That includes boundaries, work tasks, sequence of activities, pace of activities, timing of activities, choice of methods, data requirements, data analysis, people to include in the change effort, and deliverables to be produced. The result of this part of contracting is often a plan that may be more specific and detailed for the immediate next steps, such as diagnosis or preliminary education, and more general for the subsequent design, intervention, and implementation phases. It is often helpful to include key decision points in the change plan for client-consultant review or modification.

There are four types of organizational members with whom the consultant may need to contract for working relationships:

1. Direct client(s) with whom the consultant will be working;
2. Sponsors of the OD intervention, if any;
3. Key players in the power system; and
4. People who may be involved in later stages.

Some relationships will necessarily be more in-depth; some may involve limited roles and minimal content.

In contracting with the direct client, the consultant must address the full range of relationship issues and develop the working relationship. Trust and openness are issues of central importance. In addition, the consultant will find it essential to clarify what roles he or she will play for the client, what they should expect from each other, how they should work together, how they should plan together, and how they should reach critical decisions.

However, sponsors and key power players may want roles with different levels of involvement. Some may join in the change effort; others may be interested observers. Generally, contracting for these relationships involves determining how much sponsors and key power players wish to participate; how much information they want to receive; what information they want to receive; how much faith they have in the consultant's ability to pursue the objectives they seek; and how much information, support, and involvement the consultant needs from them. The consultant will need to keep the power players informed and keep asking for their input.

If the consultant knows that other people will be involved in the change effort later, he or she may find it helpful to brief them on what will be happening, determine how to keep them informed, estimate when and in what ways the change effort may impact them, and discuss, if appropriate, what they can do to prepare for participating in the change effort.

For example, in one OD intervention the direct clients consisted of a group of senior managers. The sponsor was an executive vice president, and there were about six other key power players. The consultant defined the direct clients' roles as compiling and analyzing data, and he defined his role as educating the organization, providing input options, being on call for assistance, and facilitating review and integration meetings. They agreed on what type of information to share. Agreements were also reached about the value of timeliness and the ground rules for meetings. The sponsor agreed to attend the periodic-review and integration meetings, wanted frank discussions with the consultant about the OD intervention's progress, and requested a written report at the end of the intervention.

In a meeting, the other power players were informed of the project's purpose and their roles. Their initial inputs and advice were sought. They were also reassured about confidentiality and told that the sponsor would keep them informed and share project results with them.

The most in-depth relationship contracting occurs with the consultant's direct client. The consultant is contracting primarily for the psychosocial aspects of the relationship. That includes—but is not limited to—roles and expectations, needs for involvement, information needs, contact, control, work styles, and the ground rules or principles that will be used as the consultant and the client work together. This type of contracting requires that the consultant and the client ask for what they want or need (Block, 1981; Boss, 1985).

The consultant needs to clarify his or her role. For example, will he or she serve as an expert, a helper, or a collaborator (Block, 1981)? It is equally important to clarify the client's role. For example, is the client an OD intervention manager, a co-consultant, or a decision maker? The consultant and the client also need to decide who should be most visible in relation to the OD intervention. Once the OD consultant's and the client's roles have been discussed, their expectations can develop.

Other considerations must also be addressed. Will the intervention be jointly planned or planned chiefly by the consultant or the client? Will meetings be client-led or consultant-led? The consultant and the client also will need to clarify how often they will meet, what information will need to be communicated, who will communicate the information, how the information will be communicated (for example, phone call, electronic mail, fax, presentation, memo), and when the consultant and the client will be accessible.

People's styles of working also need to be considered, especially in joint and collaborative relationships. Some people need very detailed designs and discussions; others work well with general outlines. Some people require everything to be databased; others work well from a concept, value, or vision.

Other style issues that need to be considered include how quickly each key person learns and works; whether each person works better alone or with others; and how tolerant each is about ambiguity, flexibility, and risk taking. Sometimes, work styles are compatible, and relationship contracting is easy. When the consultant's and the client's work styles are not compatible, clarity and compromise may be necessary to minimize tension and frustration.

Principles or ground rules for working together often originate from work styles, involvement, and information-sharing discussions. Agreements such as "it is okay to call me at home if we need to talk" or "we will tell each other everything and avoid surprises" provide both parties with an understanding of what is acceptable and effective. Other principles might relate to listening, equality, timeliness, how facility or reservation matters will be handled, or how each party can grow and develop in the OD intervention.

The consultant should discuss the separation policy with the client during start-up and he or she should ask the following questions:

- Who can end the OD intervention or consulting relationship? Under what circumstances?
- How will termination occur?
- What does each party owe the other party if a termination occurs?

Whether a working relationship is based on ground rules, expectations, or work styles, the consultant and the client will need to clarify and agree on how they will work together in a trusting, productive, and rewarding relationship.

For example, in one intervention, the client and consultant agreed to have follow-up meetings after key steps in the OD intervention, to discuss and enhance learning about the conceptual base of the OD intervention and to discuss specific situations or emerging problems. Because their expectations were clear, the consultant and the client had a successful working relationship. In other situations, clients and consultants have held monthly breakfasts, weekly meetings, and periodic three-way meetings with sponsors. Consultants and clients also have used written status reports or presentations at executive staff meeting.

In some OD interventions consultants need support services. Support services can be described as any task needed to see the OD intervention or change effort through to a successful conclusion. These services often include clerical help or administrative assistance. Some important questions that the consultants should ask about support services are as follows:

- Who will provide the support services?
- How/through whom will they be obtained?
- What will support services consist of?
- When will the consultant be able to use the support services?
- Who will pay for them?

Support services may be supplied by the client or by the consultant. Some consultants may need media support for their presentations or their reports. Sometimes the OD intervention requires that consultants be on-site frequently; that may necessitate office space or clerical help. Many interventions require members of the organization to supply and/or analyze data. Still other OD interventions involve travel and lodging arrangements. The questions related to these latter issues may include the following:

- Who will arrange for and pay for traveling and lodging needs?
- What class of service is involved?
- Will traveling and lodging needs be paid for directly by the organization, invoiced, or handled in some other manner?

If questions about support are left answered at the outset of the OD intervention, they may result in misunderstandings or lead to situations in which support tasks are not carried out.

For example, in one situation the client provided a support person. He was designated as part-time for the OD intervention and was to handle all administrative and logistical matters for the OD intervention team, which included the consultant.

In another situation, the client and the consultant had not clarified support services, and a misunderstanding occurred. The client did all the word processing on some materials and then deducted the cost from the consultant's invoice. Better contracting would have avoided this incident.

The last aspect of contracting involves what is being exchanged and how it is to be exchanged. The client and consultant need to reach agreement on the following issues:

- What is the consultant's pay rate?
- What consulting expenses are covered?
- What time is billable (for example, will travel time be billable)?
- How is time calculated (for example, nearest quarter hour, hour, half day)?
- How much time and money is estimated for the OD intervention?
- When should the consultant's invoices be sent?
- How should the invoices be prepared?
- What information should the invoices contain?
- Who should the invoices be sent to?
- What is the estimated timing for payments?

It is extremely important that the client and the consultant be clear about the billing and payment procedures and that these be documented in writing.

Both parties should discuss any changes that will affect the financial arrangement, such as using up budgeted amounts faster than anticipated or unanticipated budget cuts by the organization. The consultant and client should also discuss, periodically, the relationship between what is being accomplished in the change effort and the expenditures. When the relationship does not seem correlated, the client's concerns may grow: People do not want to spend substantial sums of money without witnessing visible progress toward their goals.

In one consulting situation, the consultant found it helpful to explain to the client why billable consulting days would occur earlier in the intervention rather than later and that the early bills would be larger than subsequent ones. Because the client was informed, she was not surprised by the consultant's first invoices.

With contracting, consultants need to remember that there are so many different systems and clients that contracting is almost always a process of customizing to fit each situation. Both parties must meet their individual and mutual needs in order to be satisfied. Contracting must not interfere with their working together effectively. It is a complex, human-interaction process requiring skill and flexibility.

Outcome 9: Introducing Intervention and the Consultant

Introducing the OD intervention and the consultant can be difficult. The consultant will need to know the organization's culture and systems as well as how to present the intervention properly. If people are not informed about the intervention before the consultant arrives, they might resist it. Who introduces the intervention and how he or she does it effects its credibility. If the wrong person introduces the OD intervention or uses the wrong method of communication, the intervention will begin poorly.

An introduction can benefit from more than one media. It may include a notification to everyone, followed by small-group sessions. The rationale for the intervention should be clear—what is being started and why. The involvement of key members of the organization in the introduction helps others to see the work as important; cross-organizational; and not "owned" by one person, group, faction, or department. The consultant, client, and sponsors all can have roles in the beginning of the OD intervention. Part of the introduction should be in writing in order to have a clear statement without multiple interpretations (Greiner & Metzger, 1983).

The consultant can also meet key people informally before the introduction to build comfort and rapport while minimizing feelings of concern. Providing personal as well as professional information about himself or herself at the outset of an intervention can also help portray him or her as a human being. These techniques help build the consultant's credibility and the client's confidence.

How various parts of the organization will be involved or affected by the intervention should determine how much time and effort should be devoted to its introduction. Some people should just be informed; others should be involved in two-way forums to be sure they understand the intervention and know what to expect. The consultant should know how the organization usually introduces information, but if its method is ineffective, the consultant may want to differentiate his or her change effort by creating a new introduction process.

Closing

Numerous problems in OD interventions can be traced to flaws in the start-up step. Difficulties can stem from misunderstanding the organization, ignoring issues associated with the power structure, not agreeing about work methods, and not reaching agreement on hourly rates or time commitments. These problems can be avoided if consultants take care to address them early on.

Consultants must work carefully to surface organizational issues. At the same time, they should work to instill trust and match their personal styles to the expectations of multiple players. Starting OD projects takes on great significance because change is inherently risky. Change engenders feelings of vulnerability in clients, intensifying emotions in ways that complicate helping relationships.

A consultant's authenticity and skills are central to establishing effective working relationships that contribute to successful change. The consultant cannot be too needy or too greedy, or too passive or too controlling. He or she has to remain marginal to the system yet remain close enough to the change effort and the people to obtain valid data and instill trust and confidence.

At different points in the start-up step, the "consultant as instrument" will be tested. Who the consultant is and how effective he or she will be with the client, sponsor(s), and organizational members will become evident through his or her ability to do the following:

- Communicate wants or perspectives on the issues;
- Listen to the client's message and feelings;
- Question in a probing and caring manner;
- Empathize with the client's vulnerability and fear;
- Clarify what others are struggling to communicate;

- Provide feedback to validate and support the client's thinking and behavior;
- Confront issues and people when the change effort is not going well;
- Observe effectively; and
- Facilitate the examination of issues, feelings, and differences that emerge in change efforts.

In the final analysis, consultants can see only what they have prepared themselves to see, and they can do only what they have developed themselves to do.

References

Beckhard, R., & Harris, R. (1987). *Organizational transitions* (2nd ed.). Reading, MA: Addison-Wesley.

Block, P. (1981). *Flawless consulting: A guide to getting your expertise used.* San Diego, CA: Pfeiffer & Company.

Boss, W. (1985). The psychological contract: A key to effective organization development consultation. *Consultation, 4*(4), 284-304.

Greiner, L., & Metzger, R. (1983). *Consulting to management.* Englewood Cliffs, NJ: Prentice-Hall.

Greiner, L., & Schein, V. (1988). *Power and organization development.* Reading, MA: Addison-Wesley.

Jamieson, D. (1991, March). You are the instrument. *OD Practitioner,* p. 20.

Schein, E. (1988). *Process consultation* (Vol. I). Reading, MA: Addison-Wesley.

Weisbord, M. (1973). The organization development contract. *OD Practitioner, 5*(2), 19-34.

CHAPTER 5

ASSESSMENT AND FEEDBACK

Jerry Franklin

Assessment and feedback comprise the third step in an organization development (OD) intervention. This step includes many activities that significantly influence the success of OD efforts.

Although assessment and feedback methods have been refined for decades, they are not used as much as OD experts suggest they should be. The methods used by consultants to collect and evaluate information about organizational functioning are strikingly inadequate in many OD efforts. One result of this is that some consultants initiate OD interventions without properly understanding the problems that prompted the interventions. Such interventions are often ill conceived and waste valuable resources, exacerbate existing problems, or create new problems.

In this chapter, the assessment and feedback step of an OD intervention is explored.

Assessment

Assessment is perhaps best understood as the collection and evaluation of information to identify strengths and weaknesses in a client organization. It is the basis for many OD activities. Especially critical to an assessment is a consultant's ability to identify—as much as possible—the root causes of problems, not just their observable symptoms. When causes can be distinguished from symptoms, the consultant and the client can begin to correct problems at their sources. One way to identify the cause of problems is to trace them to their sources by asking other people. Another way is to observe work processes or interactivities and attempt to trace causes through analysis.

There are two major advantages to focusing on a problem's cause. First, factors negatively affecting the organization can be addressed before they lead to serious problems. Second, the chances for developing lasting solutions are increased. If the consultant cannot identify the underlying causes, he or she may provide only temporary solutions or may succeed in suppressing only one symptom, and other symptoms from the same cause may eventually create new problems for the client.

The quality of assessment depends on the appropriateness of the focus area and the methods used to gather and evaluate information. Focus areas include an organization's environment, its internal structure and processes, and a client's desired results. Information-gathering methods include questionnaires or surveys, interviews, observations, and analyses of records. Each is described in subsequent sections of this chapter.

There are many methods that a consultant can use to gather information, and there are also many areas that he or she can assess. However, every focus area cannot be addressed and every method cannot be used in every situation. The consultant will need to limit his or her options by considering the purpose of the assessment and the client's needs. He or she also will have to contend with issues such as practical limitations, time, and money. The consultant's choices and the client's preferences will affect the usefulness of the assessment and the benefits it yields to OD activities.

Purposes of Assessment

Assessment serves four key purposes in an OD intervention. First, it provides a means by which to evaluate an organization's current situation. Assessment identifies the causes of existing problems and their possible future consequences. Second, it becomes the basis for feedback. Third, assessment provides background information for action planning. Fourth and finally, it provides a basis for tracking change and evaluating the progress of an OD intervention.

Evaluating the Current Situation. The impetus for assessing an organization's current situation often takes one of two forms in OD: A client either recognizes that there is a problem or a client wants a periodic review of the organizational environment.

In the first situation, a client realizes that there is a problem in its organization and asks a consultant to assess the situation. The consultant's efforts might lead to the identification of causes of the current problem, which also may lead to future problems.

The client's problem may be attributed to internal or external causes. Internal causes may include downsizing or reorganization; external causes may include increasing competition, changing consumer preferences, or the introduction of new technology. Typical problem symptoms include declining product quality or service quality, decreasing profitability, or lack of cooperation across divisions or departments.

In the second situation, the client asks a consultant to review the environment to prevent the occurrence of problems. The consultant identifies present trends or current conditions that could lead to future problems. In this respect, assessment becomes a form of environmental scanning, suitable for strategic planning. The consultant's goal is to anticipate, rather than merely react to, organizational problems and to address them before their symptoms appear. Regular reviews are used by more sophisticated organizations in which managers recognize the value of identifying and correcting problems in their early stages or averting them before they surface at all.

Giving Feedback. Giving clients feedback about the results of the assessment is extremely valuable. Feedback can occur at several levels, ranging from individuals to work groups to entire organizations. Giving such information to those who "own it" can serve immensely useful purposes in OD efforts. Feedback can create an impetus for change and prompt support for action by providing individuals with a better understanding of the problems they face.

Planning Change. The most obvious reason for an assessment is to use the results as the basis for planning change activities or corrective actions. As in medicine, misdiagnosis leads to useless, wasteful, or even harmful remedies. However, a thorough assessment leading to a correct diagnosis is not easy to do. One reason is that a client sometimes exerts pressure for quick action, and a consultant may be tempted to give in to the client's request even when the request is ill advised because root causes have not been identified.

Tracking Change. Assessment information also can be used to monitor the effects of external environmental changes on an organization. More commonly, the information becomes the basis for evaluating the effects of planned change on the organization and its members.

When results are positive, the information can be used to bolster support for continuing the change effort. When results are negative, the consultant can either initiate an assessment to select appropriate corrective action or stop the change effort. The consultant's decision should be based on assessment results, not on his or her or the client's intuitive impressions of what is happening.

The Client

The client is a major concern for a consultant when he or she selects appropriate assessment methods. In some cases, client characteristics may complicate the use of otherwise valuable assessment methods. For example, if a client's records are inaccurate, they should not be used.

In most cases, client characteristics provide the consultant with clues that help him or her to select appropriate assessment methods. There are many client characteristics that can affect the consultant's decision, such as size, structure, culture, previous experiences with assessment, and problem severity.

Size. An organization's size is perhaps the most obvious factor for a consultant to consider when he or she selects assessment methods. For instance, observational techniques are rarely efficient with large groups because these methods are time consuming, and large groups may contain significant variations. However, observational techniques can be effective with small groups. Assessments of small groups frequently rely on information gathered from observations and interviews.

Structure. If an organization is functionally diverse or geographically dispersed, the consultant should consider how the organization's structure may affect assessment methods. In such an organization, there is the possibility that significant differences may exist across functions or locations. Those differences should be considered because the consultant may need to take representative samples from the population.

Culture. The organization's culture also affects selection of assessment procedures. The consultant should assess the nature of the organization's work force because the employees may have different abilities. For example, the employees may read at different levels, speak different languages, or have cultural differences in regard to work, authority, and management. Culturally diverse organizations should be assessed using culturally diverse methods.

No assessment method is immune from the three client characteristics previously listed. To deal with these issues, the consultant may need to be creative and use multiple information-gathering methods to detect, analyze, and interpret the issues.

Previous Experiences. A slightly different but related issue concerns a client's previous assessment experiences. Most organizations have had to gather information for purposes ranging from attitude surveys to employee-benefits information. If such efforts were poorly managed in the past—perhaps because individual anonymity was violated—respondents naturally will be reluctant to share information and opinions freely.

The consultant should consider the client's previous experiences when he or she designs assessment activities. To detect any problems, he or she should at least ask the client questions about its experiences with information gathering. The consultant also may want to consider using more than one data-collection method so that results can be compared.

Problem Severity. When a severe problem must be tackled immediately, the consultant's initial assessment activities may have to be focused around it because of the pressure to take quick corrective action. The consultant must realize, however, that a severe problem can influence how people will respond.

For example, a conflict existed between the leaders of two interdependent units. The conflict had adversely affected the employees' performance in both units, and the client wanted the consultant to solve the problem quickly. The consultant realized that he needed to find out more about the problem to measure its impact on information-gathering methods. Moreover, the consultant was being pressured into focusing his attention on the problem itself because perception of it had already heightened. The consultant was successful because he focused on the conflict between the two leaders, bringing them together for interpersonal peacemaking. By doing so, the consultant affected employees' lagging performance, which was only a symptom and a by-product of the problem's cause.

The Focus of Assessment

An assessment may focus on many issues such as the following:

1. External factors potentially affecting an organization, such as its financial status, economic conditions, competitive pressures, and legal constraints;

2. Results of organizational activities, such as the quality and quantity of products and services, organizational profitability, and the consequences of production methods on employee health (both physical and psychological);

3. How the structure of the organization affects its functioning; and

4. How the organization's procedures and processes affect its functioning.

In addition to the large number of focus areas that a consultant must choose from, he or she must also consider from how many sources the data will be collected (levels of aggregation). For example, an assessment could be based on information concerning individuals, work groups, departments, functions, the total organization, or any combination of these.

Fortunately, information exists that, along with the client's work requirements, can help the consultant choose the focus area of an assessment and the methods he or she will use. This information includes descriptions of organizations operating in larger environments and descriptions of the inner workings of organizations.

If a consultant is working with an organization that operates in a larger environment, he or she should read about open-systems theory (Katz & Kahn, 1978). Simply stated, open-systems theory posits that organizations exist and interact within a larger environment. Organizations acquire resources (money, technology, people) from the larger environment as inputs and transform them into products or services that are returned to the environment as outputs. This transformation from inputs to outputs is affected by organizations' structures, policies, and practices, and by the behaviors of their members.

Many researchers (such as Likert, 1961, 1967; Porter, Lawler, & Hackman, 1975) have described such factors and how they are causally related—that is, how such factors affect an organization's ability to effectively transform inputs into outputs. Some of the factors associated with the transformation process appear in Exhibit 5-1. These factors, along with information concerning organizational structure, are most often focal points for OD assessments.

The focus areas of any OD assessment are influenced by such issues as project goals, consultant biases, resource limitations, and the client's expressed needs. In a worst-case scenario, assessment would be driven by a consultant's biases, his or her lack of expertise, his or her misconceptions caused by limited understanding of organizational processes, or severe resource limitations. In this case, the consultant is likely to overlook significant problems, focus his or her attention on issues of secondary importance, or miss the causes of problems. Organization development interventions based on partial information may expend valuable resources in the wrong areas and produce ineffective results.

Assessment should be based on a broader view for data-collection and analytical procedures. A consultant's goal should be to determine which areas are most critical to an organization's successful performance. To that end, the consultant must be familiar with the key factors that influence organizational performance and the relationships that exist among them. Assessment based on this broader view can identify general issues and then focus on specific ones.

Exhibit 5-1: Key Areas for Assessment in OD

Major Areas	Examples of Specific Focal Issues*
A. Systems and Policies	1. **Reward System.** The types of rewards that exist and the policies regarding their distribution.
	2. **Performance System.** The ways in which expectations are established and performance is monitored.
	3. **Career System.** Procedures for the development and advancement of people within an organization.
B. Organizational Procedures	1. **Decision Making.** How major decisions are made and who is involved in this process.
	2. **Communications.** The direction, form, and content of information flow.
	3. **Job Design.** Basic job descriptions, including the motivational potential of each job.
	4. **Bureaucracy.** The existence of practices and procedures that impede efficient functioning.
C. Leadership Behaviors	1. **Support.** Behaviors that demonstrate concern for subordinates and what they have to say.
	2. **Facilitation.** Assistance provided by supervisors (for example, planning, training, feedback) to enhance subordinates' performances.
	3. **Team Building.** Encouragement provided by supervisors to work-group members to work together and accomplish group goals.
D. Group Processes	1. **Communication**. Methods used by group members to communicate.
	2. **Activities.** Methods used by group members to plan and coordinate activities.

*These represent only a partial list of key measures.

Exhibit 5-1: Key Areas for Assessment in OD (continued)

Major Areas	Examples of Specific Focal Issues
E. Levels of Satisfaction	1. **Reactions.** How employees react to an organization's systems, including policies and procedures and how they react to the behaviors of organizational members, including supervisors and peers.

Information-Gathering Methods

Four methods are used to gather information for assessment and feedback:

1. Interviews;
2. Questionnaires;
3. Observations; and
4. Examination of records.

Some methods are more appropriate in some situations than in others. Two or more methods may be combined to balance the strengths and weaknesses of each method. The next section provides a brief explanation of each method and identifies the advantages of each.

Interviews

Interviews are classified as either structured or unstructured. Structured interviews contain a fixed number of prepared questions with preestablished response choices. Respondents are asked specific questions in a particular order. This format has the distinct advantage of providing information that covers a preset number of issues. Structured interviews also provide a basis for comparing responses across respondents.

Unstructured interviews consist of open-ended questions (for example, "How is your department structured?"). The interviewer formulates questions from responses generated by previous questions. This approach is advantageous because it allows the interviewer to probe areas of key concern.

The interviews that most consultants conduct could be described as a blend of the structured and unstructured approaches. Some consultants begin their interviews with prepared questions (the structured approach) but they subsequently modify and expand their questions based on the responses (the unstructured approach). This approach usually provides more consistent coverage than an unstructured interview. At the same time, it provides more opportunities than structured interviews to probe areas of concern.

According to Burke (1982), interviews are used more often than any other information-gathering technique in OD. It is easy to speculate on the reasons for that. Some consultants believe that interviews are easy to conduct. Interviews permit consultants to have face-to-face contact with their clients and with organizational members, and this is considered by many to be crucial to developing trust, and thus success, in OD interventions. Interviews also do not require sophisticated analytical skills—as some other information-gathering techniques do.

Questionnaires

Like interviews, questionnaires can differ greatly in form and specificity. Some resemble unstructured interviews in which respondents answer general questions. More common, however, are questionnaires that pose a fixed number of response choices. Respondents simply select one response that best approximates their answer to each question.

Questionnaires also vary in other respects. Many are designed to be used in particular settings at particular times and are tailored to the language and focus points of specific organizations. Standardized questionnaires, however, contain core items set in a fixed format. Although standardized questionnaires permit consultants to compare information across organizations and time, consultants can use both standardized and tailored questionnaires to determine the organizations' strengths and weaknesses. This approach is valuable in OD because the resultant information helps consultants determine the significance of the questionnaires' results and determine where resources can be most effectively positioned.

Standardized questionnaires with existing databases that are used for comparative purposes can be valuable to consultants, but these questionnaires must be used with caution. Their advantages include added credibility and impact (for example, comparing an individual or group with others in similar situations impresses the client) and, when the comparisons are appropriate, an enhanced meaning to results (for example, a group's score of 3.8 on a five-point scale means more if a consultant knows that the average score for a comparative group is 4.1). Additional information, such as standard deviations or distributions, may provide even more valuable information in such comparisons.

The primary risk associated with using comparative data is that consultants may compare individuals or groups that are not comparable. Especially critical are differences among those at different levels. For example, upper-level managers tend to respond differently—that is, they score higher—than do those at lower levels in organizations. Of course, other differences such as function and type of organization (for example, service, manufacturing, research) also are potentially critical in making comparisons. In order to avoid serious errors in the interpretation of results, consultants need to consider such factors when they make comparisons.

Observations

Although consultants can structure observations by using checklists and rating scales, observations rarely are as structured as other information-gathering methods. Consultants usually conduct observations in a less structured fashion and then organize and evaluate the information using their own conceptual frameworks. Observations can prove extremely useful to skilled consultants, especially when they are working with small organizations in which much of the work activity is easily viewed in a short time.

Observations are useful because they are not based on second-hand reports from others. Thus, unreliable sources and respondent biases are eliminated from information gathering. Of course, observations are subject to consultant bias and limited knowledge of the organization's work. Moreover, consultant observations can be costly to conduct because the method is time consuming and, if the departments are not located in the same area, the consultants may need to travel.

Examination of Records

Rather than setting out to gather new information, consultants can use existing data for assessment and feedback. Organizations typically collect and store information on a regular basis, including information on performance indicators such as costs, quality and quantity measures, and profitability, and information on personnel activities such as promotions, grievances, turnover rates, and absenteeism.

Consultants will find that using existing records for assessment is advantageous because records are unobtrusive. Additionally, information is readily available and it already may be in a quantifiable format that makes analysis relatively easy.

Advantages and Disadvantages of Each Method

Although a complete analysis of information-gathering methods would be lengthy, an overview of comparative advantages and disadvantages can be made possible by focusing on key criteria for judging these methods and making a few assumptions about where they might be used.

Assume that a consultant is working for a medium to large organization. His or her assignment is to gather information to assess the organization's strengths and weaknesses. This task is a preliminary step to designing OD activities. To conduct this task, the consultant will need to select an information-gathering method. He or she will use six key criteria for distinguishing among the methods.

The six criteria used for rating each method are as follows:

1. *Efficiency.* Includes such factors as the financial costs and time required to collect and analyze information from a specific number of sources.
2. *Objectivity.* Reflects how much the method is subject to consultant or respondent bias.
3. *Comparability.* Indicates how easy it is to compare results across time to determine progress.

4. *Completeness.* Indicates how well the method can cover a broad range of issues and levels of measurement.

5. *Accuracy/Validity.* Includes criteria 2, 3, and 4 and also includes the perception that the information reflects what actually exists in the organization.

6. *Flexibility.* Indicates how well the method can be modified, based on information gathered during the initial stages of the processes.

Efficiency

The efficiency of information-gathering and assessment methods is an important issue in almost every OD effort. The issue usually can be understood in terms of two frequently conflicting goals: the desire to develop a complete picture of the situation so that the problem is understood and the necessity of conserving the resources required to collect information about the problem.

The standardized questionnaire is probably the most efficient method. A consultant can modify its focus to areas known to affect organizational success and he or she can use it to gather information from many people in a brief period of time and at a relatively low cost. Further, the consultant can efficiently compile and evaluate questionnaire results through machine-scoring technology, whether the questionnaire is standardized or tailored.

The least efficient information-gathering methods are observational techniques that require much time for skilled experts to gather information about a few activities. Structured and unstructured interviews can be more or less efficient depending on their basic formats (for example, individual or group), but they are generally costly in terms of time and analysis. Records, when well-maintained, can be an efficient means for gathering information—especially if they are computerized. However, in most settings, a consultant needs to spend considerable time retrieving records in order to obtain precise information.

Objectivity

For an assessment to be useful in planning an approach to change, the methods a consultant uses to gather information and assess it must be complete and objective. The consultant's lack of objectivity can lead to his or her recommending the same solution for every problem. Unfortunately, the objectivity of some consultants is limited by the narrow range of solutions they are willing to recommend.

The least objective information usually comes from observations made by one person. Observations are dependent on the expertise and objectivity of the observer. If all observers were totally knowledgeable about every factor that influenced organizational success and had no vested interest in identifying problems for which they could offer remedies, observations would be more useful. However, consultants often have different, often conflicting, ideas about what is important and how such factors influence organizational success.

Interviewing procedures also are subject to consultant bias. However, interviews can be designed so that they focus on gathering important information. Records tend to be more objective, although records can be prepared to project a biased view of the organization or to protect someone's interests. Objectivity in using such procedures is a serious requirement for consultants.

Standardized questionnaires may be the least subject to bias for several reasons. One reason is that they typically contain a fixed number of questions focusing on predetermined issues. Another reason is that like tailored questionnaires, standardized questionnaires lend themselves to limited response possibilities for each area covered. The objectivity of this method is bolstered by standardized data-analysis procedures that are less subject to individual biases and procedural variations than other methods.

Comparability

To compare information within or between organizations or across time, a consultant must use methods that have standardized formats and provide quantifiable data. Making comparisons is important for evaluating an organization's strengths and weaknesses. Standards of comparison serve as a basis for determining how unique an issue is to a particular setting or if it is simply a reflection of measurement procedures or social trends. An apparent issue may or may not be important, depending on how it is viewed in other organizations. The efficient allocation of OD resources depends the consultant's and the client's abilities to understand the difference between apparent and actual dysfunction.

Questionnaires have a distinct advantage when comparability is an issue. A consultant's ability to compare information across sources and time periods is enhanced when he or she uses questionnaires because they have standardized information-gathering and assessment processes.

Some questionnaires have extensive databases that were developed over many years. These databases serve as a foundation for comparing results from settings that are matched by organizational criteria such as function, size, and organizational level, or by individual characteristics such as respondents' age and gender.

A consultant uses these databases to determine how one organization stands in relation to others on many issues, including communications, leadership, decision making, peer interactions, and levels of satisfaction. These issues may be important indicators for determining the true nature of an organization's strengths and weaknesses and for allocating OD resources. If nothing else, the consultant can use these databases to provide convincing evidence to skeptical line managers about comparisons between their organization and others—particularly exemplary, frequently benchmarked firms. (However, advocates of the continuous-improvement process argue that what is important is continuous improvement within an organization rather than how an organization appears to compare with others.)

Organizational records often are kept in quantitative form and thus lend themselves to easy comparisons. Unfortunately, the bases for such records may vary across organizations or even across time in one organization. Consultants should be careful when they evaluate and react to simple records such as turnover rates, profitability, grievances, and quality measures. For example, turnover in some organizations may refer to both voluntary and involuntary departures. In other organizations turnover reflects only one of these.

Consultants sometimes summarize results from carefully structured interviews and observations in a numerical format to aid comparisons. But they should be careful when interpreting these ratings because numerical interview ratings are often highly subjective and lend themselves to varying interpretations across raters.

Completeness

The quality of any assessment is based on how much it reflects all potential contributors to organizational success, including many areas previously identified in Exhibit 5-1. If any key area is omitted, a consultant and client may fail to identify sources of problems.

Structured interviews that are designed to cover key determinants of organizational success have the potential for excellent coverage of critical areas. Not only can a consultant use them to concentrate on those areas common to most organizational settings, but he or she can also modify them to capture important information unique to one organizational setting. Such flexibility permits the consultant to pursue some issues in depth and to add areas not previously considered critical. Interviews also provide the consultant with an opportunity to gather anecdotes that support and clarify issues.

Questionnaires also tend to offer advantages when completeness is an issue. Although they are not as flexible as interviews, well-structured questionnaires, validated within organizations, can cover many issues known to affect organizational success. Another advantage of questionnaires is their fixed format. Questionnaires are less subject to diversions into areas that are merely interesting to consultants or respondents but are not important to organizational success.

Observations and records are far less useful methods than the other two methods for obtaining information about critical issues. Observations tend to be obtrusive. They are limited to information that reflects what is happening in unique situations at fixed points in time. Such information may or may not be representative of typical situations or of those most important to organizational success. Records tend to be very limited in scope because they reflect the results of organizational practices rather than the practices themselves.

Accuracy/Validity

Information used as the basis for assessment must reflect what is actually occurring in an organization. Any planning that a consultant does that is based on inaccurate information has little chance of producing successful change. Furthermore, inaccurate information may be rejected by participants during feedback. Such rejection damages the credibility of OD activities associated with that information. The accuracy of assessment information will be judged by most participants on the basis of criteria such as objectivity and completeness.

All four information-gathering methods can produce accurate information. Interviews reflect what is foremost in the minds of the respondents and give authenticity to such information. Standardized questionnaires allow comparisons to be made across companies, while customized questionnaires permit comparisons across internal settings, which may increase the credibility of the results. Quantifiable questionnaires provide results that add to perceptions of accuracy. Observations gain credibility from direct encounters with real events and people. The consultant's ability to point to those events as direct evidence supporting an issue is a considerable advantage of this method. Finally, records that appear in numerical formats also take on an aura of validity even though the accuracy of such information may not warrant such judgment.

Flexibility

Flexibility refers to the ability to modify information-gathering methods or analysis activities at any stage during the assessment process. Such modification can be especially beneficial to a consultant when a significant issue that is difficult to anticipate surfaces during information gathering. Interviews hold the clear advantage over other methods because they have the greatest flexibility. Even in the most rigidly structured interview situation, a consultant usually will find opportunities to pursue issues not originally anticipated. Interviews frequently are used as part of early or exploratory information-gathering activities to identify issues for more in-depth examination.

The other three methods are not as valuable as interviews when flexibility is the chief consideration. Observations are limited by the situations that are observed. Of course, a consultant can conduct more observations, but that usually requires a redefinition of assessment activities and additional resources. A consultant can modify questionnaires, even standardized ones, to accommodate special situations prior to gathering information. A consultant may modify questionnaires or create them for specific settings if one of the following situations exists:

1. The organization includes individuals who cannot respond accurately to a standardized questionnaire (for example, if the organization has employees who speak different languages, read at different levels, do not understand technical jargon, or otherwise cannot understand and interpret standard questions).

2. The questionnaire may include terms with unusual meanings in some settings. Even such seemingly simple terms as "supervisor," "job," "employee," and "work group" can have unusual meanings in some organizations.

3. The client's focus area is not adequately represented in a standardized questionnaire. The consultant may

want to include additional items to cover the focus area, but that may or may not assist in a basic diagnosis. The inclusion of such items can be critical to the success of the OD effort because the client may take more ownership of the diagnostic process if such items are included in the data-gathering activities.

4. The consultant's initial observations or interviews have identified areas that were not adequately covered by an existing questionnaire. For example, the consultant may find that some aspect of the reward system, such as assignments to desired jobs, is a critical issue in a particular setting but that the standardized questionnaire being used does not address this issue.

The consultant can modify a questionnaire by drawing from another existing questionnaire after obtaining permission to do so or from a pool of items tested in other settings. He or she will find that using previously developed items is advantageous because the psychometric properties and databases should have already been established for the items, and the consultant will find them useful for comparative purposes. Of course, some situations and issues are truly unique and require that the consultant develop and use new items.

Once the consultant has begun to gather information using a questionnaire, he or she will not be able to modify the questionnaire. Some data-analysis procedures based on questionnaire results are flexible, but these usually concern presentation format more than results. Records are the least flexible of the four methods. Information derived from records is almost always collected for purposes other than organizational assessments. Thus, the focus of such information seldom meets the needs of the consultant as he or she develops a basis for assessment and feedback.

Selecting Appropriate Strategy

A consultant must consider the setting when he or she chooses information-gathering methods. A review of the advantages and disadvantages of the four methods suggests some general approaches. Most obvious is that each method has weaknesses. All fail to meet ideal characteristics in one or more important areas. However, interviews and questionnaires are generally the best methods for gathering information because they have significant strengths and fewer weaknesses than the other two methods. Observations and records have fewer strengths and at least two considerable weaknesses.

Considering the above points, the consultant can infer that a clear choice of strategy exists for most situations: combine interviews and questionnaires. Interestingly, interviews and questionnaires tend to be complementary. In the areas in which interview methods tend to be weakest (that is, efficiency, objectivity, comparability), questionnaire methods are strong. In the area in which questionnaires are weak (flexibility), interviews provide strength. These factors suggest that, in most situations, combining interviews and questionnaires is a good strategy for gathering assessment information.

Another factor that supports this strategy is that questionnaire results tend to be reported in numeric form, and they may be difficult for some clients to interpret and accept. Interviews, however, often provide anecdotal examples that help bring meaning to numeric summaries. Combining the two methods can produce powerful and clear results.

Feedback

Feedback is a basic component of OD efforts. Feedback is necessary for a consultant and a client to achieve a common understanding of an organization's current condition and also to identify needed change. Once members of the client organization have established their change goals, information concerning current conditions can be utilized to indicate what change is necessary and how much change is necessary.

The sources and forms of feedback information are restricted only by the limitations discussed in the previous sections. However, feedback processes most often focus on the results from interview and questionnaire procedures. In fact, the use of questionnaire results as the basis for OD feedback has a history traceable to the 1950s when Rensis Likert and Floyd Mann developed and experimented with survey feedback in organizational settings. This early work, together with later research by David Bowers (1973), indicates that feedback based on questionnaire results can be an extremely useful component of OD efforts.

Feedback in organization development takes a variety of forms and occurs in different settings. Although several approaches to feedback have been described (Nadler, 1977), three basic approaches are most common in organizational settings: data handback, survey feedback, and survey-guided development.

Data Handback

Data handback involves the return of tabulated questionnaire results to the participants, with little or no assistance from an OD consultant. The client is left to understand and use the information in the best way it can. This approach is generally ineffective and is rarely associated with current organization development practices.

Survey Feedback

Survey feedback was developed to maximize the usefulness of survey data. In its most common form, survey feedback involves a consultant summarizing questionnaire data at the work-group level. The consultant assists group members in discussions that focus on information about their interactions. Group members use these discussions to define problems and to plan ways to improve their interactions.

The widespread use of the survey-feedback approach in OD efforts has led to much experimentation and refinement. The potential uses and benefits associated with survey feedback have been reported by such authors as Mann (1957), Bowers and Franklin (1974), Nadler (1977), Franklin (1978, 1979), and Neff (1965). These reports, coupled with more stringent research comparing the effectiveness of this approach to others (Bowers, 1973), strongly indicate that survey feedback is a potentially effective means for gaining understanding and building commitment to change efforts from group members.

The accumulated experiences with survey feedback also provide a consultant with guidance in maximizing the effectiveness of feedback interactions. Among the most commonly accepted concepts are the guidelines for maximizing the usefulness of feedback presented in Exhibit 5-2.

Survey-Guided Development

Survey-guided development (SGD) builds on the survey-feedback process and emphasizes the development of an entire organization, not just improvements in individuals or specific work groups (Bowers & Franklin, 1972, 1977; Franklin,

Wissler, & Spencer, 1977; Hausser, Pecorella, & Wissler, 1977). This method includes a "waterfall" design in which a top-management group first examines its own results before other groups at each succeeding level examine theirs. Each group develops its own action plan. The focus of group discussion includes an examination of organizational issues (for example, decision-making procedures and reward systems) and work-group issues. Issues that cannot be resolved at lower organizational levels are eventually carried up the chain of command by the supervisor to the next higher level until the issues are resolved. This process increases the possibility that issues will be well defined and that resolution will occur at the lowest level possible.

Survey-guided development also emphasizes the use of information that has been summarized across major sub-groupings (for example, levels, functions, demographic groups) to better understand an organization's strengths and weaknesses. Thus, organizational members often review information that summarizes results across major subgroups within the organization in addition to information from their own work groups. This summary provides the members with a context for understanding how any particular group fits within the workings of the entire organization. It also involves a broad base of individuals in the problem-identification and problem-solving process for major organizational issues.

Survey-guided development also places a heavy emphasis on preparing for effective use of the feedback information. A consultant prepares participants to understand the results before they are exposed to their own information. He or she also trains members of the organization to better manage the process and skills associated with effective use of questionnaire results. This includes the constructive management of,

Exhibit 5-2: Characteristics of Useful Feedback

Giving Feedback	Receiving Feedback
1. Limited Deliver small amounts of information—especially when the potential emotional impact is great. **2. Descriptive** Provide recent examples for clarification whenever possible. **3. Verifiable** Support the information with other sources or recent examples. **4. Impactable** Allow the recipients to control the information. **5. Unfinalized** Deliver information that will stimulate interactions to further define issues and, where appropriate, lead to change.	**1. Understand** Listen carefully to gain a better understanding. **2. Clarify** Ask for recent, specific examples. **3. Separate Information from Emotions** Be aware of emotions and their possible sources. Emotions may be linked to any number of issues including the source of the feedback, the setting, expected consequences, and the general importance of the information to the individual or group. **4. Summarize** Repeat your understanding of the feedback to the source. **5. Evaluate the Validity** Determine if the information is accurate. **6. Ask for Suggestions** Solicit help concerning possible changes. **7. Set Objectives** Establish goals for change.

Exhibit 5-3: Major Activities in Survey-Guided Development

1. Project Planning
Establish expectations for project schedules and goals and clarify roles for all participants, including internal and external consultants. Train internal consultants.

2. Concepts Training
Prepare all members of an organization to better understand how the organization functions and how critical areas will be measured.

3. Data Collection
Administer questionnaires to everyone and conduct interviews (both individual and group) with a representative sample of the organization.

4. Feedback Training
Prepare all members of the organization to understand the feedback information and the best process for using the feedback; include skill training in giving and receiving feedback.

5. Feedback
Return information aggregated at different levels (group, department, level, function, total organization) to the appropriate individuals. Facilitate the process.

6. Problem Solving
Hold meetings to evaluate information, clarify its meaning and impact, and, where appropriate, take steps to solve problems that are having a negative impact on performance.

7. Review
Collect new information to evaluate the organization's current functioning, evaluate changes, and make further adjustments to resolve remaining issues.

and participation in, feedback meetings that are used to clarify and resolve problems. A summary of the major activities associated with survey-guided development appears in Exhibit 5-3.

Wherever planned change is to take place, feedback is critical to the following:

1. Gaining a more complete, shared understanding of current situations;

2. Determining the nature of desired modifications in existing conditions;

3. Gaining commitment to such changes; and

4. Monitoring change as it occurs.

Thus, it is not surprising that feedback procedures and tools have been used for decades to improve individual, group, and organizational performance.

References

Bowers, D. (1973). OD techniques and their results in 23 organizations. *Journal of Applied Behavioral Science, 9*(1), 21-43.

Bowers, D., & Franklin, J. (1972). Survey-guided development: Using human resources management in organization change. *Journal of Contemporary Business, 1*(3), 43-55.

Bowers, D., & Franklin, J. (1974). Basic concepts of survey feedback. In J.W. Pfeiffer & J.E. Jones (Eds.), *The 1974 annual handbook for group facilitators* (pp. 221-225). San Diego, CA: Pfeiffer & Company.

Bowers, D., & Franklin, J. (1977). *Survey-guided development I: Data-based organizational change.* San Diego, CA: Pfeiffer & Company.

Burke, W. (1982). *Organization development: Principles and practices.* New York: Little, Brown & Co.

Franklin, J. (1978). Improving the effectiveness of survey feedback. *Personnel*, 55(3), 11-17.

Franklin, J. (1979). Building interpersonal skills through survey feedback procedures. *Group and Organization Studies*, 4(3), 281-286.

Franklin, J., Wissler, A., & Spencer, G. (1977). *Survey-guided development III: A manual for concepts training*. San Diego, CA: Pfeiffer & Company.

Hausser, D., Pecorella, P., & Wissler, A. (1977). *Survey-guided development II: A manual for consultants*. San Diego, CA: Pfeiffer & Company.

Katz, D., & Kahn, R. (1978). *The social psychology of organizations* (2nd ed.). New York: John Wiley.

Likert, R. (1967). *The human organization: Its management and value*. New York: McGraw-Hill.

Likert, R. (1961). *New patterns of management*. New York: McGraw-Hill.

Mann, F. (1957). Studying and creating change: A means to understanding social organizations. In *Research in industrial human relations. Industrial Relations Research Association*, Publication No. 17.

Nadler, D. (1977). *Feedback and organization development: Using data-based methods*. Reading, MA: Addison-Wesley.

Neff, F. (1965). Survey research: A tool for problem diagnosis and improvement in organizations. In A. Gouldner & S. Miller (Eds.), *Applied sociology* (pp. 23-38). New York: Free Press.

Porter, L., Lawler, E., & Hackman, J. (1975). *Behavior in organizations*. New York: McGraw-Hill.

CHAPTER 6

ACTION PLANNING

D.D. Warrick

Action planning is the critical, fourth step in organization development (OD). When organizational changes are made without an action plan based on sound change principles, some changes fail to produce expected results, others lead to considerable resistance, and still others create unintended side effects. Sometimes the change leaves a trail of unresolved problems and distrustful people. In an attempt to avoid these problems, OD consultants should devote time and attention to action planning.

Action Planning

Even though action planning is an integral part of any OD intervention, surprisingly little has been written about it.

Action planning is implied or briefly described in the OD literature, but it is not given in-depth treatment.

Beckhard and Harris (1977) offer the most detailed description of action planning. They describe it as the process of developing strategies and action plans to manage the transition between present and future. They list four steps in the action-planning process (p. 28):

1. Determine the client's degree of choice about change (how much control do clients have in deciding whether to change and how to change?);
2. Determine what needs to be changed;
3. Determine where to intervene; and
4. Choose intervention technologies.

Beckhard and Harris also provide guidelines for developing an activity or process plan (pp. 51-52). The seven guidelines for developing a process plan are as follows:

1. The activities should be clearly linked to the goals and priorities of the identified change;
2. The activities should be clearly identified rather than broadly generalized;
3. Discrete activities should be linked;
4. The activities should be time sequenced;
5. Contingent plans should exist in case unexpected forces develop during the change process;
6. The change plan should be supported by top management; and
7. The plan should be cost effective.

Action planning in OD is the process of systematically planning a change effort using sound change models and principles. It can significantly alter how a change effort is coordinated, improve the impact of the change effort, and accelerate the time needed to accomplish lasting change in an organization.

Exhibit 6-1 depicts a planned-change model, and Exhibit 6-2 contains key change principles (Warrick, 1993). The model includes three stages of change: Stage I: Preparation, Stage II: Implementation, and Stage III: Transition. These stages correspond to Lewin's stages of unfreezing, changing, and refreezing (Lewin, 1951). However, although Lewin's model is helpful, it is not suited to an environment of dynamic change. The key to successful action planning is to ensure that the plans are organized around the three stages of change.

Planning a management-development program is a good example of how action planning makes a difference. In too many cases, management development (a comprehensive effort) is limited to management training (a limited effort). Worse, the management training is limited to Stage II of the planned-change process and the training does not consider on-the-job behavior. In fact, training may teach participants behaviors that contradict what is rewarded or what exists in the organization's culture. For instance, teamwork may be emphasized in management training, but top managers may not value teamwork or reward team efforts.

When all three stages of the change process are incorporated into the management-development program, the program is different from traditional management-development programs. Exhibit 6-3 shows a management-development program that was based on the three stages of change.

In the preparation stage, a consultant diagnoses the training needs. Then he or she asks the top managers to evaluate the results of the diagnosis, to help design the management-development program, to develop a management philosophy for the program, and to evaluate the organization's present

Exhibit 6-1: The Planned-Change Process

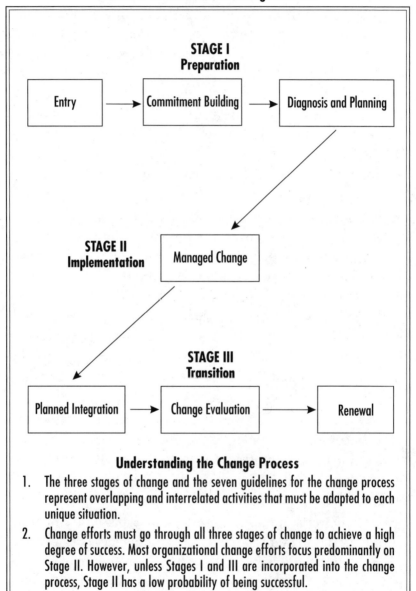

STAGE I
Preparation

Entry → Commitment Building → Diagnosis and Planning

STAGE II
Implementation

Managed Change

STAGE III
Transition

Planned Integration → Change Evaluation → Renewal

Understanding the Change Process

1. The three stages of change and the seven guidelines for the change process represent overlapping and interrelated activities that must be adapted to each unique situation.

2. Change efforts must go through all three stages of change to achieve a high degree of success. Most organizational change efforts focus predominantly on Stage II. However, unless Stages I and III are incorporated into the change process, Stage II has a low probability of being successful.

Exhibit 6-2: Key Change Principles

1. Successful change is a continual journey of learning, growing, improving, adapting, and managing the change process. Staying the same or relying on past successes is a formula for eventual failure.

2. Quick-fix solutions rarely last. A successful change effort takes time.

3. The incentives (positive or negative) for change must be greater than the incentive (reasons and excuses) for keeping the status quo (not changing).

4. Significant change usually involves varying degrees of pain and sacrifice that can be acknowledged and managed but not avoided.

5. A change effort rarely succeeds without the support of one or more change champions.

6. The change process (how change is accomplished) is equally as important as the change product (what is targeted for change). The appropriate steps must be conducted correctly for change to succeed.

7. A change effort needs to go through the three stages of change (preparation, implementation, and transition) to have a high probability of success.

8. The major focus of change should be on present realities, future ideals, and how to move step by step toward the ideals.

9. All change efforts are different. The strategies used in each effort should be a function of the type of change needed (knowledge, behavior, culture, processes, technology), the level of change desired (fine tuning, incremental, or transformational), and what the key players are willing and able to do.

10. Involving an organization's members in the change process increases their understanding, commitment, and ownership.

11. Positive change is more effective than negative change.

12. Opportunities for change disappear quickly and the momentum for change wanes as time lapses.

Exhibit 6-2: Key Change Principles (continued)

13. A consultant should focus on a few important changes instead of overloading an organization or its people with numerous changes that rarely last and may not be compatible.

14. A consultant should keep the change process simple and understandable.

15. The more that is at stake, the greater the resistance to change and the greater the need to manage the change process carefully.

16. A consultant should educate and train the members of an organization for change. Significant changes in thinking and acting often are required for change to occur. People need to understand the need for change, have the right mind set, have the skills needed to accomplish the change, have the resources to make the desired changes, and understand the change process.

17. The probability of a successful change effort can be increased through the following:

    a. A clear vision of the needed change and an understanding of how the change can be accomplished.

    b. An aligned infrastructure (mission, values, goals, philosophies, structure, rewards, and culture) to support the desired change.

    c. Planned follow-through and accountability.

    d. Top management's support and encouragement during the change process.

    e. The freedom to make reasonable mistakes and the opportunity to learn from mistakes.

    f. The ability to remove obstacles and roadblocks to change.

    g. Reasonable consequences for continued noncompliance.

18. Changes need to fit an organization's infrastructure (mission, core values, goals, philosophies, reward systems, structure, and norms), or parts of the infrastructure may need to be realigned to support the change.

19. The primary stakeholders must be involved enough in the planning and implementation of a change effort to build commitment to the change and ownership for the outcomes of change.

structure, culture, and reward systems to see if they need to be realigned to support the training needs. In the implementation stage, the consultant trains the members or the organization. He or she also discusses the organization's management philosophy and collects feedback from the members. The management philosophy promotes a common understanding of excellent management throughout the organization. In the transition stage, the consultant develops follow-up assignments for the participants to apply what they have learned, organizes meetings to share follow-up experiences, and provides any additional training that is needed.

Exhibit 6-4 shows the steps for an action-planning process. Change efforts require varying degrees of action planning, depending on the scale, complexity, and importance of the change. Therefore, based on what is needed, the model can be used as a general guideline or a step-by-step checklist.

Essential Factors for Successful Action Planning

Several factors are essential for successful action planning. They are as follows:

- Involve key stakeholders in the planning process;
- Evaluate relevant data;
- Agree on what is to be changed or improved;
- Develop a change strategy;
- Develop a system for monitoring and managing the change process; and
- Clarify change roles.

These factors are discussed in this section.

Exhibit 6-3: Management Development: An Example of Action Planning

---

Stage I Preparation (Pretraining)

Major Focus

1. Consultant interviews all members of the top-management team and some managers and supervisors.

2. Top-management team designs training program and prepares follow-up assignments.

3. Top management develops a management philosophy for the consultant to present in Stage II.

4. Consultant submits a recommended training program to top management, based on the interviews and management input.

5. Consultant builds top-management commitment to the program.

Stage II Implementation (Training)

Major Focus

1. Consultant trains program participants on the following items:

   a. The changing organizational environment and the implications for managers;

   b. Succeeding in changing times;

   c. Developing leadership skills;

   d. The changing role of managers;

Exhibit 6-3: Management Development: An Example of Action Planning (continued)

e. Developing interpersonal skills;

f. Managing "people" problems;

g. Developing skills in being a team player and team builder;

h. Managing personal and organizational change; and

i. Making personal, team, and organizational changes.

Stage III Transition (Post-Training)

Major Focus

1. Consultant organizes top-management follow-up workshop.

2. Consultant reviews program with top management.

3. Consultant and top management evaluate ideas and issues generated in Stage II.

4. Consultant plans follow-up meeting.

Involve Key Stakeholders in the Planning Process

Stakeholders include people at all levels of an organization who can influence or contribute to the success of the change effort. A common error made by consultants is to not involve key people who can influence the desired change. For this reason, the consultant's first step in action planning is to

. . . .

Exhibit 6-4: The Action-Planning Process

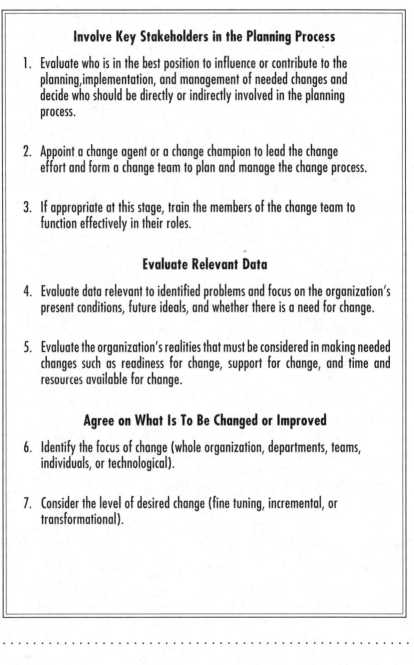

Involve Key Stakeholders in the Planning Process

1. Evaluate who is in the best position to influence or contribute to the planning, implementation, and management of needed changes and decide who should be directly or indirectly involved in the planning process.

2. Appoint a change agent or a change champion to lead the change effort and form a change team to plan and manage the change process.

3. If appropriate at this stage, train the members of the change team to function effectively in their roles.

Evaluate Relevant Data

4. Evaluate data relevant to identified problems and focus on the organization's present conditions, future ideals, and whether there is a need for change.

5. Evaluate the organization's realities that must be considered in making needed changes such as readiness for change, support for change, and time and resources available for change.

Agree on What Is To Be Changed or Improved

6. Identify the focus of change (whole organization, departments, teams, individuals, or technological).

7. Consider the level of desired change (fine tuning, incremental, or transformational).

Exhibit 6-4: The Action-Planning Process (continued)

8. Evaluate the desired change from a system perspective: consider the impact the change will have on the organization and the impact the organization willhave on the change. Explore ways to improve alignment between the change and the organization.

9. Reach an agreement on what is to be changed or improved based on what the client can do and is willing to do, and establish change or improvement goals.

Develop a Change Strategy

10. Identify any forces working for or against the desired change.

11. Explore intervention options.

12. Develop an action plan based on a sound change model and sound change principles. Decide at this stage if a broad action plan or a more detailed action plan would be most appropriate.

Develop a System for Monitoring and Managing the Change Process

13. Develop feedback mechanisms to monitor the change process.

14. Develop a system for managing the change process and increasing the probability of successful change.

Clarify Change Roles

15. Verify that the role of the change team and the roles of the key players in the change process are clear.

evaluate who will have a significant impact on the outcome of a change program, who needs to be involved in the planning process, and how much these persons need to be involved. To that end, the consultant should consider the following:

- Organizational structure (who has responsibility for approving the change and who is in charge of areas affected by the desired change?);

- Expertise (who possesses the knowledge and skill necessary to make the desired change?);

- Ongoing initiatives (who is handling projects that may affect, or be affected by, the desired change?);

- Power (who has the ability to mobilize necessary resources to support a desired change?); and

- Track records (who has been involved in past successful change efforts in the organization?)

Once the consultant has clarified these issues, he or she will need to choose a change agent or change champion to lead the effort. A *change agent* is an internal or external specialist in managing change and developing high-performance organizations, teams, and individuals. A *change champion* is a member of the organization who is responsible for championing needed changes. The consultant will need to decide whether a specialist, such as a change agent, will be needed to guide the change process. The appointed leader of the change effort usually assembles a change team to help him or her plan and manage the change process.

Occasionally, the change-agent role is filled by an external consultant or an internal consultant or an external and an internal consultant working together. An external consultant is less interested in maintaining the status quo because he or she was never socialized into the organization's culture. He or she may also enjoy instant access to, and credibility with, top managers. However, an external consultant is unfamiliar with the organization's history and politics. An internal consultant may be quite familiar with the organization's culture and politics, but he or she may not have access to, or credibility with, top managers.

A change team composed of an external and an internal change agent and the appropriate key stakeholders often is used for planning and making major changes. A team is advantageous because it taps the individual strengths—and, one hopes, the complementary strengths—of both internal and external change agents. A team also gains added advantages when its members are diverse, representing, among other variations, different ages, genders, and levels of experience.

Evaluate Relevant Data

The data used in action planning may be simplistic or sophisticated, depending on the changes being considered and the participants. However, the data a consultant uses should at least answer the following questions:

- What is the organization's present condition?
- What is the organization's desired condition? (What should the future "look like," and why is it desirable?)
- What can be done to move closer to the ideal future?
- How necessary and possible is the desired change?
- What is known about the organization's best practices?

The consultant also should evaluate the resources and time available for making the needed changes. Resources and time represent constraints affecting what can be done.

Agree on What Is to Be Changed or Improved

The consultant and the client have to decide what needs to be changed or improved. In order to agree on the change focus, they will need to consider the following:

- What can top management do to support the change effort? What is it willing to do?
- What is the target for change? Is it the whole organization, departments, teams, individuals, or technology?
- What level of change needs to happen (fine tuning, incremental change, or transformational change)?

Another consideration for the consultant is that the organization may need to be realigned to support and value the change, or the change may need to be adapted to better fit the organization. After he or she has considered all the relevant data and changes that need and can be made based on current realities, the consultant should establish goals for change.

Develop a Change Strategy

The change strategy—that is, how change is to be accomplished—is as important as the actual changes to be made.

A consultant may find a force-field analysis to be helpful in developing a change strategy. He or she can perform such an analysis by evaluating the forces driving change and the forces resisting change. This information can be very useful in planning a change strategy. (See Exhibit 6-5.)

Once the consultant has developed a change strategy, he or she should consider alternative interventions. One option is to use a small-scale, experimental pilot program to test the change. Another option is to make a change in a start-up

Exhibit 6-5: Conducting a Force-Field Analysis

What is a force-field analysis?

Force-field analysis is a problem-solving tool that is used to identify the reasons ("forces") that support two positions to a question and the strength of each force. For example, force field analysis could be used by a team to answer the question, "Should ABC Inc. establish an office in Singapore?"

How is a force-field analysis conducted?

The following steps are followed to conduct a force-field analysis:

1. State the question that is to be answered. Make sure that all participants agree on how the question is posed. It needs to be worded so that there are only two acceptable responses.

2. Use a flip chart or a blackboard and label one side of the paper or board as one of the acceptable responses, in this case "Yes," and label the other side as the other acceptable response, in this case "No." See sample chart.

Should ABC establish an office in Singapore?

Yes	No

3. Following the rules of brainstorming, have the team provide as many reasons as possible for *each* of the responses. As with any brainstorming session, no answer should be ignored and no critique is permitted during the brainstorming session. After this session, the team's force field might look like the following chart:

Exhibit 6-5: Conducting a Force-Field Analysis (continued)

Should ABC establish an office in Singapore?

Yes	No
High demand	No existing customers
Too far from Japan	Travel costs too great
Stable economy	Too much investment
Lack of competition	No employees are culturally aware
College graduates available to work for ABC	Japan can cover
Business plan shows high potential profit	Dictatorship

4. Once the team can provide no new information to the brainstorming session, the items provided should be reviewed for clarification, duplication, and so on. Items should be reworded, if necessary, for clarification.

5. The next step is to identify how strong a force each item is. There are many ways to do this. One simple way is to treat each item with a five-point Likert scale. The facilitator may handle this process in the following manner:

> "If you believe that the statement I read is a very strong argument for establishing an office in Singapore, hold up five fingers. If you believe that it is a very weak argument for the position, hold up only one finger. How strong an argument do you think 'High demand' is?"

The facilitator will then do a quick scan of the group and count the participants' responses. This number is then written on the chart. See sample chart on the following page.

Exhibit 6-5: Conducting a Force-Field Analysis (continued)

Yes	No
5 High demand	1 No existing customers
3 Too far from Japan	2 Travel costs too great
4 Stable economy	5 Too much investment
2 Lack of competition	2 No employees are culturally aware
2 College graduates available to work for ABC	5 Japan can cover
5 Business plan shows high potential profit	3 Dictatorship

6. Items that are perceived to be low in interest should be eliminated from the chart. In the sample chart above, items with a 1 or 2 would be removed. See sample chart below.

Should ABC establish an office in Singapore?

Yes	No
5 High demand	5 Too much investment
3 Too far from Japan	5 Japan can cover
4 Stable economy	3 Dictatorship
5 Business plan shows high potential profit	

7. Given the arguments that remain, participants would try to decide the question.

venture in which norms have not become fixed around one approach.

After the consultant and the change team have agreed on a change strategy, they should develop an action plan. The action plan should be flexible enough to address changing needs and conditions but should also include the following items:

- Why is the change being made?
- Where should the change be occurring?
- How should the change process unfold?
- What are the steps in the change process?
- When should each step occur?
- What is needed from the organization's members to make the change work?

The consultant can help the client develop and present the action plan in narrative form, visual form, or both. A visual model is particularly useful because it creates a clear picture of what needs to be done and simplifies communication about the change process. A narrative approach can vary from a simple plan listing action steps for each of the three stages of change to a more complex plan with goals, action plans with specific deadlines, and assigned responsibilities.

Monitoring and Managing the Change Process

A consultant needs to help the client develop a system for monitoring the change process. Various methods can be used, such as questionnaires, focus groups, and feedback sessions. The consultant should not underestimate the importance of this step. Changes can get out of control if they are not monitored effectively.

The consultant and the change team need to make a decision on how the change process will be managed and what can be done to increase the probability of success. Few successful change efforts are carried out without the sponsorship of a person or team.

Clarify Change Roles

The final step in action planning is clarifying the key players' roles in the change process. Exhibit 6-6 shows five important roles in managing change. It is possible for one person to be involved in all roles. The roles and persons fulfilling the roles may change throughout the change effort.

A *change agent* is engaged in action planning when a specialist is needed to guide the change effort or serve in an advisory capacity. A *change leader* is a person in a leadership position whose involvement and support is important in achieving the desired change. A *change champion* is an internal person who is responsible for championing the change effort and who works with a change agent or leads an effort. When a change leader also assumes the role of change champion, the change effort is greatly accelerated. A *change team* consists of the appropriate combination of change agents, change champions, change leaders, and key stakeholders who are responsible for planning, managing, and championing the change effort. Some change efforts do not require a change team. A *change supporter* assists and encourages change agents, change leaders, and change champions.

What the roles are called may vary depending on what is acceptable in the organization. Two challenges that confront

Exhibit 6-6: Critical Roles in Successfully Managing Change

Change Agent
A person who is a specialist in managing change and developing high-performance organizations, teams, and individuals.

Change Leader
A person in a leadership position who can significantly influence the success or failure of a change effort and provide the support and the leadership necessary for change to succeed.

Change Champion
A person who initiates and champions needed changes. An organization needs to develop change champions at all levels of the organization. However, it is particularly important to have change champions at the top.

Change Team
A team that is responsible for planning, managing, and championing a change effort.

Change Supporter
A person who supports needed changes in attitude and actions, offers valuable assistance in accomplishing change, and encourages the change agents, leaders, and change champions.

those who establish roles are as follows: striking a balance between too little and too much involvement and delegation of responsibility, and not creating a bureaucracy that impedes rather than facilitates change. The consultant and the change team should work at keeping the change planning and management processes as streamlined and effective as possible.

Where Should Action Planning Occur in the Planned-Change Process?

Most change models place action planning after assessment and feedback. The reason for this is that assessment produces the information needed to plan the change effort intelligently. Although most formal action planning does take place following assessment, action planning often occurs throughout an OD intervention.

During the entry step, for instance, a consultant may use action planning to explore needs for change and to develop a change proposal. He or she may modify the action plan during start-up as more people who are affected by the change become involved in the process. The consultant then reevaluates the proposal after assessment and feedback, modifies it if necessary, and makes more specific plans. During the intervention step, as needs and conditions shift, the consultant modifies the action plan. During the adoption step, the consultant may need to make further modifications as the change is fine-tuned. It is during this step that the consultant is presented with an opportunity to conduct a post-assessment to determine what has changed, what still needs to be changed, and how well the change process has worked. He or she can use this information to prepare an action plan in which additional improvements, refinements, and continuous opportunities for change are sought, thus building feedback mechanisms into the change process so that progress can be monitored and the need for new directions detected.

Action Planning: A Case Study

This section presents an illustrative case study about action planning. The name of the organization has been changed, but the circumstances are real. The goal of this case study is to give the reader a sense of the issues encountered in organization development consultation.

The events will be described first and then followed by a question about what steps should be taken by the consultant. After you have answered the question, you can read about what the consultant did.

Introduction

The Gold Company is a subsidiary of a large mining company that owns and operates five gold mines in the United States, South America, and New Zealand. The company is in the process of acquiring several additional mines that could at least double revenues for the company to over $300 million per year. The director of human resources (the director) persuaded the company's president to hire an OD consultant to conduct an assessment of the corporate headquarters in order to facilitate needed changes and prepare the company for the expected and sudden growth.

The corporate headquarters employs seventy-five people in five departments (exploration, engineering, finance, legal, and human resources). Each department is headed by a vice president. The vice presidents and the president form the top-management team. The president is a young (age 38) mining engineer who advanced quickly within the parent company. He has been president for two years and is a capable and well-liked leader. The president has had minimal formal management or leadership training, but he seems to have good leadership instincts.

The OD consultant who was hired for the project had previously worked with the company's largest mine on a program designed to develop the management team into a high-performance team, to train all of the mine managers and supervisors in the latest management skills, and to involve the managers in making high-impact improvements throughout the mine. This program was considered very successful, and the mine became the benchmark in the company in ounces of gold produced, low-cost production per ounce, and mine management. The mine manager was highly regarded in the company and mining industry.

Several meetings between the consultant, the president, and the director revealed that although the company was very successful financially and showed great promise, numerous internal problems existed. The company did not have a clear mission other than to grow and be profitable, and the company's values and goals were not clear to employees. Departments were very territorial; teamwork within and between most departments was minimal. The director was particularly concerned about the lack of teamwork among members of the top-management team. Several conflicts existed between the vice presidents, and one of the vice presidents had a history of conflicts within the organization. It was also the opinion of the director that morale was low because numerous employees had confided to her that they were either overworked, underutilized, or felt oppressed by the very performance-driven, but not people-driven, work environment.

Question One

After you have read the case study, answer the question that follows. When you have answered the question, compare what you have written to the recommended answer.

- How should the OD consultant facilitate the development of an action plan?

Suggested Answer to Question One

The initial action plan was developed by the consultant in conjunction with the president and the director. The plan focused on the first four steps of the action-planning process (Exhibit 6-4).

1. The key stakeholders available to plan the program were the president, the director, and the consultant. Although the consultant was the primary designer and facilitator of the change program, the director was the internal change champion and she worked closely with the consultant.

2. A formal diagnosis was not conducted because a model of the program needed to be developed and the top-management team's support needed to be gained.

3. The three key stakeholders considered several options in terms of what needed to be changed and what the change process should consist of. They agreed generally on what needed to be accomplished and the major components of the program.

4. Based on the recommendations of the president and the director and the consultant's experience in working with over six hundred organizations, the consultant designed

an action plan that followed the three stages of change and the seven guidelines in the change process (Exhibit 6-1). The action plan was designed to present a broad understanding of the recommended change program rather than a detailed plan because the goal was to achieve buy-in from top management. Exhibit 6-7 shows the action plan as it was presented in model form.

Question Two

After you have read about the consultant's first steps, answer the question that follows. When you have answered the question, read the recommended answer.

- What subsequent steps should be taken in the action-planning process?

Suggested Answer to Question Two

The top-management team members met with the consultant to discuss the program and then the members had several meetings of their own before deciding to proceed with the program. Three team members—including the president and the director—voiced strong commitment to the program. Two members appeared to have moderate commitment, and one member adamantly opposed the program.

The consultant surveyed all the headquarters employees by using a questionnaire that asked each employee to rate the headquarters as an organization, his or her department, and his or her immediate supervisor. The questionnaire also included several open-ended questions. The consultant also interviewed all the top-management team members and a

Exhibit 6-7: The Gold Company Organization Excellence Program

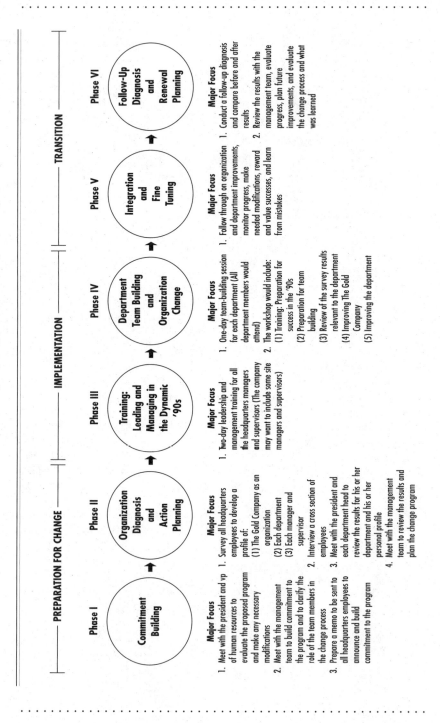

PREPARATION FOR CHANGE ——————— ||—— IMPLEMENTATION ——————— ||—— TRANSITION

Phase I

Commitment Building

Major Focus

1. Meet with the president and vp of human resources to evaluate the proposed program and make any necessary modifications

2. Meet with the management team to build commitment to the program and to clarify the role of the team members in the change process

3. Prepare a memo to be sent to all headquarters employees to announce and build commitment to the program

Phase II

Organization Diagnosis and Action Planning

Major Focus

1. Survey all headquarters employees to develop a profile of:
   (1) The Gold Company as an organization
   (2) Each department
   (3) Each manager and supervisor

2. Interview a cross section of employees

3. Meet with the president and each department head to review the results for his or her department and his or her personal profile

4. Meet with the management team to review the results and plan the change program

Phase III

Training: Leading and Managing in the Dynamic '90s

Major Focus

1. Two-day leadership and management training for all the headquarters managers and supervisors (The company may want to include some site managers and supervisors)

Phase IV

Department Team Building and Organization Change

Major Focus

1. One-day team-building session for each department (All department members would attend)

2. The workshop would include:
   (1) Training: Preparation for success in the '90s
   (2) Preparation for team building
   (3) Review of the survey results relevant to the department
   (4) Improving The Gold Company
   (5) Improving the department

Phase V

Integration and Fine Tuning

Major Focus

1. Follow through on organization and department improvements, monitor progress, make needed modifications, reward and value successes, and learn from mistakes

Phase VI

Follow-Up Diagnosis and Renewal Planning

Major Focus

1. Conduct a follow-up diagnosis and compare before and after results

2. Review the results with the management team, evaluate progress, plan future improvements, and evaluate the change process and what was learned

cross-section of employees representing the five departments at headquarters.

The results of the diagnosis provided an interesting profile of the headquarters, the departments, and the managers. Many of the president's and director's predictions proved true. Although the company performed well and had a wealth of dedicated and talented employees, it also had many internal problems. Employee morale rated a 2.6 on a seven-point scale, with seven being the highest score and one the lowest. The top-management team lacked teamwork and unity. This resulted in a lack of unity, teamwork, and direction throughout the organization. The company's culture was changing from an emphasis on involvement, openness, confidence in people to do their jobs, teamwork, and a high level of unity to a culture characterized by distrust, centralized control, blaming, and a focus on detail and housekeeping rather than on vision and results. Significant structural and communications problems also existed, and several managers received low ratings. This information, as well as other results from the diagnosis, was used to develop a more detailed action plan, again following the process shown in Exhibit 6-4.

1. A change team was formed to work with the consultant and internal-change champion (the director) to plan and manage the change program. The team included representatives from all parts and levels of the company. Although the president remained involved in reviewing the team's recommendations, he decided against participating as an active member of the team. A half-day team-building session was held with the change team to clarify its mission, responsibilities, goals, and norms and to clarify the roles and responsibilities of the team members.

2. The team members evaluated the survey results. They considered the headquarters' strengths and its opportunities for improvement and began to explore what they would like the organization to be. The members also discussed some of the obstacles they were likely to face (such as expected resistance and timing issues) in promoting needed changes.

3. The change team focused on the whole company, each department, managers' skillls, and the behaviors of employees who need to adapt to a changing environment as its targets for change. The team concluded that the obstacles warranted seeking incremental change first and, after achieving success with the incremental change, encouraging transformational change.

   The team also considered ideas to achieve a better alignment of the present structure of the organization with the desired changes. After evaluating the situation, the team dismissed several options. For example, it was clear to the team that the first step should be to develop the top-management team into a united, high-performance team that would serve as a role model. Unfortunately, top management was unwilling to pursue this option.

4. The team also evaluated forces for and against the desired change. For example, one of the vice presidents was still not committed to the program and was considered a major obstacle to its success. The exploration department was also considered a potential obstacle. That department had recently been reorganized, and a new vice president, who was not well-received, had been appointed to the department. The new vice president was unpopular because he wanted to make major changes and because he was an outsider.

Another reason the department personnel did not like him was that a well-liked and respected manager was not promoted to the vice-presidential position. In addition, the department's personnel were accustomed to working independently and they were somewhat skeptical of a collaborative change process.

It was also clear that some managers would resist the program. The team explored its options on how to nurture the forces for change and address the forces against change. A number of intervention alternatives were explored and compared to the original plan. Then the team developed a simple, but detailed, action plan and proposed the plan to top management. Some minor modifications were required before a working action plan was adopted. The team and top management agreed that the plan would be a flexible one that could be adapted to changing conditions.

5. The team developed several feedback mechanisms so it could monitor and manage the change process. Follow-up surveys also were developed. In addition, each member of the change team was responsible for giving feedback to the groups he or she represented.

6. The team reevaluated its mission, responsibilities, goals, norms, and roles and responsibilities to consider adjustments that needed to be made and additional team members that needed to be added.

Question Three

After you have read about the change team's actions, answer the question that follows. When you have answered the question, read the recommended answer.

- What remains to be done in the action-planning process?

Suggested Answer to Question Three

As the program progressed, the change team met on numerous occasions to reevaluate the action plan and to develop new action plans for special situations.

For example, at one point the uncommitted vice president became so disruptive that the change team explored numerous options for dealing with him. After all the options failed to produce results, the change team asked the consultant to speak with the president about the problem, because the vice president's resistance was beginning to undermine the credibility of the program and the president. The president rectified the problem. Although none of those involved found out what the president did, his intervention proved to be successful. The vice president suddenly became very cooperative and, for the most part, remained so.

On another occasion, the change team became frustrated because several issues, such as the company's acquisition activities, had sidetracked the program and resulted in a period of minimal activity. The consultant met with the team to revitalize it and the change program. The team developed a new action plan that targeted five, high-impact changes that were to be led by change-team members. Thus far the new action plan has proven to be successful.

References

Beckhard, R., & Harris, R. (1977). *Organization transitions: Managing complex change.* Reading, MA: Addison-Wesley.

Lewin, K. (1951). *Field theory in social science.* New York: Harper & Row.

Warrick, D.D. (1993). What executives, managers, and human resource professionals need to know about managing change. In W. French, C. Bell, & R. Zawacki (Eds.), *Organization development and transformation: Managing effective change.* Homewood, IL: Irwin.

CHAPTER 7

INTERVENTIONS IN LARGE SYSTEMS

Thomas G. Cummings and Ann E. Feyerherm

In today's rapidly changing and highly competitive environments, top managers are continually seeking ways to adapt their organizations to their environments and to design high-performance work organizations. Interventions in large systems help organizations meet the competitive demands of an increasingly complex and dynamic world. For example, change programs may be joint ventures between businesses and community organizations to resolve problems with toxic wastes, efforts to change organizational culture to enhance innovation and productivity, or the establishment of high-performance work systems in manufacturing plants.

Intervention is the fifth step in any planned-change effort. This chapter, the first of three chapters on the intervention step, defines interventions in large systems, describes their characteristics, presents examples of these change methods, and identifies the competencies needed by organization development (OD) consultants to carry them out. (For information about large-scale interventions, see Appendix IV.)

Definition of a Large-System Intervention

The purpose of an OD intervention in a large system is to make lasting change in the character and performance of an organization, a stand-alone business unit, or a large department. The *character* of an organization can be described as the pattern of exchanges between the organization and its environment and the design of the organization's internal structures, processes, and procedures that produce desired products or services. The *performance* of an organization is measured by its productivity, organizational effectiveness, market share, return on investment, and employee retention.

Organizational performance is determined by an organization's character. Specifically, an organization's performance is high when its character promotes effective exchanges with its environment and its internal-design features effectively fit together and reinforce one another (Mohrman, Mohrman, Ledford, Cummings, Lawler, & Associates, 1990).

Exhibit 7-1 illustrates these two major components of organizational character: organization-environment relations and internal-design components. The figure relies heavily on open-systems theory which views organizations as embedded in a larger environment (Morgan, 1986). The environment provides an organization with inputs (such as raw materials, people, and money) that are converted by transformation processes (such as assembly, hiring, and training) into outcomes (such as products, services, scrap, and image). The environment also provides feedback to the organization about how well it is performing. The organization's transformation processes include several interrelated design components. The key concept in open-systems theory is congruency or fit among the components. They must fit with one another to attain the most effective results (Hanna, 1988; Mohr, 1989).

Exhibit 7-1: Model of a Large System

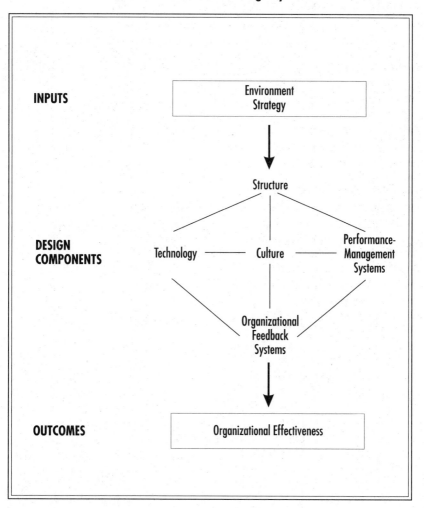

The open-systems model is appropriate for many levels within an organization, as well as the whole organization. It is an appropriate model for a large-system change effort because its components must be viewed with the total organization in mind. Therefore, the organization's environment includes other organizations, societal forces, and the turbulent and complex conditions that generally are present. The organization's internal elements also are considered. For example, in a large-system intervention, the feedback component is the feedback system for the whole organization, whereas in an intervention for a department, the feedback component might be the feedback system for individuals.

A large-system intervention attempts to improve the two key aspects of an organization's character: the organization-environment relationship (how well the inputs are suited to the organization) and the internal-design components (how well the design components fit together). An intervention directly influences the organization's character and that, in turn, affects organizational performance. Examples of interventions in both of these areas are given later in the chapter. First, the two areas are defined further.

Organization-Environment Relationship

The organization-environment relationship is defined as the fit between an organization's inputs and design components. The key inputs to a large system include strategy and environment.

Strategy is an action plan that defines how an organization will use its resources to gain a competitive advantage in the environment (Chaffee, 1985; Hofer & Schendel, 1978). It includes choices about which functions the organization will perform, which products or services it will produce, and which markets and populations it will serve. By its nature, strategy defines the relevant environment within which the organization chooses to operate (Porter, 1980).

Consequently, the *environment* consists of external elements and forces that affect an organization's ability to attain its strategic objectives. The environment includes suppliers, customers, competitors, and regulators. It also includes cultural, political, technical, and economic forces.

Environments range along a continuum from static to dynamic (Emery & Trist, 1965). A dynamic environment changes rapidly and unpredictably. It requires organizational strategies and designs that are different from those appropriate in a static environment. Research suggests that when an organization's strategy results in a highly dynamic environment, the organization's design should be organic, with flexible design components. A static environment calls for a more formalized structure that supports standardized behavior and predictability (Burns & Stalker, 1961; Lawrence & Lorsch, 1967). A consultant will need to assess an organization's environment in order to plan a large-system intervention.

Internal-Design Components

In addition to the organization-environment relationship, an organization's performance depends on the fit among the design components. The following five design components are shown in Exhibit 7-1: technology, structure, organizational feedback systems, performance-management systems, and culture.

Technology includes the methods an organization uses to convert its raw materials into products or services. It involves production methods, equipment, and work flow. Total-quality processes such as statistical process control are also part of technology.

Structure is the way in which an organization divides tasks into departments or groups and coordinates them for overall task achievement. Alternative structures are departments differentiated by function (such as engineering, manufacturing, and sales), by product and service (such as detergents, food, and paper), or by a combination of these (a matrix). An *emerging structure* is a flat organization that is based on information and temporary teams (Drucker, 1989).

Organizational feedback systems are the methods that an organization uses to gather, assess, and disseminate information about group or individual activities. For example, management-control systems help an organization to ensure that each department's activities are consistent with its objectives. Performance-review systems can serve the same function with individual employees.

Performance management systems (PM systems) focus on selecting, training, and developing people. These systems help shape people's behavior and activities within an organization. Performance-management systems also include the rewards used by an organization to induce people to join, remain, and work toward specific objectives. Reward systems combined with measurement systems are often intended to provide employees with incentives for achieving the organization's goals.

Culture is equated with the basic assumptions, values, and norms shared by organizational members (Schein, 1985). Culture is critical to guiding behaviors and making choices about organizational design. Because culture is so pervasive and central to an organization's design, it is central among the design components shown in Exhibit 7-1.

Research suggests that an organization will achieve high performance when its five design components fit with one another and mutually reinforce behaviors needed to achieve the organization's strategic objectives (Galbraith, 1973). For example, when an organization's strategy and environment call for standardized behavior, its design elements should emphasize formality and efficiency, such as those elements found in traditional bureaucracies. Conversely, when an organization's strategy and environment demand innovation and change, its design elements should promote flexibility and experimentation, such as those elements found in high-involvement organizations.

Characteristics of a Large-System Intervention

An intervention in a large system has a number of common characteristics that distinguishes it from other OD interventions. These characteristics are as follows:

1. They are triggered by environmental and internal disruptions;
2. They provoke revolutionary change;
3. They incorporate new organizing paradigms;
4. They are driven by senior executives and line managers; and
5. They require an organizational learning system (Cummings & Huse, 1989).

Environmental and internal disruptions can be compelling reasons for a large-system intervention. Such an intervention typically occurs in direct response to at least three kinds of disruptions:

1. Industry discontinuities such as dramatic changes in legal, political, economic, and technological conditions that shift an organization's ground rules;
2. Changes in a product's life cycle that require different business strategies; and
3. Internal organizational dynamics such as changes in size, strategy, or leadership (Tushman, Newman, & Romanelli, 1986).

These disruptions jolt an organization at the fundamental level and if they are identified correctly, these disruptions can provide the strong "felt need" necessary to embark on a large-system change.

A large-system intervention generally involves implementing revolutionary changes that dramatically reshape an organization. The design features that usually are affected by such an intervention are structures, feedback systems, and performance-management practices. Although evolutionary changes that fine-tune an organization can also occur during an intervention, its primary focus is revolutionary change (Greiner, 1972; Tushman & Romanelli, 1985).

Most large-system interventions attempt to restructure organizations. The goal of these interventions is to create commitment-based organizations that are better suited than the old compliance-based organizations to adapt to rapidly changing conditions. Commitment-based organizations have many mutually reinforcing elements, such as the following:

- Structures are leaner and more flexible;
- Information and decision making are diffused throughout the organization;

- Decentralized teams and business units are accountable for specific products, services, or customers;
- Participative management and teamwork;
- Strong customer orientation; and
- Total-quality concepts and practices are used.

An organization's senior executives and line managers must take active roles in a large-system intervention. Change leadership generally involves the following three critical roles:

Envisioner. Someone who articulates a clear and credible vision of the new organization and its strategy and generates pride and enthusiasm.

Energizer. Someone who demonstrates excitement for changes and models the behaviors linked to them.

Enabler. Someone who allocates resources for implementing change, uses rewards to reinforce new behaviors, and builds effective top-management teams and management practices (Tichy & Devanna, 1986; Tushman, Newman, & Nadler, 1988).

A consultant should make sure that some employees are selected to play change-agent roles along with management, because involvement should not be limited to a handful of people. The consultant should attempt to involve everyone when planning large-scale change.

The innovation and problem solving necessary for large-system change are supported by continual learning (Mohrman & Cummings, 1989). Learning also helps to manage the uncertainty involved in a major change-effort. Unlearning old ways is equally important. People's values, world views, and behaviors change as they learn new assumptions. They need to spend considerable time and effort in learning how to change themselves. The organizational members will need to institute processes and procedures and change the organization's culture so that it supports a learning orientation for the whole organization.

Examples of Selected Interventions

Organization development interventions that are applicable to large systems generally fall into two categories: those that create changes in the organization-environment relationship and those that reshape the internal-design components of an organization. Examples of both interventions are given in the following sections.

Organization-Environment-Relationship Interventions

Two interventions that are used to restructure organization-environment relationships are open-systems planning (OSP) and transorganizational development (TD).

Open-Systems Planning

The consultant can use open-systems planning to help an organization assess its larger environment and develop strategies for relating to it (Krone, 1974). This method results in a clear strategic mission for the organization and options for influencing the environment to support that mission.

Open-systems planning treats an organization as an open system that must interact with a suitable environment to survive and develop. The organization's members' perceptions play a major role in this relationship (Covin & Kilmann, 1990).

Members can choose to ignore or attend to the environment's various signals. Their responses, in turn, affect how they interact with the environment (Cummings & Srivastva, 1977).

To develop a coordinated and effective response to the environment, organizational members must share a common and accurate view of that environment. An example of an inappropriate response occurred when automobile manufacturers in the United States did not recognize or acknowledge the American public's interest in fuel-efficient cars in the early 1970s.

Open-systems planning helps an organization adapt to its environment as well as proactively influence it. A proactive stance goes beyond responding to the environment; it includes influencing it.

Open-systems planning typically is carried out in six sequential steps (Jayaram, 1976). (See Exhibit 7-2.) The first step is to identify environmental domains that affect an organization's strategy. These domains include key customers, regulatory agencies, competitors, and suppliers. Then specify the demands placed on the organization's current functioning by each domain. The second step is to assess how the organization currently responds to environmental demands, which in turn will help a consultant determine how effectively the organization is relating to its environment.

The third step is to help organizational members identify the organization's mission, its underlying purpose, and its distinctive competencies. The consultant should encourage the members to go beyond the organization's official purpose statements and attempt to clarify how well the organization's mission currently relates to its environment. The members may decide to change the organization's current mission based on their analysis.

Exhibit 7-2: Six Sequential Steps in Open-Systems Planning (OSP)

Step 1
Identify environmental domains that affect an organization's strategy.

Step 2
Assess how the organization currently responds to environmental demands.

Step 3
Help organizational members identify the organization's purpose, underlying purpose, and its distinctive competencies.

Step 4
Create a realistic future scenario of the organization's environmental demands and organizational responses.

Step 5
Create an ideal future scenario of environmental demands and organizational responses.

Step 6
Compare the organization's present situation with its ideal future and prepare an action plan to realize its ideal future.

The fourth step is to create a realistic future scenario that describes the environmental demands confronting the organization and responses to them that the organization will accept. When creating this scenario, the consultant should assume that the organization will continue to respond to the environment much as it has in the past.

The fifth step is to create an ideal future scenario that describes the environmental demands that will confront the organization and the most desirable responses to them. The consultant will need to review the first three steps and ask organizational members what they think an ideal scenario would look like. He or she should encourage the members to brainstorm and consider innovative possibilities.

The sixth step is to compare the organization's present situation with its ideal future and prepare an action plan designed to move the organization toward the desired future.

Transorganizational Development

A consultant can use transorganizational development to help an organization join in partnerships with other organizations in order to solve problems and perform tasks that are too complex and multisided for single organizations to handle alone (Cummings, 1984). Such multiorganization partnerships are called transorganizational systems (TS) and they are used increasingly to respond to the complexities of today's dynamic environments (Gray, 1989). Examples of transorganizational systems include joint ventures, research and development consortia, public-private partnerships, and customer-supplier networks. They generally are loosely coupled, nonhierarchical, and underorganized. Consequently, a TS requires an intervention that helps organizational members recognize the need for such partnerships and that develops mechanisms for organizing joint efforts.

Transorganizational development involves interventions that help organizations form TS. These interventions follow four stages that are typical of planned change in underorganized settings: identification, convention, organization, and evaluation. (See Exhibit 7-3.)

In the identification stage, a consultant identifies potential TS members. The organization that begins a TS generally takes the lead. The main activities during this stage are

Exhibit 7-3: Four Sequential Steps in Transorganizational Development

Step 1 Identification
Identify potential members of a transorganizational system (TS).

Step 2 Convention
Assess the feasibility of forming a TS.

Step 3 Organization
Form the TS and organize members for task performance.

Step 4 Evaluation
Provide feedback to the members of the TS so they can identify and resolve problems.

determining criteria for membership and identifying organizations that meet the criteria. Leadership is a key issue because many TS fail in their early stages because of lack of direction and organization.

In the convention stage, the consultant brings potential TS members together to assess the feasibility of forming a TS. At this point the potential members evaluate the costs and benefits of forming a TS and determine an appropriate task definition. Key activities in this stage include reconciling members' self-interests and working through differences.

In the organization stage, the TS is formed. Members organize themselves for task performance by creating key roles and structures. Legal obligations and member rights are determined at this point.

In the evaluation stage, the consultant gives the TS members feedback about the TS's performance so they can start identifying and resolving problems. The members assess how the TS is working and how it can be improved.

Internal-Design-Component Interventions

This section describes four interventions that reshape the internal-design components of an organization so that they fit better with one another. These interventions are sociotechnical-system (STS) design, structural design, reward system, and high-involvement organizations.

Each intervention emphasizes different design components. A sociotechnical-system-design intervention includes technology and performance-management elements; a structural design involves structure and technology; a reward-system intervention includes performance management and feedback systems; a high-involvement intervention involves changes in an organization's culture and, consequently, affects most design components.

Sociotechnical-System-Design Interventions

Sociotechnical-system design is based on the premise that an organization or a work unit is a combination of social and technical parts and that it is open to its environment (Trist, Higgin, Murray, & Pollack, 1963). Because the social and technical elements must work together to accomplish tasks, work systems produce both physical products and social/psychological outcomes. The key issue is to design work so that the two parts yield positive outcomes; this is called *joint optimization*. This method contrasts with traditional methods that first design the technical component and then fit people to it. The traditional methods often lead to mediocre performance at high social costs.

In addition to joint optimization, STS design is also concerned with the work system and its environment. This involves *boundary management*, which is a process of protecting the work system from external disruptions and facilitating the exchange of necessary resources and information (Pasmore, 1988).

The creators of STS design have developed the following guidelines for designing work (Cherns, 1987):

- Work should be organized in a way that is compatible with the organization's objectives. This often leads to a participative process that promotes employee involvement in work design.

- Only those features needed to implement the work design should be specified. The remaining features should vary according to the technical and social needs of the situation. This helps employees control technical variances quickly and close to their sources.

According to Barko and Pasmore (1986), employees who perform related tasks should be grouped together to facilitate the sharing of information, knowledge, and learning. Moreover, information, power, and authority need to be vested in those performing the work to reduce time delays in responding to problems and to enhance employee responsibility. Workers should be trained in various skills so they are flexible in changing conditions and so they have the necessary expertise to control variances. This also results in less need for supervision and staff.

Structural-Design Interventions

A structural-design intervention focuses on the technology and structure of an organization (Galbraith, 1973). A consultant divides the organization's tasks into specific groups or units and then coordinates them to achieve overall effectiveness. This results in four basic organizational structures: functional, self-contained units, matrix, and networked. When selecting a structure for an organization, the consultant needs to consider the following four factors: environment, size, technology, and goals (Daft & Steers, 1986).

The functional structure is hierarchical. Different specialized units such as research, engineering, manufacturing, marketing, and finance report upward through separate chains of command and join only at the organization's top levels. This structure offers several advantages: it reinforces specialized skills and resources, it reduces duplication of scarce resources, and it also facilitates communication within departments. The major disadvantages of a functional structure include a short-term focus on routine tasks, narrow perspectives, and reduced communication and coordination among departments. The functional structure works best when the organization's environment is stable, the organization is small to medium size, and it is engaged in routine tasks that emphasize efficiency and technical quality (McCann & Galbraith, 1981).

The self-contained-unit structure is organized around a product line, geographical area, customer base, or a common technology. Each self-contained unit includes all relevant skills and processes within its boundaries. Hence, employees with all the needed functional expertise are internal to the unit. The major advantage of this organizational structure is that the key interdependencies and resources within each unit are coordinated toward an overall outcome. The key disadvantage is that there is heavy duplication of resources and expertise. The self-contained-unit structure works well in large organizations with dynamic environments and multiple products and customer bases.

Matrix organizations are designed to take advantage of both the functional and self-contained-unit structures by imposing a lateral structure of product or program management onto the vertical, functional structure (Joyce, 1986). Consequently, some managers report to two bosses. Functional departments focus on specialized resources, and product teams concentrate on outputs. A matrix structure works best in a large organization that faces an uncertain environment, has high technological interdependencies across functions, and has product specialization and innovation goals. This structure offers the advantage of managing interdepartmental interdependencies and allowing for skill diversification and training. Its primary disadvantages are that it is difficult to introduce, employees' roles are ambiguous, and employees will face inconsistent demands and direction (Larson &

Gobeli, 1987). Bartlett and Ghoshal (1990) suggest that the disadvantages of a matrix structure can be overcome when the mindset of the employees—rather than the organization's structure—is changed.

A networked structure consists of separate units that are either internal or external to an organization. Each unit specializes in a business task or function and is held together by ad hoc (internal) or contractual (external) arrangements. Internal networks consist of temporary project teams that use specialists from throughout the organization. Drucker (1989) calls this a flat, information-based organization that has reduced levels of management.

Externally networked organizations are similar to transorganizational systems such as joint ventures, research and development consortiums, and licensing agreements across national boundaries. Networked structures have emerged in response to dynamic environments that demand complex technologies or services. These structures are highly flexible and enhance the distinctive competence of each member organization (Charan, 1991; Miles & Snow, 1986). The major disadvantages of a networked structure are that it is difficult to manage lateral relationships across many organizations and that it is difficult to sustain member commitment to the network (Galbraith & Kazanjian, 1986).

Reward-System Interventions

Reward-system interventions focus on rewarding desired behaviors and work outcomes (Lawler, 1988). Because people generally do those things for which they are rewarded, rewards can powerfully shape work behavior. Rewards can be both tangible and intangible and can be given at a variety of levels, from individual to team. Rewards are especially effective when they satisfy basic needs, are viewed as equitable, and fit individual motivations. Reward-system interventions attempt to satisfy these conditions and to assure that rewards reinforce appropriate work behaviors and outcomes (Kerr, 1975).

There are three kinds of rewards: pay, opportunity, and fringe benefits. Using money as a reward can have a profound effect on employees' behavior. Traditionally, pay is based on job classification and seniority. Although this reinforces allegiance to a particular job, it may not promote the high levels of flexibility and performance needed in today's business environment. An organization may find that alternative pay systems such as skill-based pay and pay for performance may be more appropriate for its situation. In skill-based systems, employees are paid based on the number of skills they have mastered or jobs they can perform. This is an appropriate system if an organization needs employees with high skill levels and task flexibility and if it wishes to reward growth and learning. Performance-based pay links rewards directly to measurable performance outcomes. Many organizations use this system to reward team performance which, in turn, reinforces teamwork and cooperation.

Rewards based on opportunity include promotions. However, given the trend toward downsizing, promotions are less plentiful in today's organizations. Instead, organizations are using opportunities for increased learning, task-based empowerment, special work projects, and wider job experiences as motivators and as rewards for exemplary performance.

Rewards that focus on fringe benefits can help an organization attract and retain good employees. Fringe benefits include early and flexible retirement, preretirement counseling, maternity and paternity leaves, childcare, educational funding, investment plans, and flexible work hours (La-Marke & Thompson, 1984). These benefits are sometimes administered through cafeteria-style plans that give employees some choice (Lawler, 1981). This method helps to tailor fringe benefits to individual needs, thus increasing the motivational impact of such rewards.

Reward-system interventions may influence an organization's other design components. For example, an organization may need to change its information system if rewards are based on team performance. Similarly, an organization may need to modify its training and appraisal systems if it uses skill-based pay to reward employees. A reward-system intervention can also extend beyond the workplace to affect employees' families and life styles.

High-Involvement-Organization Intervention

A high-involvement-organization intervention incorporates aspects of several interventions. A key emphasis of this change effort is a shift from a control-oriented organization to one based on commitment (Walton, 1985). A high-involvement organization seeks to diffuse power, knowledge, information, and rewards throughout the organization. This intervention is based on the fundamental belief that people are an organization's most important asset and, consequently, they need to be more involved in work-related decisions (Lawler, Ledford, & Mohrman, 1989).

A high-involvement organization generally has related design elements that mutually reinforce employee involvement. These design elements include self-managing teams, dispersed information systems, flexible structures, social and technical training, egalitarian practices, skill-based pay, pay for performance, and participative goal setting (Lawler, 1988).

A high-involvement organization has traditionally been used in new manufacturing facilities, where the design of the organization can be re-created with few existing constraints. When a traditional organization seeks to modify its practices, more difficult applications are necessary. In such a case, the organization must change most of its design components. This can require considerable time and resources as members break bureaucratic habits and learn new ways of working and relating to one another (Hanna, 1988). Exhibit 7-4 summarizes these interventions and the key design components they affect.

Exhibit 7-4: Design Interventions

Intervention	Design Components Affected
Sociotechnical-Systems Design	Technology Performance Management
Structural Design	Structure Technology
Rewards System	Performance Management Feedback Systems
High-Involvement Organizations	Culture All Design Components

Interventions in Large Systems: A Case Study

The following section contains a case study about a large-system intervention. The actual results of the OD intervention also are described.

Introduction

Banko, a large, regional financial institution, needed to implement some large-scale changes because of deregulation in the banking industry and increased competitive pressures. Banko needed to improve its market responsiveness, improve its customer service, and lower its costs.

The bank was faced with rapidly shrinking profits, and its leaders recognized the need for extensive change. They hired consultants and met with them offsite to formulate a change strategy. The consultants briefed the executives on current business thinking about organizational design and large-scale change. During the same meeting, the executives also identified Banko's values. Its values were to deliver high-quality service; to respond quickly and creatively to customers and changing conditions; to work through teams to improve the business; and to provide opportunities for growth, development, and equitable treatment for all employees.

The consultants set in motion a change process that would increase employee involvement in the bank in order to improve the bank's performance. The senior executives served as the steering committee, and it coordinated the work of two change teams. The teams comprised members from different organizational functions and levels, and the teams focused on employee involvement and market orientation respectively. The steering committee also linked the teams to the bank's business strategy.

Within weeks of announcing the change strategy, the consultants began to notice resistance to the change effort. Middle managers denied that there was a need for change. They felt that employees already enjoyed ample opportunities for involvement and that long-term customers would remain loyal to Banko. The steering committee decided that a more realistic assessment of the current organization was needed to persuade the managers that the change effort was necessary.

Because of the large-scale changes at Banko, the steering committee realized that much coordination and information-sharing would be necessary if the changes were to be success-ful. The committee felt that the right leader could facilitate the necessary coordination and information sharing. Thus, the committee chose a highly regarded executive to spearhead the change effort. She was given direct access to the steering committee and reported to the CEO. She worked directly with the external consultants and developed a cadre of internal change agents to facilitate change.

The two change teams attended an off-site orientation meeting during which members of the steering committee shared their thoughts about the bank's direction and values. The external consultants gave the participants information about organizational change, and the participants discussed the issues and choices that lay ahead. The participants also reviewed the status of the bank and its environment and spent time in their own change teams developing their plans for how the teams would operate.

The change-team members realized that they had to communicate the need for change, the new values, and the change teams' activities to the organizational members and that they needed to receive feedback from them about these issues. The team members developed a process for face-to-face communication throughout Banko that followed existing department lines. The offsite orientation meeting helped es-tablish greater employee involvement and communication during the change effort.

The external consultants spent about three months devel-oping a large-scale organizational survey for assessment. They tested and piloted it. The consultants also created a feedback process. The survey was administered in the fourth month of the change process and feedback began one month later.

The employee-involvement team and market-orientation team spent several months reading relevant information and learning what other companies were doing in their focus areas. They conducted employee focus groups within the bank and talked to managers. They met with the external consultants to discuss innovative approaches to employee involvement and market responsiveness, and they examined the survey results to uncover causes of problems.

After six months, both change teams had identified organizational changes that would fulfill their goals of achieving greater employee participation and faster market responsiveness. The teams shared these plans with the steering committee in a meeting and all participants identified contradictory and complementary change activities. This meeting resulted in a jointly developed action plan to guide the change effort. This plan was subsequently discussed throughout the organization in regular staff meetings and in special meetings that interested employees were invited to attend. Members of the steering committee and change teams were present at these special meetings to clarify issues and to collect information about reactions, concerns, and suggestions.

To overcome resistance to change during this time, the change team relied on employee participation through change-team activity and education, which the teams provided. The education was focused on sharing competitor information and the results of the internal survey.

The focus of the employee-involvement changes was to provide each operating unit in Banko with the tools needed to develop a participative, performance-improvement strategy tailored to its specific needs. Each operating unit was responsible for its own change effort, thus creating local champions and accountability. Members of the units were provided with an overview of employee involvement and with training in problem solving, quality improvement, and work-team design. They were given the freedom to begin pilot efforts that were appropriate to their own work areas.

To support these local change efforts, some managers from the operating units were trained to facilitate the changes. These positions were filled mainly by managers who had the credibility and power to initiate change.

The employee-involvement change team managed these local efforts, responded to requests and problems, and kept the steering committee informed of the units' change progress and of any additional resources that they needed. The steering committee, in turn, promoted widespread communication about the change efforts.

The market-orientation change team segmented Banko's regional market into discrete business areas. Then the change team assigned a business team to each area. Each team consisted of managers and key staff from those functions whose cooperation was required to meet customer needs. Each business team was headed by a marketing manager who had formal responsibility for the team's segment of the business. Each business team had to formulate approaches to meet customers' needs better.

The business teams were trained and were provided with skilled facilitators. Their first task was to gather information about customers in order to discover what they wanted and what organizational barriers prevented Banko from delivering needed services. This diagnosis resulted in the following relevant changes:

- A more customer-driven planning process that included diverse customer input;
- A new information system that provided information on the cost and service performance of Banko compared to each customer base; and
- A reward system geared to the performance of each business team.

This large-scale OD intervention continued for several years. The initial change effort led to a series of modifications and additional changes. The business teams changed the planning process, the information systems, and the reporting relationships. Those changes, in turn, revealed the need for team training and for a change in appraisal and development also plans.

The employee-involvement efforts began with extrinsic changes that led employees to feel good about Banko's willingness to address employee concerns and complaints. These early efforts gradually led to greater opportunities for employee involvement and to work restructuring designed to permit greater individual discretion. These changes revealed the need to modify the information system to provide comparative performance data to each work unit. This system enabled employees to detect and correct performance problems quickly and effectively. In order to facilitate greater employee control, supervisors were trained to develop and manage self-regulating work teams.

Each change was designed only after much discussion with managers and employees. Each change was followed by systematic assessment and further modification and refinement. Most changes led to additional changes, after the impact of one change in the bank required support from other components. Likewise, pressure from Banko's competitive environment required additional action.

Throughout the change process, the steering committee met regularly to review progress. It continued to promote widespread communication. The attitude survey was repeated periodically and became a barometer of organizational functioning and performance and an early warning system for detecting emerging problems. It helped to motivate each organizational unit to consider its own functioning and to develop appropriate corrective action.

The Results of the Case Study

After five years, Banko was experiencing a positive momentum because measures of costs, quality, and customer satisfaction revealed significant improvements. The attitude survey indicated increased trust, highly favorable attitudes toward many aspects of the bank, and greater understanding of its goals, values, and strategies.

References

Barko, W., & Pasmore, W. (1986). Sociotechnical systems: Innovations in designing high-performing systems. *Journal of Applied Behavioral Science, 22* (Special issue 1), 195-360.

Bartlett, C., & Ghoshal, S. (1990, July-August). Matrix management: Not a structure, a frame of mind. *Harvard Business Review,* pp. 138-145.

Burns, T., & Stalker, G.M. (1961). *The management of innovation.* London: Tavistock.

Chaffee, E. (1985). Three models of strategy. *Academy of Management Review, 10*(1), 89-98.

Charan, R. (1991, September-October). How networks reshape organizations—For results. *Harvard Business Review*, pp. 104-115.

Cherns, A. (1987). Principles of sociotechnical design revisited. *Human Relations, 40*(3), 153-162.

Covin, T., & Kilmann, R. (1990). Participation perceptions of positive and negative influences on large-scale change. *Group & Organization Studies, 15*(2), 233-248.

Cummings, T. (1984). Transorganizational development. In B. Staw & L. Cummings (Eds.), *Research in organizational behavior: Vol. 6* (pp. 367-422). Greenwich, CT: JAI.

Cummings, T., & Huse, E. (1989). *Organizational development and change* (4th ed.). St. Paul, MN: West.

Cummings, T., & Srivastva, S. (1977). *Management of work: A sociotechnical systems approach.* San Diego, CA: Pfeiffer & Company.

Daft, R., & Steers, R. (1986). *Organizations: A micro/macro approach.* Glenview, IL: Scott, Foresman.

Drucker, P. (1989). *The new realities.* New York: Harper & Row.

Emery, F., & Trist, E. (1965). The causal texture of organizational environments. *Human Relations, 18*(1), 21-32.

Galbraith, J. (1973). *Organization design.* Reading, MA: Addison-Wesley.

Galbraith, J., & Kazanjian, R. (1986). *Strategy implementation: Structure, systems and process* (2nd ed.). St. Paul, MN: West.

Gray, B. (1989). *Collaborating: Finding common ground for multiparty problems.* San Francisco, CA: Jossey-Bass.

Greiner, L. (1972, May-June). Patterns of organizational change. *Harvard Business Review, 45*, 119-130.

Hanna, D. (1988). *Designing organizations for high performance.* Reading, MA: Addison-Wesley.

Hofer, C., & Schendel, D. (1978). *Strategy formulation: Analytical concepts.* St. Paul, MN: West.

Jayaram, G. (1976). Open systems planning. In W. Bennis, K. Benne, R. Chin, & K. Corey, (Eds.), *The planning of change* (3rd ed.) (pp. 275-283). Austin, TX: Holt, Rinehart & Winston.

Joyce, W. (1986). Matrix organization: A social experiment. *Academy of Management Journal, 29*(3), 536-561.

Kerr, S. (1975). On the folly of rewarding A, while hoping for B. *Academy of Management Journal, 18*(4), 769-782.

Krone, C. (1974). Open systems redesign. In J. Adams (Ed.), *Theory and method in organization development: An evolutionary process* (pp. 364-391). Arlington, VA: NTL Institute for Applied Behavioral Science.

LaMarke, S., & Thompson, H. (1984, February). Industry-sponsored day care. *Personnel Administration,* pp. 53-65.

Larson, E., & Gobeli, D. (1987). Matrix management: Contradictions and insights. *California Management Review, 29*(4), 126-139.

Lawler, E. (1981). *Pay and organization development.* Reading, MA: Addison-Wesley.

Lawler, E. (1988). *High involvement organizations.* San Francisco, CA: Jossey-Bass.

Lawler, E., Ledford, G., & Mohrman, S. (1989). *Employee involvement: A study of contemporary practice.* Houston, TX: American Productivity and Quality Center.

Lawrence, P., & Lorsch, J. (1967). *Organizations and environment.* Cambridge, MA: Harvard University Press.

McCann, J., & Galbraith, J. (1981). Interdepartmental relations. In P.C. Nystrom & W.H. Starbuck (Eds.), *Handbook of organizational design: Remodeling organizations and their environments: Vol. 2* (pp. 60-84). New York: Oxford University Press.

Miles, R., & Snow, C. (1986). Network organizations: New concepts for new forms. *California Management Review, 28*(3), 62-73.

Mohr, B. (1989). Theory, method, and process: Key dynamics in designing high-performing organizations from an open sociotechnical systems perspective. In W. Sikes, A. Drexler, & J. Gant (Eds.), *The emerging practice of organization development* (pp. 199-211). Alexandria, VA: NTL Institute for Applied Behavioral Science/San Diego, CA: Pfeiffer & Company.

Mohrman, S., & Cummings, T. (1989). *Self-designing organizations: Learning how to create high performance.* Reading, MA: Addison-Wesley.

Mohrman, A., Mohrman, S., Ledford, G., Cummings, T., Lawler, E., & Associates. (1990). *Large scale organizational change.* San Francisco, CA: Jossey-Bass.

Morgan, G. (1986). *Images of organization.* Newbury Park, CA: Sage.

Pasmore, W. (1988). *Designing effective organizations: The sociotechnical systems perspective.* New York: John Wiley & Sons.

Porter, M. (1980). *Competitive strategy.* New York: Free Press.

Schein, E. (1985). *Organizational culture and leadership.* San Francisco, CA: Jossey-Bass.

Tichy, N., & Devanna, M. (1986). *The transformational leader.* New York: John Wiley & Sons.

Trist, E., Higgin, B., Murray, H., & Pollack, A. (1963). *Organizational choice.* London: Tavistock.

Tushman, M., Newman, M., & Nadler, D. (1988). Executive leadership and organizational evolution: Managing incremental and discontinuous change. In R. Kilmann and J. Covin (Eds.), *Corporate transformation* (pp. 102-130). San Francisco, CA: Jossey-Bass.

Tushman, M., Newman, W., & Romanelli, E. (1986, Fall). Managing the unsteady pace of organizational revolution. *California Management Review,* pp. 29-44.

Tushman, M., & Romanelli, E. (1985). Organization evolution: A metamorphosis model of convergence and re-orientation. In L.L. Cummings and B. Staw (Eds.), *Research in organizational behavior:* Vol. 7 (pp. 171-222). Greenwich, CT: JAI.

Walton, R. (1985). From control to commitment in the workplace. *Harvard Business Review, 63*(2), 76-84.

CHAPTER 8

INTERVENTIONS IN SMALL GROUPS

W. Brendan Reddy

Small groups and teams that have twelve members or less have become the building blocks of modern organizations (Goodman & Associates, 1986). With the widespread acceptance of participative management, managers and researchers alike have discovered that employees become more involved in organizational decision making and problem solving if they are placed in groups and teams (Guest & Knight, 1979; Williams, 1976). Interest in small groups has evolved through the advent of employee empowerment to include autonomous work groups, quality circles (Sims & Dean, 1985), and self-directed teams (Wellins, Byham, & Wilson, 1991).

Unfortunately, groups of any size are often called small groups or teams, thereby creating confusion about the meanings of those terms. When the membership of a group exceeds twelve people, the dynamics change from small group to large group. These changes can be dramatic. For example, in a large group there is fragmentation, more socializing, less cohesion, less openness, and the potential for regression, particularly under conditions of stress (Kreeger, 1975).

What Is a Small Group?

A small group comprises twelve or fewer members and focuses on a common goal. Depending on the small group's function, it may be known as a team, task force, planning group, problem-solving group, quality circle, self-directed team, or self-managing team. One problem confronting organization development (OD) consultants who are responsible for forming small groups is that employees often do not possess the skills to function effectively as group members. Some managers assume that employees will automatically bring their unique perspectives to the group and that group members will interact synergistically.

However, because of the complexity of group dynamics, the anxiety and ambiguity of a new group, group members' different problem-solving methods, interpersonal positioning, and group members' lack of familiarity with one another, synergistic behaviors do not occur in a new group without some assistance. For this reason, an external consultant needs to be hired or an internal consultant needs to be assigned to the group. The organization development consultant's role is to assess the small group and, in collaboration with group members, to determine what is necessary to help the group become more effective.

OD Competencies for Small-Group Interventions

The competencies an organization development consultant must possess in order to be effective with a small group are small-group theory and techniques, group-facilitation skills, and self-knowledge. These qualifications are shown in the developmental model in Exhibit 8-1. It is developmental in that new knowledge about small groups and oneself can always be added to it.

Theory is the first competency shown in the model. Numerous theories have been developed about small-group dynamics and small-group interventions in organizational contexts. Organization development practitioners should become familiar with theory associated with group dynamics, group development, group decision making, personality,

Exhibit 8-1: A Developmental Model of OD Competencies

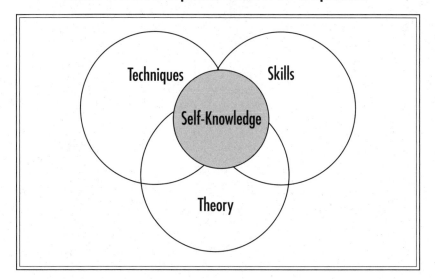

training, and team building before they undertake small-group interventions. The following are suggested readings:

- *Group Dynamics:* Napier & Gershenfeld, 1985; Shaw, 1981; Smith & Berg, 1987; Tubbs, 1988.
- *Decision Making:* Taylor, 1984.
- *Personality Theory:* Liebert & Spiegler, 1990.
- *Training:* Reddy & Henderson, 1987.
- *Team Building:* Dyer, 1977; Francis & Young, 1979; Reddy & Jamison, 1988.
- *Consultation:* Blake & Mouton, 1983; Block, 1981.
- *Process Consultation:* Schein, 1987, 1988.
- *Groups Within Organizations:* Goodman & Associates, 1986; Hackman, 1990.

Moreover, journals such as *Small Group Behavior* and *Group & Organization Studies* report on small-group cases, interventions, and research findings. Consultants should become familiar with these resources and the valuable information they contain.

Small-group techniques may be the easiest to learn of the competencies shown in the model. However, techniques are not very effective without a theory base and a knowledge of oneself. Consultants sometimes hear, "I don't know what happened. I did the same thing you did, but I failed. It must be the group." The chances are that the difference resulted from the speaker's lack of knowledge of small groups and of him- or herself.

However, a consultant does need to master some techniques in order to conduct small-group interventions. One resource he or she can use to learn techniques is the Pfeiffer &

Company *Annual* series (Pfeiffer, 1972-1995). Each *Annual* contains small-group activities, instruments, lecturettes, and articles for professionals.

A consultant needs to understand OD theory and know appropriate techniques, but these two competencies are not sufficient for facilitating small-group work. Skills, the third of the competencies shown in Exhibit 8-1, are also required. First, the consultant must learn and practice basic skills such as observing, listening, presenting, and challenging. The consultant must then master skills associated with timing, delivery, tone, emphasis, and selection of interventions. These skills can only be acquired experientially and improved with practice. The practice can be augmented by supervision and feedback.

Organization development consultants who conduct small-group interventions also need design skills (see Pfeiffer & Ballew, 1988). These skills include designing an intervention for optimal effect, easy sequence flow, and continuity from one segment to another. A consultant must relate an intervention's design to its objectives, time constraints, and participant expectations.

To use skills appropriately, an OD consultant needs self-knowledge, the fourth competency shown in Exhibit 8-1. The critical factor in an intervention is the consultant as change agent. The organization development consultant is effective only when he or she knows, and can manage, himself or herself (Reddy, 1985). The consultant must know what makes him or her angry, happy, or afraid. He or she also must know what motivates him or her to select a particular intervention. If the consultant does not have a sense of what motivates him or her, he or she may make intervention choices that do not meet the group's needs.

Phillips (1988) talks about defining who a consultant is by how he or she presents himself or herself. The consultant's effectiveness is largely determined by how well he or she performs the following facilitative roles:

- Being a model;
- Being a force that is played to, off, or against; and
- Being an energy field that affects the respective energy fields of a group or an individual (Phillips, 1988, p. 31).

Dyer (1972) describes six major themes around which interventions center. All the themes require a knowledge and management of self; they are as follows:

- Confronting, engaging, and encountering;
- Silence;
- Being open, being authentic, disclosing oneself;
- Struggling to develop trust;
- Helping the group become sensitive to the "here-and-now"; and
- Displaying care and affection (pp. 18-22).

There are many options that consultants can use to learn about themselves. Many organizations and graduate schools offer human resource (HR) workshops and courses that help the participants to recognize the impact of their behaviors on others, understand their communication styles and their reactions to other styles, give and receive feedback, and learn how to manage conflict constructively. Many courses also deal with cultural diversity and other organizational and interpersonal issues. Public workshops also are available on specific topics, such as team building and conflict management.

Another area for self-awareness is personal style—as measured by an instrument (Keirsey & Bates, 1978; Myers, 1980). Many excellent instruments are available to help OD consultants to examine their personal styles (Clawson, Kotter, Faux, & McArthur, 1992). Consultants can use instruments to compare and contrast their styles with group norms or with group members' styles. For example, if a consultant is highly introverted but the group norm is extraverted, the consultant may experience demands from group members to socialize with them. Such differences need to be understood and managed. (Exhibit 3-1 provides a list of useful instruments and descriptions of what they measure.)

Finally, OD consultants can raise their own sensitivity through continual self-examination. The following list of questions can help consultants in that examination:

- How am I feeling at the moment?
- What physical sensations accompany this feeling?
- What images and metaphors come to mind?
- What aspects of myself or my behaviors do I criticize?
- What aspects and behaviors of group members do I criticize?
- What assumptions do I make about the group or its members?
- What expectations do I have about the group or particular members?
- Do I resist members' suggestions or feedback?
- How do I react to criticism?
- What arouses my anxiety?

- Do I encourage or discourage self-disclosure about myself or group members?
- Where and what do I rationalize?
- What do I dream about after a group session?

By continually asking these questions, particularly in ambiguous and stressful circumstances, a consultant can become more sensitive to, if not insightful about, his or her own reactions, expectations, and motivations.

Consultants who are beginning small-group interventions also need to devote time to focus on their own dynamics and impact in small groups.

What Is a Small-Group Intervention?

A small-group intervention is an intended and purposive action by an OD consultant to help a small group and its members move toward explicit goals. Key parts of this definition are described in the following section.

Intended

A consultant consciously makes a statement or suggests an activity. The consultant does not make interventions in random fashion or just for effect. The consultant's intent is to help the group reach its goals.

Purposive

An effective consultant has a theoretical framework and a deliberate plan from which he or she works. The consultant knows how he or she will be directing the group so that it reaches its goals. Every intervention should be based on a framework and a plan.

By an OD Consultant

Any action—conscious or unconscious—of an OD consultant can affect the group. For the purposes of this chapter, only those interventions that are made by the consultant will be examined.

Explicit Goal

A consultant's first activity in a small-group intervention is to help the group clarify its goals and its mission. This activity is critical because group members cannot move in the same direction without clear goals. A specific goal also helps the consultant to select an intervention.

From a consultant's vantage point, an intervention has two components: strategy and choice. To select a strategy and choose an intervention, the consultant and the client must have a goal for the intervention.

Clarifying Who the Client Is

The person who initially contacts a consultant in regard to using his or her services is not necessarily the client. It is imperative that the OD consultant and the initial contact specify exactly who the client will be (Block, 1981; Neilsen, 1984). For example, it may be the contact person's boss, another manager, or a group. A manager may think that he or she, not the group, should be the client and that he or she should have special access to otherwise privileged information about group members or that he or she should be counseled individually by the consultant. However, if the consultant will be intervening directly in a group, the group should be viewed as the client. If the group is the client, the consultant should discuss any issues or problems with the group; he or she should not form a separate alliance with the manager, because the group members may then become suspicious of the consultant.

Clarifying the Contract

A clear and explicit contract is essential for successful consultation (see more on this topic in Chapter Three). A written contract is thus desirable in most cases because it makes the agreement more clear and explicit then an oral contract. The contract between the consultant and the client (individual or group) should be written as soon as possible. Both the consultant and the client need to know what is expected of them. They must agree on the action steps to be taken. The contract serves as a foundation on which the consultant can build the intervention.

The consultant also will find it useful to describe his or her values about dealing with conflict, handling confidentiality, and learning (see Exhibit 8-2).

An example may help to emphasize the usefulness of openness about values. In a small, family-owned and operated company, the president was dismayed when he learned that the OD consultant considered conflict to be natural rather than negative or destructive. The consultant's belief was in opposition to the president's.

The consultant spent considerable time educating the president about the negative effects of suppressed conflict. The consultant facilitated a skill-oriented workshop on conflict management that focused on the positive aspects of differences. The president found the experience rewarding and came to believe that dealing with conflict was not inconsistent with his own values.

Exhibit 8-2: Statement of Personal Values

The group has the right to know—at any time—my objectives and rationale for whatever I am doing.

Group members always have a choice of participating or not participating in any survey, activity, simulation, or exercise that I offer.

I will not intentionally intervene at a depth deeper than that at which group members are able to learn and I will not leave the group more disrupted than when I entered.

I will keep the members' personal information anonymous and confidential and I will not share this information with anyone except with the explicit permission of the members involved. This includes any information generated from a survey or group activity.

I assume that people learn in different ways and at different rates.

I consider conflict and resistance to be a natural outgrowth of the differences and interactions between people and I do not consider them to be negative or destructive. Although conflict and resistance may not be resolved, they can be managed.

I see my role as consultant to include protecting group members from personal embarrassment, scapegoating, or behaviors that I feel may be personally destructive to them and to the organization.

A year later, the company conducted its annual climate survey, which showed a positive change in employees' behaviors in dealing with conflict.

A consultant also may want to offer an oral contract at the start of each group meeting or intervention because it reestablishes his or her role and the members' roles and it reinforces their responsibilities (see Exhibits 8-3 and 8-4).

More specifically, the consultant should state why he or she is conducting the intervention, his or her understanding of what will happen, and why the intervention is important. If there is a discrepancy between the consultant's and the client's expectations, the consultant should discuss the discrepancy with the client and resolve it. This approach saves time and reduces the chance of frustration occurring later. It also demonstrates the consultant's credibility and professionalism.

Assessing Small Groups

A consultant needs to know how to observe a group, interview its members, use a survey, or use a combination of these methods to assess the group's functioning.

After the consultant discusses with the client his or her options for gathering data, he or she will decide how the data will be collected and whether information will come from individuals or the entire group.

Simply observing a group as it works is valuable, but the consultant needs to know what to look for. Skilled consultants know to observe who speaks most often, how alert group members appear to be, and what issues evoke the most interest. Hanson, 1972; McCall and Simmons, 1969; and Simon and Boyer, 1974, provide useful advice about how to use observation successfully.

An interview is often conducted to assess a small group. A consultant can interview group members individually, in pairs, in trios, or as a total group. Anonymity should always be assured in an individual interview—unless the respondent's consent is explicitly given to the contrary. The interviewer can

Exhibit 8-3: An Oral Contract with a Group

Before we begin the intervention, I would like to take a few minutes to talk about how I view my role.

I would like the freedom to comment on what I see happening in the group and to comment on behaviors that help the group to achieve its goal or impede the group from achieving its goal.

Although my role is to comment on the group's process—that is *how* members work together—I will not intervene in the content—the actual issue that is being worked on. I see that as the group's responsibility and the focus of the group's expertise.

My intent and hope is that you learn to observe your own processes and to perform these same interventions yourselves. Learning to do this will help the group to achieve its goals and become more effective.

Is that agreeable to each of you? [Be certain that group members comment, nod, or respond in some way.]

I would also like to know what you expect of me and I would like to discuss whether it is something that I perceive to be within my role as process consultant. [Brainstorm options.]

Exhibit 8-4: Team/Meeting Process Roles and Responsibilities

Role: *Team/Meeting Leader*

Description: The leader manages the team and meeting process. This role typically is constant.

Plan: Before the Meeting

- Decide if a meeting is necessary, based on agenda items received;
- Ensure that a date, time, and place for the meeting are decided and secured by the team;
- Develop an agenda and set a time limit for each agenda item;
- Distribute the agenda and any supporting materials prior to the meeting; and
- Consult with the process coach.

Do: During the Meeting

- Post ground rules for the meeting;
- Monitor the time for each agenda item;
- Help keep the team focused on the agenda;
- Support the presenters by summarizing and clarifying items when necessary, maintaining balanced participation, and being tactful and diplomatic;
- Be a member of the team; and
- Make sure that action items are assigned to participants when necessary.

Check: End of Meeting

- Summarize the meeting;
- Help identify agenda items for the next meeting; and
- Ensure that the meeting process is evaluated.

Act: After the Meeting

- Attend to improvements that participants identified during the meeting evaluation;
- Make a new agenda;

Exhibit 8-4: Team/Meeting Process Roles and Responsibilities (continued)

- Consult with process coach; and
- Maintain a master file of meeting minutes and track group process in the intervention.

Role: *Process Coach*

Description: The process coach acts as a consultant to the team and monitors the meeting process. He or she supplies the team with tools, methods, and feedback to improve the meeting process. (The OD consultant initially takes this role.)

Plan: Before the Meeting

- Help the team/meeting leader plan methods to collect data on the team's interactions;
- Locate resources as necessary/requested;
- Assist the leader with the development of ground rules for the meeting; and
- Determine methods to provide the team with feedback about the meeting.

Do: During the Meeting

- Suggest options to deal with a situation, especially when the team cannot think of any;
- Challenge the team to deal with uncomfortable issues;
- Be supportive of all team members;
- Use Deming's "Fourteen Points of Management" and remind the team of other appropriate teachings when necessary;
- Observe the meeting process;
- Remind the team when a ground rule has been violated;
- Assist team members in using data and in using Shewhart's (1980) plan, do, check, act (PDCA) cycle or other useful guidelines for group decision making;
- Suggest tools that will help the meeting process;
- Monitor the team's use of data; and
- Be a member of the team.

Exhibit 8-4: Team/Meeting Process Roles and Responsibilities (continued)

Check: End of Meeting

- Help the team to evaluate its meeting process;
- Summarize the behaviors observed; and
- Help the team to identify improvements that can be made.

Act: After the Meeting

- Assist with the improvement of the meeting process;
- Analyze feedback data; and
- Assist in creating the next agenda.

Role: *Scribe*

Description: This person is responsible for taking the meeting notes. This usually is a rotating role.

Plan: Before the Meeting

- Bring necessary equipment such as paper, pens, flipchart, and/or laptop computer.

Do: During the Meeting

- Record decisions;
- Summarize conclusions and discussions; ask for clarification if necessary;
- Record action items—such as who took responsibility to do what and by when;
- Assist the leader when he or she summarizes after each agenda item;
- Identify agenda items not covered and make sure these are on the next meeting's agenda;
- Keep track of topics brought up during the meeting that are future agenda items; and
- Be a member of the team.

Exhibit 8-4: Team/Meeting Process Roles and Responsibilities (continued)

Check: During the Meeting

- Record issues and ask for clarification if necessary; and
- Ensure that the meeting minutes are approved.

Act: After the Meeting

- Prepare and distribute minutes within two days.

Role: *Team Member*

Plan: Before the Meeting

- Read minutes from the previous meeting, noting changes needed;
- Review agenda for upcoming meeting;
- Complete any assigned action items;
- Notify leader of any necessary absence from meeting; and
- Provide leader with any agenda items. Note time needed and provide support documentation if necessary.

Do: During the Meeting

- Bring materials as needed;
- Practice good team skills according to the ground rules;
- Focus comments on fact rather than opinion, whenever possible;
- Assist leader throughout the meeting as needed;
- Act as group leader when presenting a topic; and
- Be a member of the team.

Check: End of Meeting

- Evaluate own behavior with respect to the ground rules; and
- Assist in evaluating the meeting process.

Exhibit 8-4: Team/Meeting Process Roles and Responsibilities (continued)

Act: After the Meeting

- Follow through with assignments; and
- Follow through with items identified to improve the meeting process.

Role: *Champion*

Description: A champion supports a specific project on which the team is working. Usually, the champion has authority to provide resources and make changes in the process being studied. This role is constant. (The role of champion often is played by a manager.)

Plan: Before the Meeting

- Clarify with the steering committee why the project was selected*;
- Assist in the selection of the team leader, process coach, and team members*;
- Meet with individual team members to ensure that they understand their assignments; and
- Meet with the team leader to help him or her develop an agenda.

Do: During the Meeting

- Provide information needed by the project team;
- Provide ongoing encouragement; and
- Be a member of the team.

Check: End of Meeting

- Determine what the team expects to be done, related to the project, prior to the next meeting.

*These tasks will be performed only before the first team meeting.

Exhibit 8-4: Team/Meeting Process Roles and Responsibilities (continued)

Act: After the Meeting

- Provide regular feedback to the steering committee about the team's progress;
- Obtain resources needed by the team;
- Meet with the manager(s) of the meeting process, the people who perform the process, and those who control the resources used within the process, when necessary, to gain cooperation;
- Meet with team members to determine and provide whatever assistance they need to carry out their assignments; and
- Provide whatever support is needed by the team leader.

---

establish rapport and minimize the respondent's defensiveness during the interview by using his or her body posture, using a calm and soothing tone when speaking, and showing interest in what the respondent is saying.

Because interviews will not always provide the consultant with information he or she needs, the consultant also needs to know how to use surveys and other instruments to assess a small group (Dunham & Smith, 1979; Nadler, 1977). Instruments can focus on specific areas such as leadership, conflict management, communication, and problem solving.

The information gathered can be reported back to the group, which can use it to make decisions (Argyris, 1970).

Collaborating with the Client

In most small-group interventions, a consultant should use a collaborative approach, working with the client in a helping, problem-solving manner, not in a prescriptive, expert, or directive manner (Schein, 1990).

Setting Obtainable Goals

An OD consultant should not promise the client easy solutions. Unfortunately, that is what the client may wish. That mentality is encapsulated in the statement "Tell me what's wrong and how to fix it." The consultant and the client need to set realistic, obtainable goals for an intervention. The concept is best described by Harrison (1970): "Intervene at a level no deeper than that required to produce enduring solutions to the problems at hand" (p. 190). The consultant should also "intervene at a level no deeper than that at which the energy and resources of the client can be committed to problem solving and to change" (p. 198).

Modeling Appropriate Behavior

One way in which people learn is by observing the behaviors of role models. If OD consultants are open, clients (both individuals and groups) will learn to be open. If OD consultants are defensive, their clients will learn to be defensive. Appropriate modeling of dynamic skills such as conflict management, communication, and giving and receiving feedback can have great impact on clients' behaviors.

Providing Follow-Up

Too often, a small-group intervention is a one-time event. A group may work with an OD consultant for a short, intensive period. Then the consultant leaves, and the group is on its own.

There is no continuity, and the group members have not had a chance to practice and improve their behavioral skills. Research on learning supports this contention. Underwood (1961) found that practice distributed across time led to larger increases in recall than a similar amount of massed practice. Zechmeister and Nyberg (1982) also determined that retention was greater after distributed practice than after massed practice. This is particularly true if the intervals between practice periods are fairly long.

Participants in one-time workshops view them simply as isolated or discrete events rather than as related parts of an ongoing process. When participants know that there will be a follow-up session with a consultant, and assignments must be completed during the interim, the probabilities increase that they will work harder. The participants become more accountable for the success of the process, the consultation is taken more seriously, and there is time from session to session to practice what is learned and to implement action steps in the work setting.

At first glance, small-group interventions may look easy. But they are complex and require a high degree of training and expertise on the part of the consultant. If possible, OD consultants should participate in supervised practice with small groups until they can facilitate interventions on their own.

Small-Group Interventions: A Case Study

This section presents an illustrative case encountered by an OD consultant working as a small-group interventionist. The objective of the following case is to provide a sense of the issues encountered in small-group consultation and the variables that should be considered.

The Case Study

The administrative council at St. Anselm Hospital was experiencing low morale and frustration, so it authorized the vice president of human resources to contact an external consultant. The council members wished to work together more effectively. The council consisted of fourteen members, including the chief executive officer (CEO), the chief operating officer (COO), and the vice presidents of nursing, finance, human resources, and administration. The other members were managers and directors of various units.

The consultant first met with the vice president of human resources to receive a briefing about the situation. She heard about the council's needs and concerns and discussed her expectations, potential role, and fee structure. She also clarified that the council would be the client rather than any individual member.

Question One

Reflect on what you have read so far and then write your answer to the question that follows. After you have answered the question, discuss your response with peers and then compare what you have written to the recommended answer.

- What would you do next in this situation? Why?

Suggested Answer to Question One

After the consultant received a broad outline of the issues from the vice president of human resources, she asked to meet with the council to accomplish the following:

- Become acquainted with the council members and establish rapport;
- Clarify that the council would be the client;
- Have council members express their perceptions of issues and concerns in order to begin building a common database;
- Determine council members' value orientations;
- Share the OD consultant's values with the council, particularly about such issues as collaboration, expression of feelings, managing conflict, and the need for action planning;
- Gather information about system (group) functioning;
- Discuss questions and strategies for further assessment; and
- Outline next steps collaboratively.

The consultant met with the council for an hour and a half. She stated her objectives, which the council found satisfactory. The format of the meeting was a simple dialogue with both the consultant and the council members raising questions and sharing information.

The members spoke quite openly about their low morale, avoidance of conflict, difficulty in making decisions, and lack of vision. They were supportive of the new CEO, her style, and the direction in which she wanted to move the council and the hospital. The members acknowledged that they had difficulty with conflict, but they wanted to learn to deal with it. They recognized differences among themselves in such areas as problem solving, decision making, and planning, and they indicated that they would like to understand and manage their differences more effectively. The conversation was accompanied by excitement, hope, and apprehension.

Finally, the consultant asked the council members what next steps seemed appropriate. The members indicated that their priority was to spend time improving their interactions. They asked the OD consultant what design she would recommend.

Question Two

Write your answer to the question that follows. When you finish, discuss your response with your peers and then compare what you have written to the recommended answer.

- What would you do next in this situation? Why?

Suggested Answer to Case Study Question Two

The consultant suggested that the council members have three separate team-building sessions. The first session would last for three days; a second session would be held in three to four months and would last for two days; and a third session would be held in six to eight months. The consultant explained that a three-day program is soon forgotten, but when participants know there will be follow-up, the likelihood of practice and commitment is increased.

The consultant's recommended design for the first team-building session required that the council members create a vision and mission for the council (Block, 1987), learn how to give and receive behavioral feedback (Jacobs, 1974), examine the impact of each member's personal style on other group members (Smith, 1980), practice communication skills, and work on "real time" issues. She explained that subsequent team-building sessions would be designed according to specific council needs and developments.

The council members then discussed the consultant's suggestion. A few members were reluctant to make a nine-month commitment without ongoing evidence that the team building was working. In response, the CEO indicated that a real commitment was necessary to accept the "program and process" and to be committed to the program's success. Her comments placed the responsibility and accountability for success directly on the shoulders of the council members.

The CEO's comments were met with much enthusiasm—even from those who had initially resisted the team-building sessions. The council members had expected the CEO to lead the effort, but instead they found themselves empowered. The council members established dates and times, and the expectations of the participants and the consultant were discussed.

During the first team-building session, the council members struggled to create a vision. They gave and received feedback with some hesitation. They learned to observe their group's processes. Issues were surfaced, but the council members felt excitement and became committed to the process.

The council members were given assignments between team-building sessions. For example, after each meeting they had to complete a one-page questionnaire about the value of that meeting. Each member had a partner with whom he or she could practice new behaviors.

By the time the second team-building session began, the council looked and behaved very differently. During the second session, the members focused on managing newly created conflicts, integrating a new member, and exploring their expectations about roles in the organization.

In the third team-building session, the council revisited its vision and mission, managed specific conflicts, and continued to work on "real time" issues. It also processed group dynamics and issues as they arose.

The members set goals and made plans for the quarterly follow-up sessions. They considered this procedure essential to the success of the change effort, so that they would not regress to old patterns and behaviors (Boss, 1983; Locke & Latham, 1984).

The council formed a committee to initiate culture change throughout the hospital. The plan is proceeding. Although there is some resistance, the hospital is experiencing positive change.

References

Argyris, C. (1970). *Intervention theory and method: A behavioral science view.* Reading, MA: Addison-Wesley.

Blake, R., & Mouton, J. (1983). *Consultation: A handbook for individual and organization development.* Reading, MA: Addison-Wesley.

Block, P. (1981). *Flawless consulting: A guide to getting your expertise used.* San Diego, CA: Pfeiffer & Company.

Block, P. (1987). *The empowered manager.* San Francisco, CA: Jossey-Bass.

Boss, R.W. (1983). Team building and the problem of regression: The personal management interview as an interview. *Journal of Applied Behavioral Science, 19*(1), 67-83.

Clawson, J., Kotter, J., Faux, V. & McArthur, C. (1992). *Self-assessment and career development.* Englewood Cliffs, NJ: Prentice-Hall.

Dunham, R., & Smith, F. (1979). *Organizational surveys: An internal assessment of organizational health.* Glenview, IL: Scott, Foresman.

Dyer, W. (1972). *Modern theory and method in group training.* New York: Van Nostrand Reinhold.

Dyer, W. (1977). *Team building: Issues and alternatives.* Reading, MA: Addison-Wesley.

Francis, D., & Young, D. (1979). *Improving work groups: A practical manual for team building.* San Diego, CA: Pfeiffer & Company.

Goodman, P., & Associates. (Eds.). (1986). *Designing effective work groups.* San Francisco, CA: Jossey-Bass.

Guest, D., & Knight, K. (Eds.). (1979). *Putting participation into practice.* Westmean, England: Gower Press.

Hackman, J. (Ed.). (1990). *Groups that work (and those that don't): Creating conditions for effective teamwork.* San Francisco, CA: Jossey-Bass.

Hanson, P. (1972). What to look for in groups: An observation guide. In J.W. Pfeiffer and J.E. Jones (Eds.), *The 1972 annual handbook for group facilitators* (pp. 19-24). San Diego, CA: Pfeiffer & Company.

Harrison, R. (1970). Choosing the depth of organizational intervention. *Journal of Applied Behavioral Science, 6*(2), 181-202.

Jacobs, A. (1974). The use of feedback in groups. In A. Jacobs and W. Spradlin (Eds.), *The group as agent of change* (pp. 408-448). New York: Behavioral Publications.

Keirsey, D., & Bates, M. (1978). *Please understand me.* Del Mar, CA: Prometheus Nemesis Books.

Kreeger, L. (1975). *The large group: Dynamics and therapy.* Itasca, IL: F.E. Peacock.

Liebert, R., & Spiegler, M. (1990). *Personality: Strategies and issues.* Pacific Grove, CA: Brooks/Cole.

Locke, E., & Latham, G. (1984). *Goal setting: A motivational technique that works!* Englewood Cliffs, NJ: Prentice-Hall.

McCall, G., & Simmons, J. (Eds.). (1969). *Issues in participant observation: A text and reader.* Reading, MA: Addison-Wesley.

Myers, I. (1980). *Gifts differing.* Palo Alto, CA: Consulting Psychologists Press.

Nadler, D. (1977). *Feedback and organizational development: Using data based methods.* Reading, MA: Addison-Wesley.

Napier, R., & Gershenfeld, M. (1985). *Groups: Theory and experience.* Boston, MA: Houghton Mifflin.

Neilsen, E. (1984). *Becoming an OD practitioner.* Englewood Cliffs, NJ: Prentice-Hall.

Pfeiffer, J.W., & Ballew, A.C. (1988). *Design skills in human resource development* (Vol. 6 in UATT series). San Diego, CA: Pfeiffer & Company.

Pfeiffer, J.W./& Jones, J.E./& Goodstein, L.D. (1972-1995). The *annual* series in human resource development. San Diego, CA: Pfeiffer & Company.

Phillips, C. (1988). The trainer as person: On the importance of developing your best intervention. In W.B. Reddy & C. Henderson (Eds.), *Training theory and practice* (pp. 29-35). Arlington, VA: NTL Institute/San Diego, CA: Pfeiffer & Company.

Reddy, W. (1985). The role of the change agent in the future of group work. *The Journal for Specialists in Group Work, 10*(2), 103-107.

Reddy, W.B., & Henderson, C. (Eds.). (1987). *Training theory and practice.* Arlington, VA: NTL Institute/San Diego, CA: Pfeiffer & Company.

Reddy, W.B., & Jamison, K. (Eds.). (1988). *Team building: Blueprints for productivity and satisfaction.* Arlington, VA: NTL Institute/San Diego, CA: Pfeiffer & Company.

Schein, E. (1987). *Process consultation volume II: Lessons for managers and consultants.* Reading, MA: Addison-Wesley.

Schein, E. (1988). *Process consultation volume I: Its roles in organization development* (Rev. ed.). Reading, MA: Addison-Wesley.

Schein, E. (1990). A general philosophy of helping: Process consultation. *Sloan Management Review, 31*(3), 57-64.

Shaw, M. (1981). *Group dynamics: The psychology of small group behavior.* New York: McGraw-Hill.

Shewhart, W.A. (1980). *The economic control of quality of manufactured product.* American Society for Quality Control. [Original edition: 1931, New York: Van Nostrand Reinhold.]

Simon, A., & Boyer, E. (Eds.). (1974). *Mirrors for behavior III: An anthology of observation instruments.* Wyncote, PA: Communication Materials Center.

Sims, H., & Dean, J. (1985). Beyond quality circles: Self-managing teams. *Personnel, 62*(1), 25-32.

Smith, K., & Berg, D. (1987). *Paradoxes of group life.* San Francisco, CA: Jossey-Bass.

Smith, P. (Ed.). (1980). *Small groups and personal change.* London: Methuen.

Taylor, R. (1984). *Behavioral decision making.* Glenview, IL: Scott, Foresman.

Tubbs, S. (1988). *A systems approach to small group interaction.* New York: Random House.

Underwood, B. (1961). Ten years of massed practice on distributed practice. *Psychological Review, 68*(3), 229-247.

Wellins, R., Byham, W., & Wilson, J. (1991). *Empowered teams: Creating self-directed work groups that improve quality, productivity, and participation.* San Francisco, CA: Jossey-Bass.

Williams, E. (Ed.). (1976). *Participative management: Concepts, theory and implementation.* Atlanta, GA: Georgia State University.

Zechmeister, E., & Nyberg, S. (1982). *Human memory: An introduction to research and theory.* Pacific Grove, CA: Brooks/Cole.

CHAPTER 9

PERSON-FOCUSED INTERVENTIONS

Udai Pareek

One concern of organization development (OD) is the development of individuals in organizations. Person-focused OD interventions have relevance for many HRD subsystems—such as training, performance counseling, and career planning—and support other OD interventions. Consultants can use several of these interventions for their development and that of their clients, peers, and subordinates.

Typology of Person-Focused Interventions

All person-focused interventions focus on individuals working in organizational contexts. Like other change efforts, these interventions involve partnerships between participants and OD consultants. Person-focused interventions can be classified in the following four ways.

1. *By the Person or Group That Initiates the Intervention.* For example, the participants, a team, the organization, or an OD consultant may be the responsible party.

2. *By Intervention Mode.* For example, the mode may be self-study, reflection, feedback, coaching, or mentoring.

3. *By Theoretical Basis.* Several theorists have contributed to the development of person-focused interventions. Among them are Freud, Jung, Erickson, Berne, Bion, Skinner, Pavlov, McClelland, Lewin, Merton, and Goffman. Freud, Jung, and Erickson are well-known for their contributions to psychoanalysis; Berne is the founder of transactional analysis (TA); Bion's work resulted in the Tavistock Institute in England and the T-group approach of the NTL (National Training Laboratories) in the U.S.; Skinner, Pavlov, and McClelland provided the basis for many training, behavior-modification, and motivational-arousal interventions; Lewin is well-known for field theory; and Merton and Goffman did work on role theory that has served as a meeting point for psychology, sociology, and anthropology.

4. *By the Person or Group That Takes the Active Role.* For example, either the participants or the OD consultant may assume this responsibility. This classification method is used in this chapter to discuss various interventions (see Exhibit 9-1).

Participant-Active Interventions

In these interventions, participants assume major responsibility for initiating change.

1. Laboratory-Training Groups

The term *laboratory-training groups* (T-groups) has various meanings. In OD's early years, T-groups were the basis for

Exhibit 9-1: Participant-Active Interventions versus OD Consultant-Active Interventions

Participant-Active Interventions	OD Consultant-Active Interventions
1. Laboratory-Training Groups	1. Training
2. Instrumentation	2. Feedback
3. Reflection	3. Coaching and Mentoring

team building and they were aimed primarily at changing individual attitudes and values. Interventions based on T-groups have been called by such names as *sensitivity training, encounter groups,* and *L-groups* ("L" standing for "learning").

Purpose of the Laboratory-Training Group. The purpose of a T-group is to provide participants with intense experiences designed to help them examine their ways of interacting with others, their styles of self-presentation, their basic life positions, their values, and other issues. The participants work in small groups of eight to twelve people for periods ranging from one to two weeks.

These groups work essentially without an agenda and with only limited guidance from OD consultants. The only announced agenda focuses on learning about self and others. A few norms are stated, and the OD consultant monitors them: The discussion centers on the present, and there is no authority hierarchy in the group. Each participant is afforded opportunities to experiment with new behaviors in an open, trusting climate that is created after several days of hard work. Each participant learns how to help others and how a group is formed.

Models of T-Groups. Two models can be used to explain the working of T-groups (Lynton & Pareek, 1990): (1) Lewin's three-stage model of learning; and (2) cognitive dissonance.

In Lewin's model, the three learning stages are *unfreezing, moving,* and *refreezing.* Unfreezing is stimulated by the nondirective and thus unexpected behavior of the OD consultant, the undefined situation, and open feedback. Moving is stimulated by the group experience itself, in which new norms and roles are established and accepted. Refreezing occurs as differentiated roles are developed, norms are stabilized, and members—including the OD consultant—are accepted by the group.

In the cognitive-dissonance model, participant development is facilitated by the dissonance or discord created. The participants need to reduce that dissonance, which stems from discrepancies between the expected and the actual in at least four key areas (Lynton & Pareek, 1990):

1. Between the participants' expectations of the consultant and actual consultant behavior. Consultants avoid all attempts made by others to seduce, force, or otherwise get them to conform to the participants' initial expectations.
2. Between a participant's self-concept and actual laboratory behavior.
3. Between the participants' expectations of the group's reactions and the group's actual reactions.
4. Between the image that a participant wishes to project and the image that others in fact perceive.

These types of dissonance make T-groups intense but disturbing experiences, and they probably also explain why T-groups produce high rates of learning retention. (Dissonance between beliefs and facts leads to discomfort, which in turn prompts learning to occur.) Research findings from the U.S. Bureau of Research place T-group retention rates at 75 percent, compared with 55 percent for visual material and 35 percent for lecture presentation (Lynton & Pareek, 1990).

T-groups do have their limitations, though:

- The OD consultants who work with such groups must be highly trained and skilled;
- In their early stages, T-groups produce high anxiety among participants;
- T-groups seem to work best with a minimum of eight and a maximum of twelve participants; and
- An effective T-group requires at least a three-day duration.

2. Instrumentation

To experience firsthand what it is like to fill out an instrument, complete Activity 1 in Exhibit 9-2 before reading this section.

What Is SAFI?

Psychological tests, projective techniques, questionnaires, checklists, and other types of inventories are called *instruments*. The use of instruments in OD interventions may be on the increase. For person-focused interventions, Self-Awareness through Feedback from Instruments (SAFI) is a very powerful intervention. In SAFI, participants take the initiative and use the scores they receive on instruments to find ways to increase their interpersonal effectiveness.

There are nine steps involved in SAFI:

Exhibit 9-2: Activity 1

Instructions: Read the following statements. To the left of each statement, note how frequently you behave in this way by writing a number that represents the frequency.

5	4	3	2	1
almost always	often	sometimes	occasionally	rarely or never

_____ 1. I assure my subordinates of my availability to them.

_____ 2. I encourage my subordinates to question me about what should or should not be done.

_____ 3. I provide my subordinates with the solutions to their problems.

_____ 4. I admonish my subordinates for not acting according to my instructions.

_____ 5. I help my subordinates to become aware of some of their strengths.

_____ 6. I help my subordinates to see the ethical dimensions of some of their actions.

_____ 7. I instruct my subordinates in detail about work problems and their solutions.

_____ 8. I reassure my subordinates of my continued help.

_____ 9. I give clear instructions to my subordinates about what should or should not be done.

_____ 10. I help my subordinates to examine the appropriateness of proposed action.

_____ 11. I encourage my subordinates to come to me frequently to seek my advice and help.

_____ 12. I clearly prescribe standards of behavior to be followed in my work unit.

From Pareek, U. (1984). Interpersonal Styles: The SPIRO Instrument. In J.W. Pfeiffer & L.D. Goodstein (Eds.), *The 1984 Annual: Developing Human Resources*, pp. 126-129. San Diego, CA: Pfeiffer & Company.

1. *Completion of the instrument*—Participants complete an instrument that has been standardized by experts.

2. *Conceptual input*—Participants read the theory associated with the instrument. This step familiarizes them with the instrument's conceptual framework. If an OD consultant is available, he or she clarifies the concepts underlying the instrument.

3. *Prediction*—Based on what the participants understand about the theory and meaning of the instrument, they predict their scores to reflect their own self-perceptions and their understanding of their own styles and behaviors.

4. *Scoring*—Participants score their completed instruments according to the procedures provided by the instrument's author.

5. *Interpretation*—Participants write down the interpretations and implications of their scores.

6. *Feedback*—Participants check the instrument feedback with other significant people whom they trust, such as managers, peers, and subordinates. They then collect factual evidence to confirm or question their interpretations and reconsider the implications of their scores.

7. *Action planning*—Participants decide to improve aspects of their personal styles or behavior and prepare plans to experiment with new styles or behave differently.

8. *Experimentation*—Participants implement their action plans, keeping detailed notes of satisfactory and frustrating experiences. An OD consultant, if one is available, provides guidance.

9. *Follow-up*—After a time lapse, the participants again complete the instrument to determine whether there is significant change in the scores. They elicit feedback from others whom they trust about any behavioral changes that have been observed.

When an OD consultant is available, he or she monitors these steps with participants, even when they work in a group. The advantage of group work is that it affords an opportunity for feedback among group members. In addition, it reinforces mutual learning.

Follow-Up for Activity 1

At this point refer to Activity 1 again. Add your ratings on the various items as shown below. The twelve items are part of an instrument on interpersonal style that is discussed in the following paragraphs.

The four style measures, shown in Exhibit 9-3, are, in the terms of transactional analysis (Harris, 1969), "OK" and "not OK" dimensions of the Parent ego state (nurturing and regulating). If your score on the Supportive style is higher than your score on the Rescuing style, you are effectively using your Nurturing Parent in your organizational role. Similarly, the operating effectiveness of your Regulating Parent is indicated by a higher ratio of Normative/Prescriptive styles. For more details read Pareek (1984).

Advantages and Disadvantages of Instruments

Using Instruments in Human Resource Development (Pfeiffer & Ballew, 1988), offers helpful suggestions to HRD professionals who wish to employ instruments. The authors also list

Exhibit 9-3: The Four Style Measures of the Instrument in Activity 1

Items	Styles	Parent	Dimension
1 + 5 + 8	Supportive	Nurturing	OK
2 + 6 + 10	Normative	Regulating	OK
3 + 7 + 11	Rescuing	Nurturing	Not OK
4 + 9 + 12	Prescriptive	Regulating	Not OK

various advantages and disadvantages of the technology of instrumentation. The list in Exhibit 9-4 is adapted from that volume.[1]

Avoiding the Disadvantages of Using Instruments

Here are a few suggestions for avoiding the disadvantages of using instruments in person-focused OD interventions:

1. Legitimize the use of instrumentation with the participants.

   - Prior to the beginning of the session, establish clear expectations concerning instruments and their value to the group experience.

   - Be ready to intervene to refocus the group discussion if participants use the instrument as a flight mechanism.

   - Minimize anxieties by explaining how the results will be used so that more learning can occur. The respondents should know that instruments are not

---

[1] From Pfeiffer, J.W., and Ballew, A.C. (1988). *Using Instruments in Human Resource Development*. San Diego, CA: Pfeiffer & Company. Adapted by permission of Pfeiffer & Company.

Exhibit 9-4: Advantages and Disadvantages of Instrumentation

Advantages

- Enables early, easy learning of theory
- Promotes personal involvement and commitment
- Develops early understanding of constructs and terminology
- Supplies personal feedback sooner than other participants are able to
- Facilitates contracting for new behavior
- Fosters open reception of feedback through low threat
- Allows comparisons of individuals with norm groups
- Promotes involvement with data and feedback process
- Surfaces latent issues
- Allows the OD consultant to focus the group and control content
- Facilitates longitudinal assessment of change

Disadvantages

- Engenders fear of exposure
- Encourages labeling
- Promotes flight from confrontation
- Generates time-consuming nitpicking
- Fosters dependence on the OD consultant
- Makes the OD consultant an "expert"; can result in feedback overload
- Triggers anger and "test anxiety"
- Makes distortion of feedback possible through manipulation of test scores

meant to be used to evaluate them and that the results will be used instead to facilitate learning or to plan change interventions.

2. Make a concerted effort to remove the aura of mystery that surrounds instrumentation.

- Discuss the margin of error and other factors that contribute to less-than-absolute results.

- Allow and encourage participants to explore the instrument thoroughly so that they see how it was designed and how their scores were derived.

- Clarify the theoretical basis of the instrument.

3. Ensure that time is made available for participants to process the data derived from the instrument.

- Provide an opportunity for participants to talk through their scores and to compare their scores with those of others.

- Emphasize and legitimize different life perspectives and orientations.

4. Assure participants that they have control over their own data.

- Carefully define the ways in which scores are to be shared or not shared.

- Emphasize that scores will not be reported to the participants' managers.

3. Reflection

Reflection is a form of self-directed study. Effective managers spend time thinking about what should be done to solve problems or seize opportunities. Schön (1983) calls such people "reflective practitioners." These managers are concerned about understanding the turbulent external environment, the dynamics inside the organization, the processes by which the organization adapts itself to changing conditions, and the means by which it influences the environment. As Schön (1983) observes:

> When practitioners do not reflect on their own inquiry, they keep their intuitive understanding tacit and are inattentive to the limits of their scope of reflective attention. The remedy to the justification of practice and to the construction of reflection-in-action is the same: a redirection of attention to the system of knowing-in-practice and to reflection-in-practice itself. (p. 282)

The relationship between an expert and a practitioner may be based on what Schön calls a traditional contract or a reflective contract. In a traditional contract, the sense of security stems from the satisfaction of finding the best available person, placing faith in the expert, and experiencing a sense of comfort by following the expert's advice. In the reflective contract, satisfaction stems from "discovering" experts and realizing mutual dependence with them.

Based on the study of reflective practitioners in several fields, Schön (1987) concludes that the practicum is the best method of developing reflective practitioners:

> A practicum is a setting designed for the task of learning a practice. Participants learn by undertaking projects that simulate and simplify practice, or they take on real-world projects under close supervision. The practicum stands in an intermediate space between the practice world, the "lay" world of ordinary life, and the esoteric world of the academy. (p. 37)

The practicum emphasizes that participants learn "a kind of reflection-in-action that goes beyond stable rules—not only by devising new methods of reasoning but also by constructing and testing new categories of understanding, strategies of action, and ways of framing problems" (Schön, 1987, p. 39).

Schön (1987, p. 40) has distinguished between three kinds of practicum: technical, thinking, and reflective. The third kind need not obviate the first and second. It helps participants to learn "to become proficient at a kind of reflection-in-action. They are reflective in the further sense that they depend on their effectiveness on a reciprocally reflective dialogue of coach and student."

Reflection as an art of analyzing problems requires both vigor (taking detailed notes on what has happened immediately after a phenomenon); detachment (looking at the notes objectively and analyzing the situation); analysis of the theory-in-action used; and reflective experimentation, usually accepting someone's help in further reflection and even in joint experimentation and exploration. All practitioners in various fields need to develop reflection-in-action and reflection on reflection-in-action.

OD Consultant-Active Interventions

Organization development consultants organize these interventions, help participants reflect and experiment, and monitor and reinforce participants' change behavior.

1. Training

Training is probably the most widely used OD intervention. Much has been written about it. Instead of rehashing descriptions of well-known training methods, this section draws attention to critical issues. Readers interested in a more in-depth discussion should refer to Lynton and Pareek (1990) and to treatments such as those found in Rothwell and Kazanas (1992) and Rothwell and Sredl (1992).

Emphasize Strategy

Greater emphasis on strategy is one way to achieve linkage between organizational/individual needs and training efforts. Several questions need to be asked before training programs are organized:

- What competencies must be acquired by individuals and groups?
- What are the goals of training as jointly determined by the work organization and the training institution?

Such questions should yield information about what training to offer so that an appropriate performance-improvement strategy can be devised (Rothwell & Kazanas, 1994).

Three phases of training strategy need detailed planning (Lynton & Pareek, 1990): (1) the pretraining phase, (2) the training phase, and (3) the post-training phase.

Effective training addresses broad, basic issues, such as purpose, options for encouraging learning, and achieving goodness of fit within the organizational and social contexts that must first support the training and then the developments that training is expected to promote.

Evaluate the Training

Measuring the effectiveness of training helps organizations to institute work-based evaluation well after participants have returned from training and establishes the total cost of training instead of only the direct costs or fee payments. Total training costs include participants' salaries, travel, lodging, and meal expenses. Also included are the costs of replacing the participants, extra organizational costs, and training overhead. Such realistic cost accounting yields figures at least twice those now commonly used and can quickly lead clients to insist on more effective training.

Ensure Organizational Readiness for Change

Organization development consultants should give much more weight to organizational readiness for change and support for improvement than they historically have given to these factors. When support is lacking, training does little or nothing to improve performance—but it does increase the frustration of the best participants and motivate them to leave for situations in which competence is valued more.

In this larger picture, the quality of training itself is secondary. More is known about how to conduct training effectively than about how to assess organizational readiness and build support for change.

Broaden the Trainer's Role

It is important to broaden the trainer's role to include consulting with participant organizations, especially matching participant selection with organizational-change strategies and ensuring organizational support for improved performance after training. While effective training depends greatly on corresponding OD efforts, the reverse is also true: Organization development interventions can be accelerated by developing competent people in key positions. The trainer plays a key role in developing both individuals and the organization.

Recognition of this fact tends to blur the distinctions between training and OD and between training and follow-up activities. More trainers will have to become competent in these related roles and more familiar with—and credible in—work settings. The inclusion of more administrators, line managers, and field staff in training departments or functions can help to build these bridges so that training and practice can reinforce each other more often than they have historically done.

Develop Consultant Competence in Action Research

Four beliefs underlie the position that all OD consultants need to undertake action research (Lynton & Pareek, 1990):

1. Solutions to problems are more effective and enduring when they emerge from systematic research than when they result from the dictates of authority or solely from an OD consultant's intuition.

2. Consultant research on problems contributes more to the solution of those problems than does research performed by others.

3. Research consists of analyzing problems, searching for solutions, and testing and evaluating solutions. These skills can be learned and developed by OD consultants; research is not the sole prerogative of experts.

4. Development of people's capabilities is the basis for improvement in practice.

Action research is the application of the scientific method to problem solving; it involves the same steps as the scientific method. (See Chapter 2 for a more complete discussion of action research.) A list of topics for action research on the part of OD consultants has been suggested by Lynton and Pareek (1990).

Take the Cultural Context into Account

Training should take into account the cultural context in which it is carried out. Training, like OD, is a means of developing or changing culture. However, trainers need to be sensitive to the societal and organizational culture. The training strategy needs to be designed to move step-by-step from where the organization is to where it "should" go. Training can become an important instrument for cultural change provided that it strikes a proper balance between being sensitive to the existing culture and attempting to change norms and values in line with what "should be" (as uncovered through action research).

2. Feedback

When feelings or perceptions are communicated to individuals about their behavior, performance, or personal styles, this information is called feedback. Interpersonal feedback occurs often in everyday work life. Managers coach their employees on performance; they share perceptions about employee achievements, pointing out strengths as well as areas in which opportunities for improvement exist. Opinions about styles and ways of behaving are expressed so that the feedback recipient may use such information to improve performance. Employees also provide their managers with feedback, for example about decisions made or actions taken that may be perceived differently from the ways in which they were intended. In addition, peers and coworkers provide one another with feedback.

The Functions of Feedback

Interpersonal feedback involves at least two people: one who gives feedback and one who receives it. The main purpose of feedback is to help the recipient to increase personal and interpersonal effectiveness. However, giving and receiving feedback can also be viewed separately in terms of the purposes served (see Exhibit 9-5). It is assumed that feedback is given and received with openness and sensitivity.

Giving Feedback Effectively. The effectiveness of feedback depends on the behaviors and responses of both people, the feedback provider and the feedback recipient. One who gives feedback, such as an OD consultant, can increase its effectiveness by ensuring that it:

- Is descriptive rather than evaluative;
- Is focused on the behavior rather than the personality of the recipient;
- Concerns behavior that is modifiable;
- Is specific and based on data rather than general and based on impressions;
- Provides data from the provider's own experience;
- Reinforces positive new behavior and what the recipient has done well;
- Suggests rather than prescribes improvement avenues;
- Is continual rather than sporadic;
- Is based on need and is elicited by the recipient;
- Is intended to help rather than wound;
- Satisfies the needs of both the provider and the recipient;

Exhibit 9-5: The Functions of Feedback

Giving Feedback

- Provides verifiable data about behavior
- Encourages collection of data from several sources
- Suggests alternatives to be considered
- Improves interpersonal communication
- Establishes culture of openness
- Promotes interpersonal trust
- Facilitates autonomy

Receiving Feedback

- Helps in processing behavioral data
- Increases self-awareness
- Increases sensitivity in picking up cues
- Encourages experimentation with new behavior
- Helps in building an integrated self
- Encourages openness
- Develops mutuality

- Lends itself to verification by the recipient;
- Is well-timed; and
- Contributes to the rapport between the provider and the recipient and enhances their relationship.

Receiving Feedback Effectively. The effectiveness of feedback depends as much on how it is received and used as it does on how it is given. If the feedback disconfirms an expectation of the recipient (for example, concerning his or her self-image), dissonance is created (see "Models of Laboratory-Training Groups" earlier in this chapter).

According to dissonance theory, disconfirming an expectation stimulates psychological tension. The feedback recipient may reduce dissonance by reacting in either a defensive or a confronting manner. Exhibit 9-6 summarizes defensive and confronting behavior.

When people feel threatened by the feedback they receive (for example, if they are criticized or blamed or are given negative feedback that they do not agree with), they tend to build a defense to protect themselves. (Freud first introduced the concept of defense mechanisms and studied them.)

Using defensive behaviors to deal with threatening feedback is like using pain-killing drugs that reduce awareness of pain but do not address its cause; defensive behaviors create an illusion of having dealt with a situation but do not change that situation. Hence, defensive behaviors reduce anxiety but do not resolve the conflict felt by the feedback recipient. Excessive reliance on defensive behaviors is likely to produce a "conflicted self."

On the other hand, if confronting behavior is used, conflict is reduced; over time the feedback recipient forms an "integrated self." Of course, defensive behavior is not always bad, and on some occasions it may be warranted. But if both people involved in giving and receiving feedback are interested in maintaining a relationship of trust and openness, then defensive behavior undermines that goal, resulting in feedback that is ineffective.

In order to benefit from feedback, a recipient should examine the defensive behaviors that he or she uses when

Exhibit 9-6: Defensive and Confronting Behavior in Dealing with Feedback

DEFENSIVE BEHAVIOR	CONFRONTING BEHAVIOR
Denial	Owning
Rationalization	Self-analysis
Projection	Empathy
Displacement	Exploration
Quick acceptance	Collecting data
Withdrawal	Expressing feelings
Aggression toward authority	Seeking help
Humor	Exhibiting and sharing concern
Cynicism	Listening
Intellectualization	Exhibiting a positive critical attitude
Generalization	Experimenting
Pairing	Relating to group
Results in conflicted self	**Results in integrated self**

receiving feedback. Then the individual should prepare a plan (preferably with the help of others) for reducing those defensive behaviors and adopting the confronting behaviors listed in Exhibit 9-6.

Confronting behavior helps a person to build relationships and collect more helpful feedback. The way in which a person receives and uses feedback also influences the way in which others give feedback. The recipient may test ideas and experiment with new behaviors on a limited basis, seeking more feedback to find out how others view his or her self-improvement efforts. This kind of effort will set in motion a self-improvement cycle leading to increased interpersonal effectiveness.

If feedback is given in the spirit of a trusting and open relationship and if it is received in the same way, it can become a most powerful instrument of change. But if feedback is not properly received, it can disrupt interpersonal relationships and undermine group development.

3. Coaching and Mentoring[2]

The Concepts, Objectives, and Processes of Coaching and Mentoring

Both managerial and nonmanagerial employees develop themselves by interacting with those whom they admire and by building trusting relationships with people who nurture, support, and guide them. The relationship involved in a mentoring situation, with an experienced person in the organization serving as mentor, is especially important; in the development of employees, there is no substitute for it. This relationship differs from any established in a training setting in its sheer intensity, its focus on establishing mutual understanding, and its confidentiality.

Although frequently associated with efforts to develop young employees, a mentoring relationship can help anyone. When young people join organizations, they need guidance and support from experienced people whom they admire and from whom they can receive advice, support, and the safety of confidentiality.

---

[2] From Pareek, U., & Rao, T. (1990). Performance Coaching. In J. Pfeiffer (Ed.), *The 1990 Annual: Developing Human Resources* (pp. 249-262.). San Diego, CA: Pfeiffer and Company. Adapted by permission of the publisher.

The word *mentor* has its origin in Greek mythology. Before going on a ten-year voyage, Odysseus left his son Telemachus in the care of an old man named Mentor, who not only helped the boy to become a competent young man but he also saved his life. This relationship became a model for what is now widely known as mentoring. The concept of mentoring centers around the emotional support and guidance given by the mentor, an experienced person, to a protégé, a less-experienced person. A mentor need not be—and preferably should not be—the protégé's manager.

Mentoring affords an opportunity for individuals to share their concerns and receive moral support and guidance for their development. The mentoring process begins when a trusting relationship is established. Mentors model behavioral norms for their protégés. They also listen to their protégés' personal and job concerns, help their protégés search for solutions to problems, share relevant experiences, respond to their protégés' emotional needs without creating inappropriate dependency, and cultivate long-lasting yet informal personal relationships.

In addition to receiving the benefits of mentoring, employees need to develop trusting and supportive relationships with their managers, who can set challenging work goals, provide support to achieve those goals, help in analyzing barriers to higher performance, and plan goals for the future. This process, called coaching, is defined as the assistance that managers provide to their employees by analyzing and guiding on-the-job performance. While mentoring centers around general development and psychological well-being, coaching is linked to the analysis of job performance and the identification of training needs.

Coaching provides a nonthreatening climate in which employees can freely express to their managers the tensions, conflicts, concerns, and problems they are experiencing. The coaching process helps employees to understand their strengths and weaknesses while increasing their understanding of the work environment. The following are additional responsibilities of coaching:

- To increase employees' personal and interpersonal effectiveness by providing not only feedback about their behavior but also assistance in analyzing their interpersonal competence;

- To review each employee's progress in achieving work objectives;

- To identify problems that are hindering progress;

- To assist in generating alternatives and a final action plan for dealing with identified problems;

- To encourage employees to set goals for continual improvement;

- To contract to provide whatever support employees need while they implement action plans; and

- To help employees realize their potential.

Both coaching and mentoring involve support offered by one person who is senior in competence, experience, expertise, or position to another person who is less senior.

Three processes are central to successful coaching and mentoring: communicating, empowering, and helping. *Communicating* means giving messages (asking questions or giving feedback and responding) and receiving messages (listening). *Empowering* involves enabling another person to exercise autonomy, providing positive reinforcement so that desirable behavior is strengthened, and helping a person to learn from the behaviors of mentors or managers by identifying with those behaviors. *Helping* behavior stems from the manager's or mentor's concern and empathy for an employee. It is also based on mutuality in the relationship; for example, the employee responds as much to the manager's needs as the manager responds to the employee's needs. Finally, helping involves identifying an employee's developmental needs so that he or she can develop and increase personal effectiveness.

An OD consultant can facilitate effective mentoring and coaching by emphasizing the importance of these processes, by helping people at all levels to improve skills associated with mentoring and coaching, and by serving as an appropriate role model of specific competencies.

Effective Listening

Effective listening, empathic response, and supportive questioning are important in mentoring and coaching. Listening deserves special consideration; it means paying careful attention to the messages that others send.

Consequently, coaching sessions should, if possible, take place in a setting that is free from interruptions so that managers can devote their undivided attention. The manager as coach must listen for content and feelings underlying the employee's literal message. Listening for hidden messages is a skill that can be practiced.

An employee needs to know that his or her manager is actively listening. A manager can demonstrate active listening by assuming attentive postures (such as leaning forward) and maintaining eye contact. When an employee has completed a message, the manager should paraphrase, mirror, or reflect what was said to ensure that the message was understood as intended. For example, an employee might say, "I'm really mad. I've tried to do my best in the past year. I've worked twice as hard as anyone else in the office, but I still haven't been promoted." The manager might respond, "You feel that you have not been shown appropriate recognition for your hard work." Managers who demonstrate that they have heard and understood employees' messages increase the effectiveness of their interaction with employees.

Complete Activity 2 (Exhibit 9-7) before reading further.

Asking Questions

During coaching sessions, managers typically pose questions to obtain information, establish rapport, clarify what was said, and stimulate thought. The questions they ask and their methods of questioning can either facilitate or impede the communication process. Some questions make employees lapse into silence or respond in a way that indicates dependence on their managers; other questions lead to openness and autonomy.

The same principle applies to OD consultants. The way in which they ask questions can either increase or decrease the effectiveness of their interventions. Questions that hinder communication are described in the following paragraphs:

Critical Questions. Such questions serve to criticize, reprimand, or express doubt about people. They lead to a "distancing effect" that separates managers from their employees or OD consultants from their clients. In addition, a sarcastic tone may be perceived as criticism even when the words are not critical. When discussing performance that has fallen short of standards, a manager should remain continually aware of his or her phraseology and tone. For example, a question such as "Why did you

Exhibit 9-7: Activity 2

Listening to Concerns

Instructions: Following are five employee statements. For each of the five, identify the employee's concern by completing the reply statement following "because" in the right column.

1. I am really mad. I have tried to do my best in the past year. I have worked twice as hard as anyone else in this office, but I still haven't been promoted.

   You feel angry because

2. I don't know why I was transferred to this department. I wasn't given any reason—they just sent me. And I don't like it.

   You feel puzzled and resentful because

3. This is absolutely ridiculous. I have only been doing this job for a few weeks, and my manager has decided to transfer me because I'm not producing as much as the others.

   You feel angry because

4. My supervisor obviously does not like me. No matter what I do, it isn't good enough. I want to change to a different department.

   You feel trapped because

5. I don't understand my boss. One day he tells me what a great worker I am, and the next day he says I'm not good at anything.

   You are puzzled because

fail to meet the deadline for your last project?" communicates criticism, whereas the question "What might account for the fact that your last project was late?" invites an examination and discussion of issues. Similarly, a question such as "How did you miss another deadline?" constitutes a reprimand, and "How can you meet your next deadline when you failed to meet the last one?" expresses doubt in the employee's abilities. Critical questions undermine an employee's self-confidence and the manager's objectives in coaching in the same way that they undermine the client's confidence and the OD consultant's objectives for a change effort. Such questions also produce resentment among people.

Evaluating or Testing Questions. These questions are posed to determine whether people are "right" or "wrong" or to discover how much they know. These questions imply that managers (or OD consultants) have a superior attitude, and they make employees (or clients) feel like witnesses who are undergoing cross-examination. For example, a manager whose objective is to find out why an employee is missing deadlines can easily slip into this kind of questioning. Again, tone is important and conveys attitude in a way that words alone do not. Testing questions are similar to critical questions in their negative effect on people.

Leading Questions. Leading questions are offered in a way designed to evoke the answers that the questioner wants, although such responses may or may not be the real answers. For example, a manager may ask, "You weren't able to meet your last deadline because the maintenance department fell behind, right?" or "Were you unable to meet your last deadline because the maintenance people wouldn't cooperate?" As another example, an OD consultant may ask, "That's really the cause of this problem, isn't it?" A leading question almost seduces the recipient into giving the desired answer. Its effect is to stop further exploration of the issue and produce misleading or incorrect information.

Other questions help rather than hinder the development of healthy relationships between managers and their employees or between OD consultants and their clients. Several of these questions are described next.

Questions Eliciting Help or Suggestions. Such questions can indicate that the questioner has faith in the respondent. For example, a manager may ask, "How do you think I should deal with this problem?" When managers and employees share open, trusting relationships, employees may also pose similar questions. The same principle applies to OD consultants and participants in a person-focused OD intervention.

Clarifying Questions. Clarifying questions yield information about performance issues and problems. Questions of this kind are frequently asked in connection with paraphrasing, mirroring, or reflecting what someone has said. An example is "You're worried about your lack of knowledge of the new system. Is that so?" Clarifying questions keep people at the same level of understanding throughout a conversation.

Empathic Questions. These questions focus on feelings. They serve to express concern rather than find solutions to problems. For example, an OD consultant might ask, "How did you feel when the shipping department sent the wrong order to the customer?" Such questions indicate concern about the impact of an event or a situation on others. Emphatic questions convey empathy, generate trust, and build the rapport that is so necessary to successful performance coaching and to successful person-focused OD interventions.

Open Questions. Open questions are those that cannot be answered with a simple "yes" or "no." Instead, they stimulate reflection and thought and require a lengthier response. Open questions usually begin with such words as who, what, when, where, why, and how. They invite people to be creative in exploring issues and in sharing ideas.

Responding

The way in which a manager responds to an employee's comments can be either useful or dysfunctional, just as the way in which an OD consultant responds to a client can be either useful or dysfunctional. Responses that are empathic, supportive, and exploratory are useful. Those that alienate, criticize, or deliver orders are dysfunctional. Exhibit 9-8 lists behaviors that are useful as well as those that are dysfunctional.

Sperry and Hess (1974) have advocated the use of contact counseling, a coaching process based on transactional analysis that makes use of techniques called keying, responding, and guiding. *Keying* means "reading" people. Managers use appropriate frames of reference to perceive what employees mean by their verbal and nonverbal responses. In *responding*, managers replay what was learned from keying in a manner that communicates understanding of the message. The final technique, *guiding*, means motivating or helping employees to change behavior in ways that help them to accomplish objectives more effectively. Organization development consultants may use the same techniques with clients in person-focused interventions.

Empowering

One objective in performance counseling, mentoring, and person-focused OD interventions is to increase individual

Exhibit 9-8: Dysfunctional and Useful Managerial Responses

DYSFUNCTIONAL BEHAVIORS	USEFUL BEHAVIORS
Alienating	**Empathic**
• Continually stressing conformity	• Leveling
• Failing to encourage	• Building rapport
• Failing to give verbal responses	• Identifying feelings
• Listening passively (rather than actively)	
	Supportive
Critical	• Acknowledging problems, concerns, feelings
• Pointing out inconsistencies	• Accepting differences of opinion
• Repeatedly mentioning weaknesses	• Showing understanding
• Belittling	• Communicating availability
	• Committing support
	• Expressing trust
Directive	**Exploring**
• Prescribing	• Asking open questions
• Giving orders	• Reflecting
• Threatening	• Sharing
• Failing to provide options	• Probing
• Quoting rules and regulations	
• Pointing out only one acceptable way	**Closing**
	• Summarizing
	• Concluding
	• Contracting for follow-up and help

potential for autonomy. One important mechanism in the empowering process, especially in mentoring relationships, is called modeling. When mentors or supervisors are viewed as positive models, employees identify with them and feel more powerful as a result. (The same principle applies to OD consultants, as emphasized repeatedly in this book.)

Levinson (1962) has stressed the importance of the process by which employees identify with their managers. One major influence that promotes employee development is the opportunity to associate and identify with people who have greater experience, skill, and influence.

According to McClelland (1976), identifying is the first stage in developing psychological maturity and is a legitimate need that should be fulfilled. Levinson (1962) identifies several ways in which influencers block identification: lack of time, intolerance for mistakes, complete rejection of dependency needs, repression of rivalry, and failure to examine the relationship shared by the influencer and the person who is influenced. Levinson suggests that to facilitate the process of identifying, managers should examine their own process of identifying with others and the needs of employees.

The ways in which managers exercise their influence over employees either empowers employees or reduces their capacity to be autonomous. Influencing is often thought to decrease the autonomy of people who are influenced and to direct them into predetermined channels. However, positive influence exercised during a coaching session has the opposite effect: The person influenced is granted a wider scope in decision making. Flanders (1970) makes a distinction between these two modes of influencing: (1) The direct mode restricts the freedom of the person who is influenced, and (2) the indirect mode increases the freedom of the person who is influenced.

Flanders classifies criticism and punishment as forms of direct influencing; encouragement is a form of indirect influencing. When people are criticized or punished, they avoid the related activities in the future. Consequently, their freedom is restricted. On the other hand, people who are praised or positively recognized are encouraged to explore new directions and thereby experience greater freedom and autonomy. For coaching to have the intended effect, managers must use the indirect mode by accepting their employees' feelings as well as their own. They should also be able to express those feelings, acknowledge and praise good ideas contributed by employees, and raise questions that prompt further exploration.

Nurturing and Helping

Coaching is essentially helping, and helping involves several processes. Helping may be offered by managers during mentoring or coaching; it may also be offered by OD consultants in the context of person-focused OD interventions.

If managers do not feel absolute positive regard for their employees, they cannot provide effective coaching. Coaches show concern by empathizing with their employees. These feelings should be reflected in the questions asked and the tone of the conversation. Managers should continually ask themselves how much concern and genuine empathy they feel for the employees whom they coach. Without genuine managerial concern, coaching will degenerate into a ritual and cannot achieve its goals.

Coaching means receiving help in addition to providing it. Unless both people involved in a coaching relationship feel free to ask for help and offer it to each other, that relationship cannot be effective. Mutuality is based on trust and the genuine perception that each person has something worthwhile to contribute to the relationship. Although coaches occupy superior positions, they continue to learn and receive help from those whom they coach.

Mutuality can be cultivated through special techniques. Morrisey (1972) has suggested a few: the *you-we technique,* the second-hand compliment, the advice-request technique, and summarizing. To employ the *you-we technique,* the manager uses "you" to compliment the employee but "we" to designate a need for improvement: "You are doing a great job; we have a problem." The *second-hand compliment* means relaying a compliment from a third party: "Mr. Reynolds says that you've done an excellent job for him." The *advice-request technique* means asking an employee for suggestions and advice about a performance issue. Finally, *summarizing* at the end of a coaching session helps to clarify what decisions have been made and who has assumed what responsibilities. Summarizing integrates the entire discussion.

The Sequential Phases of Coaching

Coaching helps employees to grow and develop in the organization. Every manager coaches employees, either knowingly or unknowingly, every day. An effective manager, functioning as a coach, helps employees to become more aware of their strengths and limitations, improve on their strengths, and overcome their limitations. By establishing mutuality and providing support as well as maintaining the proper emotional climate, managers help their employees to develop. Mutuality involves working with each employee to develop action plans for growth in the organization; support involves accepting each employee as a whole person—including both strengths and limitations—and encouraging each employee with warmth.

Coaching requires certain interpersonal skills. An OD consultant can help managers to acquire those skills, assuming that managers are genuinely interested in developing their employees. Such skills are particularly important at the time of performance review. Although a good manager coaches employees regularly whenever the need arises, a formal performance review provides an important opportunity for coaching. Such a review passes through phases corresponding to skills needed by the manager: rapport building, exploring, and action planning. Exhibit 9-9 presents these three phases, the activities that characterize them, and the coaching behaviors that help and hinder each activity. The following paragraphs discuss the three phases in more detail.

Building Rapport

In the rapport-building phase, the manager attempts to establish a climate of acceptance, warmth, support, openness, and mutuality. Such a climate is established by adopting the employee's frame of reference, by listening and becoming attuned to his or her problems and feelings, by communicating understanding to the employee, and by expressing empathy for (and genuine interest in) the employee.

A manager should thus strive to foster confidence so that the employee opens up and frankly shares perceptions, problems, concerns, and feelings. Three basic managerial activities are involved in this phase: attending, listening, and accepting.

Attending. In setting the stage for a coaching session, a manager should attend to the employee and should convey the importance of the session. Generally a coaching session is held in a private office. After taking steps to prevent disturbance from phone calls or other sources, the manager offers the employee a

Exhibit 9-9: The Sequential Phases of Performance Coaching

PHASES	HELPFUL BEHAVIORS	HINDERING BEHAVIORS
Rapport Building **Attending**	• Observing rituals • Conversing about personal matters • Smiling	• Discussing behavior immediately
Listening to feelings, concerns, and problems	• Indicating physical attention (posture) • Maintaining eye contact • Responding (verbally and nonverbally) • Eliminating or excluding telephone calls, noise, and disturbances	• Indicating distraction (paying attention to other things such as telephone calls) • Signing letters, talking to others during conversation
Accepting	• Communicating feelings and concerns • Paraphrasing feelings • Sharing one's own experience	• Failing to respond • Listening passively for a long period

Exhibit 9-9: The Sequential Phases of Performance Coaching (continued)

PHASES	HELPFUL BEHAVIORS	HINDERING BEHAVIORS
Exploring **Investigating**	• Mirroring or paraphrasing • Asking open questions • Encouraging people to explore	• Criticizing • Avoiding or hedging
Identifying the problem	• Asking questions to focus on the specific problem • Encouraging people to generate information • Narrowing the problem	• Suggesting what the problem is
Diagnosing	• Asking exploratory questions • Generating several possible causes	• Suggesting the cause
Action Planning **Searching**	• Generating alternative solutions • Asking questions about possible solutions	• Advising

Exhibit 9-9: The Sequential Phases of Performance Coaching (continued)

PHASES	HELPFUL BEHAVIORS	HINDERING BEHAVIORS
Making decisions	• Asking questions about feasibility, priority, and pros and cons	• Directing
	• Discussing solutions and jointly choosing one	• Devising an inflexible plan and holding people to it
	• Discussing an action plan	
	• Establishing a contingency plan	
Supporting	• Identifying specific help that will be needed	• Promising general help
	• Monitoring	
	• Creating a contract to provide specific support and to monitor	

chair and closes the door to ensure privacy. All such rituals must come out of the manager's genuine concern for the employee and for the objectives of the session. Most employees can tell when the manager is merely playing the part of concerned coach.

Listening. Active listening is essential to effective coaching, as it is to effective OD consulting. A manager demonstrates active listening by leaning forward and maintaining eye contact.

The manager also must remember to concentrate on nonverbal messages as well as verbal.

Accepting. Establishing a climate in which the employee feels accepted is a necessary part of establishing rapport in coaching (and in person-focused OD interventions). The employee must feel that he or she is wanted, that expressing differences of opinion is acceptable, and that the manager is interested in understanding him or her as a person rather than as merely a role incumbent. The manager establishes the appropriate climate by using active listening and by paraphrasing, mirroring, or reflecting the employee's messages. This approach makes the employee feel understood and valued. It also creates a climate that facilitates the coaching process.

Exploring

In the exploring phase, managers—or OD consultants—help employees to understand themselves and their performance problems. At this point the manager deals with the employee's strengths, weaknesses, and needs just as an OD consultant deals with those of a client. This phase requires the exercise of great skill. No one enjoys being told about weaknesses, so managers—and OD consultants—often find it preferable to assist employees in the process of discovering them. The following activities are characteristic of this phase:

Investigating. The manager helps the employee to investigate performance problems and surface special concerns. This is accomplished by asking open questions and encouraging the employee to talk about issues that concern him or her. Similarly, an OD consultant helps a client to identify issues and investigate them by asking questions and facilitating dialogue.

Identifying the Problem. After investigating, the manager asks questions designed to help the employee focus on a particular problem. These questions should make the problem more specific and generate information about it. For example, if the employee feels that others are uncooperative, the manager might pose questions designed to narrow the problem to the employee's relationships with coworkers. Follow-up questions may then be used to help the employee discover how his or her behavior hinders cooperation.

The same activity applies to OD consultants, who should ask questions to help their clients focus clearly on problems.

Diagnosing. Identifying and investigating a problem should lead to diagnosis. Without diagnosis there is no basis for problem solving. Again, open questions are useful.

Here are a few examples:

- "Why do you think people are put off when you talk with them?"
- "Can you recall occasions when you did receive full cooperation?
- "What might account for the cooperation you have received?"
- "What personal limitations especially bother you?"

Ultimately, diagnosis leads to the generation of several alternative causes of a problem.

Action Planning

In the action-planning phase, the manager and the employee jointly plan specific action steps designed to solve the performance problem and further the employee's development. Three activities are involved in the action-planning phase:

Searching. During searching, the manager helps the employee think of solutions to the identified problem. Several solutions may be discussed, such as training, job rotation, increased responsibility, or role clarification. Generating solutions should be primarily the responsibility of the employee; the manager should offer suggestions only when the employee seems to run out of ideas.

Decision Making. After solutions have been generated, the manager helps the employee to assess the advantages and disadvantages of those solutions, raise questions about the feasibility of the solutions, choose the best solution, and finalize a step-by-step action plan. Both the manager and the employee should realize that action plans may require revision after implementation has begun.

Supporting. In the final stage of coaching, the manager offers support to the employee in implementing the agreed-on action plan. After considerable discussion, the manager and the employee create contracts that detail what support the manager will provide as well as how implementation will be monitored and followed up. After the contract has been created, the coaching session is brought to a close.

Tips for Effective Coaching

The following tips about effective coaching are useful for managers and OD consultants alike:

Make Sure That the Employee Is Willing to Learn from Coaching. On some occasions an employee does not ask for performance coaching, but is (in effect) forced into it. Coaching of this type has limited value and may frustrate both the manager and the employee. In such a situation, the manager should forget about coaching and find out why the employee is not interested in growth. If the manager establishes the proper climate, this kind of discussion can encourage the employee to express his or her true feelings. However, if the employee has difficulty interacting with the manager, a problem-solving session should precede this step.

Encourage the Employee to Function Independently. Sometimes an employee is so loyal that he or she becomes totally dependent on the manager. Periodically all managers should consider whether they have unintentionally fostered such dependent relationships. It is important to allow employees to make their own decisions and thereby increase their autonomy. The same principle holds true in a coaching situation: Employees should bear the chief responsibility for determining what corrective action to take.

Minimize Arguments. One argument is sufficient to make both the manager and the employee feel defensive. The manager should try to accept everything that the employee says and build on it. Acceptance is the best way to help the employee achieve increased self-awareness.

Ensure Adequate Follow-Up. Good coaching sessions will ultimately fail to produce effective results if follow-up is inadequate. When the manager follows up through informal exchanges, he or she makes use of an approach that goes a long way toward communicating interest in the employee. But when the manager fails to follow up, the employee may feel that the coaching he or she receives is artificial and may lose interest in improving performance.

The Process of Mentoring

Levinson, Darrow, Klein, Levinson, & McKee (1978) have been instrumental in defining the mentoring process. Their concept of a mentor includes such roles as teacher, sponsor, counselor, host, guide, exemplar, developer of skills and intellect, and—most important—supporter and OD consultant. Mentoring integrates characteristics of parent-child and peer-support relationships. According to Levinson et al., young people who do not have mentors during their formative years are disadvantaged in terms of their psychological and career development.

Young people often search for and discover appropriate mentors on their own, but enlightened organizational leaders are paying more attention to mentoring and making it an official part of the training process. Young managers with high potential are often the first to be given mentoring experiences. Generally a young manager is assigned to a mentor who is senior in position and age and who sometimes occupies a position that is several hierarchical levels above that of the protégé. Mentors are not necessarily selected from their protégés' departments but are selected for their interest, availability, and "mentoring competence" (image of competence, empathy, and ability to provide emotional support). One mentor should not have more than five protégés.

There are two main phases in the mentoring process: dependence and interdependence. (Counterdependence may in some cases be an intermediate phase between the two.) During the *dependence* phase, the protégé's admiration for the mentor is followed by identification with the mentor, obtaining the mentor's guidance, and checking alternative action ideas with the mentor.

The *interdependence phase* is characterized by trust building. At this point the mentor and the protégé collaborate and provide mutual emotional support. When the mentor overwhelms and overpowers the protégé, counterdependence may develop before interdependence; in this case the protégé rejects the mentor and develops independence. To reach interdependence, the protégé must search for his or her own identity and must come to appreciate the mentor's role as well as the mentoring relationship.

The mentoring process is quite similar to the coaching process. The phases discussed in the section on coaching in this chapter are also applicable to mentoring. The ultimate goal of both coaching and mentoring is to help an employee to attain psychological maturity and effectiveness.

References

Flanders, N. (1970). *Analyzing teacher behavior.* Reading, MA: Addison-Wesley.

Harris, T.A. (1969). *I'm ok—you're ok: A practical guide to transactional analysis.* New York: Harper & Row.

Levinson, D., Darrow, C., Klein, E., Levinson, M., & McKee, B. (1978). *The seasons of a man's life.* New York: Alfred A. Knopf.

Levinson, H. (1962). A psychologist looks at executive development. *Harvard Business Review, 40,* 69-75.

Lynton, R., & Pareek, U. (1990). *Training for development* (2nd ed.). West Hartford, CT: Kumarian Press.

McClelland, D. (1976). Power is the motivator. *Harvard Business Review, 54*(2), 100-110.

Morrisey, G. (1972). *Appraisal and development through objectives and results.* Reading, MA: Addison-Wesley.

Pareek, U. (1984). Interpersonal styles: The SPIRO instrument. In J. Pfeiffer & L. Goodstein (Eds.), *The 1984 annual: Developing human resources* (pp. 119-130). San Diego, CA: Pfeiffer & Company.

Pareek, U., & Rao, T. (1990). Performance coaching. In J. Pfeiffer (Ed.), *The 1990 annual: Developing human resources* (pp. 249-262.). San Diego, CA: Pfeiffer & Company.

Pfeiffer, J. (1988). *Instrumentation kit.* San Diego, CA: Pfeiffer & Company.

Pfeiffer, J., & Ballew, A. (1988). *Using instruments in human resource development (Vol. 2: UA Training Technologies).* San Diego, CA: Pfeiffer & Company.

Rothwell, W., & Kazanas, H. (1992). *Mastering the instructional design process: A systematic approach.* San Francisco: Jossey-Bass.

Rothwell, W., & Kazanas, H. (1994). *Human resource development: A strategic approach* (rev. ed.). Amherst, MA: Human Resource Development Press.

Rothwell, W., & Sredl, H. (1992). *The ASTD reference guide to professional human resource development roles and competencies* (2nd ed.). (2 vols.) Amherst, MA: Human Resource Development Press.

Schön, D. (1983). *The reflective practitioner.* New York: Basic Books.

Schön, D. (1987). *Educating the reflective practitioner.* San Francisco: Jossey-Bass.

Sperry, L., & Hess, L. (1974). *Contact counseling.* Reading, MA: Addison-Wesley.

CHAPTER 10

EVALUATION

Gary N. McLean, Roland Sullivan, and
William J. Rothwell

Evaluation is a significant component of the action research model. As described in Chapter 2, evaluation is the sixth step in an OD intervention; however, it is the piece of the action research model that is most often omitted or abbreviated.

This chapter clarifies what evaluation means in OD, describes what encourages OD consultants to use evaluation and what discourages them from using it, presents a checklist of issues to consider when planning an evaluation, and provides expanded descriptions of the evaluation competencies. Instruments and techniques that can be used for each competency are discussed. This chapter also offers an example of how an evaluation is performed, followed by an exercise in performing an evaluation.

Definition of Evaluation

Evaluation is a set of planned, information-gathering and analytical activities undertaken to provide those responsible for the management of change with a satisfactory assessment of the effects and/or progress of the change effort (Beckhard & Harris, 1977, p. 86).

A commitment to planned evaluation should be made early in the OD process by both the consultant and the client. Planned evaluation allows a consultant to gather and examine data and to judge the value of an OD intervention, usually with the purpose of improving the intervention or deciding whether to continue it.

Workplace realities rarely facilitate the application of "pure research" methods, so OD evaluation "is likely to be more action centered, value based, collaboratively contexted, experientially rooted, situationally responsive, praxis oriented, and self-reflective than the current image" of research (Evered, 1985, p. 439). Carefully planned evaluation pays attention to both "soft" (attitudinal) data such as job satisfaction and "hard" (quantitative) data such as employee turnover rates.

The target of an OD evaluation may be the total organization or system, the organization's relationship with the external world and other organizations (transorganizational interaction), individual development, interpersonal development, intrateam and interteam development, or role development.[1]

Evaluation can occur during an intervention (formative), at the conclusion of an intervention (summative), or some time after an intervention (longitudinal). (See Exhibit 10-1.)

---

[1] These targets for evaluation are an expansion of those shown by Schmuck & Miles (1976) on the z-axis of their OD Cube.

Exhibit 10-1: Points at Which Evaluation Can Be Conducted

FORMATIVE

Evaluation conducted during the intervention.

SUMMATIVE

Evaluation conducted immediately after completion of the intervention.

LONGITUDINAL

Evaluation conducted at a specified time after completion of the intervention.

Evaluation may target either the processes in use during the change effort (see Exhibit 10-2, the x-axis of the OD Cube by Schmuck & Miles, 1976) or the outcomes of the change effort (see Exhibit 10-3, the y-axis of the OD Cube).

Advantages of Evaluation

Evaluation has many advantages for OD consultants. Some of the more important advantages are as follows.

Obtaining Corporate Support

When top management has confidence that an OD intervention is cost effective and adds value to the bottom-line effectiveness of the organization, it is more likely to allocate corporate resources for future OD efforts. Evaluation provides the means by which to build present and future corporate and management support.

Exhibit 10-2: Organization Development Research Variables—Process

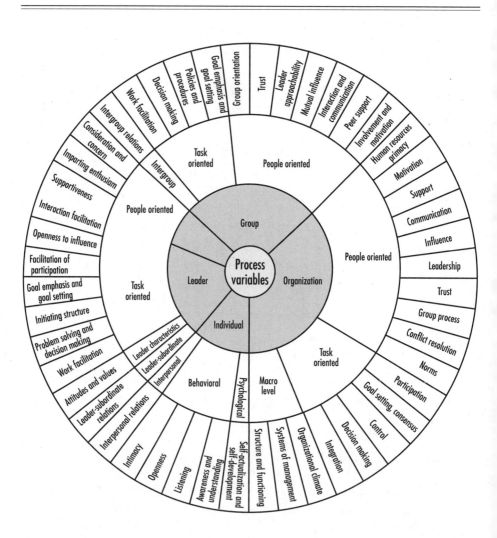

From J. Porras & P. Berg (August, 1978). The Impact of Organization Development. *Academy of Management Review,* p. 252. Used by permission of *Academy of Management Review.*

PRACTICING ORGANIZATION DEVELOPMENT

Exhibit 10-3: Organization Development Research Variables—Outcome

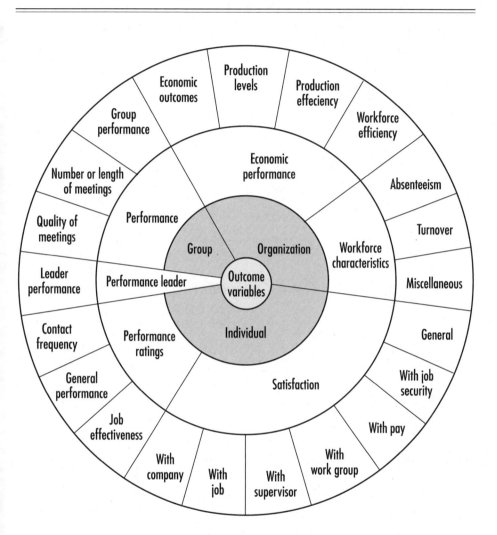

From J. Porras & P. Berg (August, 1978). The Impact of Organization Development. *Academy of Management Review*, p. 253. Used by permission of *Academy of Management Review*.

Improving Planning and Implementation Processes

Evaluation can provide a check on the effectiveness of the planning and implementation stages of the organizational development intervention—the activities planned, the personnel involved, the sequence of activities, the intervention's objectives and outcomes, and the organizational support for the changes that will result.

Gaining Participant Support

Evaluation can identify how the intervention is affecting participants and how the intervention might influence participants more positively.

Strengthening the Client-Consultant Relationship

The success of any change effort rests heavily on the quality of the relationship between the consultant and the client (Lippitt, Watson, & Westly, 1958). Evaluation can strengthen this relationship by providing feedback about the effectiveness of the relationship.

Improving the Consultant's Skills

Evaluation can reveal problems that can be related to the consultant's facilitation and group-process skills, communication of content knowledge, effectiveness of presentation, or the use of organization development processes. The consultant can then move on and focus on improving the skills targeted by the evaluation.

Meeting Professional Criteria

A consultant who acts in a professional manner plans for the evaluation of his or her work in order that he or she may improve. Consultants who are committed to maintaining their personal integrity and that of the OD profession welcome feedback on their effectiveness.

Increasing Flexibility During an Intervention

Planning for evaluation increases a consultant's ability to adjust or end an intervention if he or she discovers that it is based on incomplete information (Huse, 1980). As Porras (1984) observes, "Longer-term trends may go unnoticed and therefore not consciously be influenced by the consultant and key person" (p. 4). Evaluation increases flexibility during interventions by providing a continuing source of feedback.

Improving the Quality of the Environment

Many factors associated with the physical environment (for example, site, site staff, lighting, food, media support systems, available recreational activities) can add to or detract from the effectiveness of an intervention that is based on a laboratory learning experience. This is especially true if an offsite location is used. Evaluation can reveal how environmental factors affect an intervention.

Factors That Discourage Evaluation

It is difficult for any professional to seek input on the quality of his or her product or service and the level of his or her expertise. For this reason, some consultants create barriers—real and imagined—to planned evaluation. The following are some factors that discourage evaluation.

Lack of Money

The decision makers of a client organization may believe that the benefits of an evaluation do not warrant the expenditure for the OD consultant to conduct the evaluation. They may believe that the funds would be better spent on additional interventions. In our experience, this seems to be the major barrier to OD evaluation.

Lack of Time

An organization development consultant may find that commitments to other clients create time conflicts that will not "allow" him or her to conduct an effective evaluation. Likewise, the decision makers of an organization may be impatient to move on with an intervention and not want to take the time to conduct an evaluation.

Organizational Politics

The contact person within the client organization may have taken a significant risk in contracting with an external consultant or in championing the hiring of an internal consultant. An evaluation may lead to the conclusion that the intervention was not successful, thereby confirming the "poor judgment" of the contact person in deciding to use an OD consultant or in selecting the particular consultant.

Consultant Reputation

An OD consultant may be reluctant to conduct an evaluation. If the evaluation is positive, it may be thought that the consultant influenced the assessment of his or her own work. If the assessment is negative, the client organization—as well as the consultant—may feel that a lack of expertise is indicated. This could jeopardize the consultant's role within the contract and the client organization and could affect his or her reputation in the OD field.

Lack of Measurable Variables

Some interventions produce outcomes that are not easily measured. If this is the case, the difficulty of the evaluation task may lead the client and the consultant to avoid it.

Lack of Competence

Many OD consultants have more training and experience in conducting interventions than they do in conducting evaluations. Therefore, they feel more comfortable conducting interventions than they do conducting evaluations, so they tend to emphasize the former and avoid the latter.

Fear of Being Blamed

If fear exists within the organization, lack of cooperation may stem from fear of "being blamed." There also is an inclination within U.S. culture to use evaluation to "blame" someone. Our experiences in school exemplify the negative nature of evaluation. If the outcome of an OD effort is not everything that was desired, evaluation may create an opportunity to blame someone—if not the consultant, then the manager, the supervisor, the change-team members, or the employees.

Perceived Lack of Value of Evaluation

Previous experience or lack of understanding of the value of evaluation may create a perception that evaluation is not necessary and that it does not add value to the intervention.

The Importance of an Effective Evaluation System

Although the barriers to evaluation can be daunting, they must be overcome. The advantages of planned evaluation make it worthwhile. When a continuing evaluation effort is made, the following outcomes are likely:

- When management requests information to "prove" the value of the expenditure for OD, quality data are available or are in the process of being collected.

- Participants will have a positive attitude about OD and about the organization.

- The OD endeavor will be more efficient and effective.

- There will be increased quality and productivity in accomplishing organizational objectives.

- Additional OD needs arising from a lack of organizational support for the changes created by the intervention will be identified and may be addressed.

Exhibit 10-4 depicts an evaluation model that may be followed when conducting a planned evaluation of an OD intervention.

Exhibit 10-4: Organization Development Evaluation Model

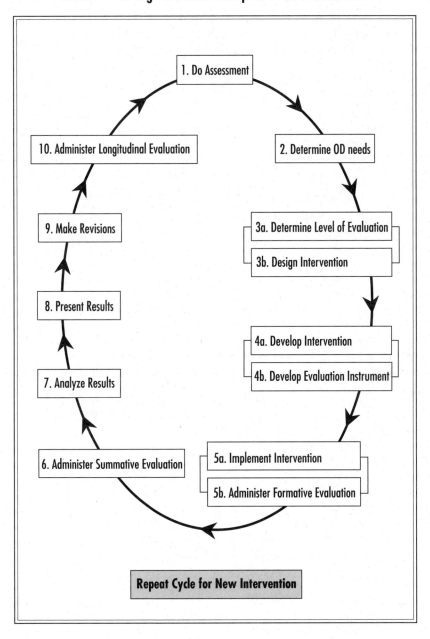

Defining Levels of Evaluation

There are many levels of evaluation. In planning an OD evaluation, it is important that an agreement is reached in the beginning about what is important and the level at which the effectiveness of the intervention is to be determined. This decision is made in the third step of the OD Evaluation Model displayed in Exhibit 10-4 ("Determine Level of Evaluation"). Donald Kirkpatrick (1959a,b; 1960a,b) suggested that there is a hierarchy of levels that can be used in the evaluation of training, and the same hierarchy can be applied to OD interventions. Each level is defined later in this chapter, and examples are provided at the end of the chapter. Exhibit 10-5 shows the four levels.

Reaction

Reaction is the first level. It is the easiest to measure and, thus, the level most often evaluated. Reaction means the participants' satisfaction with the intervention (activities, materials, consultant, facilities, etc.). A reaction form sometimes is referred to as a "happy sheet," as it is a form on which participants mark their level of satisfaction. It also can include:

- Polling members of a large group by having them raise their hands to indicate their levels of satisfaction;

- Doing a "whip" (having each member speak in turn) to obtain verbal feedback ranging from testimonies to constructive criticism;

- Asking the steering committee of the OD process or the client for subjective responses—on a daily basis (at the micro level) or as a monthly/yearly review (at the macro level).

Exhibit 10-5: Levels of Evaluation

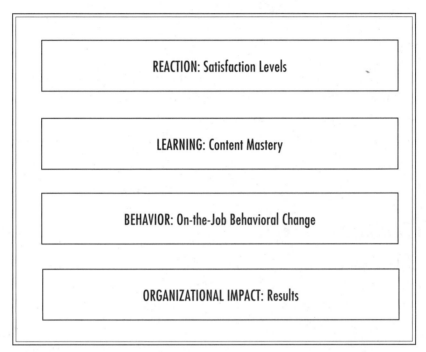

REACTION: Satisfaction Levels

LEARNING: Content Mastery

BEHAVIOR: On-the-Job Behavioral Change

ORGANIZATIONAL IMPACT: Results

Learning

Learning is the second level of Kirkpatrick's hierarchy. Some might argue that learning is more appropriate as a measurement of training; however, training is an OD intervention (see the OD Cube, Schmuck & Miles, 1976), so OD interventions that use training will benefit from evaluation of learning. Learning means how well principles, facts, and techniques are understood and absorbed. Further, since one objective of a OD consultant is to transfer OD skills and competencies to internal change agents, it would be appropriate to determine the extent to which managers or employees have learned and use OD competencies. Within OD, this is sometimes referred to as "double-loop learning" or "organizational learning."

Behavior

This level, which is generally considered to be more powerful than the previous two levels, measures on-the-job changes in individual and team behaviors and in the processes targeted by the OD intervention. Such changes are determined through pre- and post-intervention measurements, interviews, and observations.

Organizational Impact

The Organization Impact level of evaluation is usually the most difficult and, thus, the least-often used, of Kirkpatrick's hierarchy. It is designed to measure the impact of the OD intervention on the organization.

Measurement might focus on lowering turnover or absenteeism rates, reducing union grievances or product defects, increasing the quality of products or services, improving customer satisfaction, reducing costs, increasing the organization's profitability, increasing sensitivity to cultural diversity, or improving morale. As with each previous level, the appropriate measurement tool depends on the desired outcomes of the OD effort (see Exhibit 10-3). Measurement tools include surveys, interviews, secondary data, and observations.

What Level of Evaluation Should Be Used?

All four levels of evaluation should be used when possible and cost effective. Studies (for example, Coady, 1987) consistently indicate that management most prefers information on organizational impact and least prefers reaction evaluation only. The implication for a consultant is that he or she should push for the highest level of evaluation consistent with the intervention's outcomes and budget.

Evaluation Competencies

Certain competencies are required to conduct an OD evaluation. As outlined in Appendix I, internal and external OD consultants should be able to carry out the steps that are described in the next sections.

Create an Evaluation Plan

Create an appropriate, comprehensive evaluation plan (see Exhibit 10-4) that will link outcome expectations with outcome measures.

Initiate Ongoing Feedback

Expectations of the client for the consultant and of the consultant for the client should be established during the contracting stage, and a plan for ongoing feedback concerning the client-consultant relationship should be established. Regular meetings should be scheduled, and informal feedback discussions should be encouraged throughout all levels of the organization.

Select the Method and Level of Evaluation

The level of evaluation will be determined by the objectives of the intervention and the factors discussed previously. The method of measurement may be one of the following:

- Group or individual interviews
- Observations
- Secondary information
- Surveys or questionnaires
- Standardized assessment tools

In selecting the method, a consultant will need to consider:

- The amount of time that is available;
- The nature and scope of the problem;
- The degree of cooperation and trust that exists in the targeted system; and
- The role of intuition and logic in determining what is occurring.

Establish a Feedback System

A feedback system should be developed to monitor the change effort continuously, both during the intervention (formative) and after the intervention (summative). Processes and outcomes both can be evaluated at both times. Feedback may be obtained by means of periodic dialogues, surveys, interviews, and other interactions with individuals and/or groups.

Measurement before and after an intervention provides a comparison measure but has a key weakness: without a comparison group it is difficult to know whether change occurred as a result of the intervention or because of some other cause. The preferred design is to measure before, during, and after the intervention, and to compare results with a control group not included in the change effort. This type of evaluation allows for the addition of new variables, which can be important when unanticipated changes in the OD effort are required. It also permits more precise determination of what might have contributed to the change—either positive or negative—as well as building flexibility into the design of the change effort.

Sometimes only subtle clues will indicate that additional information is available or needs to be obtained. A consultant must learn to trust his or her intuition and to encourage organizational members to open up and share their perceptions with others.

Develop and Use Valid Instruments

A consultant must know how to create, administer, and evaluate reliable and practical instruments such as surveys, questionnaires, and rating scales. This particular competence is discussed in detail later in this chapter. (Pfeiffer and Ballew, 1988, also provide further information on this competence.) Kinlaw (1992) says that to be useful, an instrument must produce data that can be understood, believed, and acted on easily.

Ask the Right Questions

A consultant must ask the correct evaluation questions. In order to do this, the consultant must know not only the details of the intervention and the people and process likely to be affected but also how to ask questions that elicit further information.

Analyze and Present Data

A consultant must know how to analyze the data generated by the evaluation and how to present it to the client and others in the organization so that it is clear, credible, and useful. Data can be categorized as "hard" (measurable results) or "soft" (perceptions or attitudes). The situation will dictate whether or not the information needs to be analyzed statistically.

Anecdotes, lists, models, and many other creative means can be used to present data. Data can be presented visually as well as verbally. Attractive graphs, pie charts, flow charts, Pareto (bar) charts, cause-and-effect diagrams, histograms, run charts, scatter diagrams, and control charts all are effective ways of presenting data. This competence is discussed in more detail later in this chapter.

Integrate Feedback and Make Corrections

Once the data from an evaluation are presented, the consultant will need to work with the client and/or change team to apply the learnings from the evaluation to improve the OD effort.

Transfer Skills to the Organization

A major goal of an OD effort is to transfer OD skills to the client organization so that it can use them in the future. Golembiewski (1972) says that the laboratory approach is oriented toward helping individuals and organizations renew themselves as they "learn how to learn." In teaching OD skills, the consultant should place emphasis on the following:

- Feelings, system culture, organizational processes, and learner control;

- The experiences of the learners and the organization within social contexts.

Evered (1985, p. 426) suggests that this competence involves enhancing the ability of an organization to be self-reflective. The following list, based on Evered, describes attributes of a self-reflective organization:

- The capacity to examine its own assumptions and to raise pertinent, critical questions about its own functioning and reason for being.
- The willingness to continually ask how to know whether it is performing adequately.
- The ability to continually assess its own health, including its own criteria for health.
- The willingness to explore, to test by trying things out, and to transform itself continually.
- The encouragement of both intraorganizational and boundary-spanning (e.g., outside the organization) dialogue.
- The tolerance of dissent, criticism, and self-doubt.
- The continual search for improved ways of understanding its own nature (core learning).

Acknowledge Failure and Reinforce Progress

Effective evaluation allows a consultant to study failures and learn from his or her mistakes. A consultant also should recognize progress and make sure that all those involved know what results have been achieved, in order to motivate them to continue the change process.

Create Appropriate Closure

It is important that there be appropriate closure of a current project before the consultant and the client/change team proceed to the next cycle or project. Achieve closure by checking with the client or stakeholders who are celebrating successes or mourning over losses.

Developing Evaluation Instruments

Each evaluation level might require a different instrument for measurement. Developing such instruments requires highly technical skills. In developing skills in this area, OD consultants will find it useful to share their instruments with one another and with more experienced OD consultants, in order to benefit from critical reviews of what has been developed.

Basic Principles

There are three basic principles of instrumentation: validity, reliability, and practicability. These provide credibility and meaning to information derived from measurement.

Validity ensures that the instrument measures what it is intended to measure. Although there are many types of validity, the two most important for OD evaluation are face validity and predictive validity.

Face validity refers to the perceived accuracy and appropriateness of the instrument with respect to the stated intervention outcomes. Ultimately, such validity will be determined by whether the organization's indicated needs are met by the OD intervention. The results should "make sense" to those knowledgeable about the organization and OD and should match the information sought by stakeholders or decision makers.

Predictive validity is the ability of one measure to predict performance on some other measure. It requires the collection of data during the intervention to be correlated at a later date with "results" data gathered on the job. If there is predictive validity, there should be a high correlation between formative measures and workplace measures.

Reliability means that the instrument would obtain the same results if used several times. Reliability is associated with consistency and accuracy. It is easier to determine reliability than it is to determine validity. An instrument must be reliable if it is to be valid.

A nonnumeric approach that will improve reliability—but not show whether the instrument is, in fact, reliable—is to complete a pilot study with a small sample of employees prior to full-scale administration of the instrument. The OD consultant should check responses to identify where misunderstandings might exist, ask those completing the instrument where they encountered difficulties, and then revise the instrument based on the responses.

A "test-retest" procedure consists of administering the instrument to a pilot group and then administering it again to the same group after a brief interlude (perhaps a week). The results of both tests can then be plotted on a graph, with the scores of the first test on the graph's X axis and the scores of the second test on the Y axis. The correlation of the two sets provides a measure of stability. (For more information on conducting this procedure, see Fitz-Gibbon & Morris, 1987, p. 106.)

When an instrument has right and wrong answers (such as would be used at the learning level), there are a number of formulas that can be used to determine internal reliability. For an overview of these formulas, see Fitz-Gibbon & Morris (1987). Another approach is to determine subscores for odd-numbered questions and even-numbered questions for each respondent and obtain a correlation between the two sets of scores. The closer the correlation is to one, the higher the reliability.

Practicability means that the instrument can be completed within a reasonable amount of time with tools that are readily available. Administering the instrument to a pilot group is an excellent way to determine the clarity of items, consistency of interpretation, time needed, and administrative detail needed.

Evaluating at the Reaction Level

There are standardized questionnaires that can be used to evaluate OD interventions at the reaction level. McLean (1988) and Rothwell (1985) provide examples of climate surveys. Over one hundred instruments can be found in Pfeiffer (1988). Customized questions developed for specific programs also can provide useful information.

Many instruments are composed of statements related to the change effort; participants respond by indicating their agreement or disagreement with the statements by means of numerical scales. The type of scale most often used, developed by Rensis Likert, is a continuum divided into equal segments—usually five. The segments are numbered and labeled with descriptive words (for example, 1 = very bad, 2 = poor, 3 = o.k., 4 = good, 5 = excellent). For example:

1	2	3	4	5
Never	Sometimes	Usually	Often	Always

1. I hear about organizational changes through formal channels in a timely manner.   1 2 3 4 5

2. I know what my supervisor thinks of my work.   1 2 3 4 5

The scale numbers and labels are repeated on each page to aid the respondents in remembering the criteria. Some scales contain a "don't know" or neutral (middle of the scale) response choice to avoid forcing the respondent to make an artificial choice.

Questionnaire items should solicit information related directly to the purposes of the OD intervention and should identify areas for improvement. A consultant should resist the temptation to obtain more information than is necessary.

Questionnaire items also can consist of "open-ended" or "closed" questions, and both can be used in one instrument. An open-ended item permits a variety of responses (for example: "What do you like best about working here?"). A closed item permits only "yes" and "no" or limited responses (for example: "Do you enjoy working here?"). Because of the difficulty and time spent in analyzing the answers to open-ended questions, their use should be considered carefully. They are especially useful in determining why respondents answered as they did to closed questions and in gathering suggestions for corrective action. They also can provide information that was not solicited in the closed questions. Of course, if open-ended questions are used, adequate space should be allotted for respondents to write in their answers.

Each item in an instrument should ask only one question or contain only one topic. If more than one question, statement, or topic is presented, it is difficult for the respondent to know how to respond. It is also impossible for the surveyor to know to which part the respondents are reacting. For example, if a respondent disagrees with the statement, "This change effort met my expectations in terms of its value and quality," the surveyor will not know whether there is a problem with value or quality or both. It would be better to create two items: "This change effort met my expectations in terms of its value," and "This change effort met my expectations in terms of its quality."

Instrument items should not "lead the witness." Both the OD consultant and the client want to be able to trust the accuracy of the evaluation results. If a question suggests a desired answer, it does not yield useful information. For example, several years ago a U.S. political survey asked: "Given the outstanding economic success of President _____, how well do you think President _____ has done with his economic program?" A better question would be: "How well do you think President _____ has done with his economic program?" Another example is as follows: "In a study of our senior management, communication was identified as the primary organizational need. Do you agree?" It is difficult for respondents to disagree in such circumstances.

The layout of an instrument must encourage the respondents to complete it. This can be accomplished by means of the following:

- Leaving ample white space,
- Using large, readable type,

- Having the questionnaire typeset and using a good-quality reproduction process,

- Having good contrast between ink color and paper color, and

- Using different type styles to highlight different parts of the evaluation form.

The administration of an instrument can affect the quality of the information obtained. It is best to keep the time required to complete the form short (perhaps no longer than five minutes). It is also a good idea to have the respondents complete the form before the final activity of the event. If evaluation is the final activity, participants may not treat it seriously and may not devote the necessary time to it because of their eagerness to leave.

Other suggestions for instrument design are as follows:

- If the instrument is lengthy (more than ten items), it is helpful to randomly change the orientation (polarity, direction) of items in order to avoid a "halo effect," that is respondents who like the OD intervention choose only positive responses without giving sufficient attention to individual items.

- Randomly intersperse items that fit within different categories in order to avoid a "halo effect." Do not have all items related to a particular topic in one section.

- Ask only for essential demographic data (for example, job title, department, sex, age). Too much information can violate confidentiality by making it too easy to identify individual respondents.

- If words are used that might have different interpretations, provide clear definitions.

- If categories of responses are used, be sure they do not overlap. For example:

DO NOT USE:	USE:
a. 1 year or less	a. Less than one year
b. 1-5 years	b. 1-5 years
c. 5-10 years	c. 6-10 years

- Normally, avoid the use of value-laden words that can be interpreted differently (for example, should, good, bad, successful).
- Provide brief but adequate instructions for each section of the instrument. Test the instructions before printing the instrument.
- Avoid the use of jargon. Although certain job-specific words or phrases may be commonly used by some people in the organization, others may not understand them.

It is extremely helpful to the client organization if the OD consultant works with an in-house committee in constructing a customized instrument. The committee members can learn the steps involved by working through the process with the consultant. The skills that are transferred include:

- Interviewing
- Construction of survey items
- Technical issues, such as the avoiding "halo effect"
- Administrative processes

- Data-analysis processes
- Feedback processes
- Making recommendations based on the analysis

The committee also serves as a validation group, ensuring that survey questions are asked in the vocabulary of the organization.

Example of Evaluation at the Reaction Level

One of the authors of this chapter currently consults with organizations interested in quality transformation (Deming, 1986). The author serves as a process consultant to the senior management team, known as the transformation steering committee (TSC). Periodically, he seeks feedback regarding his role from the team members by using the form shown in Exhibit 10-6. This evaluation is at the reaction level.

Another common evaluation approach in OD is the climate survey. This instrument obtains the reactions of employees to several aspects of the work environment. Exhibit 10-7 is a sample page from a typical climate survey.

Evaluating at the Learning Level

In designing a test to determine how much learning has taken place, incorporate nothing that does not specifically measure the desired outcome(s) and that does not emerge from an objective of the OD effort being evaluated. The desired outcome(s) of a learning experience should be stated clearly, preferably in behavioral terms, at the beginning of the learning experience. An outcome should be observable and measurable.

Exhibit 10-6: Example of Reaction Evaluation

EVALUATION OF TRANSFORMATION CONSULTANT

In responding to the following questions, circle the number that corresponds with the following scale:

5 Very Satisfied	4 Satisfied	3 Neutral	2 Dissatisfied	1 Very Dissatisfied

1. How well the consultant has assisted the TSC* in
   interpreting Deming   5 4 3 2 1

2. How well the consultant has challenged the discussions
   and decisions of the TSC   5 4 3 2 1

3. How well the consultant has evaluated the progress
   and process of the TSC   5 4 3 2 1

4. How well the consultant has acted as a coach for
   senior management   5 4 3 2 1

5. How effectively the consultant has interacted with
   the Quality Coordinator   5 4 3 2 1

6. What could the consultant do to be more effective in assisting in the work of the
   TSC and the transformation process?

7. What is the consultant now doing that is not necessary for the work of the TSC
   and the transformation process and which need not be continued?

8. Any other comments?

*TSC stands for Transformation Steering Committee.

Exhibit 10-7: Sample Climate Survey

Instructions:

Read each of the following statements carefully. In the row to the right, circle the number that best describes how you feel about the statement. If you wish to make comments on any item, place the number of that item on the blank page that accompanies the survey and write in your comments. If you have no knowledge about an item, do not respond to that item.

5 Very Satisfied	4 Satisfied	3 Neutral	2 Dissatisfied	1 Very Dissatisfied

1. I am doing something really worthwhile on my job. 5 4 3 2 1

2. XYZ Company employees solve interpersonal problems well. 5 4 3 2 1

3. My supervisor is often unfair with employees. 5 4 3 2 1

4. XYZ Company makes too many changes too quickly, causing me to wonder if the company's goals are clear. 5 4 3 2 1

5. A job description exists for my position. 5 4 3 2 1

6. Employees are still identified by the company for which they were working prior to the merger of that company with XYZ Company. 5 4 3 2 1

7. My department's management is interested in my well-being. 5 4 3 2 1

8. My job is frequently dull and monotonous. 5 4 3 2 1

9. I am familiar with the current human resources policies and procedures of the company. 5 4 3 2 1

10. I usually can talk with my supervisor as often as I need to. 5 4 3 2 1

Exhibit 10-7: Sample Climate Survey (continued)

5 Very Satisfied	4 Satisfied	3 Neutral	2 Dissatisfied	1 Very Dissatisfied

11. I often think that my job contributes little to the company.   5 4 3 2 1

12. I am usually given credit for work well done.   5 4 3 2 1

13. I want to continue to work for the company as long as I can.   5 4 3 2 1

14. I have little opportunity to use my abilities in my present job.   5 4 3 2 1

15. There are too many cliques among employees.   5 4 3 2 1

16. This organization has an unfriendly atmosphere.   5 4 3 2 1

Pre- and posttesting. To ensure that learning has occurred, a test should be administered before the intervention or training, at its conclusion, and—to determine longitudinal change—when some time has elapsed after the completion of the intervention. Circumstances such as the time of day in which the test is administered, length of time required to complete the test, and test format should be the same for each test administration. If the same test is used, enough time should have elapsed since the previous administration that participants cannot remember how they responded to individual items. If different tests are used, they must be shown to be parallel so that variations in performance can be attributed to the learning that took place and not to differences in the tests.

Difficulty. It is important to control for the difficulty of a test so that the test can measure accomplishment of the desired outcomes. A test can be so easy that everyone can pass or so difficult that no one can pass. Neither is useful. The ideal test discriminates among respondents so that those who understand the material score high and those who do not understand the material score low.

Wording. If a test is not intended to measure reading ability, it should be written so that it can be understood by everyone in the target population. Words with ambiguous meanings should not be used. Test items should be tested thoroughly to ensure consistent interpretation of the words or phrases used. Each test item should focus on measuring only one objective, and each objective measured should be of importance. Items should be written in simple, clear language.

Distractors. When answers are obvious, no real evaluation occurs. To avoid this, it is often wise to use "distractors"—items that will mislead those who are not sure about the content but will not mislead the respondent who has achieved the desired learning. The difficulty of an item can be controlled by the complexity of the distractors used. For example, suppose that the following item appears on a test:

> According to Robert Mager, an instructional objective should usually have three parts. They are:
>
> A. Condition, criterion, and performance
>
> B. Resources, behavior, and results
>
> C. Condition, resources, and behavior
>
> D. Resources, behavior, and performance

The correct response is A. However, the remaining items serve as good distractions because they appear to make sense. Items C and D contain portions of the correct answer and may fool those who are not aware of the correct answer.

Answer Patterns. Particularly in true-false or multiple-choice tests, designers should avoid item patterns that can serve as cues to respondents. An effective way of avoiding patterns in a true-false test is to use a table of random numbers in a statistics book. Select a number in the table at random; if the number is odd, make the answer to the first question false; if the number is even, make the answer true. Go to the next number in the table. If that number is odd, make the answer to the second question false; if the number is even, make the answer true. Continue in this fashion until the desired response for all questions has been determined. In a similar application for multiple-choice tests, make the correct answer "a" if the number is 0 or 1; "b" if the number is 2 or 3; and "c" if the number is 4 or 5.

Types of Learning. Learning generally is classified into three types: cognitive (evaluating what participants know), psychomotor (evaluating what participants can do), and affective (evaluating what participants feel).

- *Cognitive:* Cognitive learning refers to mental abilities and skills that are subdivided into knowledge, comprehension, application, analysis, synthesis, and evaluation objectives. In OD, cognitive learning may focus around new information—such as stages in small-group development, work teams, or high-performance work organizations.

- *Psychomotor:* Psychomotor learning refers to observable physical activity. To test psychomotor learning in a controlled environment, participants can be confronted with on-the-job simulations, work samples, and in-basket exercises (in which each participant has to decide the priority for each piece of work as well as completing the work).

- *Affective:* Affective learning refers to emotions. In OD, it often refers to attitudes (such as prejudices and assumptions) that affect how people interact with others. Affective learning cannot be measured directly; it must be assumed by observing behavior and by the reports of the learners. To best measure affective learning, specify the behaviors that would be expected if the desired affect were present. Then follow the suggestions in the section that follows on evaluating at the behavioral level.

Objective Measurement. Objective measurement refers to the fact that the person conducting the evaluation does not have to be knowledgeable about the subject matter. An answer is either correct or incorrect. The answers can be compared (by an individual or by means of a computer) with an answer key to determine correctness. There are several types of objective measures. A *true-false* item requires the participants to determine if the statement is correct or incorrect. A *multiple-choice* item provides participants with an uncompleted statement (the lead-in or stem) and a set of different completion options, of which only one is correct. The participant's task is to choose the correct option. *Matching* items generally consist of two columns: one column contains stimuli for which the participant is to provide the appropriate responses from the second column. Such items are designed to measure the participants' knowledge of a series of facts, principles, interpretations, or relationships. *Completion* questions generally require a one- or two-word response. The purpose of such questions is to measure the participant's ability to recall information or to find a solution to a problem. More detailed information about test development can be found in Phillips (1991).

Exhibit 10-8 provides a checklist for objective measurement of learning.

Exhibit 10-8: A Checklist for Objective Measurement of Learning

Objectives

_____ 1. Each test item emerges from an objective of the OD effort being evaluated.

_____ 2. Each item measures only one objective.

_____ 3. The objective being measured is important.

Wording

_____ 4. The item is written in simple, clear language.

_____ 5. The item avoids ambiguous words.

_____ 6. The item is grammatically correct.

Format

_____ 7. Correct-response categories are distributed randomly to ensure that no pattern exists.

_____ 8. Directions are clear and complete.

Content

_____ 9. Reasonable distractors are used.

Technical Matters

_____ 10. The test has proven to be statistically reliable.

Subjective Measurement. Subjective measures are usually essay questions. The person who is conducting subjective measurement must be knowledgeable about the subject matter and must make a subjective judgment as to whether an answer is correct or incorrect. Although an answer key is helpful in determining correctness, judgments are required throughout.

Evaluating at the Behavior Level

The third level of evaluation—behavior or performance—requires the cooperation of supervisors, participants, external observers, peers, customers, and employees. Behavioral change can best be measured by conducting evaluation before the change effort or training intervention and again after it. Several types of instruments can be used to evaluate behavior or performance; these are listed in the sections that follow.

Critical-Incident Checklist. A critical incident is a step in a process that can "make or break" the effort. Persons who are experienced in the performance to be evaluated can be asked to identify critically important steps, as well as missteps to be avoided. The checklist can be developed from their input. Essential substeps to be followed within the procedure also should be listed, along with minimally acceptable standards, where applicable. During the evaluation, the observer marks the checklist next to each listed step, to indicate whether or not the step was completed within acceptable standards. A critical-incident checklist also can be used to evaluate the OD intervention process. For this purpose, a list of critical incidents can be solicited from experienced OD consultants.

Comparative Rating Instruments. When a consultant is asked to compare an employee's performance with the performance of other employees, a comparative rating instrument probably will be used. Most instruments of this kind require the evaluator to rate the employee according to a percentile within a norm group, or to indicate which rank the employee should be given, or to list the names of evaluated employees in order of competence.

Statistical Process Control. Organizations that are involved in quality-transformation efforts use a variety of statistical process control (SPC) tools (for example, Pareto [bar] charts, flow charts, control charts, cause-and-effect diagrams) to assess the performance of systems and of individuals within systems. Such assessment can indicate whether a system is under control. If the system is not under control, some instruments can determine whether there are special causes, such as inadequately trained individuals. The SPC approach is generally considered to provide effective measures of performance.

Action-Plan Analysis. Participants in an intervention may create an action plan that specifies in measurable language what they will do and achieve. Periodically, the OD consultant meets with the participants to review progress toward the accomplishment of the planned actions. The consultant may ask the following questions:

- Was the action completed on time?
- What percent of completion was achieved?
- If the action was not completed, do you still intend to accomplish it?
- If the action was not completed, what prevented its accomplishment?
- What did you do differently from what you had planned and why?

- What benefits did the completed activity produce?
- If you were to do it again, how would you do it differently?
- What do you plan to do now?
- If the action was completed, what is your degree of satisfaction with the outcome?
- Who will benefit the most from the action?
- Specifically, what was improved as a result of the activity?
- What money was saved or what value was added to the organization as a result of the action?
- What revenue or profit was generated as a result of the action?
- What did you, your team, and/or your organization learn?
- What did you discover about what needs to be done next?

After the participants respond, the consultant asks additional questions for clarification or to obtain for greater detail.

Interview. Supervisors and others in the organization can provide subjective information about changes that have occurred. A consultant can use an interview guide to ensure that he or she asks exactly the same questions in the same order with all interviewees. For a structured interview, the guide would be quite detailed. An unstructured interview—although less precise—allows the consultant to follow new trains of thought. The guide for an unstructured interview may contain just a few questions, such as the following:

- "What's going better for you in your job now, compared with the way it was before the intervention?"

- "What's not going as well for you in your job now, compared with the way it was before the intervention?"
- "If you could make just one change in what we are doing now, what would it be?"

Videotape. When the evaluation focuses on behavior or performance, videotaping can be a useful assessment tool. For example, if the objective of an intervention is to create more effective team meetings, a videotape of a specific team meeting prior to the intervention can be compared with a videotape of the team meeting after the intervention. This comparison can indicate the impact of the intervention on the team's meeting skills.

Journal. Increasingly, participants in an intervention are taught how to keep a journal (diary) and are then encouraged to create such a record during the intervention and for a specific amount of time after the intervention. By reflecting on the intervention—and the changes they observe taking place—participants can provide useful information for evaluation.

Observation. Observation of participant behavior before and after an intervention is another key evaluation tool. A comparison of observations of the intervention group and of a control (nonparticipant) group also can provide information about whether observed changes actually resulted from the intervention.

BARS (Behaviorally-Anchored Rating Scale). The BARS process was conceived as a way of improving the accuracy of performance appraisals. Critical components of performance are identified for each job. A behavioral anchor is a description of a specific, observable behavior that is part of a job component. For example, a behavioral anchor might be, "When confronted with questions during a break in a training session, the consultant talks to participants until their questions are answered or until the break is over." Behavioral anchors are obtained through interviews with supervisors and job incumbents. These persons are asked to describe each specific job behavior as it would appear if it were "good," "average," and "poor." The best descriptions of each behavior are selected using a rating process, and these descriptions are used in the scale. When the scale is constructed, an employee may be evaluated in terms of good, average, or poor performance for each behavioral dimension of his or her job.

Simulation Activities. For example, training to use various tools of statistical process control (SPC) is common in most quality-transformation efforts. To determine whether the concepts have been acquired, participants may be asked to take each tool (that is, a tally sheet, Pareto chart, histogram, cause-effect diagram, run chart, control chart) and use that tool in a real-life setting. After the consultant explains the use of various problem-solving tools, participants might be asked to create a flow chart of a process or to lead a brainstorming session. Although the setting in each instance is somewhat artificial—and is thus not quite at the behavior level—it does identify what the participants have learned from the training intervention.

Evaluating at the Organizational-Impact Level

An almost limitless number of sources can be used to determine the organizational impact of an OD intervention. However, because there are so many variables that can affect organizational performance, both internal and external, it becomes almost impossible to demonstrate the organizational impact resulting from a specific OD intervention.

Appropriate sources for evaluation should be identified during the development of the OD intervention (step 4b of Exhibit 10-4). If a problem prompted the OD intervention, it can furnish clues about what should be evaluated. An evaluation of organizational impact may be carried out using performance data or organizational diagnosis.

Performance Data. Performance data include turnover rates, absenteeism, safety records, defect rates, inventory levels, work-in-process levels, customer complaints, number of products/services completed per day, accuracy of forecasting, number of sales calls made, profits, return on assets, and return on investments. When used in evaluating organizational impact, performance data are compared from before and after the OD intervention.

Organizational Diagnosis. An organizational diagnosis is made to determine how employees feel about the environment in which they work. Other terms used to describe the process are climate survey, satisfaction check, employee survey, and attitude survey. Emphasis may be placed on one area of concern or on several areas. By administering the survey over several different time frames, a consultant can determine whether employee attitudes are changing in a positive or negative direction.

The most commonly used format for an organizational diagnosis is a Likert-scale questionnaire—a series of questions for which responses are provided that are on a continuum. For example:

5 Very Satisfied	4 Satisfied	3 Not Sure	2 Dissatisfied	1 Very Dissatisfied

1. How satisfied are you with the relationship between top management and the next level of management? 5 4 3 2 1

Several standardized instruments to measure organizational climate are available commercially, but a customized instrument can more effectively pinpoint issues in a specific business. A consultant can customize a questionnaire to create categories and questions to meet specific needs. McLean (1988) provides a sample questionnaire that includes the following categories:

- Corporate management's leadership
- Department management's leadership
- Supervisory effectiveness
- Interpersonal and interdepartmental relationships
- Productivity and accountability
- Communications
- Employee career development
- Training and development
- Job satisfaction
- Organizational mission and goals
- Strategic management
- Performance management
- Work flow and design
- Quality of working life
- Employee compensation
- Training options

Analyzing the Results of Evaluation

Analysis is step 7 of the evaluation model (Exhibit 10-4). Several different types of analysis are commonly used.

Means and Standard Deviations

A mean is an arithmetic average. A standard deviation is a measure of variability—that is, the smaller the standard deviation, the more the respondents agree with one another. These are the measures most often used in reporting the results of a questionnaire. Most spreadsheet and statistical computer programs can calculate means and standard deviations.

Frequencies and Percentages

A frequency is simply the number of responses obtained for each option. Percentages provide a readily understandable summary of the results. If one is reporting percentages, one should also provide the frequencies. An example can underscore the difference between frequencies and percentages. Suppose employees provided the following responses to a question and an attitude survey:

	Satisfaction				
	5 Very Satisfied	**4** Satisfied	**3** Neutral	**2** Dissatisfied	**1** Very Dissatisfied
How satisfied are you with this organization?	2(20%)	2(20%)	2(20%)	2(20%)	2(20%)
N = 10					

In this example, ten employees responded. The frequency of responses—that is, the number of employees indicating each response—is depicted by response category. Because two is 20% of ten, each response depicted represents 20% of the respondent group.

Verbal Summaries

Open-ended questions need to be summarized in the same way as numeric data. It would be very time consuming to report a long list of responses that have not been summarized. Grouping the responses by categories is one way of organizing the data. Like remarks then can be summarized together. Appropriate categories usually become evident as the responses are reviewed and can be given an appropriate label.

For example, suppose two employees responded to the question, "What other comments would you like to make?" Their responses were "Promotion policies in this organization are unfair." and "You have to be on the right side of people to be promoted here." To summarize these responses, the consultant might create a category called "concern over promotion practices" and indicate that two people raised the issue. (However, two is a small number, so the example is very simple. Most consultants in that case would probably report that small of a response by using direct quotes from the employees.)

Review what you have learned in this part of the chapter by referring to the checklist in Exhibit 10-9.

Presenting Evaluation Results

Once the evaluation has been completed, the results must be communicated (step 8 of the evaluation model in Exhibit

10-4). The objective is to develop a brief, but complete, report that can meet the needs of all of the intended audiences.

Exhibit 10-9: A Checklist for Analyzing Evaluation Results

Audiences

_____ 1. The audiences for the specific analysis were identified prior to administering the evaluation instruments.

_____ 2. The evaluation needs of the identified audiences were specified.

Types of Analysis

If numeric data:

_____ 3. Frequencies and percentages were computed.

_____ 4. Means and standard deviations were computed.

If open-ended data:

_____ 5. Categories were used.

_____ 6. Summaries were prepared.

Methods of Analysis

_____ 7. The computer was used for analysis.

Components of the Report

A report should contain a brief statement of the need that the OD intervention was designed to meet, the planned outcomes of the intervention, the stated measures of effectiveness (using as many of the evaluation levels as can be measured), and any recommendations that resulted from the evaluation. An appendix might include summaries of open-ended questions, details of how the data were gathered, or more extensive tables. Exhibit 10-10 presents the common options in presenting evaluation results.

Exhibit 10-10: Presenting Evaluation Results

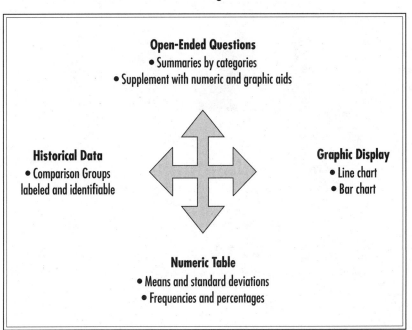

Presenting Results at the Reaction Level

Reaction-level analyses may be presented as summaries and graphs of participant responses to a survey administered after the completion of an intervention. Exhibit 10-11 displays differences between responses of males and females on four questions related to communications. Demographic comparisons (such as gender and age) should be done only when they answer important questions. Care should be taken to avoid data overload—the provision of more information than can be used in making decisions.

Exhibit 10-11: Sample Presentation of Reaction Evaluation: 1

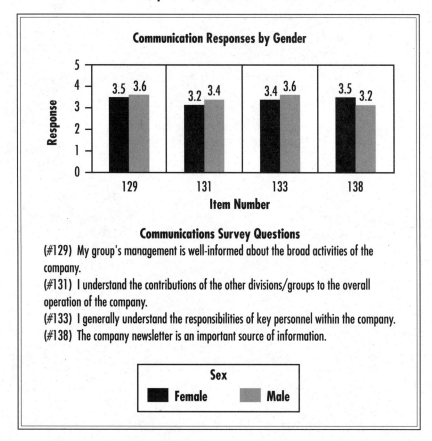

Communication Responses by Gender

Communications Survey Questions

(#129) My group's management is well-informed about the broad activities of the company.

(#131) I understand the contributions of the other divisions/groups to the overall operation of the company.

(#133) I generally understand the responsibilities of key personnel within the company.

(#138) The company newsletter is an important source of information.

When a survey is administered before and after an OD intervention, it can be used to evaluate the success of the intervention. Exhibit 10-12 is an example from an organization that repeated a climate survey after one year. The scores decreased on two questions and increased on four, although visual review would suggest that only one change was significant. It would be important to know whether there is any connection between the intervention and question six on the survey.

PRACTICING ORGANIZATION DEVELOPMENT

Exhibit 10-12: Sample Presentation of Reaction Evaluation: 2

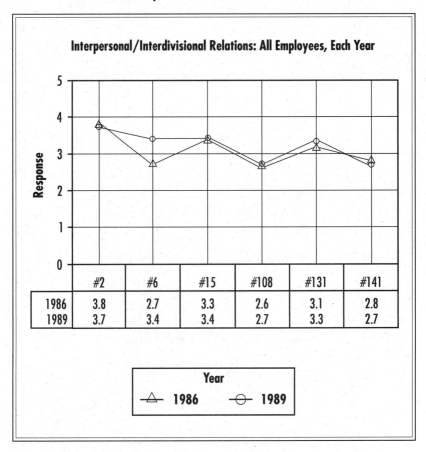

Interpersonal/Interdivisional Relations: All Employees, Each Year

	#2	#6	#15	#108	#131	#141
1986	3.8	2.7	3.3	2.6	3.1	2.8
1989	3.7	3.4	3.4	2.7	3.3	2.7

Year
△ 1986   ○ 1989

Presenting Results at the Learning Level

Learning-level analyses usually include a graph showing pre-
and posttest performance on the measures of importance in
an intervention. This information may be obtained immediately after completion of the intervention (to determine increased competence at the conclusion) or after a period of time
(to measure retention).

Presenting Results at the Behavior Level

Behavior-level analyses usually include a graph showing pre- and postintervention observation of the behaviors that the intervention was designed to alter. One example comes from a quality-transformation intervention. The facilitator helped a team to identify the norms under which team members wished to operate. One norm was "approximately equal participation."

Early in the process, the consultant created a sociogram (Exhibit 10-13, part A). The result showed that F was an isolate (this person had contributed nothing to the discussion). V, who was chairing the meeting, was the focal point of all discussion. There was little interaction among team members. Showing the diagram to the team was useful in illustrating members' actual behavior in contrast to desired behavior.

The second sociogram (Exhibit 10-13, part B) was quite different. There were no isolates. Everyone contributed to the discussion. It is impossible to tell from the diagram who was chairing the meeting. There was a good amount of interaction among members of the team, and the discussion appeared to be fairly evenly distributed among team members. Viewing this diagram provided positive feedback to team members about their improvement.

When behavior cannot actually be measured (for example, number of errors), observations of behavior often are reported on a Likert-scale questionnaire, with a supervisor, subordinates, and/or peers reporting whether an employee's competence has improved and, sometimes, by how much.

Presenting Results at the Organizational-Impact Level

Organizational-impact analyses are the most difficult to do and, thus, to report. If a causal relationship has been established

Exhibit 10-13: Sample Presentation of Behavior Evaluation

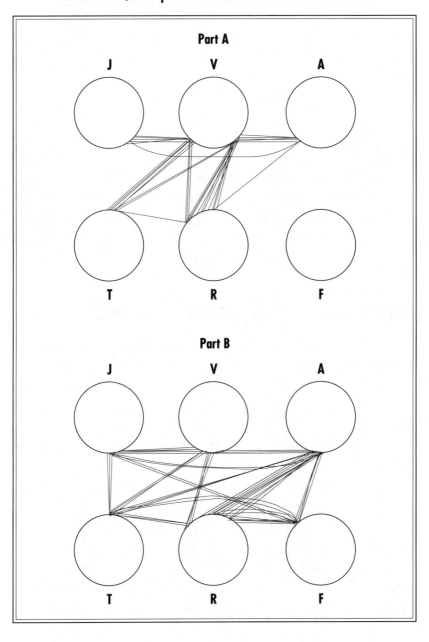

between behavior and results, organizational impact can be reported using measures such as departmental profitability, gross revenues, percentage of errors, or cost savings. If a causal relationship is not identified, it may be necessary to measure organizational impact using a Likert-scale questionnaire to obtain subjective judgments about the impact of employees' performance on the organization.

The analysis of an evaluation often generates recommendations for improvement in design, content, sequencing, time allocation, training, facilities, and whatever else will improve the effectiveness of the organization. Any barriers to, and problems encountered in, the intervention should be identified; and possible solutions should be offered. Recommendations for proceeding should be stated in sufficient detail so that they can be carried out by others.

Evaluation at the Organization-Impact Level

It is difficult to prove the organizational impact of any OD intervention. Even if all measures show positive improvement, it is difficult to show that the differences are attributable to the OD intervention rather than to changes in the organization, societal changes, competitive factors, or other variables. For this reason, the consultant and client must ask the "reasonable cause" question: "Is it reasonable to think, given what we know, that the improvements in the organization are a result of the interventions?"

McLean and Pakenham-Walsh (1987) describe several variables evaluated in a client corporation to determine whether interventions designed to improve its quality management processes had been successful. Six measures were identified as important to the business and as being affected by the intervention: product quality, cycle time, linearity, product cost, inventory, and number of suppliers. Each measure showed marked improvement. Although there were reasonable explanations for the improvements other than the OD interventions, it was clear to the consultants and the client that the interventions had significantly influenced the results. The chart for product acceptance for a key product is shown in Exhibit 10-14.

Another approach to demonstrating organizational impact is a cost-benefit analysis. An analysis of this kind explores the difference between the financial benefits resulting from the intervention and the costs of the intervention. However, it can be difficult to tie benefits directly to the intervention.

With this caveat, Sleezer, Swanson, and Geroy (1985) had HRD practitioners project the cost-benefit of a training and OD intervention in a health-care organization prior to the intervention by completing two work sheets: Net Performance Value Calculation Work Sheet (Exhibit 10-15) and Cost Analysis Work Sheet (Exhibit 10-16).

Following the intervention, the vice president of operations and the manager of marketing completed the work sheets. The benefits of the organization development intervention, according to these two individuals, are shown in Exhibit 10-17.

The HRD personnel projected significant cost benefit, although their estimates were considerably below the figures shown in the exhibit. If these figures are even close to accurate, the cost benefits are very impressive indeed. If the client does the estimates, it will probably do so quite conservatively. It is important that the OD consultant and the client contact not conduct the evaluation so that objectivity is demonstrated in the process.

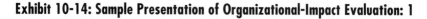

Review what you have learned in this part of the chapter by referring to the checklist in Exhibit 10-18.

Exhibit 10-14: Sample Presentation of Organizational-Impact Evaluation: 1

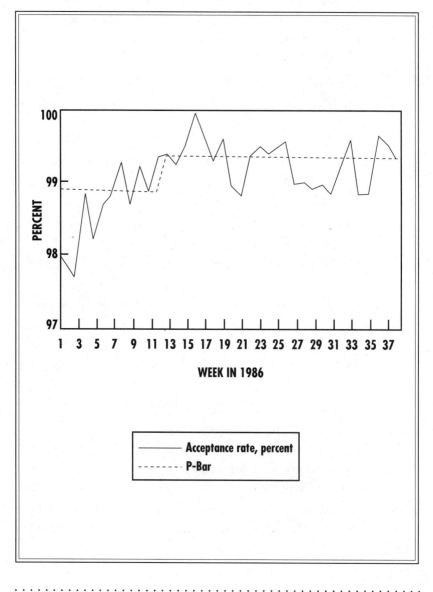

PRACTICING ORGANIZATION DEVELOPMENT

Exhibit 10-15: Sample Presentation of Organizational-Impact Evaluation: 2

Net Performance Value Calculation Work Sheet

Data Required for Calculations

(a) What is the desired performance as a result of worker training?   _____

(b) What unit(s) of measure will be used to describe the performance?   _____

(c) What is the dollar value that will be assigned to each unit of measure?   _____

(d) What is the estimated training time to reach the goal?   _____

(e) What is the current level of worker performance?   _____

(f) How many workers will participate in the training?   _____

Calculations to Determine Net Performance Value

(g) What is the estimated performance level during training?   _____

   Will trainee produce during training?

   _____ No = 0

   _____ Yes = $\dfrac{a + e}{2}$

(h) What is the length of the period being evaluated (at a minimum this will be the longest "d" of all options under consideration)?   _____

(i) What is the estimate of the total number of units (b) that will be achieved during training? [d x g]   _____

(j) What is the estimate of the total individual performance for the evaluation period? [(h - d) x a] + i   _____

(k) What is the value for the total performance for the evaluation period? [c x j]   _____

(l) What is the net performance value gain? [k - (e x c x h)]   _____

(m) Do you want to calculate the total net performance value of all trainees?   _____

   _____ Yes = l x f

   _____ No = Net Performance Value of one trainee which is value of "l"

Exhibit 10-16:
Sample Presentation of Organizational-Impact Evaluation: 3

Cost Analysis Work Sheet

Forecaster _____   Date _____

1. Needs analysis/planning
   Staff   _____
   External consultant costs   _____
   Materials   _____

   _____   _____

   _____

                                         Subtotal $ _____

2. Work behavior analysis

   Staff   _____
   External consultant costs   _____
   Materials   _____

   _____

   _____

                                         Subtotal $ _____

3. Design
   Staff   _____
   External consultant costs   _____
   External support costs   _____
   Materials   _____

   _____

   _____

                                         Subtotal $ _____

4. Development
   Staff   _____
   External consultant costs   _____
   Materials   _____

   _____
   _____

               Subtotal $ _____

5. Implementation

   Trainee   _____
   Facilities   _____
   Tuition/fees   _____
   Staff   _____
   Materials   _____

   _____
   _____

               Subtotal $ _____

6. Evaluation
   Staff   _____
   External consultant costs   _____
               Subtotal   _____

7. Total costs   Total $ _____
   (sum of all subtotals)

Exhibit 10-17: Sample Presentation of Actual Benefits of OD Program

	VP of Operations	Manager of Marketing	Average
Total Value Assigned to OD Program	$5,040,000	$7,452,000	$6,246,000
Actual Cost	455,590	455,590	455,590
Benefit	$4,584,410	$6,996,410	$5,790,410

Exhibit 10-18: A Checklist for Presenting Evaluation Results

Evaluation Report

_____ 1. Contains a statement of original need.

_____ 2. Contains specified outcomes.

_____ 3. Contains measures of effectiveness.

_____ 4. Presents measures of effectiveness in at least two formats—numeric and graphic.

_____ 5. Notes problems encountered.

_____ 6. Contains recommendations for proceeding.

_____ 7. Contains detailed information in appendices.

References

Beckhard, R., & Harris, R.T. (1977). *Organizational transitions: Managing complex change.* New York: Addison-Wesley.

Coady, M.M. (1987). *Factors that influence a technical trainer's choice of types of program evaluation.* Unpublished doctoral dissertation, University of Minnesota.

Deming, W.E. (1986). *Out of the crisis.* Cambridge, MA: Massachusetts Institute of Technology.

Evered, R.D. (1985). Transforming managerial and organizational research: Creating a science that works. In R. Tannenbaum, N. Margulies, & F. Massarik and associates (Eds), *Human systems development* (pp. 419-457). San Francisco, CA: Jossey-Bass.

Fitz-Gibbon, C., & Morris, L. (1987). *How to analyze data.* Newbury Park, CA: Sage Publications.

Golembiewski, R.T. (1972). *Renewing organizations: The laboratory approach to planned change.* Itasca, IL: F.E. Peacock.

Huse, E.F. (1980). *Organization development and change* (2nd ed.). St. Paul, MN: West.

Kinlaw, D.C. (1992). *Continuous improvement and measurement for total quality: A team-based approach.* San Diego, CA: Pfeiffer & Company.

Kirkpatrick, D. (1959a). Techniques for evaluating training programs. *Journal of the American Society of Training Directors, 13*(11), 3-9.

Kirkpatrick, D. (1959b). Techniques for evaluating training programs. *Journal of the American Society of Training Directors, 13*(12), 21-26.

Kirkpatrick, D. (1960a). Techniques for evaluating training programs. *Journal of the American Society of Training Directors, 14*(1), 13-18.

Kirkpatrick, D. (1960b). Techniques for evaluating training programs. *Journal of the American Society of Training Directors, 14*(2), 28-32.

Lippitt, R., Watson, J., & Westly, B. (1958). *The dynamics of planned change.* San Diego, CA: Harcourt Brace.

McLean, G.N. (1988). *Construction and analysis of organization climate surveys* (Project Number Twenty-Six). St. Paul, MN: Training and Development Research Center, University of Minnesota.

McLean, G.N., & Pakenham-Walsh, S. (1987, Fall). An in-process model for improving quality management processes. *Consultation, 6*(3), 158-174.

Pfeiffer, J. (1988). (Ed.) *Instrumentation kit.* 3 Vols. San Diego, CA: Pfeiffer & Company.

Pfeiffer, J.W., & Ballew, A.C. (1988). *Using instruments in human resource development* (Vol. 2 of UATT series). San Diego, CA: Pfeiffer & Company.

Phillips, J. (1991). *Handbook of training evaluation and measurement methods* (2nd ed.). Houston, TX: Gulf Publishing.

Porras, J.I. (1984, Summer). Emphasizing the research part of action research: Some guidelines for the researching practitioner. *OD Newsletter,* pp. 4-7.

Porras, J.I., & Berg, P.O. (1978, April). The impact of organization development. *Academy of Management Review.*

Rothwell, W. (1985). Administering the climate survey: A toolkit. *Journal of Technical Writing and Communication, 15*(4), 323-338.

Schmuck, R., & Miles, M. (Eds). (1976). *Organization development in schools.* San Diego, CA: Pfeiffer & Company.

Sleezer, C.M., Swanson, R.A., & Geroy, G.D. (1985). *Validation of the benefit forecasting method: Organization development program to increase health organization membership.* (Project Number Eleven). St. Paul, MN: Training and Development Research Center, University of Minnesota.

CHAPTER 11

ADOPTION

W. James Smith and Jack A. Tesmer

Many organizations are embarking on a quest for excellence. The quest goes by many names: total quality management (TQM), business process reengineering, and reduced cycle time. Even the best-run organizations are heeding the cry to become world class or even world's best. Top managers realize that their organizations must offer superlative customer service and high-quality products at competitive prices to survive in today's competitive global marketplace. Employees also realize that they must contribute to the success of their organizations in order to maintain their jobs.

Although there are many reasons for embarking on a quest for excellence, managers who lead their organizations on such a quest soon discover that there is a significant difference between desiring change and successfully implementing change. As Niccolo Machiavelli observed in *The Prince* (1513/1950):

> There is nothing more difficult to carry out, nor more doubtful of success, nor more dangerous to handle, than to initiate a new order of things. For the reformer has enemies in all those who profit by the old order, and only lukewarm defenders in all those who might profit from the new. (p. 21)

Machiavelli's words hold special meaning for organization development (OD) consultants and others who work toward constructive human and technical change. The general rule is that the greater the scope of change, the fewer the predictable outcomes. When only a small number of outcomes can be predicted accurately about change, consultants should direct their attention to the total system rather than to isolated parts of the system. Organization development consultants refer to the successful installation of change as *adoption*. The term, adoption, in this chapter will be used synonymously with implementation. Adoption is also the seventh step in any OD intervention.

Adoption means that some outcomes of a change effort have become part of an organization's culture. People have moved toward different ways of working and relating to one another; their patterns of responsibility and authority and their channels of communication and influence have changed; and they value these changes.

Adoption implies something quite different from compliance to a rigid norm during the installation of a change effort. In the context of a learning organization, adoption is the result of people in groups internalizing new patterns of action and reflection.

The Quest Metaphor

Metaphors serve us well. They are fun, they are instructive, and they offer valuable insights. Organization development consultants need to be skilled storytellers if they are to capture the attention and enlist the support of their clients. Consultants' communication skills can be strengthened through the appropriate use of metaphors and analogies.

The phrase "quest for excellence," used at the beginning of this chapter, is a metaphor for long-term change and for maintaining change. A quest for excellence, like any quest, is not a short-term undertaking but is a long-term journey. People embark on quests out of aspiration or necessity.

Some people embark on quests when they suffer economic hardships such as losing their jobs. In the same fashion, organizations undertake quests for excellence when competitors gain some of their product niche or market share.

People on quests take only those things that are of greatest value to them. They are pilgrims. They have a sense of urgency born of their desire to find something. A quest is difficult and requires sacrifice. People who embark on quests need a compelling vision to sustain them.

Quests should be led by people who understand the need—and the process—to move their followers through periods of chaos and into new beginnings. Some consultants and clients will find that it is difficult to change the status quo because employees rely on it. They may find that they will need more than just a vision of the future to motivate employees. They may have to develop a power strategy against the status quo.

Quests also require an effective organizational structure. Some consultants group employees into manageable units and set up lines of communication between them. This "marching organization" makes it easier for the leaders to motivate the employees to action and it allows them to navigate through the uncertainty of the change process.

The marching organization requires a clear-cut chain of command; it is a functional hierarchy in which tasks are divided up and authority is keyed to level. It has been used as a model for a long time by many private and public organizations. Critics of the marching-organization model think that it should no longer be used. Yet, the model is one starting point for organizing. Even today, few organizational forms can direct and execute large endeavors as efficiently as the functional hierarchy.

Quests require a transformation in the history of a community or a culture. That transformation requires organizational learning. In the rigid and functionally structured organization, only members at the top of the hierarchy are instructed by a change agent or a consultant. Lower-level change in the organization occurs by instruction from higher-level members.

An organization with a functional hierarchy that undertakes a quest for excellence will find that its organizational structure must change to one that encourages adaptation, self-management, and learning. Learning must occur much deeper in the organization than has been historically necessary. For that reason, as Perry (1990) notes, there is an increasing need to find "liberating organizational forms" that strike the right balance between bureaucracy and harder-to-explain options. One of the main barriers to achieving more effective organizational forms is a lack of knowledge about the available options.

Five Keys to Implement Change Successfully

The following five issues should be considered to implement change successfully:

1. The change should be based on business strategy and business needs;
2. The change must balance planning with flexibility;
3. The change should not rely exclusively on outside expertise;
4. The change should be the center of attention; and
5. The change must be strategy driven rather than project driven.

The Change Should Be Based on Business Strategy and Business Needs

For change to be installed successfully in an organization, the change must be based on the organization's business strategy and its business needs. In other words, managers and other organizational members must be convinced that the change will improve the organization's competitiveness and meet a "felt need."

For example, many organizations in the United States launched change efforts based on criteria for the Malcolm Baldrige National Quality Award. Those criteria were perceived to be central to the business needs and success of most organizations. It is also difficult to argue against most of the Baldrige criteria.

By the same token, change can only be implemented successfully when the change makes sense to all members of an organization, not just to managers or executives. Often, much education is needed to elicit that "felt need" throughout the organization. For example, a consultant helped managers at one organization as they worked to redesign one of their facilities. The managers talked about spending significant time giving people as much information as possible about the business. They shared critical information about costs and markets with their employees. After a year, the organization focused all measurement on the "case cost"—a relative unit of measurement for everyone. The organization spent the time to develop the necessary level of readiness and to focus the effort on issues central to business survival so that all employees, not just managers, could see and feel a need for change.

The Change Must Balance Planning with Flexibility

For change to be adopted successfully in an organization, a change agent must balance the need to have a plan for the change effort with the need to be flexible enough to take advantage of events as the change effort develops.

The need for an action plan to guide the change effort is a practical, political, and often a psychological necessity. (See Chapter 6.) However, as the change effort progresses, a rigid plan becomes a hindrance to transcending current goals or to empowering people to "seize the moment." The consultant will find that altering the plan during the change process can be a challenge. He or she will need to link innovation and development in the operational system to foster continuous improvement and to help managers learn how to change while they are changing.

For example, the top executive of one organization decided that task forces would help her organization's change effort. The executive first explained the need for change to employees and then she formed six large groups comprising managers, supervisors, and employees. The executive instructed each group to devise an action plan for the change effort. Later, the groups were assembled to report on their plans. The executive then asked each group to rework their action plans based on what they had learned from the other groups.

As a final step, the executive formed one overall task force to devise a plan based on the independent, but revised, action plans from the other six task forces. The action plan that the task force developed had significant employee involvement and it covered details that the executive would not have thought of had she developed a plan by herself. Furthermore, the change effort benefitted from the strong employee ownership that was developed by involving employees in the action-planning process.

The Change Should Not Rely Exclusively on Outside Expertise

For change to be adopted successfully in an organization, an OD consultant must gradually move the organization away from dependence on him or her. The organization must learn to keep the change effort alive on its own. The consultant must make sure that the organization has developed the requisite competence needed to maintain the change. Further, the consultant needs to make sure that the organization will devote the adequate internal resources—such as people, money, time, and leadership—to the change effort. Prevailing pressures to downsize, cut corporate operating expenses, and focus operations toward the customer require that organizations devote significant resources to the change effort and that all participants be committed to the change.

Developing an internal capability for change in the organization requires that the consultant be very patient. He or she must deal with setbacks and frustration while keeping enthusiasm for change and continuous improvement alive within the organization. For example, in one organization many employees were frustrated with their new roles as they made a transition from functional work groups to self-directed teams. The consultant set the tone by exhibiting great patience and by encouraging others to be patient.

The Change Should Be the Center of Attention

For change to be adopted successfully, a consultant must integrate it into the daily activities of the organization. By integrating the change, learning is accelerated throughout the organization because everybody is involved in a total-system improvement. The change effort must become the driving force that influences all the organization's improvement efforts. To be completely successful, the change effort must become the center of attention in the organization and must influence decision making. Some organizations do that through a total quality management effort; others use cycle time reduction or business-process reengineering.

The Change Must Be Strategy Driven Rather Than Project Driven

The fifth key issue in implementing change successfully is that the change effort must move away from being project driven and become strategy driven. This important shift in emphasis emerges after three to five years in any large-scale change effort. The relationships that are useful during the start-up of a change effort eventually become a hindrance to its success.

In the early stages of change, credibility is essential. As a result, organization development consultants often undertake projects such as developing an acquisitions process or developing new plant designs. These projects allow the consultants to introduce change in isolated areas that are separated from the established order of the corporate culture. After several projects, the consultants will have introduced change throughout the organization. At that point, the relationship between isolated projects and organizational strategy becomes critically important, and the consultants should begin to focus on total-system change.

Possible Barriers to Implementing Change

This section focuses on five barriers that may prevent an organization from adopting change. Organization development interventions are incredibly fragile for the following reasons:

- People run out of energy;
- Key executives change positions;
- Consultants "burn out";
- Timing is everything; and
- Luck is always an issue.

In a general way, barriers to facilitating the successful adoption of change stem from these reasons. The possible barriers are as follows:

- Consulting dilemmas;

- Poor consultant-client relationship;
- Failure to learn while doing;
- Failure to empower the organization; and
- Ineffective intervention processes.

Consulting Dilemmas

Facilitating the adoption of change cannot be packaged and sold in well-defined doses. Organization development consultants and clients need to be skeptical of easy answers. All OD consultants are confronted with consulting dilemmas and they will have to deal with them successfully to ensure that change is adopted.

Key Consulting Dilemmas

One difficulty of performing OD work stems from broader issues involving consulting services. When selling technical advice and expertise, most consultants work to reduce client anxiety and to solve client problems. As good salespersons, consultants must convince their clients that they can furnish workable solutions to difficult organizational problems. A consultant needs to reduce client anxiety before a client will decide to retain the consultant. Clients buy anxiety reduction.

However, it is not unusual to discover that the client is part of the problem—if not *the* problem. To confront this dilemma the consultant must raise questions that many clients would prefer to avoid. An unethical response to this dilemma is to offer a proposal that does not address the client's or management's role in a problem and keeps the client happy—and the consultant with a job. An ethical response is to address the client's or management's role in a problem even when that places the consultant at risk of losing the client.

For example, sometimes consultants must help managers to admit that they are autocrats. If this is not done very skillfully, the consultants may become unpopular with certain managers, who may try to sabotage the change effort.

Dealing with Consulting Dilemmas

Organization development is based on client requirements, and change efforts are tailored to each client's unique situation. Good OD is more learning centered than solutions oriented; it assumes that the learning process will produce unique, practical solutions. People's involvement in the learning process usually produces better solutions than those that result from unilateral decision making.

Individual, group, and organizational change often require an external consultant as a catalyst. Moreover, many organizations do not give their internal consultants enough credit and assign too much credibility to external consultants. For these reasons, it is often helpful for an internal consultant to collaborate with an external consultant when confronting organizational, personal, technical, and human barriers. The internal consultant needs the reflective feedback and fresh perspectives that the external consultant can provide. Indeed, an external consultant can ask questions that the internal consultant cannot because the external consultant does not rely on the organization's internal systems for self-validation and does not have vested interests in its outcomes.

However, external consultants cannot facilitate lasting change within most organizations as well as internal consultants and managers. Internal consultants understand their organizations' cultures better than external consultants. Also, internal consultants have a vested interest in their organizations' survival and success.

An external consultant also can benefit from working with an organization's internal consultant. By combining the credibility of the external consultant with the political knowledge of the internal consultant, the consultants can strengthen their case for adoption of change.

Poor Consultant-Client Relationship

A good consultant-client relationship is crucial to any change effort. However, no consultant can easily work with every client.

The Hazards of a Poor Relationship

Consultants should not waste time with clients who do not want to change. Clients must want to change. Change is not a product that consultants can sell; rather, it is a process, an effort that clients must engage in. If they are to be successful, OD consultants must interview prospective clients carefully and judge the chances of successful implementation before committing to a change effort. A client's resistance to change is rooted in many causes. These include the following:

- Distrust of consultants;
- Distrust, fear, and resistance among members of the client organization;
- Organizational members' inability to perceive options and their defense of the status quo; and
- The pain from which the client is presently suffering.

There may be resistance to change among people who have "grown up in" or created the existing culture and are now expected to participate in changing it. Once the consultant and client have developed a relationship founded on trust and once they have agreed on their desired outcomes, the client must use influence to support the consultant and the change effort.

A good relationship helps the client and the consultant to do the following:

- Develop a shared vision and a common understanding of organizational purpose;
- Foster motivation, faith, and ability (personal and organizational); and
- Use the organization's distinctive skills, its customs, its expertise, and its technology to support the OD effort.

Dealing with a Poor Relationship

An organization development consultant should not prematurely judge a client as unwilling to change. A consultant should be willing to work with a client who is gradually learning to be open minded.

A consultant should remember that a client's readiness for change is usually a function of situation and timing. Of course, the consultant can contribute to an impetus to change once he or she has begun to work with the client. The consultant generally has to operate in two areas at once. He or she has to respond to the client's immediate need and also look for the larger, systemic problems. As the consultant and the client learn together, resistance is understood, addressed, and, eventually, anticipated.

Poor consultant-client relationships do not permit the vulnerability that is experienced when people open themselves and their organizations to learning. People only learn as they grow to trust themselves and other people. Over time, unwilling clients can become receptive to change and can begin the learning process. For change to be successfully adopted, it must be grounded in participation, openness, and commitment.

Failure To Learn While Doing

An important task in any consultant-client partnership is designing a long-term action plan that has short-range, intermediate-range, and long-range flexible strategies. A consultant must be able to balance a client's need to design an overall plan for the change effort with the client's need to remain flexible. Managing continual change means learning while doing and adjusting as necessary. Many effective change strategies were not anticipated at the beginning of an OD intervention but developed as a result of new insights once the change had begun and participants progressed on a learning curve.

Understanding the Problems in Failure To Learn While Doing

There is an inherent uncertainty and ambiguity in learning while changing. Consultant and organizational members gradually begin to realize the truth of Kurt Lewin's observation that for people to understand an organization, they must change it. It is only through change that the forces that hold organizations in stasis are revealed. It is through action that observation and research become possible, and they, in turn, provide direction for future action.

Lewin's action-research model has been supplemented by Shewhart's plan-do-check-act (PDCA) model. (Both models are described in Chapter 2.) Continual organizational change develops and improves on its processes. (As a friend of the author says, we know where we want to end up, but drawing the map is the problem. There are no roads going to where we want to go. We create the means as we define the ends more clearly over time.)

Management is often frustrated about the lack of clear, immediate direction. Indeed, in the initial stages of most change efforts, clients insist that OD consultants tell them exactly what they should do, how it should happen, and what results to expect. Over time, clients will learn the dangers of a "quick fix" and will realize that change efforts have to mature to the point that people no longer need detailed plans to continue their efforts. This is learning in real time.

Dealing with the Failure To Learn While Doing

An OD consultant needs to bring calm to the sense of turbulence that surrounds a change effort. He or she must possess the wisdom to remain alert to both the promise of danger and the opportunity to change. The consultant must apply to change what Lao Tzu (circa 600 B.C./1972) notes about leadership:

> As for the best leaders, the people do not notice their existence. The next best the people honor and praise, the next the people fear; and the next the people hate.... When the best leader's work is done the people say, We did it ourselves! To lead the people, walk behind them.

Although the consultant must remain calm in the midst of uncertainty, he or she must also realize that if he or she does not clarify a direction and define an approach to change, chaos may result. To begin action, the consultant needs to help define the client's destination and the key steps in the change effort. The consultant may need to help the client to reroute some of the steps during the change process. But without a flexible action plan to guide change and learning, the client organization will not experience any progress.

Organizational members can learn while changing by being asked to report on the organization's external environment. Such learning is critical because most demands for organizational change originate externally with customers, competitors, suppliers, and regulators. Many approaches exist to help clients reach such understanding.

Once the organizational members understand the external environment, the second step is to translate external demand, based on the environment, into internal requirements that provide strategic direction. Organization development methods or techniques are developed for this purpose. For example, much work has been done on organizational-assessment interventions to help clients achieve in-depth understanding of their organizations' strengths and weaknesses. Organization development tools and processes are necessary to define the client's vision, analyze the client's current situation, and define the client's targets and goals. The consultant needs to develop methods to respond to each organizational need. Some methods are better for defining the ends (vision); others are better for defining the means (strategy).

To translate what is imperative in the organization's environment into an internal direction, the consultant will have to focus the organization's attention toward its customers or other stakeholders. The consultant then needs to help the client identify processes that affect organizational performance. More often than not, those processes are cross-functional, and the functional parts are suboptimized. The consultant will find that the best way to optimize those parts is to put the people who perform the work in charge of optimizing them. For change to occur, learning must occur at that level.

The third step is to translate the organization's strategic direction into operating systems that will lead toward the realization of defined goals. The consultant may need to focus client attention on creating or reexamining the following operating systems:

- The work flow and technical system;
- The structural system;
- The information and decision-making system;
- The people system; and
- The reward system.

As part of this process, the consultant will need to pay close attention to work-group boundaries, roles and responsibilities, information-sharing and decision-making processes, and work measurements and standards.

Organization development frequently involves a total-system change. Consultants must listen carefully to what clients are saying. Over the years, the clients' remarks have been changing. Not too long ago, clients said, "It is necessary to work smarter, not harder." Then they said, "It is essential to do more with less." As competitive pressures mounted, they began to say, "It is necessary to do less with less, prioritizing so that critical tasks are accomplished." Now they seem to be saying, "problems must be approached in radically new ways. Our work methods are not effective. We are stretched too thin, and we are running out of time. We cannot delegate nor can we successfully shoulder our enormous responsibilities. At the same time, matters have become so complex that we do not know how it all ties together." These are the clients who consultants must help. These are also the clients that are most willing to learn while changing.

Failure To Empower the Employees

If people are not empowered to act, change is unlikely to be adopted. In one sense, *empowerment* means giving people the skills and information they need to make good decisions and take informed, deliberate actions. Most OD consultants work toward empowering members of client organizations so organizational members can solve problems and manage change on their own. People within client organizations must be equipped with the tools and the skills to maintain change efforts so that OD consultants can disengage.

Empowerment does *not* mean "allowing people to do whatever they wish." Peter Koestenbahm (1991) defines "empowerment" by a simple equation:

$$\text{Empowerment} = \text{Direction} \times \text{Support} \times \text{Autonomy}$$

Note that the relationships are multiplicative. If any element equals 0, the product of the equation equals 0.

Problems with Empowerment

The following are some of the empowerment problems that consultants will encounter in OD interventions and that may hinder the adoption of change:

- Members of client organizations do not understand the direction in which their organizations are moving;

- Organizational members do not understand their organizations' business;
- Organizational members disagree about which priorities demand attention;
- Some organizational members think they are not trusted or sense little support from their organizations, their managers, or their peers;
- Some organizational members do not think their organizations provide necessary training and information so that employees can meet their responsibilities; and
- Some organizational members do not think they have sufficient autonomy to make improvements.

Creating Effective Empowerment

The following four issues are important in building employee empowerment:

1. An organization must achieve clarity of purpose;
2. An organization must establish its change processes collaboratively;
3. An organization must establish ways to engage employees in problem finding and problem solving; and
4. A consultant must develop an organization's internal resources to adopt and sustain the change over time.

Enabling an organization to learn and improve its performance is a critical venture for a consultant. Organizational learning starts with clarity of purpose. The consultant needs to make sure that organizational members work together collaboratively to define what the business is and what the business should become. People will benefit from in-depth discussions about organizational purpose. Indeed, clarifying organizational purpose is often a major OD intervention in its own right.

Customers and employees are often best equipped to clarify the organization's purpose. That is why the consultant must make sure that the change processes is planned and implemented collaboratively. For example, Motorola's Six Sigma Process emphasizes six components:

1. Knowing the organization's products and services;
2. Listening to, and understanding, the customer;
3. Knowing suppliers and perfecting relationships with them;
4. Understanding core processes of the business;
5. Eliminating waste and making processes mistake proof; and
6. Measuring, analyzing, and controlling.

Each item on the list is predicated on an understanding of the organization's purpose. The client organization's purpose should be a function of collaboration among its members.

Hanna (1987) talks about the need for an "outside-in" approach in which key representatives of external stakeholder groups are brought into an organization to discuss their expectations and to evaluate the organization's performance. Hanna's approach ensures that the organization does not operate exclusively by internal criteria. Indeed, probably too many organizations judge their performance and exert control through internal measures alone.

An organization also needs to maintain direct contact with its customers. A customer survey presents a key opportunity for an organization to involve its customers in defining the organization's purpose. Core production processes then can be directed toward doing the right things more effectively rather than doing the wrong things more efficiently.

A simple example should help to underscore this point. A large oil company wanted to redesign its procurement and materials-handling process. Everyone in the company had an opinion about what was wrong and what needed to be fixed. The design team systematically interviewed 250 operating supervisors to assess their needs in procurement and materials handling. After the interviews, the design team had comprehensive information on customer expectations and suggestions for improvement.

Once the consultant has established a solid understanding of the organization's purpose and the customers' needs, he or she will need to train employees to service the customers. Employees will need to be empowered to take appropriate action when customers require service.

In most change efforts, an OD consultant must help the client progress from "everyone has an opinion" to "valid information" to "possible solutions."

Ineffective Intervention Processes

Interventions are the basic technologies of OD. They are structured activities intended to help organizations to achieve new performance levels.

Much has been written about intervention theory and methods. Sherwood (1988) described the ideal redesign intervention. This type of intervention depends heavily on committed "champions" or "sponsors" for its success (see Exhibit 11-1). When sponsors appreciate the need for change, they work with a consultant to form a steering committee to guide the effort. The steering committee comprises key executives in the organization and usually has seven to fifteen members who are responsible for overseeing the effort and approving proposals for change. The sponsors, the steering committee, and the consultant work together to do the following:

1. Define the organization's vision;
2. Provide the needed resources for the change effort;
3. Achieve their own understanding of the change effort;
4. Provide educational events to employees to focus the effort;
5. Communicate the willingness to consider new approaches; and
6. Form one or more design teams to perform an analysis of the operational system.

A design team is a small, cross-functional task force comprising key people from operational systems or units that have to produce across boundaries to improve overall performance. Design teams proceed through the phases of analysis, diagnosis, design, and implementation. They produce thoughtful proposals for the steering committee. Effective design teams are mechanisms to produce the results that follow (Argyris, 1970):

1. Valid information about system performance;
2. Free and informed choice based on thoughtful alternatives; and
3. Commitment to the choices made because the process is based on user involvement.

The basic structure of the "analysis-diagnosis-design-implementation" intervention can be traced to the sociotechnical systems work of Emery and Trist (1965), Bridges and Michael Foster at the Tavistock Institute in London. Organization

Exhibit 11-1: A Model for Introducing Change into Work Organizations

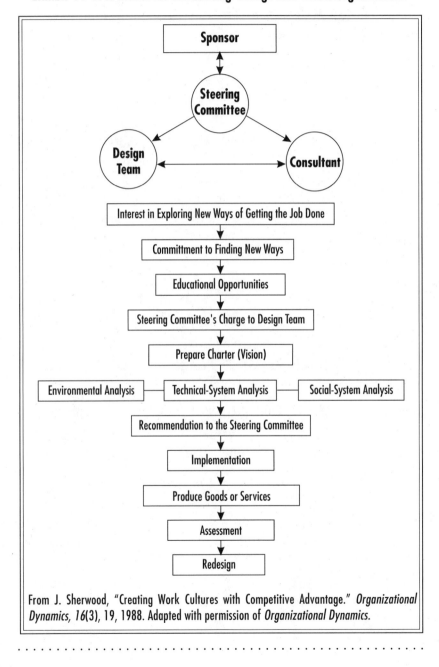

From J. Sherwood, "Creating Work Cultures with Competitive Advantage." *Organizational Dynamics, 16*(3), 19, 1988. Adapted with permission of *Organizational Dynamics.*

development consultants work to embed this structure in a broader process to achieve sustained large-system development. The analysis, diagnosis, design, and implementation phases require as long as four to six months; achieving a learning culture to carry the effort forward and to internalize the skills and new assumptions takes three to five years.

Weisbord (1987) describes the usefulness of interventions designed with "everyone in the room at once." Interventions are catalytic events with risk and opportunity for all involved. When everyone in a work group is involved in a change effort, the impetus for adopting change becomes powerful. The evolution of team building in work groups, a principle technology of OD, stems from the understanding of the importance of involving everyone.

References

Argyris, C. (1970). *Intervention theory and method.* Reading, MA: Addison-Wesley.

Emery, F., & Trist, E. (1965). The causal texture of organizational environments. *Human Relations, 18,* 21-32.

Hanna, D. (1987). *Designing organizations for high performance.* Reading, MA: Addison-Wesley.

Koestenbahm, P. (1991). *Leadership.* San Francisco, CA: Jossey-Bass.

Machiavelli, N. (1513/1950). *The prince* and *The discourses.* (The Modern Library Trans.) New York: Random House. [Original works published 1513]

Perry, L. (1990). *Offensive strategy: Forging a new competitiveness in the fires of head to head competition.* New York: Harper Business Press.

Sherwood, J. (1988, Winter). Creating work cultures with competitive advantage. *Organizational Dynamics,* pp. 5-27.

Tzu, L. (1972). *Tao te ching.* (G.F. Feng & J. English Trans.) New York: Random House. [Original work published in the 6th century B.C.]

Weisbord, M. (1987). *Productive workplaces: Organizing and managing for dignity, meaning, and community.* San Francisco, CA: Jossey-Bass.

CHAPTER 12

SEPARATION

Ann Van Eron and W. Warner Burke

S*eparation*—a term synonymous with disengagement or termination—is the process of departing from a client setting. It is the final step of the action research model and of most organization development (OD) interventions. Separation should be effectively managed by a consultant because too many OD projects may linger unproductively or may end abruptly and without adequate follow-up.

Separation Defined

Separation entails a consultant's departure from a client setting (Dougherty, 1990) and his or her assistance to a client in the continuation or maintenance of a change effort. Kolb and Frohman (1970) argue that "the consultant-client relationship is by definition 'temporary'" (p. 61) and it is successful if a consultant leaves the client setting because the organization has achieved its goals and the organization no longer needs consultative help. Lippitt, Watson, and Westley (1958) include termination in their model as the final phase of the OD process.

Termination is not always considered the final phase of the OD process (Burke, 1982a). For example, termination is not appropriate for an internal consultant, except on a project basis. Although the internal consultant may terminate specific programs and projects, he or she is nevertheless responsible for supporting an organization's new culture, following up with managers regarding the effectiveness of an intervention, and assisting with process consultation on a continual basis.

An external consultant will more frequently separate from a client setting. The external consultant's objective when he or she separates from the setting is to ensure that the client has internal human resources who can take over the change effort and who are committed to the continuing progress of the change effort.

It is a key assumption of this chapter that OD consultants can successfully separate from client organizations over a period of time. However, it is not always necessary or helpful for consultants to sever their relationships with clients. Some organizations may need periodic diagnostic reviews and assistance from external consultants. Such clients usually rehire consultants who have worked with them and who have maintained positive relationships with them. Furthermore, because of the dynamic, changing nature of organizations, managers and executives may benefit from continual consultative work.

Separation involves three stages: (1) evaluation, (2) determination of next steps, and (3) planning for post-consultation. (See Exhibit 12-1.)

Exhibit 12-1: The Separation Process

Evaulation	Determination of Next Steps	Planning for Post-Consultation
1. Project	1. Continue current initiative.	1. Develop separation plan.
2. Process	2. Start new project.	2. Transfer process to client.
	3. Stop project temporarily or permanently.	3. Reduce consultant invovlement.
		4. Address psychological issues.
		5. Complete administrative tasks and formally end project.
		6. Follow up.

Like other steps in OD interventions that are based on the action research model, separation requires careful planning and consideration. Prior to finalizing an intervention, a consultant should evaluate the project. Both the consultant and the client should evaluate the project's outcomes. In addition to evaluating the outcomes of the change effort, they should also evaluate their relationship as well as the processes used during their relationship.

After evaluating the success of the project from the perspective of its outcomes and processes, the consultant must determine what are the most suitable next steps. There are generally three options:

1. Continue the project or put more effort into the project if its goals have not been achieved;

2. Begin a new related or unrelated project; or
3. Terminate the relationship between the consultant and the client organization temporarily or permanently.

When both the client and the consultant agree that a current project should continue to achieve its desired outcomes, they then should determine the best way to achieve the project's goal. The consultant and the client should identify any obstacles to the goals, and they should plan to overcome these obstacles or any others that they may encounter later. If the client and the consultant believe that the current intervention is not yielding the desired results, they should assess the preliminary results and identify other interventions. They may need to redefine the problem.

If the organization development consultant and the client determine that the project is complete, the consultant may be able to identify new related or unrelated projects by reviewing the steps of the action research model. He or she may be able to continue the OD cycle by identifying a new project, defining its scope, developing a plan for the project, and selling it to the client.

If the consultant and the client determine that the consultant's work is complete and that there are no additional projects needed, the OD consultant should begin to develop post-consultation plans. The purpose of post-consultation planning is for the consultant to determine how to best transfer the responsibility for the change effort to the client organization. As the consultant reduces his or her involvement in the client organization, he or she needs to assist those involved with issues related to separation and the consultant may find that follow-up is needed. After he or she has submitted any final reports and invoices, the consultant can begin to formally separate from the setting. However, the consultant may maintain a continuing relationship through follow-up with the client organization.

Separation Competencies

Many skills used in earlier steps of an OD intervention are necessary in the separation step. For example, the skills employed in the contracting phase are required to confirm or renegotiate a contract. If a consultant does not get an additional project with a client he or she will still need to contract for post-consultation planning.

Some consultants incorrectly assume that if they have demonstrated these skills and have progressed through the prior steps in interventions, they will be able to progress smoothly through the separation phase. Often, however, interventions stop prematurely or linger for a period of time because of the reluctance of consultants, clients, or both to sever ties or reduce their emotional investments in one another.

A consultant will need to do the following to conduct the separation step:

Evaluate

- Provide feedback to the client on the process of the intervention and its outcomes;
- Initiate dialogue on the consultant-client relationship;
- Facilitate feedback on the consultant-client relationship; and
- Acknowledge failures and successes.

Determine Next Steps

- Facilitate discussion with the client regarding next steps for the project;

- Ask appropriate questions, analyze the situation, and identify client needs and possible new projects;

- Recognize and accept when separation is desirable;

- Initiate open discussion about separation, when appropriate; and

- Recognize when continued assistance is counterproductive.

Manage Post-Consultation

- Facilitate the separation process;

- Transfer the responsibility for the change effort to the client;

- Clarify appropriate conditions under which you could be called back;

- Address psychological issues related to separation so that consultant involvement is reduced effectively;

- Develop a follow-up plan;

- Understand and respond to post-separation emotions of consultant and client;

- Complete administrative tasks related to the project;

- Plan a departure that meets the needs of those involved; and

- Follow up with the client after departure.

A good example of a consultant not managing the post-consultation step effectively exists in Burke's *Cases in Organization Development* (1991). In an actual case, the consultant became exasperated with the company's chief executive officer (CEO) who seemed incapable of or unwilling to take action that would change the organization. The CEO did modify the structure and fired a key executive, but the OD consultant thought these changes were cosmetic and were not the fundamental changes that were required for organizational effectiveness.

Because the consultant had other clients who were more demanding at that time, he allowed the client to drift away rather than pursuing potential options for change and working on the relationship with the CEO. Separation in this case occurred because of time elapsing rather than through a managed process.

The Separation Process

The separation step is influenced by the type of consulting project, the intimacy of the consultant-client relationship, and the quality of the collaboration. Some projects, such as facilitating an off-site meeting, have clearly defined stages and endings. Short, well-defined projects generally have obvious closings that were predetermined in the contracting stage. Separation in these projects is usually less emotional and more straightforward. Longer, significant change efforts have less well-defined endings. There is more room for differences and more effort required for successful disengagement in these projects.

Evaluation

A consultant should evaluate an intervention regularly. The consultant also should evaluate the outcomes and the process of the consultation.

The OD consultant and the client should evaluate their consultant-client relationship throughout the project. This evaluation typically is not part of the more formal evaluation (Lundberg, 1985). However, the success of the change effort is to a large degree a function of the consultant-client relationship (Lippitt, Watson & Westley, 1958).

The evaluation of the consultant-client relationship is a key focus in the separation step. Just as the consultant is continually contracting, diagnosing, and intervening in the organization, he or she also should continually evaluate the change effort and the consultant-client relationship. The consultant and the client should assess the strengths and areas for improvement in their relationship, and they also should identify what they learned from the process. One way that the OD consultant can open dialogue about the consultant-client relationship is to mention it in a regular meeting he or she has with the client. For example, if they meet once a month for a progress report, the consultant should ask the client for his or her perceptions of how their relationship is proceeding. The evaluation that ensues at the end of the process is likely to reflect previous evaluations.

When reviewing the purpose of the change effort, the consultant and the client should reflect on how they defined the initial problem. They should try to remember how they determined that the change effort and the consultant's role were appropriate. The consultant and the client also need to evaluate the activities and the outcomes of all interventions. The cost effectiveness of the resultant changes should also be determined.

The client and the consultant then should identify the client's additional needs. The following are some questions that they should ask during the evaluation process:

- What was the purpose or desired outcome of the change effort?

- What were the defined roles of the consultant and the client?

- What were the results of the planned interventions?
- Was the formal evaluation of the change effort adequate and comprehensive?
- Were the results of the formal evaluation communicated appropriately?
- How could the working relationship between the consultant and the client be characterized?
- What were the strengths of the consultant-client relationship?
- What were the disappointments and areas for improvement in the consultant-client relationship?
- Was the consultation timely and cost effective?
- What has each party learned from the process?
- How could the consultant-client relationship be enhanced?
- Given the results of the change effort, what else needs to be done?
- Who should be involved in determining the next steps?
- Have the skills needed to continue the change effort been transferred to the client?
- Should the consultant-client relationship be continued? If so, toward what objective(s)?

Authenticity

An authentic consultant-client relationship based on trust will allow a candid evaluation between a consultant and a client. Although the consultant separates from the organization for a period of time, a friendship and an advisory relationship with the client may continue. Some OD consultants maintain relationships with former clients for many years. It is not uncommon for a former client to call a consultant for advice or to offer the consultant a new project.

Dependence

A part of the value system and folklore of OD is that effective consultants work themselves out of jobs. It is important for OD consultants to transfer their skills to clients and to identify resources in client organizations to carry on change efforts. At the same time, consultants must avoid becoming dependent on their clients as a means to meet their needs for work, money, or affiliation because these needs can lead to unnecessary change efforts and wasted resources. Consultants should respond to actual needs in client organizations rather than to their own needs.

As consultants embark on the separation process, they should be aware of their "need to be needed" and refrain from encountering dependence (Bell & Nadler, 1979). To avoid dependence, consultants need to train those in client organizations to continue their own change efforts.

In practice, one project with a client often leads to other projects. An effective consultant develops a good working relationship with his or her client and identifies new opportunities within the client organization. At the same time, the OD consultant should continue to transfer his or her skills to organizational members so that they are capable of facilitating their own change efforts.

The notion of dependence in the OD relationship has its origin in the assumption that the consulting relationship is equivalent to the relationship between a therapist and patient.

Although both are helping relationships, the situations are quite different. The client for an OD consultant is often an organizational system, and the OD consultant tends to work with many people from the client organization and with the interfaces between people and units. This mitigates personal dependence issues with the consultant. On the other hand, a prolonged project can create some dependence on the consultant. That is why appropriate training of organizational members is so important to effective separation.

Determining Next Steps

After the client and the consultant have reviewed the initial agreement or contract and determined the results of the change effort, they can then identify any remaining tasks and determine whether to continue the services of the OD consultant. The client and the consultant should develop an outline of next steps and decide who will be involved in the next steps. If the goals of the change effort were not realized, the consultant and the client will need to redefine the problem and/or generate new intervention options. Even if the goals of the effort were realized, there still may be additional or related work for the consultant. In this case, the process moves to one of exploring needs and contracting.

Although viewing an OD intervention as a series of steps is useful as a learning mechanism, the steps do overlap. Contracting with the client is a continual process. The consultant may begin to contract for other projects when he or she finishes a project or when his or her role changes.

A consultant or a client may reach a point in which one or both of the parties does not wish to continue or renew the relationship. In this final separation step, the client and the consultant mutually decide to terminate consultation services. Trust between the client and consultant should enable an open and rational discussion about an appropriate time to reduce consultant involvement (Schein, 1969). Abrupt termination, particularly resulting from a unilateral decision by one of the parties, can be disruptive and shocking to the whole system (Bell & Nadler, 1979).

An abrupt termination of an OD intervention may not allow the consultant or the client adequate time to alert organizational members or to plan for closure of activities. Furthermore, an abrupt termination may be an indicator of the health of the organization and/or of the consultant-client relationship. If the consultant-client relationship has been productive, the consultant and the client should be able to agree on a mutually satisfactory arrangement for termination. Although one party may feel strongly that termination is necessary, with open communication and trust, a satisfactory agreement can be negotiated.

In determining if separation is appropriate, an OD consultant should consider the following:

- The status of the intervention or the change effort;
- The client's resources and ability to maintain the OD project;
- The amount of time the consultant has available;
- The degree of cooperation and trust between the consultant and the client, as well as within the organization;
- The status of a current project prior to the consultant beginning a next project;
- The organization's readiness, openness, and commitment to move to another step or stage of change; and

- The organization's available resources to bring about change.

Some indications that the consultant may have stayed with the client for too long include the following:

- The consultant is no longer objective and has become part of the system, if not part of the problem;
- The consultant has become too dependent on the client and needs the work;
- The consultant is not growing or the consultant's personal needs are not being satisfied by affiliation with the client (the same statement holds true for the client);
- A less than healthy or negative relationship with the client evolves;
- Lack of trust between the consultant and the client becomes evident; and
- The client becomes too dependent on the consultant by making requests that the consultant believes the client knows how to do. (The consultant may help the client when the client does not have the time to finish a project or if the client is understaffed. This kind of work, however, is usually not OD.)

There are a variety of reasons for a consultant to reduce involvement in a client system. Some of these include the following:

- A contract is fulfilled;
- A budget change affects the consulting services;
- Resources for a change effort are not available or have been depleted;

- The consultant's primary client contact is transferred or leaves the organization;
- Critical skills have been successfully transferred to key members of the client organization;
- Organizational changes such as a merger or change of management call for a change of direction or termination of the change effort;
- Different consultation expertise is now required by the client;
- The client does not wish to proceed in a manner that the consultant advocates as most productive;
- Irreconcilable differences exist between the consultant and key organizational members;
- The consultant believes that nothing else can be accomplished;
- The consultant believes that his or her values will be compromised or that an ethical breach of contract will result by continuing the change effort. For example, a consultant may be asked to lie, manipulate findings for public relations purposes, or betray confidences;
- The consultant is afraid to move on and stays with a project for an extended period of time; or
- The client system wishes to continue without the assistance of a consultant.

Consultant Work Load

Both internal and external consultants must manage work schedules. A primary reason a consultant separates from a client setting is to focus on other projects. However, if a consultant does not have other projects scheduled, he or she may prolong the consultant's work with the current client. If the consultant becomes financially dependent on the client, he or she may make biased decisions about termination or other issues. The consultant needs to understand and manage these influences.

Need for Responsive Initiatives

In the process of determining the next steps, a consultant and a client may identify problems in the implementation process. For example, if they determine that the consultant made an error in analyzing the available data or that he or she failed to follow through on a commitment, the consultant should agree to rectify the situation at no additional cost to the organization. However, the consultant and the client should not be held responsible for what is outside their spheres of influence, such as the departure or transfer of a key staff person.

Sometimes a client may expect a consultant to absorb the cost of remedial work even if the consultant is not directly responsible. An open, honest relationship is invaluable in these circumstances. When disagreement over uncompensated tasks arises, the consultant must determine whether the cost of performing the work without additional pay outweighs the cost of client dissatisfaction (Kelley, 1981).

Post-Consultation Planning

As a part of post-consultation planning, an OD consultant should do the following:

- Develop a separation plan;

- Transfer the process to the client;
- Reduce consultant involvement;
- Address psychological issues;
- Complete administrative tasks and formally leave the setting; and
- Follow up.

Develop a Separation Plan

Separation planning begins when a client and a consultant decide that there are no current or future roles for the consultant. Post-consultation planning enhances the likelihood that the outcomes of an OD intervention will be maintained and supported in an organization.

Key parties who are influenced by the consulting process should be involved in the post-consultation planning. While plans are made between the consultant and the client, the consultant should solicit input from other organizational members who were affected. The key players should develop and approve the post-consultation plans. The more involved the consultant has been with the client system, the more time and effort he or she may need to prepare for separation.

Transfer the Process to the Client

The adoption step (described in Chapter 11) addresses the process of stabilizing positive learning and change in the organization and transferring the OD process to the person or department trained to be the OD resource in the system. While the transfer of learning takes place throughout the organization, the consultant may need to develop more aggressive plans to ensure that the outcomes of the process are integrated into the organizational system.

The organization development consultant should establish a follow-up plan and an agenda of activities by using the same planning process applied in previous phases of the change effort. The process includes defining objectives, establishing procedures, assigning responsibilities, and evaluating cost effectiveness and feasibility (Bittel, 1972).

As part of post-consultation planning, the consultant should have a meeting with the client to formally review the consultant's final report. This meeting also provides them with an opportunity to deal with unresolved issues (Bell & Nadler, 1979; Dougherty, 1990). A final date for the consultant's departure also can be determined at this meeting. According to Parsons & Meyers (1984), establishing a definite termination point prevents unnecessary dependence by the consultant or the client.

Reduce Consultant Involvement

A good consultant-client relationship can involve a protracted process of contracting and disengagement. After the decision has been made that the consultant will terminate activities with the client, the consultant should begin to reduce his or her involvement with the client setting. Critical parties of the change effort should be notified of the ending of the consultation in an appropriate and timely way.

The consultant needs to make sure that appropriate support systems are in place as disengagement proceeds and he or she may need to conduct additional training. A sound method of reducing involvement is *fading* (Dougherty, 1990). In this method, contact with the client is gradually reduced.

For example, if the consultant had been meeting with the client twice a week, he or she should begin to meet with the client only once a week, then every other week, then once each month, then once a quarter, and finally once after several quarters. As the role of the consultant fades, the client organization begins to assume responsibilities previously held by the consultant. The reduced involvement allows the client and the consultant to reassess the appropriate timing for disengagement. If the timing is not appropriate, renegotiation of the contract is possible.

According to Schein (1969), the reduced involvement must be negotiated between the client and the consultant to assure the client that reduced involvement is not equivalent to no involvement. Very low involvement such as attending occasional meetings creates opportunities for the consultant to become involved more easily than complete termination. Bell and Nadler (1979) contend that the consultant should be available on an "as-needed" basis while the client organization manages the changes brought about by the consulting effort.

Address Psychological Issues

The client and the consultant may experience a sense of loss that may result in depression and dependence as a positive working relationship comes to a close (Kelley, 1981). In some societies, endings often initiate anxiety, discomfort, sadness, or depression. Therefore, some people may avoid terminating relationships. They may postpone completing projects by beginning new projects or by procrastinating in completing assignments.

The client and the consultant may have shared important experiences and are likely to have developed a mutual interdependence. It is important that the consultant initiate a discussion to address and deal with the emotions associated with disengagement. Otherwise, these feelings may not go away (Kelley, 1981) and they could lead to anger or an unproductive extension of the consulting process (Dougherty, 1990).

In a healthy but terminating OD relationship, the client may miss the confidential, candid, and stimulating discussions he or she had with the consultant. Both the client and the consultant experience the loss of friendship. The consultant may also sense a loss of challenge.

The process of jointly evaluating the appropriate time to terminate the relationship allows the client and the consultant an opportunity to share their feelings and perspectives. An open discussion about the discomfort in separation is important and healthy. The consultant and the client will find it valuable to understand the stages and the behavioral outcomes of the mourning process for long-term relationships. Bridge's (1980) book on transitions presents one view of this process.

The consultant may express concern about the well-being of the client. In addition, discussing future possibilities for working together can ease the stress of termination (Dougherty, 1990) and can validate the friendship.

The consultant should plan to fill the emotional gap that he or she experiences when a major project is completed. It is not uncommon for consultants to experience depression after successfully completing major projects. Many OD consultants immediately begin new and challenging projects; others plan relaxation time. It is helpful to acknowledge that low feelings are natural and to learn how to manage them (Kelley, 1981).

Complete Administrative Tasks and Formally Leave the Setting

The consultant should complete all necessary reports and documentation required by the organization before leaving the client setting. In addition, final invoices for services and expenses should be submitted.

The consultant also should send a letter documenting the disengagement agreement and the date of the final termination when he or she sends the final invoice. This letter should summarize the results of the project and the benefits experienced by the client organization. In addition, the consultant should thank the client for the opportunity to work with the organization. The OD consultant also should summarize the follow-up plan developed with the client and reiterate that the client should feel free to contact the consultant if problems or new projects develop.

The consultant's failure to send a final invoice or provide a final report may indicate his or her reluctance to acknowledge departure and completion of the project. In fact, it is not uncommon for consultants to delay submitting their last invoices.

Although terminating a project is difficult for the consultant and the client, a formal closure that allows all parties involved to celebrate their accomplishments promotes positive morale. An undefined closure leaves individuals feeling unfinished and, perhaps, angry or hurt. In addition, an undefined closure can influence post-consultation plans and the consultant's possibility of contracting for future projects with the client. As a means for recognizing achievements, the consultant and the client may plan to make a joint presentation at a conference or to publish what they have learned.

Follow-Up

An action plan, designed to facilitate follow-up, assures the consultant and the client that their work outcomes will be revisited later. According to Kelley (1981), follow-up affords an opportunity to salvage plans that have not been adequately implemented. Moreover, the consultant's future availability can be clarified during this time.

During follow-up, the client can contact the consultant if problems arise. The consultant agrees to check in with the client and other designated individuals on a regular basis to maintain the relationship and monitor the project. This follow-up serves as an early warning system for problems. The consultant can also maintain contact with the client by calling or sending pertinent publications and articles.

Some consultants build remuneration for follow-up with associated costs into their initial proposals. Others renegotiate their contracts for this service at disengagement. Often, however, consultants absorb the cost of follow-up as part of the cost of being in business. Advantages of follow-up include the opportunity to assure the success of a project, to identify other client needs, and to remind the client of the consultant's services and availability.

Learning Activities Related to Separation

The best way for consultants to prepare for the separation process is to practice and become comfortable with separation discussion. Sample role-play activities follow. For each role play, a consultant should find a colleague with experience in OD with whom he or she can spend about ten minutes. The consultant should read the role-play description, act out the role, and then discuss issues that occur as a result of the role-play activity with his or her colleague.

- Role play an evaluation discussion that would occur after working for one month with a new client. In this situation, the consultant is meeting with the client's steering committee to give the members data on the organization's climate and to give the members and the client feedback.

- Role play an evaluation discussion in which the consultant is frustrated because the client is not interested in taking the course of action the consultant strongly believes is warranted.

- Role play an evaluation discussion in which the client believes that the consultant received erroneous information during an off-site management meeting that the consultant facilitated. The client is worried that the consultant will make decisions based on that information.

- Role play a planning session between the client and the consultant. This discussion would occur after they have analyzed a formal survey of a cultural-change process.

- Role play a discussion between the consultant and the client in which they have determined that the current project has been completed and the consultant is contracting for a new, related project.

- Role play a discussion between the consultant and the client in which the client has indicated that the project has been completed and there are no additional funds for a new project.

- Role play a discussion between the client and the consultant in which, after three years, the consultant believes that the necessary skills have been transferred to the client and that there is no need to continue the OD intervention.
- Role play a discussion between the consultant and the client in which the client wants to end the project and the consultant believes separation is premature.
- Role play a discussion between the consultant and a newly appointed CEO who has a different value system and style from previous management.
- Role play a post-consultation planning discussion between the consultant and the client in which the consultant provides an outline for how the responsibility for the project will be transferred to the client, a separation schedule, and a follow-up plan.
- Role play a post-consultation planning discussion between the consultant and the client in which the OD consultant talks with the client about the emotional issues related to separating after four years of working together.
- Role play a discussion between the consultant and the client in which the consultant believes that he or she has been asked to do something he or she considers to be unethical, such as revealing sources of confidential information from a series of interviews with managers.

After each role play, the consultant should write a list of issues for future exploration and learning and then discuss the issues on that list with professional colleagues in OD as opportunities present themselves.

References

Bell, C.R., & Nadler, L. (1979). Disengagement and closure. In C.R. Bell and L. Nadler (Eds.), *The client-consultant handbook* (pp. 210-214). Houston, TX: Gulf.

Bittel, L.R. (1972). *The nine master keys of management.* New York: McGraw-Hill.

Bridge, W. (1980). *Transitions: Making sense of life's changes.* Reading, MA: Addison-Wesley.

Burke, W.W. (1982a). *Principles and practices of organization development.* New York: Harper Collins.

Burke, W.W. (1991). Engineered materials. In A.M. Glassman & T.G. Cummings (Eds.), *Cases in organization development* (pp. 68-77). Homewood, IL: Irwin.

Dougherty, A.M. (1990). *Consultation: Practice and perspectives.* Pacific Grove, CA: Brooks/Cole.

Kelley, R.E. (1981). *Consulting: The complete guide to a profitable career.* New York: Scribner's.

Kolb, D.A., & Frohman, A.L. (1970). An organization development approach to consulting. *Sloan Management Review, 12*(1), 51-65.

Lippitt, R., Watson, J., & Westley, B. (1958). *Dynamics of planned change.* San Diego, CA: Harcourt Brace.

Lundberg, C.C. (1985). Consultant feedback: A metaphor technique. *Consultation, 4*(2), 145-151.

Parsons, R.D., & Meyers, J. (1984). *Developing consultation skills.* San Francisco, CA: Jossey-Bass.

Schein, E.H. (1969). *Process consultation: Its role in organization development.* Reading, MA: Addison-Wesley.

P A R T III

INTERNATIONAL COMPETENCIES AND ETHICS IN OD

Part III covers international competencies and the ethics of OD consultants.

CHAPTER 13

INTERNATIONAL OD

David C. Wigglesworth

Wˢith the onset of the single European market, the changes in Eastern Europe, the expansion in the Pacific Rim, and the increased globalization of business, managers around the world are recognizing that their national perceptions, values, and modes of conducting business can have either a positive or negative impact on their success in the international arena.

Although the roots of organization development (OD) are in the United States and the United Kingdom (Wigglesworth, 1987), OD is an expanding force in international business. It is being applied in countries that have different behavioral patterns, value systems, and perceptual frameworks. However, OD is effective only when consultants understand that different approaches and competencies may be required in Jakarta or Paris from those that are required in New York or London.

Likewise, the cultural issues that consultants confront when working internationally may affect those who work with a culturally diverse workforce in the U.S. or U.K.

Many think that all people share the same experience in the same way, regardless of cultural differences. Yet Whorf (1956) has pointed out that cultural patterns structure experience; an observer from one culture may perceive reality in ways totally different from an observer from another culture. The implications of this for OD are apparent. Even though all human beings may be more alike than different, it is the differences that can exacerbate a problem, impede an intervention, and mitigate effectiveness.

Child (1981) suggests that although organizations throughout the world are growing more alike at the macro-level (structure and technology), within these organizations individual behavior at the micro-level (communication and interaction) maintains its cultural specificity. Doyle (1989) quotes Beckhard as stating that "our experience is so different in the developed West, we need patience—to be able to get inside people's heads because we can't have their background—to see the world as others see it so the processes that we eventually codesign are appropriate for the specific situations" (p. 4).

Commenting on a group experience in the Soviet Union, Dibble, Scott, Steele, Barbie, Barnes, and Lewitt (1990) make the same point: "The group returned humbled by their experience. Their blithe assumption that OD as we practice it has something to offer people and organizations functioning in such a dramatically different culture proved naive and presumptuous" (p. 22). In the same paper, Scott observed that "we are yet culture bound by our organization experience in a free market economic system" (p. 23).

Organization development consultants who function internationally or in different cultures need to realize that the role of the economy, the position of the state, the ways of doing business, and the culture all impact the effectiveness of any OD intervention. Organization development consultants have an important role to play. As Eisen, Steele, and Cherbeneau (1990) point out, "OD can lead the way in helping clients think more globally, strategically, and in the future tense, whether we work locally or at world corporate headquarters. To do this, we need to become more aware of our cultural assumptions and behavior—and to adopt new practices. This means developing a strong awareness of multi-level cross-cultural differences, and knowing how to foster better cultural understanding between national groups and among diverse work place cultures" (p. 2).

Transferring OD to other cultures must be viewed as a transfer of technology that must fit organically. Wigglesworth (1989b) says, "Organically appropriate technology must have a consistent integrity that makes the new technology function effectively within the cultural framework of the recipient society" (p. 11). When OD is transferred to other countries and cultures, OD consultants must recognize and maintain the cultural integrity of the host country if they are to be effective.

OD Competencies and Their Requisite Skills

Like all people, OD consultants make sense of reality by comparing experiences to their internal road maps. Maps are developed in an individual's formative years and retain their value throughout the individual's life. International OD consultants need to understand the road maps of others. Bryan (1987) states that "for Americans [those from the United

States] practicing OD in Canada, it is like having to remake your map while in the middle of the journey, sometimes like having to rely on someone else's more up-to-date map, and sometimes like discovering that where you are isn't on the map" (p. 4). For many OD consultants, practicing OD in places farther from home and among people with whom they have less in common makes the task more difficult.

Fundamental competencies for practicing OD internationally, derived, in part, from Casse (1982), are as follows:

- Linking skills;
- Self-awareness;
- Understanding of others;
- Interaction skills;
- Tolerance of ambiguity; and
- Persistence.

Within each competence are basic skills—also derived from Casse (1982). Knowledge of these skills is a prerequisite for any successful international OD practice.

Linking Skills

Organization development consultants who work internationally must be capable of linking theory and practice within their own country. They must have the requisite background, knowledge, theory base, and proficiency of skills to be effective within their home environments.

Self-Awareness

Consultants who work internationally need to be well-grounded about themselves. More specifically, they need to be:

- *Aware of their own cultures.* It is essential that consultants be aware of their own cultures and understand that their images of the world are highly dependent on their cultural assumptions, values, and beliefs.

- *Aware of their own limitations.* Consultants should know that their constructs of reality are highly dependent on the natures and structures of their own psyches.

Understanding of Others

Organization development consultants who work internationally need to understand others. More specifically, they need to:

- *Practice empathy.* Being able to see the world as other people see it is a powerful tool, because people prefer to work with those who give the impression that they understand things from the viewpoints of others.

- *Respect other cultures.* Tolerance and respect are indispensable for effective cross-cultural interaction, and clients value those who demonstrate respect.

- *Learn from interactions.* To learn how to learn is a key skill, because each situation is different and requires the OD consultant to adapt.

- *Avoid attributions.* To explain other people's behavior using one's own frame of reference leads to misunderstandings and communication problems.

- *Be nonjudgmental.* Controlling one's natural tendency to make judgments about other people is essential in international work.

- *Avoid rigid stereotypes.* Generalizations can lead to misinterpretations and ineffectiveness.

Interaction Skills

Consultants who work internationally need to be able to interact effectively with others. Intercultural interaction requires OD consultants to be able to:

- *Communicate.* Effective intercultural communication requires the use of basic skills such as asking open-ended questions, using silence, paraphrasing, and reflecting feelings.

- *Relate to people.* Consultants need to pay special attention to the "maintenance" part of their role. Too much emphasis on the "task" side of the role can jeopardize effectiveness.

- *Listen and observe.* OD consultants must be able to listen to other people and observe other people's behavior as well as their own.

- *Demonstrate flexibility.* In an international or intercultural setting, OD consultants must expand their range of options and choices in order to deal effectively with various situations.

- *Adjust according to people's reactions.* Consultants need to be able to utilize all of their personal and professional resources to adapt their actions at any time in order to suit the situation.

Tolerance of Ambiguity

Organization development consultants who work internationally need to be able to tolerate ambiguity in order to cope with some of the unavoidable stresses and uncertainties of international/intercultural settings.

Persistence

Organization development consultants who work internationally need to be persistent. To flee or withdraw, although perhaps justifiable in the short term, can create problems and lead to deadlock in the long term. The multicultural OD consultant must be patiently persistent.

Key Factors that Affect International OD

Stereotypes are often based on observations, perceptions, value judgments, and prejudices. Stereotyping tends to place the clients of OD consultants at a disadvantage in the global business arena.

An organization's international success depends on many factors, including financial strength; quality of products; marketing ability; faith in its endeavors; respect for its employees and associates; and dedication to making its international venture succeed. There are also uncontrollable variables, including global economics and domestic and international politics.

International negotiations, intercultural communications, and international/intercultural OD are affected by what have been called *cultural determinants* (Wigglesworth, 1989a). These can either enhance or defeat a project. Values, perceptions, cultural heritage, and unique ways of doing business are some of the cultural determinants that can make or break an international venture.

As an example of how important cultural determinants can be, consider that Nelson and Browning (1990) have documented a bitter and prolonged cultural clash during GE's acquisition of Cie. Generale de Radiologie that resulted in declining morale and productivity and prompted an exodus of French engineers and managers from the acquired company. Similarly, when Hachette of France acquired the U.S.-based publishing group, Dimandis Communications, in New York, Reilly (1991) reported the cultural clashes that worked to the detriment of the acquisition.

When OD consultants find themselves faced with startlingly different values, it is clear that they need to encourage cross-cultural communication if they are to be effective. It is not enough to know merely the cultural folkways and taboos of particular clients. Consultants also need to know how their clients perceive things, their knowledge bases, their value systems, their behavioral customs, their similarities and differences with the consultants' cultures, how they process information, and what their responses mean.

In order to place the above information in perspective, OD consultants also must understand themselves. They need to know how knowledge of such cultural data can help them to build on similarities and mitigate differences, how an agenda can be communicated across cultures, and how synergistic approaches can be developed.

Organization development consultants must solicit, observe, and reflect on clients' needs. To help clients to effect change, OD consultants must be able to communicate with them. It is especially helpful to be able to speak and understand the client's language, but even if the consultant does not know the language, he or she needs to be aware that not everyone communicates in the same way. For example, in some languages of Southeast Asia, there is no word for "no," and these languages lack an imperative verb form. Even if clients speak English, their customary use of language may impede effective cross-cultural communication.

Other factors that need to be considered are as follows:

- When people talk about other cultures, they tend to describe the differences, not the similarities.

- What may seem logical, sensible, and reasonable to a person from one culture may seem irrational, stupid, and unimportant to a person from another culture.

- Differences between cultures are generally seen as threatening and tend to be described in negative terms.

- Norms of social interaction in other cultures may be quite different from those of the consultant or those of traditional OD. For example, the role of physical distance and its relationship to authority and power is not the same in all cultures (Hofsted, 1984).

- Consultants need to accept the fact that their reality is not the only reality and that those in other cultures often perceive life from a different base of assumptions. For example, Nigerian farmers, when shown a drawing of a hoe, a tool they use most every day, see only a man walking down a long lane. The Chinese Taoist philosopher Chuan Tzu stated that "disputation is proof of not seeing clearly." Part of OD involves helping others to be aware that their reality is not the only reality.

- Perception also differs among individuals, as is exemplified by eyewitness accounts of accidents.

- Language is another factor that can impact international OD. Some languages have hundreds of thousands more words than others, and some languages do not even have words for things that are commonly referred to in other languages. Language can reveal ethnocentrism or denial that differences exist between cultures.

- Body language is not the same in all cultures. Gestures that are acceptable in one country may be highly objectionable in other countries. For example, the gesture of making a circle with the thumb and first finger signifies that something is just right in the U.S.; the same gesture is obscene in Brazil, means zilch or zero in France, and means money in Japan. When Japanese people scratch their heads and suck in their breath (saying "saah"), they may be indicating that they do not understand. If one fails to recognize this cue, communication may go awry.

- Eye contact and touching have different meanings in different cultures. For example, U.S. residents expect eye contact to be maintained, but Japanese residents find it uncomfortable.

- The way in which information is processed varies in different countries. Kohls (1986) says that inductive reasoning—which emphasizes moving from the specific to the general—appears to predominate in the United States, Ireland, Canada, Australia, Denmark, New Zealand, the Netherlands, Sweden and Norway—countries in which OD has been widely accepted. However, most of the world, including much of Western Europe, has a strong preference for deductive reasoning, with its emphasis on moving from the general to the specific.

- Relatively "field-independent" people, often found in the U.S. and U.K., display greater skill in solving the type of problem that requires isolating certain elements from their context and making use of them in a different context (Jahoda, 1980). "Field-dependent" people, found in much of the developing world and parts of Europe, are more sensitive to the prevailing social field and therefore are more likely to respond to social cues or conform to social pressures (Witkin, Dyk, Paterson, Goodenough, & Karp, 1962).

Organization development consultants need to remember that cultural differences exist and that they must be handled approriately.

Cultural Determinants

From an organization development perspective, cultural determinants are cultural factors that enable or prevent an effective intervention. From an international management perspective, cultural determinants are cultural factors that impede productivity, organizational growth, and profitability. The determinants are often intangible and sometimes unpredictable, but always have their roots in the values and belief systems of those involved. Cultural determinants may be styles of doing business, perceptions of others' behavior, or fundamental acceptance or rejection of some aspect of another's culture. Although cultural determinants are present in any intercultural interface, they may not be apparent, although their effects may be.

Organization development consultants who work internationally would do well to review the works of the American anthropologists Edward T. and Mildred Reed Hall (1990); the Dutch industrial psychologist Geert Hofstede (1984), and the Dutch social-systems scientist Fons Trompenaars (1993).

The Work of Edward and Mildred Hall

Communication

Hall (1959, 1976) and Hall and Hall (1990) contend that although culture is many things, it is fundamentally communication—a process for creating, sending, storing, and processing information. They perceive communication from three perspectives: words, material things, and behavior. Words are the medium of business, politics, and diplomacy. Material things are usually indicators of status and power. Behavior provides feedback about how people feel and includes techniques for avoiding confrontation. An international or intercultural OD consultant needs to understand how clients from different nations or cultures communicate from all three perspectives. The consultant should learn how words, material things, and behavior are perceived and valued in the clients' cultures.

Cultural Interfacing

Recognizing that, generally, it is far more difficult to succeed in a foreign environment than in a familiar one, and that the top managers of a foreign subsidiary are crucial to the success of meaningful interfacing, the Halls believe it be essential to recognize four basic principles of cultural interfacing: context, space, time, and message flow.

Context is the first of the four principles of cultural interfacing. Hall (1959) describes low-context cultures and high-context cultures. People from low-context cultures (those who use the English language, Scandinavians, and Germans) transmit information in explicit codes such as words. Meaning and understanding are achieved by sending and receiving accurate messages, usually by being articulate and "spelling it out."

On the other hand, people from high-context cultures rely on information that exists either in the physical context or within the person. Meaning and understanding are implicit in what is not said—in the nonverbal communication and body language, in the silences and pauses, and in relationships and empathy. People in high-context cultures communicate by not stating things.

High-context cultures require more conformance in behavior and therefore allow less deviation in role performance. Low-context cultures permit more deviance from ideal role models and tend to have looser social structures.

In terms of interpersonal relationships, the emotionally charged, interpersonally oriented approach is characteristic of high-context cultures. Bonds between people in high-context cultures are stronger, and there is a tendency to subordinate individual interests for the sake of the relationship or group.

A functionally oriented, specialized approach is characteristic of low-context cultures. Communication is a means to an end or goal. Interpersonal bonds are fragile. This is exemplified by the way in which people move away or withdraw with relative ease if a relationship is not developing satisfactorily.

Space is the second of the Halls' basic principles of cultural interfacing. Space can be separated into territoriality and personal space. People in low-context cultures often have a highly developed sense of territory, marking off (for example) "my room," "my kitchen," "my office," or "my lab." In organizations in low-context cultures, territoriality can communicate power by the location of an office, its size, and whether it has a door that closes. In organizations in high-context cultures, such as France, top executives tend to want their offices centrally located, surrounded by subordinates, so they can stay informed and can exert control.

Personal space represents another form of territoriality. The amount of space that we require around us (that is, the physical distance that others maintain in interacting with us) is influenced by our cultural backgrounds. In low-context cultures, comfortable interaction distance literally is "at arm's length," and people are expected to "keep their distance." In high-context cultures, the acceptable space between persons may be very small.

In facilitating change within an international setting comprising people from high-context and low-context cultures, an OD consultant must be sensitive to the issues of territoriality and personal space.

Time is the Halls' third principle of cultural interfacing. The Halls describe monochronic time and polychronic time.

Monochronic time is characteristic of low-context cultures. Time is considered to be something that can be "spent," "saved," "wasted," and "lost." It is scheduled, compartmentalized, and is often viewed as sacred and unalterable. It tends to seal individuals off from one another and can intensify some relationships while diminishing others.

Polychronic time is characteristic of high-context cultures in which there is simultaneous occurrence of a number of things and great involvement with people. The emphasis is not on meeting schedules but on completing human transactions.

In the U.S., it is commonly said that there is a time and place for everything. People from other cultures may perceive that U.S. businesspersons do not practice what they preach. In the U.S., business can be discussed almost everywhere. On the other hand, people in high-context cultures tend to place greater social and psychological significance on feeling "right" about the time and place of an interaction. In India, people are rarely permitted to talk about business when visiting someone's home. In some Asian cultures, it is common practice to go to a relaxing eating or drinking establishment to initiate business talks, and the preliminary steps in a business negotiation may take place on the golf course.

Message flow is the fourth principle of cultural interfacing. In low-context cultures, information does not flow freely and is often highly focused, compartmentalized, and controlled. It may be used to gain position or power. In high-context cultures, message flow seems to have an independent life of its own. Information flows freely and spreads rapidly because interpersonal contact takes precedence over everything else. The time and space values of high-context cultures expedite information sharing.

Organization development consultants who work internationally would do well to understand and practice the Halls' five basic principles of cultural interfacing. These principles are:

1. The higher the context of either the culture or the industry, the more difficult the interface.
2. The greater the complexity of the elements, the more difficult the interface.
3. The greater the cultural distance, the more difficult the interface.
4. The greater the number of levels in the system, the more difficult the interface.
5. Very simple, low-context, highly evolved, mechanical systems tend to produce fewer interface problems than do multiple-level systems of great complexity that depend on human talent for their success.

The Work of Geert Hofstede

Hofstede (1984) addresses the cultural determinants of differences in social styles (norms of social interaction), which may be diametrically opposed in different cultures. His four dimensions are power distance, uncertainty avoidance, individualism, and masculinity.

Power distance measures how much the less powerful members of a society accept the unequal distribution of power. *Uncertainty avoidance* measures how much members of a society feel threatened by ambiguous situations and try to avoid these situations. Hofstede's studies reveal that the role of physical distance and its relationship to authority and power and uncertainty avoidance varies along a continua among diverse cultures. Low power distance and weak levels of uncertainty avoidance are found in countries such as the United States, Great Britain, New Zealand, and Denmark; whereas high power distance and strong levels of uncertainty avoidance are more likely to be found in Latin America, France, and the Middle East.

The Work of Fons Trompenaars

Trompenaars (1993) addresses a number of the topics discussed by the Halls and Hofstede and reaches similar conclusions. He describes an implicit culture composed of basic assumptions that produce the norms and values that show themselves in such manifestations of the explicit culture as music, architecture, and food. He defines culture as "things taken for granted," "shared meanings," and the "unconscious," with three fundamental elements: time, humans, and nature.

Time. In discussing time, Trompenaars cites St. Augustine: "The only thing that exists is the present. We have maps of the past and maps of the future in our minds." The past and future do not exist because only the present is real. Trompenaars suggests that the Swiss and the Swedish are very definite about divisions of times in relation to appointments; U.S. residents show up for appointments within five minutes of the meeting time; the Italians and Spanish are fifteen minutes early or late; the French are usually late; and the Arabs have a much wider time frame for appointments. Trompenaars divides cultures into *sequential* time cultures, in which things are done in a linear fashion, one at a time, and *synchronic* time cultures (similar to Hall's polychronic time) in which several things occur at once and there are numerous and possibly interchangeable steps on the way to reaching the goal.

Humans. The meanings Trompenaars assigns to human relationships are also culture bound. He contrasts cultures along several continua:

- Universalism versus particularism, that is, differences in societal versus personal obligations;
- Individualism versus collectivism, that is, differences between personal and group goals;
- Neutral versus affective relationships, that is, emotional involvement in relationships;
- Specific versus diffuse relationships, that is, degrees of involvement; and
- Achievement versus ascription, that is, legitimization of power and status.

In this discussion, Trompenaars includes the dimension of space. He contrasts the noncontact societies, such as the

U.S. and Germany, with the contact societies, such as Latin America and the Middle East.

Nature. Trompenaars perceives nature on a continuum, running from "internal control" (with nature equating with mechanism—that is, dominance over nature) through "harmony" to "external control" (with nature equating with organism—that is, subjugation to nature).

Trompenaars' studies reveal that individual countries or cultures have their own places on the continua of time, humans, and nature. From looking at these, one can determine where a culture is in relationship to the issues within an organization.

The Halls, Hofstede, and Trompenaars provide substantial data to indicate the roles of cultural determinants in organizations. When these are linked to the field-dependent and field-independent work of researchers such as Jahoda (1980) and Witkin et al. (1962), it becomes apparent that OD consultants who work internationally need to be well aware of the roles of cultural determinants in their work.

To be effective when interfacing with people from other cultures, OD consultants need to have the ability to receive and transmit information effectively in order to be able to appreciate and develop the expertise that needs to be applied in international OD. This includes:

- *Knowing how the information flows.* In most low-context cultures, information is generated with people outside authority and flows to a manager. The system works because responsibility is delegated and initiative is valued. In cultures in which authority is more centralized, the reverse is true, and employees take less responsibility to keep their managers informed, so the managers must take the initiative to seek out information. In countries in which many people are involved in a decision, there are customary patterns of information flow that might leave out the foreign OD consultant who is not familiar with the dynamics.

- *Not pushing to get straight to the point.* For most people in low-context cultures, getting straight to the point is an important aspect of business. OD consultants should not try to make deals while those from high-context cultures are still trying to get to know them. Low-context people are specific and like facts; high-context people tend to imply things and like suggestions. The low-context emphasis on linear thinking (going from "a" to "b" to "c") cuts off loops in other people's thinking and can cause resentment that can negatively affect the interaction.

- *Speaking simply, but not simple-mindedly, to people who do not speak one's language.* When speaking in one's own language to a client who is not fluent in it, an organization development consultant should speak slowly and enunciate distinctly enough to be heard clearly and should avoid complicated words, jargon, and slang. However, speaking too slowly, enunciating too deliberately, or raising one's voice as though the person were deaf is condescending and insulting. The consultant should keep his or her sentences short and pause between sentences. It is also a good idea to check for understanding by asking questions that call for more than simple "yes" or "no" responses.

- *Distinguishing between a courteous answer and the truth.* In many cultures, naked candor is not valued as much as courtesy, sensitivity to feelings, loyalty to family, and saving "face." With some Asians, for example, the emotional quality of an interaction is more important than the meaning of the words or sentences. Form is more important than the actual communication, and social harmony is the primary function of speech. One of the most futile requests that can be made to an Asian is "give me a simple yes or no answer." In Japan, for example, there are over sixteen ways to avoid saying no.

- *Knowing the context so as to know the meaning.* Ambiguity is common in other languages and cultures. OD consultants may get only the information they specifically request, no matter how relevant the additional information might be. Incompleteness is often exacerbated by indirection. Such words as "perhaps," "maybe," and "we'll consider it" are common Chinese phrases, and "inconvenient" can mean impossible.

- *Making sure that personal style of expression does not communicate things unintentionally.* It is necessary to remember that expressions of anger are unacceptable in many cultures and that public anger is taboo. Humor does not often translate well across cultures, and the popular practice of "kidding around" in the U.S. may well be inappropriate in an intercultural environment.

- *Recognizing that silence is part of communication and not interrupting it.* People in the U.S. have a tendency to rush to fill silences, to talk rather than to wait patiently. In many cultures, silences are part of communication and should not be interrupted.

- *Not misjudging the competence of others just because they do not speak one's language.* Speaking or not speaking a particular language in addition to one's own does not mean that an individual is more or less intelligent or that he or she has more or less business acumen or competence.

The international practice of OD requires finely-honed communication skills and other interpersonal skills; high sensitivity to intercultural issues; a reasonable knowledge of one's own cultural determinants; and awareness of the client's national, ethnic, and corporate cultures. Organization development consultants who function internationally must be able to provide adaptive mechanisms, constructs, and paradigms to facilitate interventions appropriately.

Those who work internationally have an unprecedented opportunity. If humankind eventually wants to arrive at a more secure and peaceful world, human beings need to begin by changing the process of their interactions across divergent viewpoints. Schindler and Lapid (1989) note: "Our survival and prosperity in the 21st century hinge upon our ability as a species to develop new modes and processes of communication and conflict management appropriate to our global interdependence" (p. 15).

Francis (1989) points out that those who work with people from other cultures, in professions whose techniques may be foreign and at odds with local cultural values, have three choices. One choice is to discard their own values and preferred techniques. Another is to impose their values and preferred techniques on others. The third choice is to compromise and improvise. The alternative for international OD consultants is not listed. It is to understand the cultures of their clients so the consultants can adapt the clients' values and preferred techniques, adapt their own values and preferred techniques, and compromise and improvise in a synergistic way.

According to Eisen et al. (1990), "OD practitioners need to be proficient at tying together theory and practice in ways that correlate with a competitive advantage. There is thus a growing interest in strategic planning, market research, and related approaches, especially those based in systems perspectives for making sense of our complex world. Consultants must also have an understanding of the special vocabulary, values, and processes of a wide range of clients" (p. 2).

References

Bryan, J. (1987, June). Differences: An American reflecting on practicing OD in Canada. *OD Practitioner, 19*(2), 1-4.

Casse, P. (1982). *Training for the multicultural manager.* Washington, D.C.: Society for Intercultural Education, Training and Research.

Child, J. (1981). Culture, contingency and capitalism in the cross-national study of organizations. In *Research in organizational behavior* (Vol. 3). Greenwich, CT: JAI Publishers.

Dibble, L., Scott, B., Steele, H., Barbie, M., Barnes, K., & Lewitt, D. (1990, June). Perspectives on consulting in the Soviet Union. *Vision/Action, 9*(2), 21-25.

Doyle, M. (1989, March). Now is the time for all good OD consultants to come to the aid of their planet. *Vision/Action, 8*(1), 1-5.

Eisen, S., Steele, H., & Cherbeneau, J. (1990, June). Developing OD competencies for the 90's and beyond: Conclusions from a Delphi conference. *OD Practitioner, 22*(2), 1-4.

Francis, J. (1989, March). The cultural relativity of training techniques. *Vision/Action, 8*(1), 16-19.

Hall. E. (1959). *The silent language.* New York: Doubleday.

Hall, E. (1976). *Beyond culture.* New York: Doubleday.

Hall, E., & Hall, M. (1990). *Understanding cultural differences.* Yarmouth, ME: Intercultural Press.

Hofstede, G. (1984). *Culture's consequences.* Newbury Park, CA: Sage.

Jahoda, G. (1980). Theoretical and systematic approaches. In Triandis & Lambert (Eds.), *Handbook of cross-cultural psychology* (Vol. 1). New York: Allyn & Bacon.

Kohls, R. (1986). *Square pegs into round holes.* An address at an invitational international roundtable: International training and human resource development practices and their effectiveness. Washington, D.C.: ASTD/World Bank.

Nelson, M., & Browning, E. (1990, July 31). GE's culture turns sour at French unit. *The Wall Street Journal,* p. A-10.

Reilly, P. (1991, February 15). Egos, culture clash when French firm buys U.S. magazines. *The Wall Street Journal,* p. A-1.

Schindler. C., & Lapid, G. (1989, September). Mediated dialogue and conflict management. *Vision/Action,* 8(3), 13-16.

Trompenaars, F. (1993). *Riding the waves of culture.* London: The Economist Press.

Whorf, B. (1956). *Language, thought and reality.* New York: John Wiley & Sons.

Wigglesworth, D. (1989a, March). New challenges: Global management: The cultural determinants. *Sundridge Park Management Review.*

Wigglesworth, D. (1989b, March). Seeing intercultural OD as technology transfer. *Vision/Action,* 8(1), 10-12.

Wigglesworth, D. (1987, Fall). Is OD basically Anglo-Saxon? *Leadership & Organization Development Journal (U.K.),* 8(2), 29-31.

Witkin, H., Dyk, R., Paterson, H., Goodenough, D., & Karp, S. (1962). *Psychological differentiation.* New York: John Wiley & Sons.

CHAPTER 14

ETHICS IN OD

Susan H. DeVogel, Roland Sullivan,
Gary N. McLean, and William J. Rothwell

O rganization development (OD) is a value-driven profession; thus it is imperative that OD consultants exemplify OD values in their professional conduct with clients, peers, society, and themselves. Organization development consultants deal with the vulnerabilities of client systems and the individual members of those systems. Those vulnerabilities and the competing interests that arise in OD interventions can place the consultants in positions in which they must make difficult choices based on values. Such positions can be called *ethical dilemmas.*

This chapter includes recommendations to help OD consultants recognize and deal with ethical dilemmas. It suggests that OD consultants form peer groups that will help them to reflect on their ethical dilemmas, make responsible choices about resolution strategies, and commit to developing greater awareness of what drives their personal decision-making approaches. This chapter also includes an instrument for individual or group reflection and guidelines for an ethics-reflection group.

Professional Ethics and How They Relate to OD

Although much has been written about ethics in OD practice, few of these writings suggest a systematic or reasoned approach to the subject. Further, the range of desirable virtues for OD consultants is as diverse as the writers who describe them.

Defining Professional Ethics

Webster's Ninth Collegiate Dictionary (1989) defines ethics as "the discipline dealing with what is good and bad and with moral duty and obligation, ...a set of moral principles or virtues...a theory or system of moral values...the principles of conduct governing an individual or group" (p. 426).

Bayles (1981) provides an extensive definition of a profession and describes several features common to all consulting professions. The features usually found in the consulting professions are as follows:

- Extensive specialized training;
- The use of primarily intellectual skill to provide advice about matters not generally understood by the average person; and
- The provision of an important service in society.

Bayles (1981) describes six additional features commonly, but not always, found among professions. These include:

- Certification or licensure. However, a license does not make an individual a professional, nor does the absence of licensure make an occupation nonprofessional;

- The existence of an organization that represents the profession;

- Autonomy in one's work, including the independent exercise of judgment and the use of one's own discretion in carrying out the work;

- The provision of important services to society by serving basic values;

- The monopoly over the provision of services and an attempt to define the sphere of appropriate practice; and

- Self-regulation or the absence of public or external control.

DeGeorge (1986) notes that "an individual can only be a member of a profession if he or she is part of a constituted, self-regulated, properly defined group" (p. 340). *Professional codes*—statements to members and the outside world about the ideals claimed by the profession—are a part of this self-regulation. Lippitt and Lippitt (1978) add that a professional code of ethics protects clients and ensures their fair treatment by outlining definable rules of conduct. A professional code also demonstrates a professional's willingness to submit to self-discipline.

Lippitt and Lippitt (1978) add that the hallmarks of a professional include elements of dedication, placing great importance on one's ethical positions, taking pride in applying one's knowledge and skills, functioning with integrity, and "a willingness to be alert to novel situations and to respond to them as they develop" (p. 78).

Lippitt and Lippitt (1978) add that effective functioning as a professional also means the following:

- Acquiring the knowledge of the profession and learning its disciplines;

- Learning to apply professional knowledge and skills effectively;

- Always putting client interests ahead of one's own interests or those of the group to which one belongs;

- Maintaining high standards for serving clients; and

- Behaving at all times with a professional bearing (p. 14).

Organization development meets many, if not all, of the requirements previously stated. It is, at the very least, an "emerging profession" as defined by Barber (1988).

For Benne (1959), one of the early OD thinkers, the question of ethics is fairly simple:

> If the statement of the confronting problem involves ethical predicates—"right," "wrong," "should," "shouldn't"—it is primarily ethical. (pp. 60-61)

Lippitt and Lippitt (1978), however, believe that such a dichotomous approach to morality is insufficient because the meanings of "right" and "wrong" are not always clear. They argue that when dealing with people it is more important to consider human relations than codes. This position reflects Joseph Fletcher's (1966) situation-ethics approach. Lippitt and Lippitt do acknowledge that a situational approach may call for a greater commitment to values and more disciplined discernment than the average person can muster.

Professional ethics, then, encompasses an individual's personal ethics, the global field of "ordinary" ethics, the legitimate interests of society, and the concerns specific to the individual profession. Veatch (1972) notes that the dark side of professional ethics is the false claim that professionals are sometimes exempt from ordinary ethical principles.

Types of Ethical Norms

Bayles (1981) suggests that there are three major types of ethical norms:

1. Standards, which describe an individual's qualifications and values;
2. Principles, which describe the individual's responsibilities, with latitude for individual interpretation; and
3. Rules, which describe the individual's absolute duties or obligations.

For Bayles, the ethical task is to balance the various principles and/or responsibilities.

Rules, Standards, and Values

There are few rules in professions. Presently, there are no absolute qualifications or standards in organization development. However, there is considerable concern about the values of OD consultants and the principles by which they make ethical decisions. Organization development writers have proposed many values, responsibilities, and principles to govern the conduct of OD consultants.

Gellermann, Frankel, and Ladenson's (1990) "Statement of Values and Ethics by Professionals in Organization and Human Systems Development" (the statement) contains an exhaustive discussion of the beliefs and values held by hundreds of OD professionals. White and Wooten (1986), who are acquainted with the early stages of Gellerman's work, describe the statement as a code but maintain that without refined methodologies and practices (science), educational standards, accreditation, and professional licensure, a code of ethics cannot be fully formulated (p. 80).

Some of the values included by Gellermann, Frankel, and Ladenson (1990) are as follows:

> ...life and the quest for happiness...justice...human potential and empowerment...respect, dignity, integrity, worth, and fundamental rights of individuals and other human authenticity, congruence, honesty and openness, understanding and acceptance... flexibility, change, and proaction...learning, development, growth, and transformation...whole-win attitudes, cooperation-collaboration, trust, community, and diversity...widespread, meaningful participation in system affairs, democracy, and appropriate decision-making...and effectiveness, efficiency, and alignment. (pp. 375-376)

Pfeiffer and Jones (1977) describe *caring* as a critical element of the character of a consulting professional. They also believe that it is the consultant's responsibility to stay mentally and physically healthy and to get his or her needs met outside of consulting relationships.

Other writers in the field of ethics have described additional professional values, such as competence, loyalty, discretion, honesty, diligence, and candor (Bayles, 1981, p. 22). Campbell (1982) stresses the importance in any profession of self-discipline; moral autonomy; and the ability to make moral judgments independent of a higher authority, in a systematic way, and with accountability to a peer group. Lebacqz (1985) adds fidelity, courage, truthfulness, and prudence.

Lebacqz's (1985) meta-analysis of older ethics sources yields additional virtues, including a professional's responsibility to have or demonstrate a sense of calling or commitment; his or her concern for justice; the professional's belief that service is primary and remuneration secondary; his or her concern for consumers' rights and well-being; the professional's affirmation of good citizenship; his or her sense of the worth of the individual; and the professional's respect for others. Additional qualities essential for an ethical OD consultant include a commitment to doing good, to not doing harm, and to honesty.

Kultgen (1988) describes critical intellectual virtues that should be possessed by a professional. The professional should have proficiency, which Kultgen defines as the combination of technical (specific to the profession) and moral (dealing with people) skills. Elements of this combination include understanding the client's needs, having good sense, the ability to integrate abstract concepts, understanding the context in which the work is done, knowing when to speak and when to be silent, having good communication skills, and possessing the ability to analyze the soundness of his or her own ideas and work.

Principles

The Gellermann, Frankel, and Ladenson (1990) statement includes four ethical principles:

1. Serve the good of the whole.
2. Do unto others as we would have them do unto us.

3. Always treat people as ends, never only as means; respect their "being" and never use them only for their ability to "do"; treat them as persons and never as objects.

4. Act so we do not increase power by more powerful stakeholders over the less powerful. (pp. 377-378)

The statement also contains a comprehensive list of responsibilities to a professional's self—including integrity, self-development, and self-awareness—as well as responsibilities for the development of the profession and responsibilities to clients and society in general.

An eleven-page discussion of guidelines on applying these values and principles is also included in the statement. Examples of these guidelines follow:

> Neither seek nor accept assignments outside our limits without clear understanding by clients when exploration at the edge of our competence is reasonable. (Gellermann, Frankel, & Ladenson, 1990, p. 380)

> Avoid automatic confirmation of predetermined conclusions about the client's situation or what needs to be done by either the client or ourselves. (p. 380)

> Inform them [participants] in a way that supports their freedom of choice about their participation in activities initiated by us; also acknowledge that it may be appropriate for us to undertake activities initiated by recognized authorities in which participants do not have full freedom of choice. (p. 381)

Other OD writers have, of course, addressed specific ethical responsibilities of OD consultants. Miles (1979) stresses that consultants must be honest with themselves about their own values before accepting work with clients whose values differ. Pfeiffer and Jones (1977) address the responsibility of consultants to be honest about their credentials, qualifications, and limitations. Pfeiffer and Jones (1977) also state that, during the start-up step, consultants should promise only what they can control; during the evaluation step, consultants are responsible for evaluating their own work and assessing its effectiveness, at least privately. Pfeiffer and Jones also believe that consultants should avoid speaking ill of colleagues in the presence of others and, instead, should privately confront anyone who seems incompetent, unethical, or unprofessional.

According to Benne (1959), each consultant must relate to a client with flexibility and integrity in a mode of mutual accommodation. Pfeiffer and Jones (1977) add that trainers and consultants must be aware of the inequality of power and be sensitive to clients' resulting expectations.

Practical Issues and Dilemmas

A host of potential ethical dilemmas exist in the practice of OD. Given the responsibilities previously listed, it is not difficult to envision violations of these principles. The following ethical dilemmas are described in the OD literature.

Building on the work of Katz and Kahn (1966), White and Wooten (1986) see role conflict as the underlying cause of most ethical dilemmas:

> Interrole conflict on the part of change agents often occurs when he/she is expected to be a nurturing person, while at the same time having to confront others about negative aspects of their behavior. Change agents also frequently experience person-role conflict when role requirements request them to violate moral or ethical values. (p. 97)

White and Wooten (1986) describe five categories of ethical dilemmas that occur in OD: "(1) misrepresentation and collusion, (2) misuse of data, (3) manipulation and coercion, (4) values and goal conflict, and (5) technical ineptness" (p. 149).

Consultants must address potential value conflicts early in their consultant-client relationships. Pfeiffer and Jones (1977) state that "consultants need to determine what the values of a client organization are, and if they cannot accept those values, either they have to get out or they have to try to change the organization's values" (p. 222).

McLean, Sims, Mangham, & Tuffield (1982) cite the pressure on external consultants to be "gurus" during initial interviews. White and Wooten (1983) mention the problem of determining who the real client is. Warrick and Thompson (1980) discuss the ethical danger of consultants' creating unrealistic expectations in clients.

Miles (1979) describes several potential ethical problems involving data collection and feedback, including confidentiality, privacy, a consultant's biases, how much feedback the consultant should give to a client, and to whom to give it. White and Wooten (1986) observe that a consultant may distort or delete data during diagnosis and feedback. They agree with Miles (1979) about the problem of ownership of data:

> Ownership of the data is as well a frequently occurring dilemma for the parties to the change. This occurs when survey feedback or process observation is not shared with all contributing members (White & Wooten, 1986, p. 161).

White and Wooten (1983) note that a consultant may face dilemmas during the feedback stage caused by inappropriate assimilation into the client culture. These dilemmas may also impede intervention planning. Walton and Warwick (1973) say that a consultant may be obligated to clarify the power implications of any intervention to participants, rather than pretend that all interventions are value neutral.

McLean et al. (1982) question whether organization development is even concerned with "planned" change. Many of the respondents in their study reported that much that happens is not planned; much that is planned may be unacceptable or may be altered by organizational politics. Many consultants maximize the benefits of opportunities and issues as they arise. McLean et al. (1982) contend that at this stage, a consultant may be tempted to prescribe or sell an intervention that he or she enjoys doing or does well.

Warrick and Thompson (1980) describe the problem of using the action-planning step as an opportunity to uncover or rehash more problems, leading to continuous employment for a consultant but not developing problem solving within an organization.

As a consultant implements change efforts, new ethical dilemmas arise. Miles (1979) questions whether an organizational member can truly choose to enter or depart from an intervention and whether there is pressure from superiors to participate.

During interventions, other ethically difficult situations can arise. For example, during a team-building intervention, participants may be forced to reveal more of themselves than they wish (Walter, 1984; Walton & Warwick, 1973). They can be harmed if the facilitator does not know how to handle difficult group dynamics (Walter, 1984). *Overload* is a term used by Walton and Warwick (1973) to describe an ethical problem that is:

[A] situation in which an individual receives more aversive feedback than he has bargained for or can handle. The result may be increased psychological pain for the person, a loss of esteem in the eyes of others, and a deterioration in organizational performance without other redeeming features. (p. 693)

Walter (1984) claims that changes resulting from OD efforts may weaken or destroy years of individual career development. He suggests that "perhaps OD should not aspire to change things of fundamental importance to the long-term career plans of organization members" (p. 432). Pfeiffer and Jones (1977) caution that a consultant may be asked to conduct interventions or gain information that will give cause for terminating employees. This, they say, is neither ethical nor prudent. However, McLean et al. (1982) note that this happens frequently and that consultants often comply with these requests.

Evaluation, according to White and Wooten (1983, 1986), includes the potential for misuse, deletion, or distortion of data. During the evaluation step, Sullivan (1989) advises a consultant to acknowledge any mistakes and avoid blaming others. Sullivan also notes that the termination of a consulting relationship should be handled in a timely manner, without unhealthy dependence, and with provisions for a client's need for closure.

Ethical Decision Making

The OD literature yields little practical advice—or philosophical help—on resolving ethical dilemmas that OD consultants face. What discussion there is frequently begins with Kant's categorical imperative (DeGeorge, 1986; Jaspers, 1957), in which one must treat others as ends rather than solely as means. Jaspers writes, "Act as though the maxim of your action, through your will, were to become a universal law of nature" (p. 65). In short, people should not use other people for their own purposes.

Bayles (1981) provides the following three-step resolution process:

> First, one must identify and weigh the values of the client against those of others who will be affected.... Second, one must consider the general probability of one being in either position—client or affected third party. This consideration is especially important for issues in which many persons are affected. Third, one must remember that one is considering rules for professional roles; one is not deciding a particular case and one will not be able to give a different answer for a later similar case. In general, the procedure is designed to foster asking whether one would rather live in a society with professionals governed by one set of norms or another (p. 100).

White and Wooten (1986) say that any change agent has only two resolution strategies available, "employing past practices" or negotiating an "agreement between the change parties" (p. 179).

Snell (1986) proposes that the best way for consultants to deal with ethical dilemmas is to discuss them with other consultants at the time the dilemmas arise. In a context of trust, consultants can evaluate and criticize one another's ethical criteria.

Gellermann, Frankel, and Ladenson (1990) suggest that learning to practice ethically is a developmental process. They describe the importance of developing one's ethical "fluency" (p. 64)—which involves understanding and commitment—as a preparation for rational decision making that is based on a more structured form of problem analysis and ethical analysis.

Exhibit 14-1: A Five-Step Model for Ethical Thought and Action

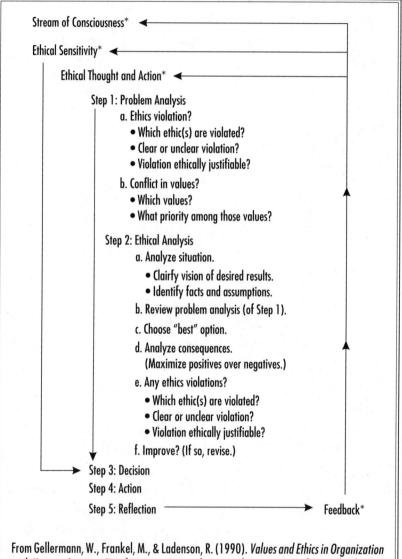

Stream of Consciousness*

Ethical Sensitivity*

    Ethical Thought and Action*

        Step 1: Problem Analysis
           a. Ethics violation?
              • Which ethic(s) are violated?
              • Clear or unclear violation?
              • Violation ethically justifiable?
           b. Conflict in values?
              • Which values?
              • What priority among those values?

        Step 2: Ethical Analysis
           a. Analyze situation.
              • Clairfy vision of desired results.
              • Identify facts and assumptions.
           b. Review problem analysis (of Step 1).
           c. Choose "best" option.
           d. Analyze consequences.
              (Maximize positives over negatives.)
           e. Any ethics violations?
              • Which ethic(s) are violated?
              • Clear or unclear violation?
              • Violation ethically justifiable?
           f. Improve? (If so, revise.)

    Step 3: Decision

    Step 4: Action

    Step 5: Reflection ⟶ Feedback*

From Gellermann, W., Frankel, M., & Ladenson, R. (1990). *Values and Ethics in Organization and Human Systems Development: Responding to Dilemmas in Professional Life.* San Francisco: Jossey-Bass, pp. 65-66. Used by permission of Jossey-Bass and the American Association for the Advancement of Science.

Note: Drawing on our store of knowledge and experience, our "stream of consciousness" calls attention to our need for "ethical sensitivity." The ethical thing to do may be clear immediately, in which case we can make a decision without further thought. Or we may need to consider our situation more carefully, in which case our thinking, with reference to our ethics and values, can help clarify whether we have an ethical problem (Step 1). This may enable us to make a decision without futher thought, but, if necessary, we can analyze our situation even more closely (Step 2). This thought process involves a combination of reason and intuition. Our ethical competence depends in large part on the extent to which we have (1) informed our intuition with clear vision, accurate beliefs, clearly understood values and ethics, and an understanding of our potential ethical problems, (2) reflected on our experience and given feedback to our store of knowledge, and (3) practiced the use of our values and ethics in ways similar to those outlined in the model, so that they are available to our minds when we need them.

The consultant develops ethical sensitivity through intuition and reflection on his or her beliefs, values, and hypothetical or experienced ethical dilemmas. This leads to the consultant consciously choosing his or her values and ethical standards. The decision-making model rests, ultimately, on clarifying one's personal values and learning to apply them in a systematic fashion.

McLean et al. (1982) conducted an interview study of actual OD practices and found that the reality of OD differs significantly from what appears in OD theory and texts. Consultants reported pushing clients toward certain purposes, actions, agreements, and conclusions.

Ethical Dilemmas in the Real World of OD

Based on the study previously described, DeVogel (1992) conducted thirty-four interviews and surveyed 182 OD consultants to determine which ethical dilemmas occurred most frequently in actual OD practice. The survey pool was a random sample of members of the OD Professional Practice Area of the American Society for Training and Development (ASTD). A questionnaire containing thirty-nine potential dilemmas was used, and respondents were asked how often they encountered these dilemmas.

Of the thirty-nine dilemmas listed, thirteen were reported by at least 40 percent of the respondents as occurring occasionally, frequently, or almost always. The thirteen, in decreasing order of frequency, are discussed in the following sections.

1. Illusion of Participation

"Employees are given the illusion of participatory decision making when management's mind is already made up." Seventy-one percent of respondents reported that they face this dilemma at least occasionally. The most common methods of handling it are confronting the client (44 percent) and negotiating an alternative approach (18 percent). Few respondents refused to cooperate or terminated the consulting relationship based on this client behavior.

2. Skip the Diagnosis

"I am asked to skip a needs assessment or diagnosis and just do an intervention (for example, training or team building)." Sixty-five percent of respondents reported that they face this dilemma at least occasionally. The most common methods of handling it are negotiating an alternative approach (35 percent) and confronting the client (25 percent). Eight percent of

the respondents refuse to comply. None reported terminating the consulting relationship.

3. Inappropriate Intervention

"I am asked to conduct an OD intervention (for example, team building) which I think is inappropriate for the organization." Sixty-one percent report this dilemma as occurring at least occasionally. Negotiation (32 percent), action research (30 percent), and confrontation (28 percent) are the most common methods for handling it. Few respondents refused to comply; none reported terminating a consulting relationship.

4. Stretch the Limits of My Competence

"I try a new intervention with a client that might stretch beyond my competency or skill." Fifty-eight percent of respondents face this situation at least occasionally. The most common methods of handling it include using action research (43 percent) and taking independent action (24 percent). Some respondents (17 percent) report that they do not consider this to be a problem. Very few (14 percent) discussed it with their clients.

5. Coercion

"Employees are forced to participate in an intervention against their will." Fifty-seven percent of respondents report confronting this dilemma at least occasionally. The most common methods of handling it are to negotiate (37 percent), confront the problem (23 percent), or gather more information using

action research (23 percent). None of the respondents refused to cooperate or terminated the consulting relationship.

6. Political Pressure

"I find my behavior shaped by the internal policies of the client organization." This dilemma is reported by 57 percent of the respondents as occurring at least occasionally. There is little consensus on how to deal with this problem. The most frequent approaches used by respondents are applying action research (23 percent) and taking independent action (23 percent). Others negotiated (18 percent), responded indirectly (17 percent), or simply do not consider it to be a problem (15 percent).

7. Informed Consent

"Employees are drawn into an intervention without really knowing what they are getting into." Fifty-six percent of respondents report that this occurs at least occasionally. They deal with this problem through negotiation (34 percent), action research (21 percent), independent action (18 percent), or confrontation (18 percent). None of the respondents reported refusing to cooperate or leaving the consulting relationship. Five percent do not consider this to be a problem.

8. Client Has Misled the Consultant

"I discover that the client has misled me about the nature of the problems in the organization or his or her willingness to cooperate." Fifty-four percent of respondents report that this occurs at least occasionally. The most common methods of han-

dling this problem are confrontation (46 percent) and action research (25 percent). Few respondents terminated their consulting relationships with clients because of this problem.

9. Misuse of Information

"A manager asks me for information with the intent to use that information for administrative purposes (for example, promotions, dismissals)." Fifty percent of respondents report that this occurs at least occasionally. There is no clear consensus on how to approach this dilemma. The most frequent response is to refuse flatly (23 percent). Other respondents will negotiate an alternative approach (17 percent), confront the problem (15 percent), or conduct action research (13 percent). Fifteen percent did not consider this to be a problem.

10. Violate Confidentiality

"A manager asks me to divulge information that I have explicitly promised not to share with others (for example, what happened in a team-building session)." This is at least occasionally a problem for 47 percent of the respondents. Of that group, 47 percent handle it by refusing to comply, and an additional 29 percent confront the problem by saying they did not like it (without necessarily refusing).

11. Priority of Interests

"I struggle with whose interests should take precedence: management's or employees'." Forty-six percent of the respondents report that this occurs at least occasionally. The most common

methods of handling this problem are action research (40 percent) and negotiation (26 percent).

12. Role Expectations

"I get caught between my view of the consultant's role and the expectations the client has about what my role should be." This dilemma is experienced at least occasionally by 44 percent of the respondents. Negotiation (38 percent) and confrontation (31 percent) are the most typical methods of handling the problem.

13. Conflict with Co-Consultant

"I disagree with a co-consultant about what to do with the client." This dilemma is reported as occurring at least occasionally by 43 percent of respondents. They are most likely to negotiate (44 percent), conduct action research (27 percent), or confront the problem (22 percent) in order to resolve the dilemma.

Decision-Making Styles or Methods

Perhaps the most striking results of DeVogel's research, from a practical point of view, are the insights gained about how OD consultants decide what to do about their ethical dilemmas. Research subjects were asked to describe their decision-making styles or approaches.

Overwhelmingly, the subjects in the study relied on two decision-making approaches: internal processes (such as values, personal ethics, reason, feelings, and intuition) and discussion with other people (such as colleagues, members of the client organization, friends, bosses, or spouses). Sometimes the respondents were able to develop parameters based on their experiences in various organizations. Sometimes their decisions were based on pragmatic concerns. The majority of respondents described their decision-making processes as intuitive and feeling-based rather than as rational. Organization development consultants in both the interview and survey phases of DeVogel's research rarely, if ever, used decision-making models such as the one proposed by Gellermann, Frankel, and Ladenson, (1990).

Essential Ethical Competencies for OD Consultants

Because there is no professional organization that speaks with authority for the entire OD field, there is no standard of professional ethical practice. Organization development writers and others interested in professional ethics have described ethical standards, values, and principles. However, such lists do not help an OD consultant to decide which value or principle takes precedence when he or she is confronting an ethical dilemma or an ethically ambiguous situation. Professional ethical competence is the ability to sort and sift through values and principles and make reasonable choices that would stand up to the scrutiny of one's peers, as well as allow one to sleep at night.

To become ethically competent, a consultant may begin, as suggested by Gellermann, Frankel, and Ladenson (1990), by becoming ethically sensitive. A consultant can become ethically sensitivity by facing ambiguity as well as his or her own motivations and interests. The consultant also can work to develop the following competencies:

- Knowledge of the codes of the organizations concerned with OD;

- Continual personal reflection and self-awareness—including clarifying one's values and developing rational ethical principles that can be resources in times of crisis, when self-interest might cloud one's judgment; and

- Conversations with other consultants about ethical issues and choices, with a willingness to present one's own decisions for scrutiny by others and to assist others with their ethical dilemmas.

Implications for Professional Practice

DeVogel's (1992) research indicates that out of a potentially vast array of ethical dilemmas, only a small group occurs with notable frequency. This group of dilemmas calls forth a variety of response strategies, and these responses are derived through consultants' personal reflection and consultation with peers. The research also suggests that rational tools such as decision-making models may not appeal to many OD consultants and, therefore, may not be used even when they are understood. Therefore, this chapter offers three tools for consultants—a checklist to guide their personal reflections, guidelines for an ethics-reflection group, and case studies.

Individual Reflection

Ethical reasoning, as a logical process, is perhaps best done when a consultant is not facing a crisis or difficult decision, when self-interest or other emotional factors might cloud his or her judgment. Individual reflection can take many forms, including studying the codes of the profession, clarifying personal values, and mentally solving hypothetical dilemmas, using the principles and values one has adopted.

Activity I: Codes

Three codes are printed in Appendix III: the code of the OD Network; the code of The Organization Development Institute (The O.D. Institute), which is quite similar to the statement found in Gellermann, Frankel, and Ladenson, 1990; and the code of the ASTD. The memberships of the OD Network and The O.D. Institute consist almost entirely of OD consultants; ASTD membership includes OD consultants and persons in a variety of other human resource development (HRD) roles whose work may encompass OD.

Review the codes in Appendix III and ponder the following questions:

1. Which of the three codes matches your personal thinking and values?
2. Select the sentence(s) or idea(s) in each code that best reflect your moral beliefs. Why do they mean so much to you?
3. Have you ever experienced a crisis of conscience—an ethical dilemma—in which your values or principles were called on? How did you resolve that crisis or dilemma?
4. The next time you experience a crisis of conscience, how could you use the code(s) to guide your decision making?

5. Would you be willing to have your professional behavior scrutinized by other OD consultants according to the principles in the code(s) you have chosen? Why or why not?

6. To what extent do you think that the OD professional associations should be able to use the codes to endorse or repudiate the actions of their members? Why?

Activity I may also be a useful resource for an ethics-reflection group.

Activity II: OD Value-Clarification Instrument

Exhibit 14-2 contains an instrument that is designed to help individuals clarify their values. Participants can score and interpret their instruments using the sheet in Exhibit 14-3.

The following list explains what each value of the instrument indicates:

Client autonomy, broadly defined, means that the authority for decision making about the OD process rests with the client. The data are owned by the client, as are choices about contracting and interventions.

Informed consent means that an organization and its members have the rights of informed consent (they understand and agree to the purpose and methods of an intervention before participating) and freedom from coercion (nobody is forced to participate in an OD intervention, particularly if personal disclosures will be requested).

Collaboration means that an OD consultant chooses to conduct his or her relationship with a client from a perspective of equality. Although the OD consultant has specialized skills and knowledge, he or she believes that the ultimate resource for solving the organization's problems is to be found within the client group. The style that the consultant adopts is thus a nonexpert, collaborative approach.

Objectivity and independence mean that an OD consultant, whether internal or external, places a high value on maintaining objectivity with regard to the client system. He or she makes an effort to stay out of organizational politics. The consultant does not get involved in the client system's dynamics or collude consciously or unconsciously with the client's desire to avoid unpleasant issues. The consultant is able to sort through the conflicting messages and demands coming from the client system. Objectivity and independence also mean that the needs of the client and standards of sound professional practice come before considerations of the consultant's contract, job security, or friendships within the client organization. The consultant does not seek to benefit financially from the relationship.

Confidentiality means that a consultant has a high concern for protecting privileged information and informants. The consultant is careful to uphold his or her promises, to maintain the trust of individuals, and to safeguard sensitive information about the organization. The consultant also protects the privacy of clients.

Truth telling means that a consultant is open and honest with a client about such matters as the limits of his or her skill or knowledge. The consultant also explains to the client the full cost, possible risks, and hoped-for benefits of an intervention, even when doing so might result in the termination of a contract. The value of truth telling may sometimes conflict with the value of preserving confidentiality.

Professional development means that a consultant has a high concern for improving his or her own skills and for contributing to the advancement of the profession. The consultant gives credit to others when it is due and he or she shares materials.

Social justice means that a consultant is concerned about the value issues pertaining to society, such as race, gender, and equality. The consultant is concerned about economic justice in the organization's business or management practices, such as producing hazardous waste or involving the consultant in downsizing and layoff decisions.

Recognizing limits means that a consultant is aware of the limitations of his or her ability to serve a client responsibly. These limitations include his or her availability, knowledge, skill, cultural awareness, idiosyncrasies, and conflicts of interest, such as the consultant's financial involvement with the client or his or her involvement with the client's competitors. Recognizing limits means that the consultant has a clear sense of boundaries.

Group Guidelines

As a professional issue, ethics suggests the notions of peer review and accountability. The input of colleagues can help a consultant resolve an ethical problem. Peer input also can help a OD consultant to develop and exercise dispassionate judgment. Like the process of individual ethical reflection, group reflection or peer accountability can help a consultant to balance emotional factors and self-interest.

Each ethics-reflection meeting is focused on a particular case. One member of the group may volunteer to serve as the meeting facilitator in order to ensure that the discussion is focused and meaningful. One member then presents a current example from his or her OD practice of a situation containing an ethical struggle for him or her. The member presents an organized narrative of his or her situation and addresses the following questions:

- What is the main ethical problem within this story?
- What action was taken to resolve the ethical problem?
- How was the decision made? Describe the reflective process that led to the action taken. Was it a rational process? Was it intuitive? Was a model used?
- What were the values and principles that influenced the decision?

The remaining members of the group offer other resolution strategies and critique the presenter's decision-making process by answering the following questions:

- Was the decision-making process consistent with OD values?
- Was the process consistent with the values espoused by the presenter?
- Do the presenter's values agree with the logic and the application of the principles espoused?

If time allows, a second case may be presented and discussed during the meeting. The following guidelines are offered for the formation of an ethics-reflection group.

Group Size: Research in small-group discussion methods indicates that five to seven people is the optimum size for maximum participation by group members.

Meeting Length: One and one-half to two hours. The group members will need to use the first few minutes and the last few minutes of the meeting to care for the group's inclusion and closure needs. Group members should not ignore the importance of tending to these social requirements because they increase the productivity of the group.

Meeting Frequency: The group will need to experiment with a timetable that meets the needs of the members. Meetings should be frequent enough to build commitment and cohesiveness within the group. A monthly meeting may work well.

Alternative Resources: To keep the group from running out of ideas, occasionally a member may present new concepts from the OD literature or the group may invite a guest speaker.

Case Studies

After reading each case study, imagine (or discuss with a colleague) what you would have done and why. Developing your reasons may be more important than achieving agreement on how to handle the situation.

Case Study 1. "I was hired very early in my consulting career to work in a church headquarters. I had conducted a number of interviews as part of the organizational diagnosis. In one of the interviews, all of which had been conducted under conditions of anonymity, I was told by a lower-level manager about some budget practices that were being used by another manager at his level. The practices were questionable at best and may have violated the law. This information was included in my feedback to senior management. The senior managers insisted that they had to know the names of both managers. I reminded them of the agreement regarding anonymity. Their perspective was that it was more important to handle the situation than to honor the commitment to anonymity. We reached an impasse, so I left the contract."

Case Study 2. "I had been working on a long-term contract with a client for about seven years. During that time, I had developed a social relationship with the company president. The president's style was at the root of many of the problems within the organization. I began to question my ability to maintain objectivity and a confrontational mode with the president, given the evolving relationship. I talked about the situation with the president and I decided to separate from the company and refer another consultant. I continued my social relationship with the company president for more than ten years after the separation."

Case Study 3. "I was working with a colleague in a nonprofit organization in which we had contracted with the executive director, whom we viewed as the client. We conducted an organizational diagnosis, consisting of both interviews and a survey, and discovered that the executive director was a primary cause of the problems being experienced by employees. He was an alcoholic and was carrying on an open affair that the employees viewed as very disruptive to the organization. The director was not interested in receiving this feedback. Our ethical dilemma was whether we should continue to work with the client on other issues, report our findings to the board of directors, or leave the contract. We left the contract."

Case Study 4. "I was conducting an organizational diagnosis for a fast-food chain that had over twenty stores within its franchise. As part of the diagnosis, I interviewed employees from various stores. During one interview, an employee asked me whether the interviews were being conducted under a commitment to anonymity, and I confirmed this. She then said that she wanted to share something with me, but that I could not share any of the specifics of the information such as name of the store, other employees involved, or the nature of her experience. Having received that commitment, she then told me about her experience. It was a vivid story of sexual harassment and possibly sexual assault. I heard a similar story from another employee at that store. Clearly, it was a serious problem that needed correction. How could that be done without violating my commitment to both anonymity and confidentiality? I ended up reporting to senior management that the company had a serious problem of sexual harassment within its system and that senior management had better find it to reduce the company's liability exposure. Within two days, senior management had identified the source of the problem, which already was widely known, and that manager was fired."

Conclusion

An ethical OD consultant respects and practices the following key principles:

Client Autonomy. An ethical consultant honors a client's preferences, pace, direction, judgment, and decisions, and he or she allows the client to decide how far to extend the OD process and when to terminate a consulting contract.

Client Freedom. The consultant ensures that each person involved in an intervention is participating willingly, understands why the intervention is being conducted and how it will work, and has the right to choose which of his or her opinions to disclose to others.

Collaboration. The OD consultant offers advice, choices, and recommendations rather than prescriptions; he or she does not act as an expert, but as a facilitator who helps a client to identify problems and find solutions.

Objectivity and Independence. The OD consultant remains neutral in the face of organizational politics, conflicting stories, or opposing emotional needs of organizational members. He or she insists on raising difficult issues when necessary, regardless of the potential reaction to them.

Anonymity. The OD consultant does not share specific information about any intervention, client, or employee without the clear consent of the person or people involved. He or she does not ever gather information in order to help terminate an employee.

Truthfulness. An OD consultant is forthright about the risks, estimated cost, estimated time, and potential effectiveness of a proposed intervention, as well as about his or her own experience, viewpoint, biases, concerns, and doubts.

Professional Development. In order to remain effective, an OD consultant keeps up with the OD field by attending professional meetings, reading the current literature, discussing problems with colleagues, and serving as a mentor.

Social Justice. The OD consultant refuses to work for any client whose goals, products, or services violate his or her own values. The consultant speaks out against any and all discrimination that he or she sees in a client organization.

Recognition of Limits. The OD consultant contracts only with clients whom he or she has the time and skills to serve well; he or she maintains clear boundaries between personal and professional relationships; and he or she is aware of his or her own biases and idiosyncrasies, seeking outside guidance on these issues if necessary.

Exhibit 14-2: OD Values-Clarification Instrument

Susan H. DeVogel

Instructions: This instrument consists of pairs of statements related to OD values. Read each pair. For each pair, indicate how important each statement is to you by rating the statements according to their relative values. You must allocate a total of three points to each pair of statements, but the points may be distributed however you like. For example, you may give all three points to one statement if you think the other is completely unimportant or if you like both statements, you might allocate two points to the statement you prefer and allocate one point to the other.

Although there will be some repetition of ideas throughout the instrument, treat each pair of statements independently. Do not struggle long over any decision; go with your initial instinct. If you are bothered by the strength of any statement, mentally add the words "generally" or "usually" to it.

Example:

It is important to me that...

___3___ a. I can go to the beach during the summer.

___0___ b. I have fresh vegetables.

___2___ a. I have fresh fruit.

___1___ b. I can go to the beach during the summer.

It is important to me that...

_____ 1a the client decides how far the OD process should be pushed through the organization.

_____ 1b all participants understand why an intervention is being conducted.

It is important to me that...

_____ 2a   I abide by a client's preference for a certain intervention, whether or not a diagnosis has indicated that it is needed.

_____ 2b   when I have reached the limits of my ability to serve a client, I discuss the situation with the client and offer options.

_____ 3a   when I am asked to give advice about an organizational problem, I assist the client in exploring the problem further rather than offering my opinion.

_____ 3b   I try to remain neutral when I encounter a client system's politics.

_____ 4a   I refuse to share what went on during an intervention with people who were not present in the group.

_____ 4b   if I have doubts about the effectiveness of a requested or proposed intervention, I share those doubts with the client.

_____ 5a   I am willing to discuss my professional ethical dilemmas with colleagues.

_____ 5b   I do not remain silent when I see evidence of gender discrimination or sexual harassment in a client organization.

It is important to me that...

_____ 6a   all participants in an intervention should be there willingly.

_____ 6b   when a manager asks me for feedback about his or her personal effectiveness, I give my honest views.

_____ 7a   I try to remain neutral even when I have friends within an organization.

_____ 7b   I serve as a mentor to somebody who wishes to enter the field of OD or who is less experienced.

_____ 8a   I trust the client's judgment when the client believes that an OD process has proceeded far enough.

_____ 8b   I give recommendations rather than instructions about how the OD process should proceed.

_____ 9a   when alternative interventions seem to be equally beneficial, I let the client choose the intervention.

_____ 9b   I refuse to share what went on during an intervention with people who were not present in the group.

_____ 10a   when a manager asks me for feedback about his or her personal effectiveness, I give my honest views.

_____ 10b   I do not participate in organizational processes that will result in people losing their jobs.

It is important to me that...

_____11a I do not work for a client whose product or service conflicts with my personal values.

_____11b I keep clear boundaries between my personal and professional relationships.

_____12a all participants understand how an intervention will proceed before we begin.

_____12b I view myself as a facilitator rather than as an expert.

_____13a I do not downplay the estimated time or cost when preparing an intervention proposal.

_____13b I attend as many meetings of professional organizations as I can.

_____14a I insist that the organization confront difficult issues when I believe that the client prefers to avoid them.

_____14b I do not reveal the names of my clients to others without the express permission of my client.

_____15a before I try a new intervention, I study the theory behind it.

_____15b I try to be aware of the biases I bring to any interaction, including my own cultural and gender biases.

It is important to me that...

_____16a the client should determine which interventions are appropriate for the organization.

_____16b I insist that the organization confront difficult issues when I believe that the client prefers to avoid them.

_____17a I do not share personal information that I know about an employee, regardless of how I gained it.

_____17b I do not take on consulting projects in areas in which I have little knowledge or experience.

_____18a when alternative interventions seem to be equally beneficial, I let the client choose the intervention.

_____18b I do not work for a client whose product or service conflicts with my personal values.

_____19a the client should determine which interventions are appropriate for the organization.

_____19b I am willing to discuss my difficult cases with colleagues.

_____20a all participants understand why an intervention is being conducted.

_____20b I try to remain neutral when I get caught between conflicting emotional needs of organizational members.

It is important to me that...

_____21a I insist on raising difficult issues, even if I know that doing so might jeopardize my contract or job.

_____21b I am honest with a client about the extent of the potential benefits that might be expected from an intervention.

_____22a I view myself as a facilitator rather than as an expert.

_____22b I do not take on consulting projects in areas in which I have little knowledge or experience.

_____23a employees have the right to decide how much of their personal opinions to disclose to others during an OD intervention.

_____23b I never share information if I have promised to keep it confidential.

_____24a I try to remain neutral even when I have friends within an organization.

_____24b I only take on as many clients as I have time to serve well.

_____25a if a manager asks me to gather information to help fire somebody, I refuse.

_____25b before I try a new intervention, I study the theory behind it.

It is important to me that...

_____26a   I abide by a client's preference for a certain intervention, whether or not a diagnosis has indicated that it is needed.

_____26b   I refuse to give recommendations about who should be laid off, based on information I have gained during an OD intervention.

_____27a   when I am asked to give advice about an organizational problem, I assist the client in exploring the problem further rather than offering my opinion.

_____27b   If I have doubts about the effectiveness of a requested or proposed intervention, I share those doubts with the client.

_____28a   when asked by a client about a specific intervention, I am truthful about whether or not I have ever tried it.

_____28b   I keep clear boundaries between my personal and professional relationships.

_____29a   employees should not be forced by their supervisor or manager to participate in an OD activity.

_____29b   I do not remain silent when I see evidence of discrimination against persons with differing abilities in a client organization.

It is important to me that...

_____30a I trust the group to find the answers to organizational problems.

_____30b I am willing to discuss my difficult cases with colleagues.

_____31a I usually refuse to share what went on during an intervention with people who were not present in the group.

_____31b I do not remain silent when I see evidence of gender discrimination or sexual harassment in a client organization.

_____32a I allow the client to determine the pace and direction of the consulting relationship.

_____32b I disclose the risks of an intervention, even if I believe the potential benefits greatly outweigh the risks.

_____33a I try to remain neutral when I get caught between conflicting emotional needs of organizational members.

_____33b I do not keep silent when I see evidence of racism in a client organization.

_____34a all participants in an intervention should be there willingly.

_____34b before I try a new intervention, I study the theory behind it.

It is important to me that...

_____35a I allow the client to determine the pace and direction of the consulting relationship.

_____35b I do not participate in organizational processes that will result in people losing their jobs.

_____36a all participants understand how an intervention will proceed before we begin.

_____36b I keep clear boundaries between my personal and professional relationships.

Exhibit 14-3: OD Values Scoring

Instructions: Transfer your scores from the instrument to this scoring form. Note that the items are *not* listed sequentially. When you have filled in all the blanks, total each of the nine columns.

Client Autonomy	Informed Consent	Collaboration
1a. _____	1b. _____	3a. _____
2a. _____	6a. _____	8b. _____
8a. _____	12a. _____	9a. _____
16a. _____	20a. _____	12b. _____
19a. _____	23a. _____	18a. _____
26a. _____	29a. _____	22a. _____
32a. _____	34a. _____	27a. _____
35a. _____	36a. _____	30a. _____
Total _____	Total _____	Total _____

Objectivity & Independence	Confidentiality	Truth Telling
3b. _____	4a. _____	4b. _____
7a. _____	9b. _____	6b. _____
14a. _____	14b. _____	10a. _____
16b. _____	17a. _____	13a. _____
20b. _____	23b. _____	21b. _____
21a. _____	25a. _____	27b. _____
24a. _____	26b. _____	28a. _____
33a. _____	31a. _____	32b. _____
Total _____	Total _____	Total _____

Professional Development	Social Justice	Recognizing Limits
5a. _____	5b. _____	2b. _____
7b. _____	10b. _____	11b. _____
13b. _____	11a. _____	15b. _____
15a. _____	18b. _____	17b. _____
19b. _____	29b. _____	22b. _____
25b. _____	31b. _____	24b. _____
30b. _____	33b. _____	28b. _____
34b. _____	35b. _____	36b. _____
Total _____	Total _____	Total _____

Exhibit 14-3: OD Values Scoring (Continued)

Instructions: Transfer your total score for each of the nine values on the scoring form to the chart below.

OD Value	Score
Client Autonomy	_____
Informed Consent	_____
Collaboration	_____
Objectivity and Independence	_____
Confidentiality	_____
Truth Telling	_____
Professional Development	_____
Social Justice	_____
Recognizing Limits	_____

The higher your total score for a particular value, the more important that value is to you. On the lines provided, rank order each value according to the score you have accumulated for each. The resulting list may help you gain insight into how you resolve ethical conflicts, particularly when you must choose between two values that are both important to you.

Value preferences:

_____

_____

_____

_____

_____

_____

References

Barber, B. (1988). Professions and emerging professions. In J.C. Callahan (Ed.), *Ethical issues in professional life* (pp. 35-39). New York: Oxford University Press.

Bayles, M.D. (1981). *Professional ethics.* Belmont, CA: Wadsworth.

Benne, K.D. (1959). Some ethical problems in group and organizational consultation. *Journal of Social Issues, 15*(2), 60-67.

Campbell, D.M. (1982). *Doctors, lawyers, ministers: Christian ethics in professional practice.* Nashville, TN: Abingdon.

DeGeorge, R.T. (1986). *Business ethics.* New York: Macmillan.

DeVogel, S.H. (1992). *Ethical decision making in organization development: Current theory and practice.* Unpublished doctoral dissertation, University of Minnesota.

Fletcher, J.F. (1966). *Situation ethics.* Philadelphia, PA: Westminster.

Gellermann, W., Frankel, M., & Ladenson, R. (1990). *Values and ethics in organization and human systems development: Responding to dilemmas in professional life.* San Francisco, CA: Jossey-Bass.

Jaspers, K. (1957). *Kant.* New York: Harcourt Brace.

Katz, D., & Kahn, R.L. (1966). *The social psychology of organizations.* New York: John Wiley & Sons.

Kultgen, J. (1988). *Ethics and professionalism.* Philadelphia, PA: University of Pennsylvania Press.

Lebacqz, K. (1985). *Professional ethics: Power and paradox.* Nashville, TN: Abingdon.

Lippitt, G.L., & Lippitt, R. (1978). *The consulting process in action.* San Diego, CA: Pfeiffer & Company.

McLean, A.J., Sims, D.B.P., Mangham, I.L., & Tuffield, D. (1982). *Organization development in transition: Evidence of an evolving profession.* Chichester, England: John Wiley & Sons.

Miles, M.B. (1979). Ethical issues in OD interventions. *OD Practitioner, 11*(3), 115-123.

Pfeiffer, J.W., & Jones, J.E. (1977). Ethical considerations in consulting. In J.W. Pfeiffer & J.E. Jones (Eds.), *The 1977 annual handbook for group facilitators* (pp. 217-223). San Diego, CA: Pfeiffer & Company.

Snell, R. (1986). Questioning the ethics of management development: A critical review. *Management Education and Development, 17*(1), 43-64.

Sullivan, R. (1989). Personal ethical OD canons. *Minnesota Education and Development, 17*(1), 43-64.

Veatch, R. (1972). Medical ethics: Professional or universal? *Harvard Theological Review, 65*(4), 531.

Walter, G.A. (1984). Organization development and individual rights. *Journal of Applied Behavioral Science, 20*(4), 423-439.

Walton, R.E., & Warwick, D.P. (1973). The ethics of organization development. *Journal of Applied Behavioral Science, 9*(6), 681-697.

Warrick, D.D., & Thompson, J.T. (1980). Still crazy after all these years. *Training and Development Journal, 34*(4), 16-22.

Webster's Ninth New Collegiate Dictionary. (1989). Springfield, MA: G. & C. Merriam.

White, L.P., & Wooten, K.C. (1983). Ethical dilemmas in various stages of organizational development. *Academy of Management Review, 8*(4), 690-697.

White, L.P., & Wooten, K.C. (1986). *Professional ethics and practices in organization development: A systematic analysis of issues, alternatives, and approaches.* New York: Praeger.

P A R T IV

DEVELOPING FUTURE
OD COMPETENCIES

Part IV concludes the book. It addresses possible future competencies that OD consultants may need.

CHAPTER 15

DEVELOPING OD COMPETENCE FOR THE FUTURE

*Saul Eisen, Hoy Steele, and
Jeanne Cherbeneau*

Many organization development (OD) consultants wonder how the accelerating rate of change in the world is affecting—and will continue to affect—the needs of their client systems and, consequently, the nature of their work. In particular, OD consultants may be wondering what new competencies they will need in the future. This chapter summarizes the results of a four-year study that explored the competencies OD consultants would need in the future.

The Aims and Background of the Study

The study was directed at eliciting an exploratory, future-oriented dialogue about how the OD field is evolving and how

OD consultants can continue to develop and maintain professional competence. The research process used in the study involved both electronic conferencing and face-to-face group discussions. The authors of this chapter presented, discussed, and elaborated on the outcome of the initial on-line conferences on the Fulcrum Network[1](Fulcrum) at an Organization Development Network (OD Network) conference in Seattle, Washington. Subsequent on-line conferences took place on Fulcrum, and the authors collected and presented that data at OD Network conferences in Boston, Massachusetts, San Diego, California, and San Francisco, California.

Some three hundred participants participated in the study. The participants represented diverse ages, professional experiences, and roles. They were men and women from various national, ethnic, and racial backgrounds. Although they cannot all be acknowledged by name here, the authors are grateful for their contributions to this research project.

This research was not statistically based. The participants were not randomly selected to represent a profile of the OD profession, and their tallied responses were not analyzed quantitatively. Furthermore, only a few participants representing other organizational functions—and, perhaps, other perspectives—were involved. If participants from other functions had participated in greater numbers, their input would have been valuable; perhaps it could have revealed new areas for investigation and served to balance the perspectives of the internal and external OD consultants whose responses predominated.

This study used a qualitative, consensus-based process. Each group of participants responded to the results of a pre-

---

[1] The Fulcrum Network is an on-line service for OD consultants who want to share their experiences and discuss their ideas. For more information about it, write to the Department of Management, Sonoma State University, Rohnert Park, CA 94928.

vious electronic conference or face-to-face group discussion. Data were modified and supplemented based on each group's discussion and its sense of the relative importance of various trends or issues and their effect on OD practice. Some ideas that did not represent a consensus were taken out. Although it was not structured as a traditional Delphi study, in which chosen experts respond to a series of related surveys, the research process was inspired by the Delphi technique. The study was also influenced by the systems perspective.

The methodology of the study was simple. As a first step, the researchers presented to each group of participants the challenge of accelerating change as it might affect client organizations and consulting practices. The researchers then guided the groups in brainstorming sessions and helped them prioritize their responses to a series of questions. The responses were prioritized by means of a multivoting technique. The priorities developed on the first list provided the background for the next brainstorming session. Small-group discussions provided opportunities for in-depth inquiry and for challenging assumptions.

Summary of Themes and Needed Competencies

The following questions were addressed by the study:

1. What are the trends (events, changes) in the relevant environments of organizations that are having or will have an important impact on OD consultants' work and how they perform it?
2. What competencies are needed by consultants to respond effectively to these trends?

As the researchers reviewed the responses to the first question, they found that the participants' responses could be organized thematically into the following five major categories:

1. Broadened frameworks in a global environment;
2. Clients and client systems;
3. Cultural and demographic diversity and change;
4. Values and ethics; and
5. Trends within OD.

The following sections summarize the key trends identified by the participants and the competencies needed by OD consultants for each trend. (The individual trends and competencies in the self-assessment instrument are found in Exhibit 15-2.) The researchers combined the participants' actual statements to make them more understandable.

Broadened Frameworks in a Global Environment

Trends

Global interdependence is increasing (Drucker, 1989). Different constituencies are becoming interconnected socially, politically, economically, and technologically. The world is becoming increasingly turbulent as nations, corporations, and financial institutions instantly react to singular events. There are growing strains among international firms and nations. Old sociopolitical systems are breaking down under the weight of democratic movements and ethnic nationalism.

Global competition is unrelenting and expanding on multiple fronts. The emerging corporate financial and global perspective has led to expansion, downsizing, mergers, acquisitions, joint ventures, and multiorganizational structures.

Newly merged global entities are larger and more centralized. Issues between the northern and southern hemispheres and between developed and developing nations are emerging. Issues include debt, capitalization, competition for markets, and the dominance of multinationals over cottage industries. As a result, OD has expanded into cross-cultural and international work.

Additionally, there is a growing awareness that the earth is a closed, fragile ecosystem (Laabs, 1992). This awareness has profound implications related to an OD consultant's personal and professional values and behavior. It suggests the possibility of assuming more proactive advocacy roles related to social and environmental concerns in the context of strategic planning interventions.

Competencies

Organization development consultants need to become proficient at combining theory and practice with competitive advantage. Interest is growing in strategic planning, market research, and related approaches—especially those based in a systems perspectives for making sense of a complex world. Consultants must also have an understanding of the special vocabularies, values, products, services, and processes of highly diverse clients.

There is a strong need for OD consultants to move beyond assisting/helping process roles to proactive, content/substantive leadership roles. Internal and external OD consultants should assume more active leadership roles in helping clients think globally and strategically (Rhinesmith, 1992). To expand their roles, OD consultants need to become more aware of their own assumptions, biases, knowledge gaps, and behavioral patterns—and how they affect OD interventions (Neuman, Edwards, Namsbury, & Raju, 1989). Beyond awareness, they need to work through—and change—inaccurate assumptions and biases, educate themselves as needed, and adopt new or more effective practices (Senge, 1990). That includes developing a strong awareness of multilevel, cross-cultural differences and knowing how to foster better cultural understanding among national and ethnic groups as well as among diverse workplace cultures.

Clients and Client Systems

Trends

In response to increasing government and marketplace demand for economic efficiencies, many organizations are downsizing, merging, unmerging, and experimenting with a wide range of organizational structures (Darraugh, 1990). Managers in many organizations are seeking sophisticated approaches to organizational change that go beyond increasing productivity (Steinburg, 1992). They want to release the potential of their employees, but these managers either do not know how to accomplish this goal or fear changing the management styles that got them to their current positions. This pressure frequently results in managers' demanding superficial solutions or the latest fads—and this may also lead to calls for help that are made too late.

There is an increase in the integration and interdependence of business, human, and technical systems. Fluidity is created as people work in dispersed networks, with temporary or changing assignments. More people feel powerless to influence the systems in which they live and work.

Many people are losing their jobs as a result of downsizing (Darraugh, 1990). Senior or long-term employees and managers are often affected. Middle-management positions and promotion opportunities have decreased, but the demand for employees to assume greater responsibility and demonstrate greater competence has increased. For example, middle managers must manage a broader scope of work and perform multiple functions—and they are usually expected to achieve increased outputs with decreased inputs.

In some settings, labor relations are becoming increasingly complex and volatile as organizations attempt to respond to economic pressures and experiment with new structures and new ways of managing. Additionally, employee-benefit expenses for employers have increased in the United States to an average of more than $3,000 per employee per year due to escalating healthcare costs, stress reactions, and poor health habits.

Competencies

Organization development consultants need to know how to make a difference more efficiently, without resorting to "quick fixes." They need to be able to help managers understand and use better strategies and processes for quicker organizational healing, learning, and change. Consultants need to use practical, easy-to-understand approaches that are tied to the bottom line as they also contribute to organizational healing, optimal employee health, and performance.

Organization development consultants need a better understanding of planning and organizational change efforts. The ability to examine organizational culture, norms, and managerial practices—as well as organizational structures and designs—will be even more important in the future. Organization development efforts need to be integrated with all organizational systems, including human resource management, financial, and information systems.

Consultants must develop leadership skills and methods that will improve employee performance without adding more tasks and activities for their clients. High-level conflict-management skills are increasingly essential to help organizations address interpersonal and intergroup conflict effectively. For example, consultants may need to help management and unions settle their disagreements (Appelbaum, 1991; Pascale, 1990). Conflict-management skills, when taught to employees, might also help them to cope with stress-related and health-related disorders.

Cultural and Demographic Diversity and Change

Trends

Workforce diversity has emerged as a key management issue for several reasons. Some of them are population shifts; older workers; single parents; changes in immigration laws, labor regulations, and labor laws; economic pressures resulting in dual-career couples; and the advancement of more people of color and women in organizations (Coates, Jarratt, Mahaffie, 1990; Jamieson & O'Mara, 1991). Yet some may wonder how much support for workforce diversity exists at senior-management levels.

The increasing number of senior employees in organizations means that there are fewer opportunities for promotion.

A bipolar pattern of employees also is emerging—that is, there are increasingly larger groups of both undereducated and overeducated employees.

Consumer trends also are affected by demographic shifts. New demands are being placed on organizations to change their traditional methods of hiring, training, promoting, and rewarding employees; determining what products and services to offer; making products or delivering services; and marketing and selling to consumers.

Competencies

Organization development consultants need to develop problem-solving and organizational-change skills that are task focused and culturally sensitive. Consultants also need to be able to frame the process of major change in a way that fosters diversity and links it positively to the bottom line.

Demographic changes require OD consultants to be able to develop organizational structures and systems that adjust to the needs of diverse employees such as different ethnic groups, older workers, single parents, dual-career couples, disabled workers, and employees who care for elderly relatives. Consultants also need to understand, keep up to date with, and integrate their work with legal issues such as equal employment opportunities and affirmative action. Consultants should go beyond purely legal issues to encourage, even celebrate, workforce diversity.

An organization development consultant needs to have a multicultural awareness that is linked to self-awareness of his or her own biases and prejudices. The consultant also needs to adopt a clinical focus regarding the personal stressors surrounding discrimination, integration, changing roles of men and women, and demands placed on dual-career couples and single parents. Skills in career and personal counseling and in interpersonal and intergroup conflict resolution are also critical to an OD consultant.

Values and Ethics

Trends

Many employees are demanding physically and psychologically healthier workplaces and acknowledgement of their roles in enhancing productivity (McPartland, 1991). Many employees seek increased integration of their work and personal values. For example, a growing number of people are dissatisfied with materialism as a central motivator. Some employees express a reduced commitment to their careers and organizations and an increased commitment to their personal "quality of life" and family needs (Johnson, 1991).

Many managers and OD consultants are finding that existing reward systems do not support the changing workforce values or related values espoused by OD, organizational transformation (OT), quality of work life (QWL), employee involvement (EI), or total quality management (TQM). Thus, they are beginning to question the legitimacy of the status quo, including how power is used in organizations.

There is greater awareness and publicity regarding individual and business ethics. (See Chapter 14.) Many organizations are beginning to focus on defining and communicating to employees their expectations regarding business ethics and personal conduct. Additionally, many organizations are assuming more social responsibility by encouraging their employees to volunteer and by supporting employee time spent in community activities.

Competencies

Organizations may experience greater return on investment (ROI) if OD consultants work more closely with other organizational functions, such as human resource management and finance, to design new structures and reward systems to support changing employee values and thinking. Consultants need to know how to assist organizations to create organizational environments that are motivating and meaningful on all levels. This alignment often means helping organizations draw on employees' personal visions to create organizational visions.

In carrying out this work, consultants need to know themselves and to remember that they are the instruments of their works. They can foster individual and organizational self-examination and renewal when they have gone through sufficient self-examination and possess the kind of humility and compassion that supports others in their own self-reflection. (See excerpts from on-line discussion in Exhibit 15-1.) Consultants also need advanced knowledge and skills to assist individuals and organizations in examining, defining, communicating, and building commitment to their desired organizational values and ethics.

Additionally, honest self-reflection and self-scrutiny will help OD consultants to pay attention to, and take responsibility for, the impact of their personal and professional values, ethics, and behavior on clients, colleagues, and the OD field.

The importance of personal maturity and self-knowledge was discussed in some depth during one on-line conference. The conference participants saw professional development of OD consultants as a lifelong process that culminates in the level of masterful practitioner. Participants commented that the masterful practice of OD requires certain "higher competencies" that, although difficult to define, are nevertheless important as part of an integral definition of OD consulting. Furthermore, they felt that these higher competencies are becoming increasingly important and should be acknowledged in professional-development programs. Excerpts from this on-line discussion are shown in Exhibit 15-1.

Trends within OD

Trends

As many new people enter the OD field, they bring with them a broad range of skills. Unfortunately, some OD consultants may have a limited knowledge of OD and they may take on consulting assignments outside their areas of expertise. This practice could produce undesirable results such as damaging the client system and creating unnecessary expense.

As some OD consultants begin to work for high-paying clients, they may become more materialistic and less concerned with the social values that are associated with the OD field. The lack of coherence within the OD field and among its practitioners can create confusion among clients regarding what to expect.

Organization development efforts have begun taking a total-systems approach. More attention is being given to the requirements of organizational cultural change and the role of managers as leaders. There seems to be increasing confusion regarding the relationship of OD to TQM and reengineering efforts and whether there is really any significant difference among them. Clearly there are increasing links among OD efforts, customer satisfaction, and quality initiatives within organizations. Similar blurred and perhaps nonexistent boundaries appear between OD and OT, EI, and QWL.

Exhibit 15-1: Excerpts from the Fulcrum Computer Conference*

Saul Eisen

Conceptual models used in OD are trending toward the more complex and metaphorical frameworks. They deal increasingly with aspects of organizational behavior such as spirited work, culture, and "energy."

An emerging area of competence for practitioners may be the knowledge and broad understanding of these emerging conceptual frameworks, and our ability to apply them correctly as part of our intervention strategy.

Furthermore, this implies the required ability to understand and use metaphor and nonrational approaches for working with aspects of organization culture such as "work spirit."

Donald Haselwood

The competencies for dealing with organizations via the nonrational, holistic requires a different kind of analytic skill and it is a different kind of complexity we deal with: different from the more linear, logic based models.

Saul Eisen

There are times in my professional interaction with others...when we all become part of something larger; my interventions are not my own, any more than water is created by a faucet. Yet magic happens. Hope blooms. Trust overwhelms us. Hidden potentials are manifested. Those are sacred moments for me, and they put me in touch with spiritual aspects of the practice of OD. They're too important to talk about; easy to misunderstand. There are no techniques for creating them.

In terms of competencies and professional development this aspect of our practice, I believe, is at the top of a hierarchy of learning and growth. The "how-to" is not available to a neophyte in an article on organizational transformation or flow state dynamics (though it can be recognized there by those who already know it). It's a curriculum one does not graduate from, but rather work that constantly

*From "Core and Emerging Areas of Competence for Masterful Practice in OD," 1990, *OD Practitioner, 22*(2), 14-15. Used by permission of *OD Practitioner.*

Exhibit 15-1: Excerpts from the Fulcrum Computer Conference
(Continued)

needs doing. To skip one's homework and go for the glamorous work can be folly, or worse—a power manipulation leading to great harm. Practitioners need to work on the spectrum of areas which support this level of work: personal maturity and psychological health, interpersonal and group process awareness and skill; organization and system theory; socio-cultural processes and structures; and a meditational practice or discipline.

Michael Marlowe

I wonder if there aren't layers of competencies; for example, for the new practitioner it might be learning to teach my internal experience (feelings, thoughts, wants) and using this to track the common points of human experience to create empathy, and speak the family secrets. I know sometimes when I work with scientists and say things like "well I'm feeling x as you describe this situation to me," and then extrapolate what they might be experiencing, they are often amazed that I could know this.

Maybe a more advanced version of using self as a resource involves evoking the "higher self" to guide interventions and give help directly from the heart—talking to clients on deep levels. This certainly was the gift of folks like Milton Erickson or Fritz Perls.

Andrew McColl

Elements of spirituality, feelings, culture and other non-rational constructs exist in large systems, often unconsciously or without acknowledgement. If OD can be defined as the design and development of high performing human systems (today's definition), then the development of OD professionals is the development of powerful, whole, high performing individuals. For me, the main reason OD professionals need to become aware of their own non-rational elements is so that they can also bring these elements of the client system into the awareness of the client. Surfacing these things so that the client can make conscious (that is, design) choices about them is clearly a major area of competence for OD professionals.

**Exhibit 15-1: Excerpts from the Fulcrum Computer Conference
(Continued)**

Donald Haselwood

What are the characteristics, competencies that distinguish the excellent from the OK [consultants]? A couple of things pop up:

- An ability to grasp the situation from the overall level (for example, business and social trends), down to the nitty-gritty level; on a number of dimensions (for example, technical/business, group dynamics, psychology).
- The capacity, leadership, ability, energy—but not necessarily content know how-to run the business at the level that he/she would be working at.
- Living "authentically" or, as one VP said, "when you talk to 'X' you know you're dealing with someone who is 'real.' Most top executives are pretty good at seeing through facades and fronts in others.

Mary Fewel

I like and agree with (Michael's) ideas about "higher self" and consulting. But tools first. And basic tools at that.

I now approach the end of my first year of OD-related studies. I'm changed by the learning, like I'm wearing stronger shoes, got something worthwhile in my knapsack, I understand my map and compass, have a more discerning eye for the landscape (and, not coincidentally, for my own inscape as well).

Bob Thurston

Mary, I like your thoughts about the tools-compass and map—but, I think it is best described as a journey, where one learns the most by sometimes being the most lost. My most exciting work has come when I least understood or anticipated what the outcomes would be.

Mary Fewel

Bob, for me, the whole point of map, compass, good shoes, etc., is the journey. Thank you for telling about the unknown aspect of consulting. For me, of course, at this point, each new intervention phase presents a bit of it. Glad to know the thrill may still be there for me when I'm a veteran like you. (Perhaps "derring-do" is a desirable quality in consultants?)

**Exhibit 15-1: Excerpts from the Fulcrum Computer Conference
(Continued)**

David Noer

I am struck by two things: 1) the arrogance and elitism of the concept that OD professionals have a "corner" on the means for nurturing work spirit and legitimizing non-rational modes of thinking in the work place. 2) The "heavy" burden of knowing the right way, and needing to transfer that "enlightenment" to "them"—those others who can't find the way without us! To me, a competency that is seldom articulated is that of humility.

When you look at some of the great practitioners—people like Shepard and Tannenbaum—you find a basic humility, not the sophomoric arrogance of knowing something different or of a higher order than clients.

Mary Fewel

I wonder if humility is a competency? I see it as a quality. And qualities are not taught so much as caught, I think.

From where I sit (in class, mostly), I would cite humility as an essential quality not only in OD practitioners, but even more so in teachers of OD. Students, like clients, need behaviors modeled for them, but will ultimately pick up on/absorb what's really there, behind the behavior (that is, false humility). Real humility is the soil out of which great authentic behaviors grow.

Saul Eisen

I believe that genuine humility emerges from self-esteem and emotional maturity. I agree that these cannot be taught, but they certainly can be fostered, by experiences such as therapy, t-groups, and mentoring, and these may be important aspects of professional development and academic training.

So, perhaps our discussion is leading us to broaden the framework, from discussing competencies such as skills and techniques, toward higher order qualities which may not be teachable as much as learnable, or in Mary's image, "catchable." Tannenbaum has consistently and eloquently reminded us of the centrality of self-knowledge in our practice.

Exhibit 15-1: Excerpts from the Fulcrum Computer Conference
(Continued)

Shepard often spoke about another such quality, courage. (His house in Connecticut, in fact, was called Fort Courage.) It was his willingness to take those outrageous but well-targeted risks which characterized his genius. It was not a reckless courage, but a well-targeted, intuition-based, inspired sort of courage. I think he taught courage by being courageous. Bob and Mary may be referring to that quality here when they write about trekking into the unknown.

A third quality of masterful consulting is what Jeanne Cherbeneau calls compassion; not the narrow sympathy for other's problems, but the high understanding of the human and social predicament, and of the dignity of all who struggle within it, including oneself.

Bob Thurston

In 1973, Tannenbaum gave a talk at the San Diego National OD Network entitled, "Does This Path Have a Heart?" The essence of the talk was dedicated to the thought that the "journey" only has meaning when it combines the vision of purpose with the essence of the whole person. This was the first public lecture that he gave after his severe heart attack and the soul searching about his purpose (spiritual values) if you will.

Since that time, I have looked in organizations for people to link up with, who can articulate their "paths" and "journeys." Each time I have found such a person, I have found a person who can bring about major organizational change. There is something about knowing what the path is and having the heart to pursue it.

Pressures are mounting in organizations to assess the outcomes of OD interventions in qualitative and quantitative terms (Head & Sorenson, 1990). There are indications that OD is changing from a function that is directed by a staff manager to a function that is directed by a line manager (Steinburg, 1992).

Competencies

The need for project management and evaluation requires that OD consultants have general knowledge of business operations, specific knowledge about clients industries, an understanding of financial analysis, and a variety of methods that contribute to key success factors. Consultants also need skills in statistics to translate knowledge of business operations into ROI relative to OD activity. Qualitative research and evaluation methods continue to be important. Some OD consultants may need to work with other consultants who have the skills they lack in either qualitative or quantitative methods in order to ensure that both sets of skills are available in change efforts.

Organization development consultants need better process approaches to total-systems diagnoses and interventions. They need an enhanced ability to work with total organizations, to see the Gestalt and the interlinkages, and to foster an appreciation of the whole by key stakeholders. Consultants need to be able to translate cultural variables into understandable terms for their clients. They also need to become more effective in educating managers about OD—especially about their own roles in the change process.

Self-Assessment and Planning Instruments

Exhibit 15-2 is an instrument that the researchers have found to be useful in workshops at OD Network conferences on developing OD competencies for the future. The instrument lists the twenty-four major trends and future competence areas that will be needed by OD consultants to prepare for those trends. For each competence there are two scales: one scale for assessing the degree of knowledge or skill a respondent presently possesses and a second scale for prioritizing its importance in the respondent's continuing professional-development planning. The instrument contains blank spaces for listing additional trends and competencies that are specifically relevant to the respondent.

After completing this Self-Assessment Instrument, go to Exhibit 15-3. It provides a planning process for identifying the component knowledge, skills, and attitudes required for each competence listed. There may be significant overlap among the learning required for each of the areas, and this is addressed in the exhibit. The exhibit also includes specific learning activities, together with relevant milestones for assessing progress, and a time frame for completing each part of the plan.

Conclusion

The intention of the research project described in this chapter was to provide a context for thoughtful consideration of how organization development consultants, working inside or outside organizations, learn to function effectively and how effective functioning can be defined. This project was not an attempt to regulate or control what is taught in the OD field or how it is taught. Certainly a diversity of formats and approaches is an important and even a healthier aspect of the professional-development process and the organization development field itself.

Exhibit 15-2: Self-Assessment Instrument

Instructions: For each of the following twenty-four items, write 1, 2, 3, 4, or 5 in the space provided to indicate your degree of knowledge/skill in a particular competence. If you do not have a particular competence listed, or if your knowledge of it is low, then write 1, 2, 3, 4, or 5 in the space provided to indicate your development priority for that skill.

Trends and Competencies	Knowledge/ Skill		Development Priority	
	Weak Strong 1 2 3 4 5		Low High 1 2 3 4 5	
Theme: Broadened Frameworks in a Global Environment				
1. *Global competition on multiple fronts* Can combine OD theory and practice to correlate with a competitive advantage.	_____		_____	
2. *Interdependence between organizations and turbulent economic, political, and technological environments* Can guide strategic-planning process.	_____		_____	
3. *Strains in organizations that are in global economic and information environments, but national political order* Can assist organizations to cope with economic changes and simultaneous information processing.	_____		_____	

Exhibit 15-2: Self-Assessment Instrument (continued)

Trends and Competencies	Knowledge/ Skill					Development Priority				
	Weak				Strong	Low				High
	1	2	3	4	5	1	2	3	4	5
Theme: Broadened Frameworks in a Global Environment (continued)										
4. *Increased numbers of whole-system innovations* Can develop processes involving both technical and applied behavioral science expertise.			_____					_____		
5. *An expansion of OD into cross-cultural and international work* Can increase cultural understanding between national groups and among diverse workplace cultures.			_____					_____		
6. *Awareness that individuals are paying a high price for ethnocentrism* Awareness of cultural assumptions and behaviors; can adopt new and effective practices.			_____					_____		
7. *Growing awareness of the earth as a closed and fragile system* Can lead the way in helping clients to think more globally, strategically, and futuristically.			_____					_____		

Exhibit 15-2: Self-Assessment Instrument (continued)

Trends and Competencies	Knowledge/ Skill		Development Priority	
	Weak　　　Strong		Low　　　High	
	1　2　3　4　5		1　2　3　4　5	
Theme: Clients and Clients' Issues				
1. *More sophisticated approaches to change that are beyond purely technical approaches to increasing productivity*				
Have a broad understanding of change efforts and a variety of methods for planning and organizing them.	_____		_____	
2. *Owners and managers of small businesses are looking for better ways to organize and operate their businesses*				
Can develop practical, easy-to-understand approaches that are suitable for small systems.	_____		_____	
3. *The OD process within the business environment is being tied more closely to bottom-line concerns*				
Can tie objectives of interventions to, and measure results in, bottom-line terms.	_____		_____	

Exhibit 15-2: Self-Assessment Instrument (continued)

Trends and Competencies	Knowledge/ Skill		Development Priority	
	Weak　　　Strong 1　2　3　4　5		Low　　　　High 1　2　3　4　5	
Theme: Clients and Clients' Issues (continued)				
4. *Manufacturing and other industries are working under greater time constraints and with less space and they are doing more with less*				
Can develop methods to improve performance with minimal addition of more tasks and activities.	_____		_____	
5. *Employees are losing their jobs as a result of downsizing; fewer middle managers*				
Can create processes for organizational healing and responsive models for career development and employee assistance that address these issues on both individual and organizational levels.	_____		_____	
6. *More and more people feel alienated from mainstream systems and feel powerless to influence them*				
Can work at both systems and individual levels to:	_____		_____	

Exhibit 15-2: Self-Assessment Instrument (continued)

Trends and Competencies	Knowledge/ Skill					Development Priority				
	Weak				Strong	Low				High
	1	2	3	4	5	1	2	3	4	5
Theme: Clients and Clients' Issues (continued)										
a. Assist organizations to assess systemic and procedural blocks to employee empowerment and commitment to organizational mission and goals.			____					____		
b. Assist managers to examine organizational culture, norms, and management practices that block empowerment.			____					____		
c. Assist employees and managers to develop effective approaches to remove the blocks in *a* and *b* and to enhance their own skills at self-empowerment.			____					____		
7. *Poor health habits and stress lead to hidden overhead costs of approximately $3,000 per employee per year in the United States*										
Can develop approaches that generate optimal health and optimal performance in client organizations.			____					____		

Exhibit 15-2: Self-Assessment Instrument (continued)

Trends and Competencies	Knowledge/ Skill					Development Priority				
	Weak				Strong	Low				High
	1	2	3	4	5	1	2	3	4	5
Theme: Cultural and Demographic Diversity and Change										
1. *Increasing diversity of cultural backgrounds in the work force* Can develop problem-solving approaches that are sensitive to and effective within a wide variety of cultures and value systems.			_____					_____		
2. *More minorities and caucasian women are working in organizations and are being promoted; there are also more diversified work forces— for example, older workers, single parents, dual-career couples, disabled workers, and individuals who care for elderly relatives*			_____					_____		
Can help organizations create organizational cultures and structures that value and integrate the best from all their diverse employees.			_____					_____		

Exhibit 15-2: Self-Assessment Instrument (continued)

Trends and Competencies	Knowledge/ Skill		Development Priority	
	Weak Strong 1 2 3 4 5		Low High 1 2 3 4 5	
Theme: Cultural and Demographic Diversity and Change (continued)				
3. *Increasing numbers of smart, competent people are opting to work for themselves, which is possibly lowering the quality of managers and workers in large organizations* Can assist organizations to assess why people are leaving and to help them develop appropriate responses.	_____		_____	
4. *As a result of cultural and demographic diversity, organizations are changing their traditional ways of hiring training, promoting, and rewarding employees; determining what products are to be sold and what services are to be offered; producing products and delivering services; and marketing and selling to consumers* Have a multicultural awareness grounded in my self-awareness of my own biases and prejudices and an openness to active innovation in all aspects of the organization and its activities to respond to diversity and changing demographics.	_____		_____	

Exhibit 15-2: Self-Assessment Instrument (continued)

Trends and Competencies	Knowledge/ Skill					Development Priority				
	Weak				Strong	Low				High
	1	2	3	4	5	1	2	3	4	5
Theme: Values and Ethics										
1. *Dissatisfaction with materialism*										
Can assist organizations to create meaningful environments that are motivating on all levels.			_____					_____		
Can help organizations draw on employees' personal visions in creating organizational visions.			_____					_____		
2. *Increasing complexity of, and attention to, business ethics and practices*										
Can reflect honestly on my own behavior and take responsibility for the impact of my personal and professional values, ethics, and behavior on individual clients organizations, colleagues, and OD the profession.			_____					_____		
Can assist organizations to recognize and assess ethical issues and to address them effectively.			_____					_____		

Exhibit 15-2: Self-Assessment Instrument (continued)

Trends and Competencies	Knowledge/ Skill		Development Priority	
	Weak 1 2 3 4 5	Strong	Low 1 2 3 4 5	High
Theme: Values and Ethics (continued)				
3. *Most existing reward systems do not support the values being introduced or supported by OD, organizational-transformation, and quality-of-work-life efforts*				
Can design new reward systems that support new values and thinking.	_____		_____	
4. *Reduced commitment to career and organization, increasing commitment to personal quality of life*				
Can help organizations to rethink expectations of employees and to accept and implement a wellness model.	_____		_____	
5. *More individuals in organizations are exploring their own spirituality and higher consciousness and are less impressed with and tolerant of consultants who focus on ego/power/ success*				
Possesses humility; can support others in their self-reflection.	_____		_____	

Exhibit 15-2: Self-Assessment Instrument (continued)

Trends and Competencies	Knowledge/ Skill	Development Priority
	Weak Strong 1 2 3 4 5	Low High 1 2 3 4 5
Theme: Trends Within OD		
1. *A move from OD being a function that is directed by staff managers to function that is directed by line managers* Can assist line managers to understand the OD function, to evaluate it and its practitioners, and to represent it effectively to the rest of their organizations.	_____	_____
2. *Some consultants have a narrow focus and they only see and focus on issues related to their own areas of expertise* Can conduct a total-system diagnosis and analysis.	_____	_____
3. *Increasingly materialistic approach by some consultants, rather than attention to both business effectiveness and social values, is leading to confused client expectations* Can work with clients in ways that integrate and maximize both business and social goals.	_____	_____

Exhibit 15-2: Self-Assessment Instrument (continued)

Trends and Competencies	Knowledge/ Skill		Development Priority	
	Weak Strong 1 2 3 4 5		Low High 1 2 3 4 5	
Theme: Trends Within OD (continued)				
4. Growing confusion regarding the relationship of OD to total-quality-management, sociotechnical systems, organization-transformation, employee-involvement, and quality-of-work-life programs Have a broad knowledge of current and emerging OD methods and ability to articulate the similarities and differences between them and OD.	_____		_____	
5. Some organizations are beginning to assess the outcomes of OD interventions in both qualitative and quantitative terms Can use qualitative research, evaluation methods, and my skills in statistics and computing to translate knowledge of business operations into ROI relative to OD activity.	_____		_____	

PRACTICING ORGANIZATION DEVELOPMENT

Exhibit 15-2: Self-Assessment Instrument (continued)

Instructions: If there are any additional trends or competencies that are specifically relevant to you that were not listed in Exhibit 15-2, use this form to list and rank them.

Trends and Competencies	Knowledge/ Skill		Development Priority	
	Weak 1 2 3	Strong 4 5	Low 1 2 3	High 4 5
Self-Assessment Instrument				
Trend:				
Competence:	_____		_____	
Trend:				
Competence:	_____		_____	
Trend:				
Competence:	_____		_____	

Exhibit 15-2: Self-Assessment Instrument (continued)

Trends and Competencies	Knowledge/ Skill		Development Priority	
	Weak Strong 1 2 3 4 5		Low High 1 2 3 4 5	
Self-Assessment Instrument				
Trend:				
Competence:	_____		_____	
Trend:				
Competence:	_____		_____	
Trend:				
Competence:	_____		_____	

Exhibit 15-3: Action Plan for Acquiring Competencies

Instructions: Use this form to develop an action plan for your competencies generated from Exhibit 15-2.

1. List your three desired competencies, in order of priority:

   a.

   b.

   c.

2. For each competence, identify to what extent it consists of knowledge, skill(s), or attitude(s). Rank order these for each competence:

   a. _____ skills _____ knowledge _____ attitudes

   b. _____ skills _____ knowledge _____ attitudes

   c. _____ skills _____ knowledge _____ attitudes

3. For each competence, identify and write out as precisely as possible the knowledge, skills, and attitudes needed:

a. knowledge:

   skills:

   attitudes:

b. knowledge:

   skills:

   attitudes:

c. knowledge:

   skills:

   attitudes:

Exhibit 15-3: Action Plan for Acquiring Competencies (continued)

4. Can skills for more than one competence be learned at the same time or in the same way?

   Notes:

5. Now think about your current practice—your clients, the type of work you do—and assess to what extent you can learn your new desired competencies in the normal course of your practice.

   Notes:

6. Which competencies still need to be learned? What will you have to do differently?

   Notes:

Exhibit 15-3: Action Plan for Acquiring Competencies (continued)

7. *Action Plan:* Write out how you will acquire the components parts of each competence. Indicate several milestones for each competence (that is, how you will recognize you are making progress) and a timetable for each one. The last milestone should mark completion of your acquisition of that particular knowledge, skill, or attitude.

Competence a.	How acquired	Milestones	Timetable
knowledge:			
skills:			
attitudes:			

Competence b.	How acquired	Milestones	Timetable
knowledge:			
skills:			
attitudes:			

Competence c.	How acquired	Milestones	Timetable
knowledge:			
skills:			
attitudes:			

In "The Irony of a Mature Helping Profession," Herb Shepard (1983) suggests that the typical progression for such professions leads professionals to practices that risk the negation of their own values:

> After initial periods of innovation and then product differentiation, there is a period of legitimation, accreditation and development of ethical codes. Then there is often a period of monopolization: control over entry and other practices to eliminate competition. This then leads to a period of exploitation, subordinating clients' needs, and finally, to a defensive period when clients begin to rebel. What is needed is an awareness of this process, and its pitfalls, and of the need for integrative order. The great challenge to our profession is to transcend the tendencies of the later stages. To do this, we must address the issues of our profession in the same ways we address the issues of our clients.

As a continuing objective of this study, the authors of this chapter are forming a network of OD educators called OD CONSORTIUM. The purpose of this network is to link the growing number of OD programs and training activities around the world so that OD consultants can share their experiences and interests, learn from one another, and address issues of common concern. As one step toward the formation of such a network, the authors are creating a database of all professional-development programs. It will include participants from the faculties of academic OD programs as well as providers of professional-development workshops and training conferences.[2] Through this research project and the for-

---

[2] An on-line conference for this network has been established on the Fulcrum Network. Information on how to participate in OD CONSORTIUM and join the on-line conference is available from Saul Eisen at Sonoma State University, Rohnert Park, CA 94928. It can also be obtained by calling Saul at 707-664-2516.

mation of a network of OD educators, we hope to begin moving toward more integrative order in the OD profession.

References

Appelbaum, S. (1991). Resolving conflict via team building: The physician-nurse case. *Organization Development Journal, 9*(4), 81-87.

Coates, J., Jarratt, J., & Mahaffie, J. (1990). *Future work: Seven critical factors reshaping work and the work force in North America.* San Francisco, CA: Jossey-Bass.

Darraugh, B. (Ed.). (1990, October). How to survive mergers and downsizings. *Info-Line*, pp. 1-15.

Drucker, P. (1989). *The new realities: In government and politics/in economics and business/in society and world view.* New York: Harper & Row.

Jamieson, D., & O'Mara, J. (1991). *Managing workforce 2000.* San Francisco, CA: Jossey-Bass.

Johnson, A. (Ed.). (1991). *Work-family roundtable.* New York: The Conference Board.

Head, T., & Sorenson, P. (1990). Critical contingencies for the evaluation of OD interventions. *Organization Development Journal, 8*(2), 58-63.

Laabs, J. (1992). The greening of HR. *Personnel Journal, 71*(8), 60-63, 66-71.

McPartland, P. (1991). How adults learn to become fit in the work setting. *Journal of Healthcare Education and Training, 6*(1), 2-6.

Neuman, G., Edwards, J., Namsbury, S., & Raju, (1989). Organizational development interventions: A meta-analysis of their effects on satisfaction and other attitudes. *Personnel Psychology, 42*(3), 461-489.

Pascale, R. (1990). *Managing on the edge: How the smartest companies use conflict to stay ahead.* New York: Simon & Schuster.

Rhinesmith, S. (1992). A global human resource agenda. *Cultural Diversity at Work, 4*(3), 1, 10, 12.

Senge, P. (1990). *The fifth discipline.* New York: Doubleday.

Shepard, H. (1983, Summer). The irony of a mature helping profession. *CCI News,* pp. 6-7.

Steinburg, C. (1992). Making choices about change: Taking charge of change. *Training & Development, 46*(3), 24-32.

AFTERWORD

Donald W. Cole

In the late 1970s I began receiving a number of strange telephone calls. I got a call from someone who introduced himself as an employee of a major corporation in the United States. The caller had just been hired as an OD consultant for the corporation, but he had no OD training and no OD experience. His manager wanted him to conduct a team-building session with the corporation's management team, and the caller wanted information on a weekend workshop that he could attend in order to learn how to conduct a team-building session.

About the same time I got another call from a professor at a university in the midwestern U.S. The professor's dean wanted him to start an OD program. The professor had no OD training and no OD experience. He wanted the name of a good book on OD that he could read.

During this period, students of an OD program at another midwestern university had conducted a "touchy-feely" T-group in a local manufacturing division of a U.S. company. A member of that company's personnel department later told me that most of the participants who had attended the T-group had been fired or transferred because they had returned from the program engaging in behaviors that management felt were inappropriate for the company.

After a number of such experiences, it became obvious to me that there was a Gresham's law of OD: Without some controls, bad OD might eventually drive out good OD. I felt we should put some boundaries around this new field. Not everyone who attends a weekend workshop on OD should be able to lay claim to being an OD expert.

I felt that the field of OD needed to become a profession, and in order to become a profession a number of things were needed. The most important was a code of ethics, a statement on the unique body of knowledge and skills that OD people must possess, and a visible boundary around the field so that the public could tell who was a competent OD practitioner and who was not.

As a charter member of the Organization Development Network (OD Network) and a member of its board of directors from 1979 to 1981, I tried to get the OD Network involved in developing an OD code of ethics and building the OD field into a profession. However, I was told that "we are not that kind of an organization," so I decided to do it myself, with help from the OD Institute.

In 1981 I wrote the first OD code of ethics. It was published in the OD Institute's monthly newsletter, and readers were asked for their comments. A revised version was published in the 1982 edition of *The International Registry of OD Professionals* and *The OD Handbook*.

In the fall of 1981, Dr. William Gellerman agreed to handle later revisions. Dr. Gellerman has done a wonderful job of revising the ethics code into one that can be used by OD professionals worldwide. The code of ethics has now gone through twenty-two revisions and has been translated into numerous languages.

National Training Laboratories (NTL) has gotten sued because it "certified" people. The OD Institute did not want to get into that kind of difficulty, so instead of certifying people, the organization registers them. The members of the OD Institute had some heated discussions as to who could be registered and who was competent to decide who was competent. I felt, however, that some set of objective criteria should be used. For a time the problem seemed unsolvable. Eventually, in good OD fashion, the members developed an integrative solution. The OD Institute established the initials RODP (registered organization development professional) for people who judged themselves to be competent and the initials RODC (registered organization development consultant) for people who met the OD Institute's more stringent requirements. The members are not yet completely happy with either of these designations, and the OD Institute has a committee working to improve them.

In deciding how to qualify people who could use the initials RODC, the members saw the need for a knowledge test of some kind. Dr. Warner Burke, a member of the OD Institute's advisory board, agreed to prepare such a test. In 1983, Dr. Warner completed the Assessment Questionnaire for Knowledge and Understanding of OD. (In 1990, Dr. Burke was given the Outstanding OD Consultant of the Year Award for this and other important contributions to the field.) The questionnaire was based on questions proposed by OD students, which were reviewed, modified, and refined by one hundred highly qualified OD practitioners in the United States. These questions were not based on explicitly defined OD knowledge because such a body of knowledge had not yet been codified. There were no questions on ethics and no input from the international OD community. Dr. Benton Randolph, RODC, currently heads a committee to revise this test.

The OD Institute also became concerned about what students were learning and, more importantly, what they were not learning. Over half of the OD/OB academic programs in the U.S. do not teach the OD code of ethics and do not subscribe to journals being published in the field. Furthermore, based on evidence currently available, most students graduating from OD programs have never had their papers published.

In developing and revising the questionnaire, and in evaluating what should be taught in OD academic programs, it became obvious to me that the field needed a statement on the knowledge and skills necessary for competence in OD. The OD Institute is delighted that such a statement has, at long last, been written, approved, and adopted.

We at the OD Institute are vary grateful to Roland Sullivan, RODP and the team of people he collected for the tremendous job they have done in developing this book. In particular I wish to thank Dr. Gary McLean, RODC, and Dr. William Rothwell, RODC, for the prodigious amounts of time and effort they contributed to this project. Well done, gentlemen.

A P P E N D I X   I

ESSENTIAL COMPETENCIES FOR INTERNAL AND EXTERNAL OD CONSULTANTS

Background

This is the fifteenth revision of the organization development professional competencies list. From 1977 to 1993, over two thousand practitioners and change management academicians from around the world contributed their inputs. The current list was revised at the 13th International O.D. Congress, held in Monterrey, Mexico; the 1994 National OD Conference, held in Baltimore, Maryland and the Twenty Fourth Annual Information Exchange, held in Lake Geneva, Wisconsin. An estimated 1,400 professionals had an opportunity to review and critique the list.

If you would like to contribute to the sixteenth revision of the OD competencies list, you can send your input electronically by means of the gopher command to: (gopher.tmn.com), then select Organization and Management.

If you are not on-line, please mail or fax your input and feedback to the following address: Roland and Kristine Sullivan, 20020 Vine Street, Deephaven, MN 55331; telephone: 612-474-8363; FAX: 612-470-0481.

We are specially interested in any relevant research or articles.

Step 1: Entry

Marketing Phase

1. Fluently and convincingly convey your qualifications, knowledge, and skills to prospective clients with minimal OD jargon.
2. Use your awareness of the business environment to identify organizations that are presently undergoing crises or accelerated changes or growth.
3. Locate and match the size, character, structure, and commitment for change of potential clients with your skills and abilities.

Initial Contact Phase

4. Understand and become familiar with the nature of a prospective client's business.
5. Adapt to and use the language of the client system.
6. Determine who the appropriate decision makers are, establish contact with these people, build rapport with them, and model attitudes and behaviors that will lead to client trust.
7. Determine what is necessary to establish a mutually satisfying relationship with your contacts.
8. Conduct a miniassessment to determine:

   a. The client's values, history, philosophy, visions, key challenges, and degree of sensitivity to change;
   b. The organization's size, product/service lines, profitability, and so on;
   c. The areas of the organization that need to be examined during the initial diagnosis; and

d. The unique nomenclature and characteristics of the client system.

9. Help the client organization reflect on its own motivations and on the discrepancies of goals within the system that are creating dissatisfaction.

10. In collaboration with the client, identify and clarify outcomes to be achieved by a change effort.

11. Evaluate the client's hopes and expectations in a realistic manner, and based on your knowledge from and experience with other change efforts.

12. Communicate to the client the intricacies and complexities of a system and how changes in one area impact other areas.

13. Recognize and respond to concerns about your qualifications, competence, expertise, and credibility.

14. Articulate to the client the OD process you recommend and the anticipated effect on bottom-line results.

15. Present and discuss the theoretical foundations of system/organizational change in a concise and accurate manner.

16. "Know thyself" and try to remain objective in your observations during the entire change process.

17. Contract with the client for cooperation, collaboration, and joint responsibility, and then model these essential behaviors.

18. Model appropriate personal motivations, expectations, values, boundaries, abilities, and limitations; model those behaviors that the client will be asked to accept.

19. Stay grounded in the OD consultant's role as a catalyst for change; avoid taking on the organization's responsibility for implementing and accepting change.

20. Identify the elements and timing of receiving feedback regarding the project from the client.

21. Use, and be able to explain, a clear, straightforward compensation structure and billing process.

22. Determine if the client is willing and able to pay your fee. Be creative in finding ways to meet the client's needs.

23. Solicit from the client an appropriate commitment of human and other resources or factor these costs into the fee structure if such resources are not available.

Step 2: Start-Up

24. Continue the development of processes begun in the entry step by gathering more detailed information and by continuing to build rapport with the client. These efforts will include, but are not be limited to, the following:

   a. Identifying the critical success factors, as seen by the client at that time;

   b. Understanding and appreciating the world the client comes from and the reality and perceptions within which it operates;

   c. Further assessing and clarifying the real issues as they continue to surface and seeking to dramatize natural tensions and discrepancies as appropriate;

   d. Acknowledging differences and understanding the implications of those differences;

   e. Helping the client reflect on motivations for change;

   f. Creating a focus on the future and a vision based on the client's current reality that helps the client see its own set of possibilities; and

   g. Being aware of how your own biases can influence the process.

25. Identify the formal and informal power in the client organization in order to gain further commitment and mobilize people in a common direction.

26. Ensure that the client's desired changes are aligned with the organization's goals and objectives.
27. Develop relationships at all levels in the organization that are grounded in trust and credibility.
28. Seek commitment and participation from all those affected by the changes.
29. Deal effectively with resistance as it surfaces.
30. With the client, define the roles of leaders, internal and external consultants, and all other participants in promoting and implementing the desired changes.
31. Create an adjustable plan with the client for managing the change process.
32. Recognize what is required to solve the client's longstanding problems or recurring conflicts and seek the experiences that will give you the proper skill level.
33. Maintain patience during the change process, especially when working through issues that are complex or emotionally charged.

Step 3: Assessment and Feedback

34. Determine the types and amounts of data that are needed to help the organization focus on the issues and maximize its efforts.
35. Take a broad view for data collection and analysis in order to identify general issues.
36. Utilize an appropriate mix of data-gathering methods to ensure efficiency, objectivity, comparability, completeness, validity, reliability, and flexibility.
37. Ensure that the chosen data-gathering method fits organizational needs, the consultant's skill level, and the time available.
38. Clarify boundaries of confidentiality in order to facilitate honest disclosure by the client system.

39. Understand and explain to the client how diversity will affect the diagnosis of the culture.

40. Be alert to possible misconceptions or misunderstandings brought about by cultural differences.

41. Focus on collecting relevant and valid information about existing paradigms.

42. Probe issues as they surface, researching and identifying root causes rather than symptoms.

43. Help the organization identify and obtain missing data.

44. Continue to be open to additional concerns to be assessed (and to different avenues through which to locate and assess them).

45. Observe accurately; note behavioral data as they occur.

46. Observe and document what exists without making judgments.

47. Stay centered in the present and focus on the ongoing process.

48. Assess dissatisfaction with existing organizational goals and its potential impact on the attainment of them.

49. Obtain information on the lack of congruence between the espoused organizational culture and the actual culture.

50. Identify the sources of anxiety and discrepancy in the system in order to dramatize real and perceived differences.

51. Observe behavior that affects the informal systems, such as the flow of information and dynamics of power.

52. Focus on major system outputs and trace them as they flow through the system.

53. Gather quantities of data in a fast and comprehensive manner (for example, administer an instrument to as many people as possible at one time).

54. When gathering data, maintain an appropriate balance between completeness and usefulness.

55. Use statistical models and computer technology to analyze data.

56. Involve individuals and groups creatively in the interpretation of the data, thereby generating ownership by the participants.

57. Make comparisons across information sources and time periods.

58. Look for and identify patterns that emerge throughout the data-gathering process and know how data from different levels of the organization relate.

59. Using the data, determine where the organization is and where it wants to be.

60. Make observations based on assessment results, not on impressions or personal views (either your own or the client's).

61. Synthesize data into appropriate themes, factors, groups, and so on.

62. Determine what information is relevant and useful and what is not.

63. Identify the relationships between the formal and informal systems within the organization.

64. Probe and explore hidden causes in order to develop a thorough understanding of the problem.

65. Trace the existing or potential consequences of a specific action or behavior as it affects different parts of the organization.

66. Get commitments from relevant organizational members that there will be no retaliation to those people who are honest.

67. Create and maintain a nonthreatening atmosphere in which the client feels that working with the feedback data will result in beneficial outcomes.

68. Respond to discomforting concerns sensitively, compassionately, and courageously.

69. Understand the impacts that diverse cultural norms of timing, communication styles, and relationship building will have on the reception of feedback.

70. Facilitate a healthy group process that will allow resistance to the data to come out through free and open dialogue.

71. Ensure that the relevant people fully discuss the implications of the data.

72. Present data that is:

    a. Relevant;

    b. Descriptive;

    c. Verifiable;

    d. Timely;

    e. Limited;

    f. Comparative;

    g. Understandable; and

    h. Appropriate.

73. Help the client understand, clarify, and own the relevant data.

74. Help those who provided the data to understand, clarify, and own the data.

75. Discuss how the data directly relate to organizational effectiveness and validate the accuracy of the assessment.

76. Ensure that all conclusions and propositions are directed toward organizational changes that are relevant and feasible.

77. Simplify, narrow, and reduce the change focus at the appropriate time so that the next steps are identified for the client.

78. Develop and begin appropriate and meaningful interventions.

79. Facilitate a visioning process that leads to establishing the first steps for change.

Step 4: Action Planning

80. Help participants move from focusing on pain and problems toward envisioning a positive future. Teach them the process for planning the transition state.

81. Facilitate a participative, decision-making process that critically judges the choice of intervention.

82. Help participants brainstorm and generate imaginative and creative options.

83. Facilitate a mental rehearsal of the intervention to anticipate any likely consequences, side effects, and potential gains.

84. Envision and describe to the client the first steps toward adopting new paradigm as part of the change process.

85. When considering "quick fix" solutions, consider long-term strategies that can be initiated at the same time.

86. Ensure that there is a connection between the organizational goal, the intervention, the support from top management, the cost, and other persons and teams in the system.

87. Focus first on the area that will generate the greatest amount of positive change at the lowest cost and in the least amount of time.

88. Obtain a preliminary commitment from the client for support of the implementation of the action plan.

89. Determine what resources are available and allocate them appropriately.

90. Clarify all roles, responsibilities, and due dates for all implementation tasks.

91. Co-create, with as much of the client system as possible, a written implementation plan that is concrete, cost effective, measurable, simple, clear, flexible, results oriented, and logically sequenced.

92. Help as many people and levels in the organization as possible to determine the next steps for moving toward the preferred future and/or new paradigm.
93. Obtain a clear commitment to review and evaluate outcomes early.
94. Design and communicate the plan so that buy-in exists at all levels of the client system.
95. Manage resistance effectively.
96. Help the client to develop a reward system that supports the new, desired state.

Step 5: Intervention

97. Apply management, organizational, and systems theories by being aware of how organizational dynamics are affected by what you do.
98. Display a good sense of timing in order to gain the greatest amount of impact.
99. Help the organization deal with the effects that changes in one part of the system have on other parts.
100. Help the client work through resistance and prepare it for the change.
101. Intervene at an appropriate depth, neither too shallow nor too deep.
102. Balance risk and experimentation safely in the intervention.
103. Be spontaneous, redesigning the intervention in response to the needs of the moment.
104. Facilitate concurrent interventions.
105. Use group- and intergroup-facilitation skills.
106. Facilitate interactions among people that build community.
107. Be aware of potentially damaging consequences to the organization.

108. Help the client system to realize individual and group potential.

Phase 6: Evaluation

109. Choose the appropriate evaluation method (the same options that were available for the initial assessment) and level (reaction, learning, behavior, or organizational impact).
110. Establish a feedback system to monitor the change effort continually, both during the intervention (formative evaluation) and at the end (summative evaluation).
111. Develop and administer valid, reliable, and practical evaluative instruments.
112. Analyze evaluation data, link outcome expectations with outcome measurements, and present results clearly and in a useful manner.
113. Evaluate the results of the intervention in terms of added value to the bottom line and in terms of the increased overall effectiveness of the organization.
114. Identify any changes in the organizational culture, performance, quality, safety, turnover, and so on.
115. Recognize progress relative to the change goals.
116. Identify the degree to which the action plan was implemented successfully.
117. Reinforce positive change and correct negative change.
118. Determine if the pain within the organization has been reduced and if the members of the organization feel that they have been helped.
119. Identify top management's response to the progress of the implementation.
120. Integrate feedback and learning from the evaluation into the plan and continue correction and adjustment of the change effort.

121. Ensure that your actual time and costs are in line with original estimates.

Step 7: Adoption

122. Balance the plan for the change effort with the flexibility to react to events as the change effort unfolds.
123. Link the ongoing change process to both the organization's structure and its daily operations.
124. Base future changes on organizational strategy and business needs.
125. Shift the emphasis of the effort from project-driven change to strategy-driven change.
126. Get a commitment from top management as well as from a wide organizational mix of people to carry on the continual transformation.
127. Mobilize internal resources and support for ongoing self-direction, self-learning, and self-renewal.
128. Work to diffuse the innovation beyond early or prototype efforts into the daily activities of the organization.
129. Introduce the change process to other parts of the organization or division that are ready for it.
130. Give special attention to areas where slippage into old attitudes or behaviors begins to occur.
131. Gradually wean the client organization away from dependence on the consultant.
132. Transfer OD skills to members of the client organization so that participants learn how to learn and move closer to being self-dependent and sustaining.
133. Transfer the OD process to the person or department trained to be the OD resource within the system.
134. Work with the members of the organization to accept ownership of the change process.

Step 8: Separation

135. Recognize and accept when separation is desirable and when continued assistance in the change process can be counterproductive.
136. Initiate open discussion about disengagement.
137. Facilitate a discussion with the client regarding the next steps for the change project.
138. Ask appropriate questions, analyze the situation, and identify client needs and possible follow-up initiatives.
139. Decide whether to continue the current project, begin a new unrelated or related project, or disengage temporarily or permanently.
140. Ensure that improvement will continue in the organization after disengagement.
141. Complete all administrative tasks related to separation.
142. Transfer the process and responsibility for continuing progress to the client.
143. Address psychological issues related to separation so as to reduce your involvement effectively.
144. Plan a departure that meets the needs of all those involved.
145. Plan for post-separation consultation contact with the client, if appropriate.
146. Understand and respond to the post-separation emotions of all parties, including your own.
147. Follow up with the client when appropriate.

General Competencies

148. Develop skills in listening to others. Learn to adapt to different communication styles.
149. Clarify personal values and boundaries that you wish to hold amid multiple perspectives.

150. Be creative and increase your capacity to tolerate uncertainty, complexity, ambiguity, and chaos.

151. Develop self-awareness of the influences of cultural dynamics on your beliefs.

152. Know your biases, assumptions, judgments, conventions, and habits.

153. Know your boundaries when amid conflict.

154. Develop trusting and helpful relationships with clients and with all members of client systems.

155. Stay focused and centered and look for meaning amid chaos.

156. Be willing to compromise and develop new ways to combine present beliefs with new knowledge.

157. Face emotional situations with a minimum amount of personal defensiveness.

158. Facilitate clear, meaningful contact between yourself and the client system.

159. Demonstrate sensitivity to the sensory and physical functioning of yourself and others.

160. Remain physically and mentally healthy while under stress.

161. Tune into the emotional reactions of others and yourself.

162. Resolve ethical issues with integrity and in accordance with the OD profession's code of ethics.

163. Exhibit self-awareness and be aware when your personal needs are being satisfied by client affiliation.

164. Invite, acknowledge, and respond appropriately to feedback.

165. Model what clients are asked to accept.

166. Exhibit self-control and discipline.

167. Energize others and yourself.

168. Use spiritual and inner power sources for the benefit of the larger universal system.

169. Forgive yourself when you fail to attain perfection. Model forgiveness with the client.

170. Stay aware of what is happening.

171. Commit yourself authentically to clients.

172. Pay attention to spontaneous and informal events.

173. Consistently maintain confidentiality.

174. Play multiple roles and, when necessary, switch among them and announce that you are switching.

175. Tap the energy in the client system.

176. Tolerate and deal with the poor interpersonal skills of others, while modeling good interpersonal skills.

177. Use technology effectively (for example, computer packages, electronic mail, and faxes).

178. Interpret cross-cultural influences in a helpful manner.

179. Recognize the influence of your interactions on others and groups.

180. Utilize a solid conceptual framework based on research.

181. Be comfortable with quantum leaps, radical shifts, and paradigm changes.

182. Help to bring individual and groups' into consciousness.

183. Act with intention and understand the consequences of each intention.

184. Use humor creatively and effectively to create catharsis.

185. Preserve the best from the OD profession and continue to improve OD knowledge and skill.

186. Model creativity and bring it out within each system.

187. Continually learn how to learn and be open to being taught by others.

APPENDIX II

SAMPLE CONSULTING PROPOSAL

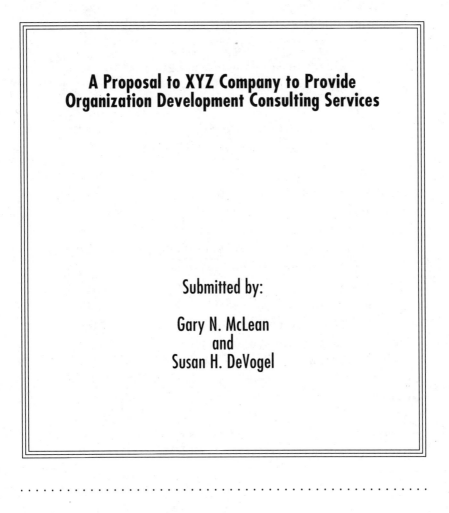

**A Proposal to XYZ Company to Provide
Organization Development Consulting Services**

Submitted by:

Gary N. McLean
and
Susan H. DeVogel

Introduction

This proposal is in response to a request for a joint proposal and individual proposals for organization development work within XYZ Company. It outlines an intervention proposed by co-consultants Gary N. McLean and Susan H. DeVogel to do the following:

- Provide executive/management development;
- Provide leadership in assessing the culture of XYZ Company;
- Facilitate organization development interventions to improve the efficiency and effectiveness of XYZ Company and to improve the working climate;
- Take the first steps in providing a foundation to ensure readiness for a continuous-quality-improvement process; and
- Reassess the culture two years after an intervention to determine progress made and challenges that remain.

The intervention is planned in phases so that the management team of XYZ Company can identify specific tasks to be undertaken, the processes to be followed, and the costs associated with each phase. Such an approach will also permit XYZ Company to determine areas in which it may have internal expertise to supplement the work of the consultants and thus reduce costs.

The action research model, which was presented during the interviews with the consultants, will guide and direct the consultants' work. The first step will be to conduct in-depth interviews with members of the management team and to facilitate the development of individual development plans for them. This will be followed with an assessment of the climate and culture of XYZ Company. The consultants will then provide feedback to the management team and to all employees. The consultants also will facilitate action planning around the diagnosed needs. The consultants will then support the implementation of change activities with the goals of improving the performance of the company, the leadership of the management team, the morale of the employees, and the perception of the company within the broader context of the parent company, all in preparation for full participation in the company-wide initiative related to quality.

The action research model is a data-based approach that is responsive to the needs of individual work units, as well as the company as a whole. It is a participative model in which the company leaders participate with the consultants to identify intervention issues and to plan an intervention and its evaluation. It is an educational model in which the consulting and facilitation skills of the consultants are shared with the personnel in the company so that they will be better equipped to conduct additional problem-solving and change activities after the conclusion of the contract.

The co-consultants, Gary N. McLean and Susan H. DeVogel, have worked together for many years in a variety of educational and consulting activities. Both consultants have wide experience in the activities detailed in this proposal. Their skills and experience include organizational restructuring, team building, quality management by the Deming method, strategic planning, training-needs assessment, climate surveys, career development, conflict management, coaching, and management development.

In this consulting-team arrangement, DeVogel will serve as contact between the XYZ Company staff and the consulting team. Both consultants will be responsible for coordinating the consultation activities.

Advantages of Joint vs. Individual Proposals

The consultants recommend that the XYZ Company give top consideration to a joint proposal. Following are the advantages of such an approach:

1. Using a consulting team takes advantage of the synergy and strength of a team approach to problem solving and various

other tasks. Such an approach also models collaboration to the management team and to employees.

2. The gender mix enriches the sensitivity to, and awareness of, subtleties within the company's culture and processes.

3. Greater flexibility is built into the contract with two consultants. When one consultant is not available, the other is likely to be. Given current restrictions, it is probable that this two-year proposal would stretch to a three- to four-year process if either consultant were working alone.

4. The consultants bring with them a variety of experiences that complement one another. McLean has over twenty years of experience in organization development, was a pioneer in the quality-management field, and has experience in unionized environments. DeVogel brings extensive experience in research instrumentation, organization development, and quality transformation.

5. Networking opportunities are extensive through the contacts of the two consultants. Such contacts will provide access to greater resources that may ultimately emerge as benchmarking partners.

Intervention Approach and Budget Estimates for Organization Development Consultation

The consultants are committed to an approach in which change is based on an understanding of:

- The present state of the company;
- The desired future state of the company; and
- The readiness of the company for change.
- The services to be provided are detailed below.

Phase One: Executive Coaching and Management Mentoring

The first phase is designed to provide support and assistance to the president and his staff. This is seen by the consultants as the top priority. This phase could stand alone if resources are not available for the other phases. The following steps/processes will be followed:

1. Interview all personnel at the senior-management level. This will serve the dual purpose of assessing individual managerial-development needs and providing initial input on issues that need to be added to the customized needs-assessment instrument.

2. Share the organizational results of the interviews in summary format with the senior-management team. Any issues related to individuals will be shared with the individuals, and an individual-development plan (IDP) may be created for each manager, based on the outcomes of the assessment.

3. Meet with the managers on a mutually agreed basis to monitor the IDPs and to provide advice/support/counsel, as needed.

Phase Two: Climate Assessment

An evaluation of the company's current climate is necessary in order to establish a deeper understanding of the current state of the company and its readiness for change. This process will result in the identification of issues and policies that need to be addressed and will provide a foundation for organizational change. The following steps/processes will be followed:

1. Review existing data that could reveal the company's problems and strengths.

2. Tour the facilities.

3. Interview a cross-section of employees, including both supervisory and nonsupervisory personnel, in order to obtain a clear understanding of the present culture. Interviews will include but are not limited to the following:

    - How decisions are made;
    - Trust;
    - Formal and informal patterns of leadership;
    - Gaps between formal and informal systems of communication, power, and norms; and
    - Management/union relationships.

Individual interviews will take approximately one hour each and will continue until the information that is surfacing does not warrant continued interviews—approximately fifteen interviews.

4. Construct a customized climate survey from the existing database by modifying existing questions, eliminating unrelated questions, and adding new questions, based on the information gathered. The climate survey will include questions about topics such as decision making, trust, cohesiveness, behavioral norms, formal and informal-communication systems, and supervision within the company. (Although the consultants do not recommend it, if resources are a concern, the questionnaire used by XYZ's parent company could be used, with minor modifications made in consultation with a committee of XYZ Company supervisory and nonsupervisory employees. This would save about thirty hours of consultant time.)

5. Work with an internal committee for validation of the survey prior to its administration.

6. Develop guidelines for administration of the survey. The consultants encourage the use of external administrators, either one of the consultants or, for cost effectiveness, a subcontractor. The survey will be administered on site to all employees. A response rate as close as

possible to 100 percent is desirable in order to be able to generalize the results to the total organization.

7. Monitor subcontractors, if personnel and facilities are not available within XYZ Company to accomplish these tasks, while they scan response sheets, analyze information, produce feedback graphs, and analyze open-ended questions.

8. Provide written feedback report on the interviews, the climate survey, and other data and present it to the management team.

9. Coach the management team in providing feedback to all employees.

10. Provide a feedback report, in executive-summary format, that can be distributed to all employees. All written reports produced by the consultants, as well as oral communications, will protect the privacy and anonymity of all participants. Patterns, general issues, and system problems/strengths will be discussed.

Phase Three: Action Planning

Based on the results of the organizational assessment, including the interviews, climate survey, and other information generated during the feedback sessions, a separate meeting between the management team and the consultants will be held. During this meeting, issues will be prioritized and an action plan will be developed to address those issues. A full-day meeting will be planned; depending on the group's need, less time actually may be used. The result of this meeting will be a plan for systematic organizational change through organization development interventions.

Phase Four: Organization Development Interventions

Depending on the issues identified in the earlier phases of this process and the outcomes of the action planning, the consultants will facilitate interventions as needed with employees, supervisors, and management. Such interventions may focus on:

- Supervisory styles and issues;
- Role clarification and negotiation or responsibility charting;
- Conflict management;
- Assessment and improvement of work processes;
- Team-building activities;
- Meeting-effectiveness training and process observation;
- Individual coaching with employees and supervisors;
- Ethics workshops;
- Training in using quality-improvement tools;
- Decision-making and problem-solving skills; and
- Interpersonal and intrateam communications skills, including giving and receiving feedback.

Phase Five: Evaluation

1. Two years after the project, the survey and feedback sessions will be repeated to determine if appropriate progress has been made. Although it is impossible to ascribe a cause-and-effect relationship between consultant activities and organizational change, it will be possible to determine what changes have occurred and to identify further needs for change. It will also be possible to determine whether the organization is prepared for a quality-transformation intervention.

2. The consultants suggest a monthly, two-hour meeting and frequent telephone contact with the client to discuss the progress of the consulting effort.

It is the consultants' belief that an effective consultant-client relationship is based on honest and straightforward communication.

Evaluation of the process is greatly enhanced if the client fully participates by providing continual feedback throughout the consulting process.

The advantages of continual feedback are:

- The client becomes a partner in, rather than a consumer of, the organization development process;

- Small problems are addressed before they become big problems;

- Opportunities for enhancement and improvement of methods are less likely to be overlooked;

- Victories can be celebrated throughout the organization as they happen; and

- The consultants quickly learn what is needed by the organization and its subsystems, enabling them to provide more effective service.

Potential Cost-Reduction Strategies

The hours indicated on the following two tables are estimates. Only actual time and expenses will be billed. Many of the activities previously listed could involve a variety of configurations of personnel. Decisions about who will be involved in which activities will be made jointly between the client and the consultants. Thus, within each phase, significant savings can occur, depending on the results of the assessments and the desires of the management team.

For example, savings can occur if:

- The parent company's survey is used instead of a customized survey;

- XYZ Company personnel administer the survey, analyze the open-ended questions, prepare the graphs, and so on;

- Monthly coaching/mentoring sessions are not held;

- The extent of the organization development interventions can be reduced; and

- Monthly meetings with the management team are reduced to bimonthly meetings.

In each instance, however, the consultants believe that, in the long run, the resultant savings may not be worth the potential loss of trust from the employees and the inadequacies in the organizational change design.

The contract and the phases presented are open to continual assessment and reevaluation.

Two-Year Budget Estimates for Nonpersonnel Items

Phase One: Executive Coaching and Management Mentoring

Costs for the first phase will depend on needs identified by the consultants and costs for management/executive development. These two items should already be included in budgets.

Phases Two and Five:	Climate Assessments	
	Year 1	Year 2
Printing of surveys for optical scanning	$1,000	$1,000
Administration of survey (12 hours at $15)	180	180
Scanning of instruments	100	100
Computer time and supplies	500	500
Statistical analysis	750	750
Analysis of open-ended questions on survey	500	500
Production of graphs for feedback	1,000	1,000
Copying, overheads, and so on	500	500
Printing of report	750	750
Total add-on costs for Phases Two and Five:	$5,280	$5,280

XYZ Company Process Timelines for a Joint Consultancy, First Year (1992-3)

Activities	Jul	Aug	Sep	Oct	Nov	Dec	Jan	Feb	Mar	Apr	May	Jun
1.1 Mgmt Interviews	20											
1.2 Feedback	10											
1.3 Coaching		6+4	6+4	6+4	3+2	3+2	3+2	3+2	3+2	3+2	3+2	3+2
2.1 Review Documents	5											
2.2 Tour Facility	2/2											
2.3 Interview Employees		8+8										
2.4 Construct Survey		10/5										
2.5 Committee Validation		10										
2.6 Administration Monitoring			1									
2.7 Monitor Analysis			3									
2.8 Full Feedback Report and Present to Mgmt				20								
2.9 Coach Mgmt—Feedback				1								
2.10 Summary Feedback Report				2								
3.1 Action Planning					9/9							
4.1 OD Interventions						5+10	5+10	5+10	5+10	5+10	5+10	5+10
5.1 Repeat Survey/Feedback												
5.2 Monthly Mgmt Meeting	2/2	2/2	2/2	2/2	2/2	2/2	2/2	2/2	2/2	2/2	2/2	2/2
Consultant Conference	1/1	1/1	1/1	1/1	1/1	1/1	1/1	1/1	1/1	1/1	1/1	1/1

Note: 2/2 = both consultants present; 2 + 2 = both consultants involved, working separately. McLean's hours in a joint consultancy are underscored; DeVogel's are not.

XYZ Company Process Timelines for a Joint Consultancy, Second Year (1993-4)

Activities	Jul	Aug	Sep	Oct	Nov	Dec	Jan	Feb	Mar	Apr	May	Jun
1.3 Coaching	3+2	3+2	3+2	3+2	3+2	3+2	3+2	3+2	3+2	3+2	3+2	3+2
3.1 Action Planning												9/9
4.1 OD Interventions	5+10	5+10	5+10	5+10	5+10	5+10	5+10	5+10	5+10	5+10	5+10	5+10
5.1 Repeat Survey/Feedback											11+25	
5.2 Monthly Mgmt Meeting	2/2	2/2	2/2	2/2	2/2	2/2	2/2	2/2	2/2	2/2	2/2	2/2
Consultant Conference	1/1	1/1	1/1	1/1	1/1	1/1	1/1	1/1	1/1	1/1	1/1	1/1

NOTE: 2/2 = both consultants present; 2 + 2 = both consultants involved, working separately. McLean's hours in a joint consultancy are underscored; DeVogel's are not.

XYZ Company Budget Estimates for Two Years (1992-4) Under Joint and Separate Consulting Arrangements

First Year, 1992-93

Phase	Hours	McLean Separately	DeVogel Separately	Joint*
1 Coaching and Mentoring	100	$13,500	$8,000	9,720 / 2,240
2 Climate Assessment	70	9,450	5,600	4,725 / 3,360
3 Action Planning	9	1,215	720	1,215 / 720
4 OD Interventions	105	14,175	8,400	4,725 / 5,600
5.1 Repeat Survey/Feedback	0			
5.2 Monthly Mgmt	24	3,240	1,920	3,240 / 1,920
Consultant Conference	12			1,620 / 960
PERSONNEL TOTALS	320	$41,580	$24,640	$25,245 / $14,800 / $40,045

Second Year, 1993-94

Phase	Hours	McLean Separately	DeVogel Separately	Joint*
1 Coaching and Mentoring	60	$8,100	$4,800	$4,860 / 1,920
2 Climate Assessment	0			
3 Action Planning	9	1,215	720	1,215 / 720
4 OD Interventions	180	24,300	14,400	8,100 / 9,600
5.1 Repeat Survey/Feedback	36	4,860	2,880	1,485 / 2,000
5.2 Monthly Mgmt	24	3,240	1,920	3,240 / 1,920
Consultant Conference	12			1,620 / 960
PERSONNEL TOTALS	321	$41,715	$24,720	$20,520 / $17,120 / $37,640

*McLean's figures, based on $135 per hour, are listed first, followed by DeVogel's at $80 per hour.

Phase Three: Action Planning

XYZ Company will need to make arrangements for a one-day retreat. For example, reservations for a conference room and an afternoon meal may need to be made at a local hotel.

Phase Four: Organization Development Interventions

Without knowing which interventions are going to be necessary, this phase is impossible to predict. It may include duplication of printed materials, purchase of training materials and references, and so on.

Additional
Mileage at .275: 2,400 miles per year = $660 each year

Consultant Availability

Both McLean and DeVogel agree not to undertake additional work during the period of this effort that would make it impossible for them to fulfill their obligations as described earlier. If separate consultancy is preferred, then the rate of delivery of the services outlined will be reduced.

A P P E N D I X III

ETHICS STATEMENTS FOR OD

Statement of Values and Ethics for Professionals in Organization and Human System Development * (January 1986)[1]

Organization and Human System Development (OD/HSD)[2] is an emerging profession rooted in human values and relevant theory whose purpose is to help individuals, organizations, and other human systems achieve excellence.

Preamble

This Statement is intended to serve as an inspirational guide, a statement of ideals toward which OD/HSD professionals can strive.[3] Its purposes are to:

1. Increase professional consciousness and responsibility among OD/HSD professionals by:

    Stimulating a widespread discussion of values and ethics underlying OD/HSD practice;

    Highlighting and clarifying major differences in OD/HSD values and ethics and seeking to resolve them; and

_____

* Used by permission of the Organization Development Network.

Identifying those OD/HSD values and ethical guidelines that are generally accepted.

2. Enable OD/HSD professionals to make more informed ethical choices about their practice by referring to a generally accepted set of guidelines. [4]
3. Contribute to enabling the OD/HSD profession to achieve excellence in its own functioning.

Our intention is to serve all of those purposes for OD/HSD professionals throughout the world to enhance their sense of membership in a global professional community.

Since this Statement has been developed from within the cultural perspective of the United States, as was OD/HSD itself, we recognize that it includes concepts, beliefs, assumptions, and values unique to that country's culture. We also recognize that practice according to the Assumptions and Guidelines outlined in this Statement may be precluded by certain cultural conditions. Our expectation is that discussion stimulated by this Statement will help us identify specific cross-cultural differences and similarities underlying the practice of OD/HSD.

Those who use this Statement should keep in mind that it is continually evolving and will change and grow as our profession matures. [5] Our ultimate goal is a widely shared learning and discovery process dedicated to the creation of professional excellence and lives that are fully worth living.

A basic assumption of these guidelines is that violating them might result in harm to the client, the organization, its members, other stakeholders, the OD/HSD professional, the OD/HSD profession, society, and/or life on Earth.

The guidelines provide a reasonable standard for the protection of all those who are affected by the practice of OD/HSD. OD/HSD professionals are encouraged to share their ethical positions with their clients; clients are encouraged to discuss those positions with their OD/HSD professionals and, in case of questions or differences, work together on clarification and mutually satisfactory resolution.

Since we view ethical practice as a continuing, developmental process, we encourage OD/HSD professionals to:

- Involve themselves actively in that process by becoming more sensitive to their ethical dilemmas; and

- Share the results of that process with other OD/HSD professionals [6] and, when appropriate, with their clients.

Assumptions Underlying the Ethical Guidelines of OD/HSD Professionals

1. Human beings are:
    a. Interdependent economically, politically, socially, culturally, and spiritually and they are responsible for the choices they make within that context;
    b. Rightfully responsible for and capable of:
        (1) Making choices, taking charge of their lives, and functioning autonomously within a context of interdependence; and [7]
        (2) Controlling their own growth and the pace of that growth. [8]
    c. Inherently of equal worth as human beings, regardless of race, creed, age, nationality, gender, socioeconomic status, or sexual preference; and [9]
    d. Rightfully entitled to equal opportunity in their workplaces and other human systems.

2. All human systems—including individuals, groups, organizations, communities, and societies—are:

    a. Wholes comprised of parts/subsystems that are interdependent with one another, with the whole, and with the macrosystem(s) of which the whole is a part;

b. Interdependent, open systems whose actions influence and are influenced by a variety of different stakeholders. For example, the stakeholders of a business organization may include customers, managers, workers, suppliers, clients, patrons, investors, labor organizations, committees, communities, governments, societies, and, ultimately, the world;

c. Shaped by the tensions among system, subsystem, and macrosystem dynamics, with concrete possibilities for more mature forms of being evolving out of those tensions; and

d. Unique combinations of beliefs and values, purposes, goals, resources, and needs that enable them to make unique contributions to the world; their purposes are to bring their contributions into being.

3. A major aim of OD/HSD is to help the system become conscious of and able to fulfill its purpose by:

a. Enabling the system as a whole and each part within it to:

(1) Understand their purposes and interdependence with one another;

(2) Review their purposes and revise them over time as conditions and their awareness of conditions change; and

(3) Clarify and refine their relationships so they can align themselves.

b. Helping individuals within the system to:

(1) Accept responsibility for their lives;

(2) Recognize both the extent of and the constraints on their freedom, their power to choose how they live their lives within the system, and the impact of the system on their lives; and

    (3)   Recognize the possibilities for promoting social justice.

  c. Helping each higher order subsystem (team, department, division, and so on) understand its purpose and interdependence and accept its responsibility for fulfilling its role within the system;

  d. Providing for equitable distribution of the fruits of the system's productivity;

  e. Creating and supporting a climate within which freedom, equality, mutual trust, respect, and love prevail;

  f. Helping people align both individual and system purposes with:

    (1)   The needs and purposes of all the system's stakeholders; and

    (2)   The welfare of all the people of Earth, all living things, and their environment.

4. A human system whose parts are integrated and consciously aligned with the system's overall purpose and its environmental context will function more effectively and efficiently because:

  a. The system will avoid wasting energy on counterproductive behavior; and

  b. The environment will support the system if the system is aligned with the environment. (Note: This does not deny the possibility of productive behavior by the system directed at changing the environment in order to achieve more enduring alignment.)

5. OD/HSD professionals:

  a. Acknowledge the important and pervasive influence of values and ethics on the effectiveness and potential for growth of individuals, organizations, and more inclusive human systems and consider them in the process and content of their OD/HSD practice;

b. Place high value [10] on:

(1) Consciousness of values—knowing what they consider most important/desirable/worthy;

(2) Excellence—people doing the best they can with their potential, individually and collectively;

(3) System effectiveness and efficiency—achieving desired results (purposes, goals and objectives) at minimum cost;

(4) Holistic, systemic view—understanding human behavior from the perspective of whole system(s) that influence and are influenced by that behavior and conceiving of the dynamics of systems in terms of the interdependent parts/subsystems that comprise them and of the macrosystem(s) within which the systems are parts;

(5) Stakeholder orientation—recognizing the interests that different people have in the system's results and valuing those interests equitably;

(6) Human potential—viewing people as having unique potential that can be realized through contribution to collective achievement and valuing the full realization of that potential;

(7) Quality of life—recognizing that the whole experience of life is important (not only those uses of life that serve system purposes) and that worklife should serve both system and personal purposes;

(8) Individual dignity, integrity, worth and fundamental human rights; [11]

(9) The dignity, integrity, and worth of organizations, communities, societies, and other human systems;

(10) Authenticity in relationships and openness in communication; and [12]

(11) Wide participation in system affairs, confrontation of issues leading to effective problem solving and democratic decision making. [13]

c. Realize that they are in a service profession in which they make available their expertise and personality, and are prepared to discuss the way they do this with colleagues and participants in the consulting process;

d. Recognize the responsibilities of individuals to the groups, organizations, and other human systems of which they are members;

e. See themselves as members of a global professional community and accept their responsibilities to that community; recognize that the accomplishments of the OD/HSD profession are the results of both individual and collective effort;

f. Recognize that choices which may seem unethical in the short run may be ethical in the long run, such as not responding to a request for a quick fix in order to allow conditions to emerge under which more authentic help is possible;

g. Recognize that along with respecting the right of free choice goes the responsibility for discussing with clients the consequences of their choices and how those choices might be changed to yield different consequences; and

h. Recognize the need for balance in cases where the above values conflict and recognize further that practice according to the values and ethics described in this Statement may be precluded by certain cultural conditions. [14]

Ethical Guidelines for an OD/HSD Professional

As an OD/HSD professional, I commit to supporting and acting in accordance with the following guidelines:

I. Responsibility for Professional Development and Competence

A. Accept responsibility for the consequences of my acts and make every effort to ensure that my services are properly used; [15]

B. Recognize the limits of my competence, culture, and experience in providing services and using techniques; neither seek nor accept assignments outside those limits without clear understanding by the client when exploration at the edge of my competence is reasonable; refer client to other professionals when appropriate;

C. Strive to attain and maintain a professional level of competence in the field, [16] including:

1. Broad knowledge of theory and practice in:
   a. Applied behavioral science generally;
   b. Management, administration, organizational behavior, and system behavior specifically;
   c. Multicultural issues, including issues of color and gender; and
   d. Other relevant fields of knowledge and practice.

2. Ability to:
   a. Relate effectively with individuals and groups;
   b. Relate effectively to the dynamics of large, complex systems;
   c. Provide consultation using theory and methods of the applied behavioral sciences; and

d. Articulate theory and direct its application, including creation of learning experiences for individual,
small and large groups, and for whole systems.

D. Strive continually for self-knowledge and personal growth;
be aware that "what is in me" (my perceptions of myself in
my world) and "what is outside me" (the realities that exist
apart from me) are not the same; be aware that my values,
beliefs, and aspirations can both limit and empower me and
that these are primary determinants of my perceptions, my
behavior, and my personal and professional effectiveness;

E. Recognize my own personal needs and desires and deal
with them responsibly in the performance of my professional roles; and

F. Obtain consultation from OD/HSD professionals who are
native to and aware of the specific cultures within which I
work when those cultures are different from my own. [17]

II. Responsibility to Clients and Significant Others

A. Serve the short- and long-term welfare, interests, and development of the client system and all its stakeholders;
maintain balance in the timing, pace, and magnitude of
planned change so as to support a mutually beneficial
relationship between the system and its environment;

B. Discuss candidly and fully goals, costs, risks, limitations,
and anticipated outcomes of any program or other professional relationship under consideration; seek to avoid auto-
matic confirmation of predetermined conclusions, either
the client's or my own; seek optimum involvement by client
system members in every step of the process, including
managers and workers' representatives; fully inform client
system members about my role, contribution and strategy
in working with them;

C. Fully inform participants in any activity or procedure as to its sponsorship, nature, purpose, implications, and any significant risk associated with it so that they can freely choose their participation in any activity initiated by me; acknowledge that their choice may be limited with activity initiated by recognized authorities; be particularly sensitive to implications and risks when I work with people from cultures other than my own;

D. Be aware of my own personal values, my values as an OD/HSD professional, the values of my native culture, the values of the people with whom I am working, and the values of their cultures; involve the client system in making relevant cultural differences explicit and exploring the possible implications of any OD/HSD intervention for all the stakeholders involved; be prepared to make explicit my assumptions, values, and standards as an OD/HSD professional:

E. Help all stakeholders while developing OD/HSD approaches, programs, and the like, if they wish such help; for example, this could include workers' representatives as well as managers in the case of work with a business organization;

F. Work cooperatively with other internal and external consultants serving the same client system and resolve conflicts in terms of the balanced best interests of the client system and all its stakeholders; make appropriate arrangements with other internal and external consultants about how responsibilities will be shared;

G. Encourage and enable my clients to provide for themselves the services I provide rather than foster continued reliance on me; encourage, foster, and support self-education and self-development by individuals, groups, and all other human systems;

H. Cease work with a client when it is clear that the client is not benefiting or the contract has been completed; do not accept an assignment if its scope is so limited that the client will not benefit or it would involve serious conflict with the values and ethics outlined in this Statement;

I. Avoid conflicts of interest:

1. Fully inform the client of my opinion about serving similar or competing organizations; be clear with myself, my clients, and other concerned stakeholders about my loyalties and responsibilities when conflicts of interest arise; keep parties informed of these conflicts; cease work with the client if the conflicts cannot be adequately resolved;

2. Seek to act impartially when involved in conflicts between parties in the client system; help them resolve their conflicts themselves, without taking sides; if necessary to change my role from serving as impartial consultant, do so explicitly; cease work with the client, if necessary;

3. Identify and respond to any major differences in professionally relevant values or ethics between myself and my clients with the understanding that conditions may require ceasing work with the client; and

4. Accept differences in the expectations and interests of different stakeholders and realize that those differences cannot be reconciled all the time.

J. Seek consultation and feedback from neutral third parties in case of conflict between myself and my client; [18]

K. Define and protect the confidentiality of my client-professional relationships;

1. Make limits of confidentiality clear to clients/ participants;

2. Reveal information accepted in confidence only to appropriate or agreed-upon recipients or authorities;

3. Use information obtained during professional work in writings, lectures, or other public forums only with prior consent or when disguised so that it is impossible from my presentations alone to identify the individuals or systems with whom I have worked; and

4. Make adequate provisions for maintaining confidentiality in the storage and disposal of records; make provisions for responsibly preserving records in the event of my retirement or disability.

L. Establish mutual agreement on a contract covering services and remuneration:

1. Ensure a clear understanding of and mutual agreement on the services to be performed; do not shift from that agreement without both a clearly defined professional rationale for making the shift and the informed consent of the clients/participants; withdraw from the agreement if circumstances beyond my control prevent proper fulfillment;

2. Ensure mutual understanding and agreement by putting the contract in writing to the extent feasible, yet recognize that:

   a. The spirit of professional responsibility encompasses more than the letter of the contract; and

   b. Some contracts are necessarily incomplete because complete information is not available at the outset.

3. Safeguard the best interests of the client, the profession, and the public by making sure that financial arrangements are fair and in keeping with appropriate statutes, regulations, and professional standards.

M. Provide for my own accountability by evaluating and assessing the effects of my work:

1. Make all reasonable efforts to determine if my activities have accomplished the agreed-upon goals and have not had other undesirable consequences; seek to undo any undesirable consequences, and do not attempt to cover up these situations;

2. Actively solicit and respond with an open mind to feedback regarding my work and seek to improve; and

3. Develop, publish, and use assessment techniques that promote the welfare and best interests of clients/participants; guard against the misuse of assessment results.

N. Make public statements of all kinds accurately, including promotion and advertising, and give service as advertised:

1. Base public statements providing professional opinions or information on scientifically acceptable findings and techniques as much as possible, with full recognition of the limits and uncertainties of such evidence;

2. Seek to help people make informed choices when making statements as part of promotion or advertising; and

3. Deliver services as advertised and do not shift without a clear professional rationale and the informed consent of the participants/clients.

III. Responsibility to the Profession

A. Act with due regard for the needs, special competencies, and obligations of my colleagues in OD/HSD and other professions; respect the prerogatives and obligations of the institutions or organizations with which these other colleagues are associated.

B. Be aware of the possible impact of my public behavior upon the ability of colleagues to perform their professional work;

perform professional activity in a way that will bring credit to the profession.

C. Work actively for ethical practice by individuals and organizations engaged in OD/HSD activities and, in case of questionable practice, use appropriate channels for confronting it, including:

1. Direct discussion when feasible;

2. Joint consultation and feedback, using other professionals as third parties;

3. Enforcement procedures of existing professional organizations; and

4. Public confrontation.

D. Contribute to continuing professional development by:

1. Supporting the development of other professionals, including mentoring with less experienced professionals; and

2. Contributing ideas, methods, findings, and other useful information to the body of OD/HSD knowledge and skill.

E. Promote the sharing of OD/HSD knowledge and skill by various means including:

1. Granting use of my copyrighted material as freely as possible, subject to a minimum of conditions, including a reasonable price defined on the basis of professional as well as commercial values; and

2. Giving credit for the ideas and products of others.

IV. SOCIAL RESPONSIBILITY

A. Strive for the preservation and protection of fundamental human rights[19] and the promotion of social justice.

B. Be aware that I bear a heavy social responsibility because my recommendations and professional actions may alter the lives and well-being of individuals within my client systems, the systems themselves, and the larger systems of which they are sub-systems.

C. Contribute knowledge, skill, and other resources in support of organizations, programs, and activities that seek to improve human welfare; be prepared to accept clients who do not have sufficient resources to pay my full fees at reduced fees or no charge.

D. Respect the cultures of the organization, community, country, or other human system within which I work (including the cultures, traditions, values, and moral and ethical expectations and their implications), yet recognize and constructively confront the counterproductive aspects of those cultures whenever feasible; be sensitive to cross-cultural differences and their implications; be aware of the cultural filters which bias my view of the world.

E. Recognize that accepting this Statement as a guide for my behavior involves holding myself to a standard that may be more exacting than the laws of any country in which I practice.

F. Contribute to the quality of life in human society at large; work towards and support a culture based on mutual respect for each other's rights as human beings; encourage the development of love, trust, openness, mutual responsibility, authentic and harmonious relationships, empowerment, participation, and involvement in a spirit of freedom and self-discipline as elements of this culture.

G. Engage in self-generated or collaborative endeavor to develop means for helping across cultures.

H. Serve the welfare of all the people of Earth, all living things, and their environment.

Notes

1.
   a. This Statement is built upon the foundation of several prior statements and contributions, including those from the Association for Creative Change; the Academy of Management; the American Psychological Association; the NTL Institute of Applied Behavioral Science; Certified Consultants International; the National Organization Development Network; the Dutch Association of Organizational Experts and Advisors; the Gestalt Institute of Cleveland; International Consultants Foundation; the Organization Alignment Project of The Institute for the Study of Conscious Evolution; the International Registry of Organization Development Professionals; the OD Institute; the OD Division of the American Society for Training and Development; Organization Renewal, Inc.; the International Human Resources Development Corporation; the Societe Internationale pour le Development des Organisations; OD Network—United Kingdom; Gesellschaft fur Organisationentwicklung; Society for Applied Anthropology; a study group from Reseau OD Canada; the OD study group of SANNO Institute of Business Administration (Japan); the European Institute for Trans-National Studies in Group and Organizational Development; the American Society for Personnel Administration; and the National Association of Social Workers. In addition, many other groups and individuals have contributed to its current state of evolution, including groups from Poland, South Africa, and Spain.

   b. We have sought to make this Statement an expression of a substantial consensus by the OD/HSD profession. When significant differences within the profession have been identified, they have been acknowledged in the Issues Discussion which should be read as a companion document to this statement.

2. The field we call Organization and Human System Development (OD/HSD) is most generally recognized by the name Organization Development (OD) since most of its practitioners focus primarily on organizations. It is also known by the names Change Facilitation, Human Resource Development, Human Systems Development (because the profession works with such diverse systems as Individuals, families, communities, and even more inclusive systems) and Applied Behavioral Science (since the profession bases much of its practice on applying the sciences of psychology, sociology, anthropology, and other behavioral sciences).

3. This Statement is not intended as a regulatory code, buttressed by rules to govern behavior. (The profession does not presently have the monitoring and enforcement structure, with sanctions and supports, that such a code would require. Since there are so many associations of OD/HSD professionals throughout the world, a single, widely acceptable code and enforcement structure are unlikely in the near future and, even if they could be developed, at present there is no indication that professionals or their associations would like to develop them.)

In contrast, this Statement is the beginning of an educational code, which seeks to describe and explain professional norms in a way that can be applied precisely in resolving the ethical dilemmas experienced by practitioners. Our expectation is that such a code, along with case studies and other educational materials, will be developed in time. (And, at least for the present, this seems to be where most professionals and their associations would like to concentrate their attention.)

4. OD/HSD professionals who also identify with an organization or professional association that has a formal Code of Ethics may use that code to guide their behavior. When the other code covers matters not covered in these guidelines or is in conflict with them, the people responsible for updating this code should be informed as a step toward resolving significant differences.

5. Among other things, as our knowledge increases so too will the precision of our ethical guidelines and principles.

6. In time, we expect OD/HSD professionals to share the results of their attention to ethical dilemmas so that we can accumulate the information (case studies and other educational materials) needed to create and maintain an educational code of the kind referred to in Note 4 of this Statement.

7. As much as possible, we proceed on the assumption that the ability to act responsibly, or at least the potential for it, exists. We recognize, however, that people may live under economic, social, and political conditions that severely limit their freedom in the exercise of that ability. We also recognize that some human beings may not act responsibly or be capable of making responsible choices. For example, emotionally disturbed people or persons whose life experiences have disempowered them—based on such conditions as poverty, discrimination, and oppression—need to be approached with sensitivity to and consideration for the effects of these experiences.

8. We generally believe that if people try to shift responsibility for their growth to others or if others try to take it from them, their growth will be fundamentally hindered. But we recognize that people can help one

another by suggesting alternatives that enable them to reexamine and accept responsibility for their choices, and we consider such help an important part of our role. We also recognize that not all people are able to control their own growth, for such reasons as those mentioned in Note 1.

9. OD/HSD professionals recognize that people have different characteristics and competencies and may be valued differently by societies, but as human beings we view them as of equal inherent worth.

10. For a fuller discussion of values central to the practice of OD/HSD, see the Issues Discussion associated with this Statement.

11. Specific fundamental rights we value include rights to:

    a. Life, liberty, and security of person;

    b. Freedom of thought, conscience, and religion;

    c. Freedom of opinion and expression; and

    d. Freedom of choice.

    In general, we accept as a guide the United Nations Universal Declaration of Human Rights.

12. We recognize that there are conditions under which people cannot realistically be authentic and open. For example, conditions of dependence and oppression clearly would make such behavior dangerous if not suicidal. However, even when such behavior is not realistic, we value it and value changing conditions so that it can become realistic.

13. OD/HSD professionals recognize that democratic participation in decision making is not effective or practical under all conditions, but we are committed to bringing about the conditions that make such participation practical under all conditions where it is consistent with human excellence.

14. When cultural conditions preclude following these guidelines, we accept responsibility for the consequences of our action or inaction and will seek to be clear about the guidelines we choose to guide our action in their place.

15. Each of us accepts responsibility for being our own judge of "proper" use of our services; among other things we include making every effort to ensure that our services are used to promote, rather than obstruct, movements toward peace, justice, freedom, and responsibility.

16. Collectively our practice extends from practitioners who concentrate on the personal/professional development of individuals to the development of transnational human systems; each of us strives to attain and maintain a professional level of competence within our own area(s) of concentration and, in addition, sufficient competence in relation to other areas of concentration that we can work cooperatively with other OD/HSD professionals in serving our clients' needs. As noted in the section on assumptions, "OD/HSD professionals recognize that the accomplishments of the OD/HSD profession are the results of both individual and collective effort." (Assumption 5-e)

17. Consultation with someone who knows the culture may be brief if we are confident that our own cultural limitations will not have a negative impact on the client system or the larger system within which it functions. However, we recognize that our own cultural conditioning may blind us to such negative impact and so we undertake at least a minimal consultation.

18. We recognize that perfect neutrality may not be possible, but we will seek to find a third party who approximates it.

19. See Note 11 above.

THE ORGANIZATION DEVELOPMENT CODE OF ETHICS

(DECEMBER, 1991, 22ND REVISION)*

Our purpose in developing an O.D. Code of Ethics is threefold: to increase professional and ethical consciousness among O.D. professionals; to guide O.D. professionals in making more informed ethical choices; and to help the O.D. profession itself function at the fullness of its potential.

We recognize that for us to exist as a profession, a substantial consensus is necessary among the members of our profession about what we profess, particularly our values and ethics. This statement represents a step toward such a consensus.

Values of O.D. Professionals

As an O.D. professional, I acknowledge the fundamental importance of the following values both for myself and my profession:

1.   Quality of life—people being satisfied with their whole life experience;

---

* Reprinted from *The International Registry of Organization Development Professionals and Organization Development Handbook.* (1992). Cleveland, OH: The Organization Development Institute, pp. 42-46. Used by permission of The Organization Development Institute.

2. Health, human potential, empowerment, growth and excellence—people being healthy, aware of the fullness of their potential, recognizing their power to bring that potential into being, growing into it, living it, and, generally, doing the best they can with it, individually and collectively;

3. Freedom and responsibility—people being free and responsible in choosing how they will live their lives;

4. Justice—people living lives whose results are fair and right for everyone;

5. Dignity, integrity, worth, and fundamental rights of individuals, organizations, communities, societies, and other human systems;

6. All-win attitudes and cooperation—people caring about one another and about working together to achieve results that work for everyone, individually and collectively;

7. Authenticity and openness in relationships;

8. Effectiveness, efficiency, and alignment—people achieving the maximum of desired results, at minimum cost, in ways that coordinate their individual energies and purposes with those of the system-as-a-whole, the subsystems of which they are parts, and the larger system of which their system is a part;

9. Holistic, systemic view and stakeholder orientation—understanding human behavior from the perspective of whole system(s) that influence and are influenced by that behavior; recognizing the interests that different people have in the system's results and valuing those interests fairly and justly; and

10. Wide participation in system affairs, confrontation of issues leading to effective problem solving, and democratic decision making.

Ethical Guidelines for O.D. Professionals

As an O.D. professional, I commit myself to supporting and acting in accordance with the following ethical guidelines:

I. Responsibility to Self

    A. Act with integrity; be authentic and true to myself.

    B. Strive continually for self-knowledge and personal growth.

    C. Recognize my personal needs and desires and, when they conflict with other responsibilities, seek all-win resolutions of those conflicts.

    D. Assert my own economic and financial interests in ways that are fair and equitable to me as well as to my clients and their stakeholders.

II. Responsibility for Professional Development and Competence

    A. Accept responsibility for the consequences of my acts and make reasonable efforts to ensure that my services are properly used; terminate my services if they are not properly used and do what I can to see that any abuses are corrected.

    B. Strive to achieve and maintain a level of competence for both myself and my profession by developing the full range of my own competence and by establishing collegial and cooperative relations with other O.D. professionals.

    C. Recognize my own personal needs and desires and deal with them responsibly in the performance of my professional roles.

    D. Practice within the limits of my competence, culture, and experience in providing services and using techniques.

E. Practice in cultures different from my own only with consultation from people native to or knowledgeable about those specific cultures.

III. Responsibility to Clients and Significant Others

A. Serve the long-term well-being, interests, and development of the client system and all its stakeholders, even when the work being done has a short-term focus.
B. Conduct any professional activity, program, or relationship in ways that are honest, responsible, and appropriately open.
C. Establish mutual agreement on a contract covering services and remuneration.
D. Deal with conflicts constructively and avoid conflicts of interest as much as possible.
E. Define and protect the confidentiality of my client-professional relationships.
F. Make public statements of all kinds accurately, including promotion and advertising, and give service as advertised.

IV. Responsibility to the Profession

A. Contribute to continuing professional development for myself, other practitioners, and the profession.
B. Promote the sharing of O.D. knowledge and skill.
C. Work with other O.D. professionals in ways that exemplify what our profession says we stand for.
D. Work actively for ethical practice by individuals and organizations engaged in O.D. activities and, in case of questionable practice, use appropriate channels for dealing with it.
E. Act in ways that bring credit to the O.D. profession and with due regard for colleagues in other professions.

V. Social Responsibility

A. Act with sensitivity to the fact that my recommendations and actions may alter the lives and well-being of people within my client systems and the larger systems of which they are subsystems.

B. Act with awareness of the cultural filters which affect my view of the world, respect cultures different from my own, and be sensitive to cross-cultural and multicultural differences and their implications.

C. Promote justice and serve the well-being of all life on Earth.

D. Recognize that accepting this Statement as a guide for my behavior involves holding myself to a standard that may be more exacting than the laws of any countries in which I practice, the guidelines of any professional associations to which I belong, or the expectations of any of my clients.

Notes

The process which produced this Statement (currently in its 22nd version) was begun in 1981. It has been supported by most O.D. oriented professional organizations, associations, and networks in the United States. It was also supported unanimously by the participants at the 1984 OD World Congress in Southhampton, England. To date, more than two hundred people from more than fifteen countries have participated in the process. (Note: The endorsements are of the process and not the statement.) The process has included drafting a version, sending it out with a request for comments and suggestions, redrafting based on the responses, sending it out again and so on.

Our aim has been to use the process to establish a substantial consensus including acknowledgement of the differences among us. By providing a common reference for O.D. professionals throughout the world, we seek to enhance our sense of identity as a global professional community. Because this statement was initially developed within the United States, adapting it to other cultures may be necessary.

Editor's Note: A more complete discussion of organization development values and ethics can be found in the following material:

Gellermann, W., Frankel, M., & Ladenson, R. (1990). *Values and ethics in organization and human systems development: Responding to dilemmas in professional life.* San Francisco, CA: Jossey-Bass.

Frankel, M. (1987). *Values and ethics in organization and human systems development: An annotated bibliography.* AAAS Publication.

White, L., & Wooten, K. (1986). *Professional ethics and practice in organization development.* New York, NY: Praeger.

THE ASTD CODE OF ETHICS *

Τ he ASTD Code of Ethics provides guidance to members to be self-managed human resource development professionals. Clients and employers should expect from ASTD members the highest possible standards of personal integrity, professional competence, sound judgment, and discretion. Developed by the profession for the profession, the ASTD Code of Ethics is the Society's public declaration of its members' obligations to themselves, their profession, and society.

I strive to...

- Recognize the rights and dignities of each individual.

- Develop human potential.

- Provide my employer, clients, and learners with the highest quality education, training, and development.

- Comply with all copyright laws and the laws and regulations governing my position.

- Keep informed of pertinent knowledge and competence in the human resource field.

- Maintain confidentiality and integrity in the practice of my profession.

---

* Reprinted from *Who's Who in Training & Development*. (1992). Alexandria, VA: The American Society for Training and Development, p. 6. Used by permission of The American Society for Training and Development.

- Support my peers and to avoid conduct which impedes their practicing their profession.
- Conduct myself in an ethical and honest manner.
- Improve the public understanding of human resource development and management.
- Fairly and accurately represent my human resource development/human resource management credentials, qualifications, experience, and ability.
- Contribute to the continuing growth of the Society and its members.

Rules of Behavior for Members

Members of the Society shall...

- Refrain from any overt statements or pointed humor which disparages the rightful dignity and social equity of any individual or group when presenting from any Society platform.
- When using the Society's name or in introductions to presentations, make clear the ideas presented are personal and do not represent those of the Society.
- Refrain from using the Society's platform to directly sell, promote, or otherwise encourage participants to purchase or use the speaker's products or services.

Rules for Leaders

National leaders of the Society...

- Will not solicit or receive anything of value for services rendered in the Society's name or using the Society's materials.
- Will not use any Society funds for their personal gain.

- National leaders are defined as national elected officers, board of directors, board of governors, council representatives, regional directors, industry group directors, members of executive committees; members of appointed positions: committees, task forces, and special projects.

APPENDIX IV

REAL-TIME STRATEGIC-CHANGE TECHNOLOGY: SPEEDING UP SYSTEM-WIDE CHANGE

Roland J. Loup

Introduction

An intervention that involves large groups of employees provides a process to help effect system-wide organizational change. Bunker and Alban (1992) provide a historic overview of large-group interventions. They trace the development of work in organizations, whole systems, community development, and organizational development, and they demonstrate that large-group work has existed in several forms for some time. The rapid organizational change required by today's organizations has helped place large-group technology closer to the mainstream of organization development consultation.

Large-group interventions are currently being practiced in several forms. Perhaps the most widely known is the *search conference* described in Weisbord's (1980) *Productive Workplaces*. The search conference began in 1960 with the work of Emery and Trist. In a search-conference session, participants work together to build a preferred future (Lippitt, 1983) for their system and to develop a plan to realize that preferred future.

Other applications of large-group interventions include open-space technology (Owen, 1992), the conference model (Axelrod, 1992), and work-out. Each intervention has its own approach and application, but all the interventions address whole systems and incorporate interventions with groups larger than those of traditional organization development consultations. (Large-group interventions have successfully involved over 2,200 people working in concurrent sessions of about 550.)

Real-Time Strategic-Change Technology

Work on the real-time strategic-change technology (RTSC) began at Ford Motor Company in Detroit, Michigan in 1981 when an executive vice president of the Diversified Products Organization realized that in order to be successful, his organization was going to need new ways of working at every level and across all functions. He asked a group of internal and external consultants to train his managers quickly to be more participative. The consultants suggested a different type of "seminar," one that would bring about a significant paradigm shift in how the managers viewed the workplace. This seminar became a five-day program consisting of sixty to 150 participants. The initial sessions included representatives from each organizational function and the top four to five levels of management. The seminar was then brought to plants and offices to support the changes begun by management. (For a more complete discussion of this work, see Albert, Dannemiller, Loup, and Jacobs, 1994.)

The five-day seminar formed the basis for the continuing development of RTSC and its applications in a variety of change situations, including strategic planning, total quality management, joint ventures/mergers, cultural diversity, and sociotechnical systems.

The Conceptual Framework

Four basic theories/models provide the conceptual framework for the large-scale events in the RTSC. One essential component of the change process is the development of a large system-wide team as well as smaller, cross-functional, work teams. This macrolevel change needs to begin with the way in which individuals and teams work together. Jack Gibb's (1970) team-building theory was used for this purpose. Gibb's theory states that the three major elements of team building are as follows:

1. Membership;
2. Control; and
3. Goal formation.

Every group cycles through these elements; however, the most effective team building results when the three elements are addressed in the following order:

Membership. This element consists of issues concerning acceptance of an individual into a group. Acceptance is increased when group members believe it is safe to honestly voice their feelings, values, and beliefs.

Control. After a group explores membership issues, concerns about control begin to surface. Issues at this stage involve how the group is going to work together; relative positions of influence, power, and leadership; and needs for inclusion.

Goal Formation. When a group has addressed the first two elements, its attention shifts toward its objectives. The integration of individual goals into the group's goals becomes a core issue in this stage.

Team development involves repeatedly cycling through the three elements. This process deepens the team members' ability to work together. A basic change formula that Beckhard and Harris (1987) attribute to Gleicher formed the second conceptual construct used in this intervention. Gleicher's change formula is used as a diagnostic tool and as a planning model. The elements of Gleicher's formula were revised as follows for ease of recognition and application:

$$D \times V \times F > R$$

Gleicher's formula states that change will occur when the product of dissatisfaction (D) with the present situation, a vision (V) of what is possible, and first steps (F) toward reaching the vision are greater than the resistance to change (R). If D, V, or F is zero or near zero, the product of the three will also be zero or near zero, and, therefore, the resistance to change will not be overcome. In an organization-wide change effort, a significant number of organizational members needs to share a common understanding and agreement on each of the three elements in order for change to occur. The large-scale process creates an opportunity for this to occur.

The third theory emerged as a response to learnings gathered by the consulting team at Ford during the diagnostic phase of the intervention. Dannemiller (1988) created the arthritic-organization theory from an analysis of the impact of Weber's (1947) work on bureaucracy and Taylor's (1915) work on task specialization in organizations. Dannemiller proposed that as an organization ages, horizontal hierarchies intersecting with the vertical chimneys created by specialization lead to a rigidity, or arthritis, of the joints (see Exhibit 1). This means that the organization as a system is neither flexible nor adaptable to either the internal-workflow requirements or the changing external environments. Organizations with reduced flexibility are facing a competitive, fast-changing environment that requires quick response. The RTSC process involves the whole system and thus provides the possibility of increased information flow, system focus, and quicker response.

Exhibit 1: Arthritic Theory

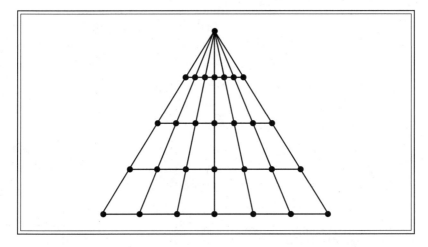

The fourth part of the conceptual framework is the strategic-planning model that describes how to develop a strategy that meets the needs of all the organization's stakeholders. Using a large-scale event to identify the needs of key stakeholders is an important part of forming a strategy. As those present at a large-scale event learn the needs of stakeholders, the participants begin to see the organization from a broader perspective. This perspective allows them to think, plan, and act according to the strategic plan.

A strategy that is representative of the whole system focuses the organization into a strong direction and helps to ensure that the strategy will be implemented. An organization is focused if a significant number of its members make decisions based on the organization's goals and objectives.

The Nine Phases of the RTSC Process

The nine-phase RTSC process are explained in this section. The phases are presented, for simplicity, in a linear and sequential fashion. However, they seldom occur sequentially. The actual format of each phase changes to fit the individual client situation.

1. *Contracting with the Leadership Team of the Change Effort.* The purpose of the first phase is for a consulting team to establish a collaborative working relationship with a leadership team. Both teams need to clarify what they bring to the process and what they need from it. The teams also need to agree on their roles and what work needs to be done.

2. *Building Alignment, Ownership, and Commitment to the Process in the Leadership Team.* The purpose of the second phase is for the consulting team to ensure that the leadership team is committed to the change process. The consultants and the leadership team need to work together to develop measures of success for the change effort, an initial project plan for the intervention, and the roles of the team members and the team. Key decisions that may need to be made by the leadership team during the change effort are identified. The leader of the organization can be instrumental in helping to gain the commitment of the team members to the change effort.

3. *Developing an Organizational Strategy for the Change Effort.* In the third phase, the leadership team drafts a strategy for the change effort. This draft often is presented at a large-scale event to solicit feedback from the total group. The strategy can be finalized by the leadership team during the event. This approval approach helps to establish the leadership of the change effort and builds commitment to the strategy among those who have to implement it.

4. *Designing the Real-Time Strategic-Change Event.* In the fourth phase, the leadership team selects members for a design team. The members are representative of those who will be attending the large-scale event. They will work with the consultant team. The design team ensures that the large-scale event is client-focused by reminding the consultants about the organization's actual circumstances. The design team provides the consultants with data about the organization and it determines what results should be sought from the large-scale event.

Exhibit 2: Strategic-Planning Model

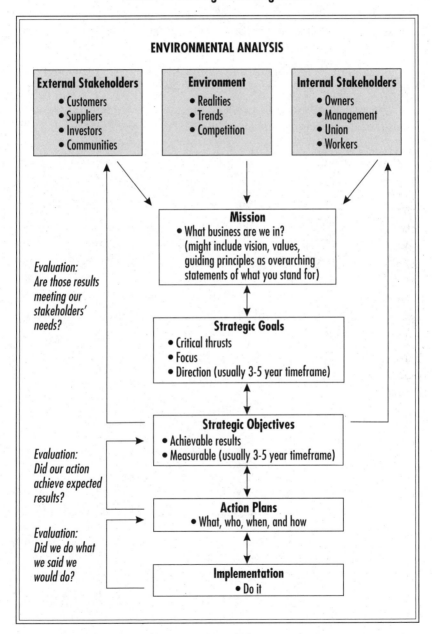

ENVIRONMENTAL ANALYSIS

External Stakeholders
- Customers
- Suppliers
- Investors
- Communities

Environment
- Realities
- Trends
- Competition

Internal Stakeholders
- Owners
- Management
- Union
- Workers

Mission
- What business are we in?
  (might include vision, values,
  guiding principles as overarching
  statements of what you stand for)

Strategic Goals
- Critical thrusts
- Focus
- Direction (usually 3-5 year timeframe)

Strategic Objectives
- Achievable results
- Measurable (usually 3-5 year timeframe)

Action Plans
- What, who, when, and how

Implementation
- Do it

*Evaluation:
Are those results
meeting our
stakeholders'
needs?*

*Evaluation:
Did our action
achieve expected
results?*

*Evaluation:
Did we do what
we said we
would do?*

The team meets with the consultants to design a large-scale event that will meet everyone's needs. The design team often takes on other assignments to help the event take place, such as helping to recruit speakers, promoting the meeting, and making special seating arrangements.

5. *Meeting Planning for the Event.* In this phase, a selected team member is responsible for making the arrangements that will lead to success in the large-scale event. There are two major issues to be considered at this point: making the usual arrangements for any meeting of several hundred people (for example, location, meals, breaks, and parking) and organizing materials such as newsprint charts, marking pens, and tape for use at round tables typically seating eight to ten.

6. *Planning Follow-Up Initiatives to the Event.* Some participants may believe that the large-scale event is the total intervention. In phase two, the leadership team defines possible initiatives that would complement the large-scale event. In the sixth phase the leadership team—often working with others such as the design team—and the consultants identify possible activities that can complement the large-scale event by using the information that was generated earlier. These activities can include:

- Agreeing to the need for task forces to carry out action plans developed at the large-scale event;

- Planning ways to communicate with others in the organization who will not attend the large-scale event;

- Developing training plans for internal staff in the design and facilitation of large-scale meetings; or

- Identifying potential assignments for the leadership team or other groups within the organization to continue the change process.

Final decisions on these initiatives may need to be made during or after the large-scale event, based on what is learned at the event itself. However, the initial thinking should precede the event.

7. *Staging Day for the Event.* The purpose of the seventh phase, which usually takes place the day before the event, is to be sure that everyone (leaders, team members, consultants, speakers, participants, and so on) is ready to make the event a success. On this day, for example, the leadership team may meet to focus on its task and role, speakers may receive final coaching, consultants may review their roles and assignments, team members set up the meeting room, team members review materials to be distributed, someone checks the sound system and audiovisual system, and the appointed team member reviews meal arrangements with the catering staff.

8. *Holding the Event.* During this phase, the consultant team facilitates the meeting. Each team members will find himself or herself performing various roles, such as large-group facilitator; coach to speakers, participants, and leaders; designer; member of the consultant team; and member of the logistics-consulting team.

9. *Implementing Follow-Up Change Initiatives.* In the final phase, the leadership team takes responsibility for establishing follow-up activities and monitoring their progress. The consultants make sure that plans, responsibilities, and initial steps are established and known by everyone at the event before the event adjourns. The consulting team may have roles in the facilitation of these activities.

Skills and Knowledge Needed for RTSC

Real-time strategic-change technology is based on the process consultation model. The skills necessary for process consultation are basic to RTSC consultation. Working knowledge of the concepts are presented in Schein (1988) and Block (1981).

The following skills are also essential to a successful large-scale process consultant. These skills are not listed in any order.

Staying Client Focused. A consultant needs to be in charge of the RTSC process and to have the client in charge of the content. To stay client focused, a consultant must listen to stakeholders in a client system throughout the RTSC process and he or she must concentrate on the success of the process, not its outcomes.

Dealing with the Chaos of System-Wide Change. Organizations that are involved in system-wide change efforts are in a state of chaos. People in these organizations often know that everything is chaotic, feel that they do not have control over the chaos, and long for everything to return to "normal." A consultant needs to understand that organizational members will sometimes act irrationally, that events will not always seem to make sense, and that often there is little that anyone can do besides accept chaos as part of the process. A consultant will need to stay calm and remind his or her client that the apparent irrationality is part of the process.

Managing the Project. The RTSC is a complex process that a client often needs help managing. A consultant needs to know how to help plan and manage the overall project, which includes facilitating strategy-development sessions; scheduling, designing, and facilitating large-scale events; training internal consultants in the large-scale process; and scheduling, designing, and facilitating special meetings of the leadership team.

Designing Large-Group Meetings. The skills needed to design a large-group meeting are based on the work of Lippitt and Schindler-Rainman (1975) and Schindler-Rainman and Lippitt (1980), in which specific activities for large groups are designed to follow a process flow, usually defined by one or more models such as the change model or a planning model. A consultant must be able to work successfully with design teams to arrive at designs that are client focused and that will achieve the outcomes and purpose of the event. He or she must also write clear instructions for activities and plan large meetings. (For more information, see Albert, et al., [1994].)

Facilitating Large-Group Meetings. Specific skills required to facilitate a large-group meeting include framing specific assignments so that they make sense to all participants, changing the design of the session if necessary, perceiving group energy, and keeping well ahead of the action in order to foresee possible problems.

Coaching. Successfully coaching leaders, the leadership team, internal consultants, internal and external stakeholders, and team leaders and members is essential to the success of a large-scale process. A consultant needs a variety of coaching styles for these various groups.

Leadership. Leading a consulting team is a critical skill. The team comprises the team leader, at least one other consultant, and the team member who is responsible for logistics. Other members may include internal staff members who are process trainees. A consultant needs to be able to lead a consulting team effectively throughout a large-scale process.

Consensus Building. Building consensus among members of various groups is essential to the success of a large-scale process. For example, consensus is important when developing strategic goals, a mission, or a vision with a leadership team. A consultant needs the skills to help these teams with this important process.

Training. A consultant is continually training a variety of people throughout the RTSC. Some of the training is conducted in formal training sessions, such as training employees to act as consultants in a large-scale process. Other training is informal, such as helping members of a leadership team learn how to lead the changes necessary to develop a new culture or implement a new strategy. Skills in both informal and formal training techniques are essential.

Large-group interventions provide a technology for helping bring about system-wide organizational change. Building on values and assumptions of organization development consulting, approaches to whole-system change, and technologies of large-group interventions, large-scale interventions are emerging as one way to help systems change more rapidly than traditional organizational interventions.

The continued development of real-time strategic-change technology is important to the future development of organizations.

References

Albert, R., Dannemiller, K., Loup, R., & Jacobs, R. (1994). *Real time strategic change: A consultant's guide to large scale meetings.* Ann Arbor, MI: Dannemiller Tyson Associates.

Axelrod, D. (1992). Getting everyone involved: How one organization involved its employees, supervisors, and managers in redesigning the organization. *Journal of Applied Behavioral Science, 28*(4), 499-509.

Beckhard, R., & Harris, R. (1987). *Organizational transitions.* Reading, MA: Addison-Wesley.

Block, P. (1981). *Flawless consulting: A guide to getting your expertise used.* San Diego, CA: Pfeiffer & Company.

Bunker, B., & Alban, B. (1992). The large group interaction—A new social innovation? *Journal of Applied Behavioral Science, 28*(4), 473-479.

Dannemiller, K. (1988). Team building at a macro level, or "Ben Gay" for arthritic organizations. In W.B. Reddy & K. Jamison (Eds.), *Team building: Blueprints for productivity and satisfaction.* Alexandria, VA: NTL Institute.

Dannemiller, K., & Jacobs, R. (1992). Changing the way organizations change: A revolution of common sense. *Journal of Applied Behavioral Science, 28*(4), 480-498.

Gibb, J. (1970). *The basic reader: Reading in laboratory training.* Detroit, MI: The Episcopal Church, Province V.

Jacobs, R. (1994). *Real time strategic change: How to involve an entire organization in fast and far-reaching change.* San Francisco, CA: Berrett-Koehler.

Lippitt, R. (1983). Future before you plan. In *NTL managers' handbook.* Arlington, VA: NTL Institute.

Lippitt, R., & Schindler-Rainman, E. (1975). *Taking your meetings out of the doldrums.* (2nd Ed.) San Diego, CA: Pfeiffer & Company.

Owen, H. (1992). *Open space technology: A user's guide.* Potomac, MD: Abbott.

Schein, E. (1988). *Process consultation: Its role in organizational development* (Vol. 1). Reading, MA: Addison-Wesley.

Schindler-Rainman, E., & Lippitt, R. (1980). *Building the collaborative community: Mobilizing citizens for action.* Riverside, CA: University of California Extension.

Taylor, F. (1915). *The principles of scientific management.* New York: Harper & Row.

Weber, M. (1947). *The theory of social and economic organizations* (A.M. Henderson & T. Parsons, Trans; T. Parsons, Ed.). New York: Free Press.

Weisbord, M. (1980). *Productive workplaces: Organizing and managing for dignity, meaning and community.* San Francisco, CA: Jossey-Bass.

List of Exhibits

INDEX

B

Background research, 54-55, 93
  See also Orientation
Barriers, to change, 377-392
BARS (Behaviorally-Anchored
  Rating Scale), 348-349
Beginning
  See Start-up
Behavior level, in evaluation step,
  345-349, 358-360
Beta change, 9
Bias, consultant, 147, 498
  See also Objectivity
Block, Peter, 126
Boundary management, 218
Burke, W. Warner, 91
Business process reengineering, 30

C

Career Development (CD), 32, 35
Certification, 447
Change
  in action research, 51-52
  barriers to, 377-392
  in critical research, 48-49
  five keys to, 373-377
  introducing (exhibit), 391
  leadership, 211
  models, 47-69
  planning, 142-143
  Shewharts' PDCA cycle, 49-50
  strategy, 184-189
  tracking, 143
Change roles, 10, 182, 189-190
Character, of an organization, 204
Client
  and assessment, 143-145

defined, 10-11
  and future trends, 498-500
  identifying, 111-113, 243-244
Climate survey (exhibit) 339-340
Closure, 329, 414
Coaching, 286-308
  See also Mentoring
  in action planning, 304-305
  effective, 305-306
  empowering in, 294, 296-297
  exploring in, 303-304
  helping in, 297-298
  listening in, 289-290
  questions in, 290, 292-294
  and rapport, 299, 302-303
  responding in, 294, (exhibit)
    295
  sequential phases 298-299,
    (exhibit) 300-302
Coercion, and ethics, 461
Coercive approach, as alternative
  to OD, 40
Cognitive dissonance, 268-269
Collaboration, with client, 253-254
Communication
  in coaching, 288
  Hall and Hall on, 432
Comparability, in information-
  gathering, 153, 156-158
Comparative rating instruments,
  345-346
Compensation, disagreement
  over, 409
  See also Financial arrangements
Competence
  See also Credibility
  in action research, 280-281
  and ethics, 461
  for future, 493-529

step, 53, 60, 67
when conducted (exhibit), 313
Exploring, in coaching, 303-304

F

Fading, 411-412
Feedback
  See also Assessment and
    Feedback
  forms of, 162-168
  giving, 142
  in interventions, 281-286
  in large systems, 206, 208
  in SAFI, 271
  and survey research, 22, 26-29
  system 325-326
Financial arrangements, contracting for, 111, 133-134
Flexibility
  of change effort, 374-375
  increasing, 317
  in information-gathering, 154,
    159-161
Focus of attention, 59-60
Follow-up, 254-255, 415
Force-field analysis (exhibit),
  185-187
Formative evaluation, 60, 67
Freud, Sigmund, 18
Fulcrum Network, 494, 505-509
Future, and OD, 493-529
  study on, 493-495
  competencies for, 495-510
  and clients, 498-500
  trends, 495-510
  self-assessment and planning
    (instruments), 510-511

G

Gamma change, 9
Gantt, Henry L., 15
Gilbreth, Frank and Lillian, 14-15
Ginzberg, Eli, 17
Globalization, 421, 496-498
Goals, setting, 254
Groups, and ethics, 470-472

H

Hall, Edward and Mildred,
  432-435
Helping, in coaching, 289, 297-298
Herzberg, Frederick, 18, 20
High-involvement-organization
  intervention, 223-224
Hofsted, Geert, 436
Human resource fields, and OD,
  30-35
Human Resource Wheel, 32-35
Humans, defined by Trompenaars,
  437-438

I

Implementation. *See* Adoption
Individual development
  See Person-focused interventions
Ineffective intervention processes,
  389-390, 392
Information gathering
  advantages and disadvantages
    of, 153-162
  methods of, 149-153
  strategies, 162
Initial contact, in marketing, 95-99

R

Rapport, in coaching, 299, 302-303

Reaction level, in evaluation, 322, 331-336, 338, 355-357

Readiness, for change, 279, 381

Real-time strategic change technology, 601-613

Records, examining, 152-153, 154-161

Reflection
and ethics, 466-467
in person-focused interventions, 275-277

Registered Organizational Development Professional (RODP), 91

Registered Organization Development Consultant (RODC), 91-92

Relationship
See also Dependence
client-consultant, 109-110, 118-120, 316
poor, 380-382

Reliability, 330

Resistance, to change, 380-381

Resisters, identifying, 124

Responding, in coaching, 294-295

Results
analyzing, 351-353
presenting, 353-367

Reward-system intervention, 221-223

Rewards, three kinds of, 222

Rogers, Carl, 18

Role clarity, 189-191

Role model, consultant as, 77, 87-88, 95, 119, 254.

Role-play
See Activities

Roles
in change, 182, 189-190
in groups (exhibit), 248-253

S

SAFI
See Self-awareness through feedback from instrument

Schools of thought, in management thinking, 14-22

Self, conflicted vs. integrated, 284

Self-assessment instruments, 510-511, (exhibit) 82-83, (exhibit) 512-524

Self-awareness, 466

Self-awareness, for international consultants, 424-425

Self-awareness through feedback from instrument (SAFI), 269-272

Self-knowledge
and consulting, 76-81
in future, 503
in international OD, 428
in small-group OD, 237, 239-242

Selling
See Marketing

Sensitivity training, 267

Separation, discussing during start-up, 131

Separation, 395-417
administrative tasks of, 414
competencies in, 399-401
and consultant work load, 408-409
defined, 395-399

Separation (continued)
  and follow-up, 415
  learning activities, 415, 417
  post-consultation planning,
    405-408, 409-413
  process, 401-405
  step, 53, 68-69
  three stages of (exhibit), 397
Shewhart's PDCA cycle, 49-50
Simulation activities, 349
Skills, 107-108, 136-137, 316
  See also Competencies
Skinner, B.F., 18
Slippage, 67-68
Small-group interventions,
  235-260
  assessment in, 246-247, 253
  case study, 255, 260
  defined 242-243
  and follow-up, 254-255
  OD competencies for, 237-242
Social justice, 470
Sociotechnical-system-design
  interventions, 218-219
Space, cultural views on, 433-434
Spencer, Herbert, 15
Sponsor, 12, 111-113
Stakeholder, defined, 12
Standard deviation, 352
Standards, professional, 449-451
Start-up, 105-137
  common conditions of, 105-106
    (exhibit), 107
  step, 52, 55-57
Statement of Values and Ethics...,
  by Gellerman et al, 450
Statistical process control (SPC),
  346

Steps, of interventions, 52-69
Stereotypes, 425, 427
  See also Cultural issues
Strategic change technology,
  601-613
Strategic Planning, 7, 607
Strategy, defined, 206
Structural-design intervention,
  219-221
Subsystem, 12
Success, conditions for, 36-38
Success rates, for OD, 67
Summative evaluation, 60-67
Support services, contracting for
  131-132
Survey research, and feedback,
  22, 26-29
System, 12-13

T

T-group, 25, 266-269
Tavistock Sociotechnical Systems,
  22, 29-30
Taylor, Frederick, 14-15
Technology, 208
Termination, 396, 406
Theories X and Y, McGregor's
  (exhibit), 21
Therapy, for consultants, 79
Time, cultural views on, 434-435,
  437
Timing, of intervention, 60
TQM, 30
Trainer, role of, 279-280
Training and Development
  (T&D), 32-33

- Editor:

  Socorro P. Gonzalez

- Production Editor:

  Dawn Kilgore

- Indexer:

  Kathleen Deming

- Cover and Interior Page Design, Page Composition:

  Susan G. Odelson

- Page Composition Assistance:

  Judy Whalen

  Nicola Ruskin

- Graphic Assistance:

  Jean Komick

  Lee Ann Hubbard

This book was edited and formatted using 486 PC platforms with 8MB RAM and high resolution, dual-page monitors. The copy was produced using WordPerfect software: pages were composed with Corel Ventura Publisher software; and cover and art were produced with CorelDRAW software. The text is set twelve on fifteen New Calendonia, and the heads are set in Futura Condensed Medium and Bold Italic.